Gillian Beer's landmark book demonstrates how Darwin overturned fundamental cultural assumptions by revising the stories he inherited, how George Eliot, Thomas Hardy and other writers pursued and resisted the contradictory implications of his narratives, and how the stories he produced about natural selection and the struggle for life now underpin our culture. This second edition of *Darwin's Plots* incorporates an extensive new preface by the author and a foreword by the distinguished American scholar George Levine.

'The only problem with this book is deciding what to praise first. It draws on a breadth of knowledge in many fields, its literary readings are alert and original, it has a profound grasp of idea and form. It must be read by the scientist, the student of Victorian thought and art and the educated person in the street . . . The book is so exciting as a work of literary criticism – among much else – that it must provoke and disturb old interpretations and judgements.' Barbara Hardy, *New Statesman*.

'. . . Gillian Beer's superb study . . . a work of criticism that takes its modest place among the other "cloudy triumphs" of English genius.' Michael Neve, *Sunday Times*.

'Offers fresh insights into familiar themes in the history of science by dealing with them in quite a new way.' John Durant, *The Times Literary Supplement*.

Gillian Beer is King Edward VII Professor of English Literature at the University of Cambridge and President of Clare Hall, Cambridge. Her previous books include *Arguing with the Past: Essays in Narrative from Woolf to Sidney* (1989), *Forging the Missing Link: Interdisciplinary Stories* (1992), *Open Fields: Science in Cultural Encounter* (1996) and *Virginia Woolf: the Common Ground: Essays by Gillian Beer* (1996).

DARWIN'S PLOTS

*Evolutionary Narrative in Darwin, George Eliot
and Nineteenth-Century Fiction*

Second Edition

GILLIAN BEER

CAMBRIDGE
UNIVERSITY PRESS

PUBLISHED BY THE PRESS SYNDICATE OF THE UNIVERSITY OF CAMBRIDGE
The Pitt Building, Trumpington Street, Cambridge, United Kingdom

CAMBRIDGE UNIVERSITY PRESS
The Edinburgh Building, Cambridge CB2 2RU, UK   www.cup.cam.ac.uk
40 West 20th Street, New York, NY10011–4211, USA   www.cup.org
10 Stanford Road, Oakleigh, Melbourne 3166, Australia
Ruiz de Alarcón 13, 28014 Madrid, Spain

First published by Routledge & Paul plc 1983
Art paperback edition 1985
Second edition published by Cambridge University Press 2000

Printed in the United Kingdom at the University Press, Cambridge

Typeset in 11/12½pt M. Baskerville   [GT]

A catalogue record for this book is available from the British Library

ISBN 0 521 78008 X hardback
ISBN 0 521 78392 5 paperback

Nature, if we believed all that is said of her, would be the most extraordinary being. She has horrors (horror vacui), she indulges in freaks (lusus naturae), she commits blunders (errores naturae, monstra). She is sometimes at war with herself, for, as Giraldus told us, 'Nature produced barnacles against Nature'; and of late years we have heard much of her power of selection.

Max Müller, *Lectures on the Science of Language*, second series, 1864, p. 566.

Contents

Foreword

George Levine

Early in *Darwin's Plots*, Gillian Beer argues that *On the Origin of Species* is 'one of the most extraordinary examples of a work which included more than the maker of it at the time knew, despite all that he *did* know'. With these words Professor Beer initiated an enterprise that itself probably included more than she knew, despite all that she *did* know – which, to say the least, was a lot. For the book remains as alive and important now as it was when it appeared in 1983, on the first crest of the booming 'Darwin Industry', which has in the past fifteen years expanded even beyond the imagination of those who already understood how enormously rich and fertile Darwin's thought remained. Unlike most great scientists of the past, whose work has been absorbed by science (and often by culture) and marked as a brilliant stage toward later developments, Darwin remains strangely and almost charismatically alive – he 'has grown younger in recent years', says Professor Beer – and evolutionary biology remains an active force in science and beyond.

Darwin's Plots identifies a 'remnant of the mythical' in his arguments, a not quite complete fit 'between material and theory', a willingness to fall back on 'unknown laws', a passion for multiplicity and for aberrations. In teaching us how Darwin's metaphors and language work, by refusing any simple placement of his thought, either historical or philosophical, Professor Beer in effect predicted his continuing power to fertilise and disturb.

Darwin's name long ago entered the language to mark off a dog-eat-dog, cruelly competitive world. But, as Beer demonstrates, Darwin's language had shown him as much a believer in cooperation and what Kropotkin called 'mutual aid' as in ruthless competition. Beyond the popular imagination, up through the continuing human interest of the *Beagle* voyage and the continuing worry over the religious implications of evolutionary theory, the sustained interest of scholars and scientists

ix

in his work has made him perhaps the most discussed writer in English besides Shakespeare. Like the language that Professor Beer so brilliantly analyses, Darwin has remained endlessly interpretable, and the work of understanding him and using his ideas has accelerated during the past two decades.

As Professor Beer herself notes, the most impressive achievement of the Darwin industry in that time has been the extraordinary edition of Darwin letters, which to the moment of this writing, through nine volumes, takes us only up to 1861, that is, two years after the publication of *On the Origin of Species*. The notebooks – richly suggestive in their indications of the way Darwin was thinking in the run-up to his great work – have been published. An enormously useful register and summary of all his correspondence is now available. Perhaps most interestingly of all, as a result of the crucial archival work that produced the *Letters*, several notable biographies have appeared, particularly *Voyaging*, by Janet Browne, and *Charles Darwin*, by Adrian Desmond and James Moore. These studies, while refusing anything like the traditional hagiographical approach and while thickening our understanding of Darwin as a creature of his moment and a complex and multiply motivated man, give us a Darwin who might begin to correspond in life to the complex artist/ scientist who produced the language that Professor Beer so richly analyses. But, as she rightly notes in addressing the Desmond–Moore biography, her own approach, fastening on the particularities of the complex and remarkably flexible language of Darwin's texts, undercuts the implication that Darwin was absolutely a man of his time, explicable in terms of the conventions of the middle-class society to which he so nervously and doggedly adhered.

At the same time as the biographical and archival interest in Darwin has intensified, there has been an explosion of interest in Darwinian theory, particularly through evolutionary psychology: Daniel Dennett has pronounced Darwin's idea 'dangerous' in a study that provocatively follows out the line that sees Darwin as unrelentingly and courageously materialist and antimetaphysical. Richard Dawkins has carried the myth of Darwin's commitment to a pervasively competitive world deep into microbiology with his theory of *The Selfish Gene*. E. O. Wilson and Steven Pinker, prominently among others, take Darwin as the patron saint of sociobiology and evolutionary psychology, which pursue reductionism into the intricacies of human consciousness and behaviour. Each of these writers claims Darwin as his own but in effect together they simply multiply the number of different Darwins his posterity has created. The Darwin Gillian Beer gives us will not stand still for such unequivocal cooptations. Her new preface gives us some sense of how the approach of *Darwin's Plots* would have handled these later versions of Darwin, would have placed *them* inside the myths of our own culture and of the cultures they presume to transcend, and would have raised the kinds of questions that would make resting in their extreme versions of Darwin impossible. And beyond these struggles, within the limits of yet stricter science, Darwin remains controversial in the continuing combat between palaeontological and microbiological evolutionary biology. Outside of the official confines of science, the Victorian battle between God and Darwinian materialism continues in the attacks of creationism. *Darwin's Plots* prepared us for the tensions within and against Darwinian thought, as it worried the forms of our 'plots', the possibilities of meaning, order, futurity, development, death.

It is a mark of the significance of *Darwin's Plots* that it remains undeniably the single indispensable study of Darwin as a *writer* and as a presence in the language and consciousness of modern literature. Nobody has so rigorously and imaginatively addressed Darwin's work as literature, or so insistently read him as a creative writer, on an imaginative par with Charles Dickens or Thomas Hardy or George Eliot or Virginia Woolf.

Though it is deliberately 'literary' in its approach and sets out to read Darwin as a writer who also happened to be a scientist, it is also thoroughly multidisciplinary. The new preface gives another sharp glimpse of the way Professor Beer's remarkable attention to language extends beyond language into the widest range of intellectual and cultural connections. She demonstrates again that Darwin's language has its significance not merely in its literal meanings, but in the way tone, syntax, semantic substance play against each other and help shape thought and open up more possibilities than it can openly articulate. Such analysis has helped this book outreach the best of literary studies that have followed it, and to anticipate many of the moves made in current studies of Darwin and evolution. It is entirely compatible with the views promulgated by sociologists and historians of science with increasing force after its publication that ideas must be seen in the flesh-and-blood context of the moment of their production. Yet it refuses historical or social reductionism; Professor Beer historicises but she never loses sight of the ramifying possibilities of Darwin's special genius.

Thus she never adopts the extreme position, so prominent in much contemporary history and sociology of science and in cultural studies, that the social provides total explanation – that it is not a matter of ideas half-perceived, half-created, but of ideas virtually entirely 'constructed'. She notes bemusedly in the new preface how some people read the book as arguing that science is merely a 'fiction'. But her point, richly made over and over again, is that the language in which Darwin's theory is articulated is thick with the culture in which Darwin lived and that fully to understand the 'science', one must recognise how the language contributed to it, evoked resistances, entailed compliance. The language and the arguments cannot be disentangled. So the book marks the strenuous, inevitably incomplete resistances of the theory to the cultural forces that shape it. Beer's study, emphasising the implication of Darwin's thought in culture, responsibly worries through the question of the degree to which Darwin can be thought of as 'discoverer' or as 'inventor'. Tracing much of Darwin's thought back to Romantic predecessors, in poetry as well as in science, Professor Beer shows through both argument and enactment that the recognition of the creative and imaginative aspects of science does not in any way diminish the importance or distinctness of scientific work. Though nobody can come away from a reading of the book without a sense that science is thoroughly and crucially (and creatively) inside of culture, every reader must also see that it brilliantly enriches our understanding of our own culture precisely because it enriches our understanding of Darwin and the enormous difficulty of his enterprise.

The distinctiveness of *Darwin's Plots* even now has not been adequately assimilated into literary study. What distinguished the book, and what continues to distinguish it in literary study, is not only its meticulous attention to Darwin's language, but a bold and convincing demonstration that Darwin should be read not only as someone whose ideas profoundly influenced his culture, but as someone whose ideas were also importantly shaped by culture. *Darwin's Plots*, that is to say, indicates that the cultural traffic ran both ways. Finding echoes in Darwin's writings of Milton (whose works, along with Lyell's *Principles of Geology* accompanied him everywhere on the *Beagle*), of Wordsworth and Coleridge and Dickens, Professor Beer identifies Darwin as a Romantic materialist and traces the movement of literary language thick with assumptions of intention and agency into arguments that deny those very assumptions.

Earlier interest in Darwin and literature usually manifested itself in the useful work of locating Darwinian ideas moving from him to writers, from science to literature and politics. Some pioneering studies like Lionel Stevenson's important *Darwin Among the Poets* (1932) focussed almost entirely on Darwin's 'influence' on later writers. Darwin was a figure difficult to ignore even for the most literary of critics. But while there had been some earlier work that attended to the language of Darwin's books, particularly Stanley Edgar Hyman's *The Tangled Bank* (1962), nobody before Professor Beer had attended so meticulously and learnedly to the texture of Darwin's language and its deep historical roots. Nobody before Professor Beer traced so carefully the constraints of inherited language on the shaping of Darwin's arguments, or recognised the creative implications of his resistance to the traditions he used, or thought through so carefully and yet imaginatively the ways in which his metaphors opened up possibilities and created an argument that included more than the maker of it knew. Darwin's metaphors, Professor Beer argues, 'attempt to press upon the boundaries of the knowable within a human order'. *Darwin's Plots*, then, describes adventures in language and its possibilities, moves from the minute particulars of individual words to a recognition of how Darwin's work transformed the fundamental myths of the culture, myths upon which its language was built and whose vestiges help give Darwin's writing its capacity to escape monolithic impositions of meaning.

'Discourse', Professor Beer claims, 'can never be expunged from scientific *enquiry*'. Professor Beer's 'discourse' has its own distinctive and really inimitable qualities. *Darwin's Plots* marks the emergence of an unmistakable critical voice that speaks with authority and grace across a broad range of intellectual disciplines. Its strength comes in part from an unusual angularity, its capacity to evoke unexpected meanings and connections, to point toward multiplicity and contradiction. Beer's prose both entices and, one might say in a Beerism, disequilibrates: it makes it impossible for readers to relax, for it forces them to see that language does not hold still, neither Darwin's nor her own. Her words are never casual and serve not only the obvious utilitarian effect of getting it right but of getting it right in ways that expand possibilities and intimate abundance; they press to a broader realisation of how much might emerge from a creative imagination watching the play of words shifted from context to context. Such shifting is not only a function of the self-conscious human perceiver; it is the (Darwinian) way of the world. The seductive strenuousness of Beer's prose derives from her sense of the relentless fluidity of language and experience, the multiple possibilities of relationships, between ideas, people, cultures, disciplines.

This is the voice that makes *Darwin's Plots* one of the indispensable critical works of the past two decades and that accounts for its remarkable capacity to open out into the intellectual struggles over Darwin, Darwinism, science and culture which followed in the years after first publication of the book. While in her new preface Professor Beer suggests ways in which she might have changed the book were she to be writing it now, what we have needs no alteration, in part because, like the Darwinian language Professor Beer explores, it suggests more than it can literally say. Professor Beer has set the standard for how to read Darwin and how to connect his amazing enterprise to the stories our culture has been able to tell itself, and continues to tell. She has shown that the language of Darwin's arguments is 'not a layer that can be skimmed off without loss'. *Darwin's Plots* takes us through that language into the cultural centres of Darwin's thinking and into a recognition of the ways in which it continues to proliferate and to enrich us.

Preface to the first edition

This work has filled and extended my life over several years. During that time I have been continuously grateful for the resources of the Cambridge University Library, the English Faculty Library, and the Girton College Library, and for the helpfulness of their librarians.

The English faculty office has come to my aid from time to time by typing draft sections and I would like to thank all the members of staff. Dr Jenny Fellows, and members of my family, have read proofs and checked references. Historians and philosophers of science as well as my colleagues in literary studies have been most kind in inviting me to try out my ideas in discussions, seminars, and lectures. I could not have completed the work without the stimulation of friends working in a variety of fields who have been generous of their knowledge, offering me references to pursue, arguments to consider, and scepticism to combat. It is hard to name a few among so many individuals to whom I feel gratitude, but I would particularly mention the importance of conversation over the years with John Beer, Jina Politi, Sally Shuttleworth, Allon White, and Ludmilla Jordanova. More recently, Howard Gruber, David Kohn, Mary Jacobus, and George Levine have offered invaluable help. Gordon Haight and Barbara Hardy have been of help to me since the beginning of my career and, like all those engaged with George Eliot, I am indebted to them for their work. Some very interesting writing on George Eliot and the relations between scientific and literary culture has not yet been published: I would particularly mention dissertations by John Durant, Simon During, Sally Shuttleworth and Margot Waddell.

Sections of the present book have appeared, in somewhat different form, in *This Particular Web* (ed. Ian Adam), *The Listener, Comparative Criticism* II (ed. Elinor Shaffer), *Women Writing and Writing about Women* (ed. Mary Jacobus), *Cahiers Victoriens et Edouardiens, The Journal for the History of the Behavioural Sciences*. In addition, I have written two forthcoming essays which supplement the present work. 'Darwin's Reading and the Fictions of Development' in *The Darwinian Heritage* (ed. David Kohn, Princeton University Press) examines in much greater detail Darwin's literary reading at the period of theory formation and precipitation; 'Virginia Woolf and Prehistory' in *Virginia Woolf Centenary Essays* (ed. Eric Warner, Macmillan) shows the longer-term effects of Darwin's work in a twentieth-century writer.

Bearing and rearing children made me need to understand, first, evolutionary process, and then, the power of Darwin's writing in our culture. So it is to my mother and my sons that I dedicate this book – though without my husband, much would have been impossible.

Gillian Beer
Girton College, Cambridge

Preface to the second edition

Darwin has grown younger in recent years. He is no longer the authoritative old man with a beard substituting for God. Instead his work and life are again in contention and debate. Sociologists, microbiologists, linguists, sociobiologists, philosophers, feminists, psychologists, biographers, geneticists, novelists, poets, post-colonialists, have their say. Moreover, the publication, volume by tremendous volume since 1985, of the Darwin *Correspondence*[1] has shown us that, so far as Darwin's theories go, everything started with a young man, eager for knowledge and adventure, who set out on a journey round the world just before his twenty-third birthday: the age of a postgraduate student now. The letters bring out the vivid engagement of the young Darwin on his *Beagle* travels, the ardour of his response to the natural world and the immediacy of his engagement with societies he encountered. His vacillations in language register how hard he found it to settle his opinions of other tribes. His struggles with categories break open settled taxonomies. The stamina of his mental exploration gives the lie to the outworn assumption that once back from the *Beagle* he merely settled into a comfortable humdrum life. He was still on his world journeys while he sat in his armchair, his mind packed with the materiality of the physical world and sharpened by exceptions noted. His greenhousee could harbour questions that unsettled the assumptions of the western world – and he determined to engage with those questions.

When I came to write *Darwin's Plots* the best part of twenty years ago I first approached Charles Darwin's work through thinking about Victorian fantasy. Why was evolutionary theory abroad in so many guises? What anxieties did it arouse? What pleasures did it promise? And what new mental freedoms gave it its allure? As I began to investigate these

[1] Frederick Burkhardt; Sydney Smith; David Kohn; William Montgomery, eds. *The Correspondence of Charles Darwin, 1821–1882*, volume I (Cambridge, 1985); volume XI has now appeared and the edition is going forward strongly, with new editors added at present, through the 1860s.

questions I came to realise that the intellectual and emotional excitement generated by *The Origin of Species* was partly the outcome of Darwin's struggle to find a language to think in. He was working in a milieu where natural theology had set the terms for natural historians. The key concepts for natural theologians seeking to display God's workings in the material world were *design* and *creation*. Darwin, on the contrary, was trying to precipitate a theory based on *production* and *mutation*. How to think these ideas against the grain of the language available? One means was to invent a phrase poised on the edge of metaphor, a phrase that, moreover, alluded to its predecessor, even as it undermined it: 'natural selection' is a pithy rejoinder to 'natural theology'. Instead of an initiating godhead, Darwin suggests, diversification and selection have generated the history of the present world. Instead of teleology and forward plan, the future is an uncontrollable welter of possibilities. In the world he proposed there was no crucial explanatory function for God, nor indeed was there any special place assigned to the human in his argument. Those lacks, moreover, were not presented as lacks: the world of nature is always full.

I speak of 'natural selection' as poised on the edge of metaphor because of the way it claimed an explanatory role before contemporaries had learnt what it meant. They puzzled, as people have puzzled since, over its individual elements: natural as opposed to unnatural, or man-made? selected by whom or what? Part of Darwin's triumph is that the phrase, in the event, quite rapidly passed from this unruly question-raising, context-rich status into technical description. It came to seem honed, even simple.

Yet much of the power of 'natural selection' as a tool for thought comes from the opposing conceptual elements it encompasses. There is an awkward fit between the first two necessary elements and the third: the liberal emphasis on profusion, and variability, is constrained by the frugality of the selective process. There must be hyperproductivity; there must be difference; there must be death. Few organisms will survive through their progeny beyond a parsimonious number of generations. Yet, over aeons of time, all organisms are in some measure related to each other. Prodigality and rigour are the basis of his argument, as they are the characteristics of his prose.

Darwin affirmed at every stage of his argument and examples the linked concepts of diversification and selection. His metaphors of the tree and the great family in the *Origin* went some way to articulate his emphasis on unlikeness, transformation, and kinship – though they did not have a complete explanatory fit. But he did not face the second outcome of his theories head on: the loss of future plan. He prophesies knowledge of the past but not of what is to come.

> When we better know the many means of migration, then, by the light which geology now throws, and will continue to throw, on former changes of climate and of the level of the land, we shall surely be enabled to trace in an admirable manner the former migrations of the inhabitants of the whole world.

When, then, surely: understanding will allow us to track *former* changes and migrations. Nowhere does Darwin give a glimpse of future forms: and rightly so, since it is fundamental to his argument that they are unforeseeable, produced out of too many variables to be plotted in advance.

He countered the reader's eschatological appetite by fastening our attention on a backward story told laterally. His narrative demonstrated in every field of understanding the processes by which the variety of the present world had been arrived at. It was a form of history and had to be so since the full array of experimental evidence no longer survived – and could not do so if the theory of natural selection, with its emphasis on extinction and the vanishing of earlier forms, was sound. So although Darwin himself gave some considerable emphasis to the language of progress and improvement, generating an onward and upward motion in much of his storytelling, these tales were constantly under the pressure of other, darker stories – of rapine, degradation, and loss.

> Nothing is easier than to admit in words the truth of the universal struggle for life, or more difficult – at least I have found it so – than constantly to bear this conclusion in mind. . . . We behold the face of nature bright with gladness, we often see superabundance of food; we do not see, or we forget that the birds which are idly singing round us mostly live on insects or seeds, and are thus constantly destroying life.[2]

Gladness and destruction: life, making and destroying itself; the individual, swamped and yet demanded as a medium for mutation; the human, everywhere and nowhere in his argument: these tensions were what so intensely interested me in the *Origin*. The energies of these conflicting narratives poured into Victorian responses. They set peculiar tasks for novelists where the writer's prospecting eye is expected to take responsibility for the futures inscribed. Those futures, or fictional 'events',

---

[2] Charles Darwin, *The Origin of Species*, ed. Gillian Beer (Oxford, 1996) pp. 393, 52–3. This edition is referred to in this preface only; in the main text page-references are to ed. John Burrow (Harmondsworth, 1968).

take place, moreover, within the multiple hypothesised futures the reader is encouraged to produce in the process of reading the story. *Middlemarch* works with these multiplicities. Darwin's narratives set another challenge, too, because the scope of the individual's lifespan is both very slight in evolutionary terms: once progeny are produced the individual is done with, biologically; yet, the individual also carries the freight of evolutionary change through the slight variations encoded in each organism or person. Hardy, in particular, responded to this double chanciness.

Samuel Butler, who deserves and has received attention elsewhere but not in this book,[3] saw the problem implied: in human affairs, biological evolution takes place across another evolutionary form, that of cultural memory. Through record and language, through tools and machines, futures are built and change is released – though at the same time the process is understood as settling society and grounding knowledge. No human lifespan is long enough to invent the fundamental tools and conditions for living which we take for granted (wheels, telephones, democracy, one-party rule) and which are donated by the historical culture within which the human person is born already embedded. That idea is now enjoying renewed currency through the idea of 'memes',[4] a term that draws language into evolutionary theory and insists on what Stephen Pinker calls 'the rococo complexity of human grammar' as an outcome of the selective process.[5]

I suspect that evolving humans lived in a world in which language was woven into the intrigues of politics, economics, technology, family, sex, and friendship that played key roles in individual reproductive success. They could no more live with a Me-Tarzan-you-Jane level of grammar than we could.

Such argument also emphasises primordial continuities in our most sophisticated products. George Dyson puts that second point in an approachable form in *Darwin Among the Machines*:[6]

Evolution is traditionally portrayed as a succession of discrete layers, those of geology and biology gathered into chapters like the pages of a book. A layer of dinosaurs is followed by a layer of mammals. But the precursors of mammals were there all along. If you could ask mammals how long they had been around, they wouldn't answer, 'Since the dinosaurs left,' they would answer,

---

[3] George Dyson, *Darwin among the Machines* (London, 1997); Elinor Shaffer, *Erewhons of the Eye: Samuel Butler as Painter, Photographer and Art Critic* (London, 1988).

[4] See especially Daniel C. Dennett, *Darwin's Dangerous Idea: Evolution and the Meanings of Life* (New York, 1995), pp. 335–369.

[5] Stephen Pinker, *The Language Instinct* (London, 1995) p. 368.

[6] Dyson, *Darwin among the Machines*, p. 202.

'Since life began.' If you could ask the same question of machines such as microprocessors, you might get an answer that begins not with the age of computers but with the age of bifacial stones.

Even now, the articulation of Darwinian theory is fraught with multiple meanings that Darwin himself sought to control – or which he never fully and consciously confronted. We see it in the continuing debates around sociobiology and genetics; in the arguments that arose in the mid-1970s between the mechanistic and yet anthropomorphic concept of the 'selfish gene' of Dawkins and the environmental emphasis of Lewontin's genetics: 'context and interaction are of the essence'.[7] The severely directive arguments concerning human achievement that were fashionable in the sociobiology of that time, particularly in the debate that raged around E. O. Wilson's *Sociobiology: the New Synthesis*,[8] have gradually given way to a renewed fascination with variability, as we see in Wilson's own later work.[9]

The works of David Worster and Richard Grove, for example, have made manifest the link between ideological practices and ecological management.[10] Indeed, it is remarkable that the chapter on 'Natural Selection' that among Darwin's contemporaries was often read as an argument for competition 'in the great and complex battle of life' now reads so strongly also as an ecological text:

Let it be borne in mind how infinitely complex and close-fitting are the mutual relations of all organic beings to each other and to their physical conditions of life.[11]

Darwin can be seen either as providing a grounding vocabulary for colonialism, or, as I have elsewhere argued, equally as resisting 'intrusion' and idealising the closed environment of island spaces because they give opportunities for the most 'natural' form of natural selection in which the indigenous inhabitants uncover among themselves more and more ecological niches through the action of variation.[12]

[7] Richard Dawkins, *The Selfish Gene* (Oxford, 1976), passim; Richard Lewontin, *The Genetic Basis of Evolutionary Change* (New York, 1974) p. 318.

[8] (Cambridge, Mass., 1975); *On Human Nature* (Cambridge, Mass., 1978); *The Diversity of Life* (Cambridge, Mass., 1992).

[9] *Naturalist* (Washington, DC, 1994); *Consilience: the Unity of Knowledge* (London, 1998).

[10] David Worster, *Nature's Economy: a History of Western Ecological Ideas* (Cambridge, 1985); Richard Grove, *Green Imperialism: Colonial Expansion, Tropical Island Edens and the Origins of Environmentalism, 1600–1800* (Cambridge, 1995).

[11] Charles Darwin, *The Origin of Species* ed. Gillian Beer (Oxford, 1996) p. 67. For discussion see Introduction pp. xxvi–xxviii.

[12] 'Writing Darwin's Islands: England and the Insular Condition', in Timothy Lenoir (ed.), *Inscribing Science: Scientific Texts and the Materiality of Communication* (Stanford, 1998), pp. 118–139.

One of the most spirited and sophisticated recent interventions into the issue of competition and variability, determinism and the random, has been Daniel Dennett's *Darwin's Dangerous Idea*.[13] Dennett avoids personification as well as the problem of the individual by placing the 'dangerous idea' at a level that refuses such concerns: the algorithmic. Dennett characterises algorithms as having 'substrate neutrality', 'underlying mindlessness', and 'guaranteed results'. He then presents his fundamental assertion:

Here, then, is Darwin's dangerous idea: the algorithmic level *is* the level that best accounts for the speed of the antelope, the wing of the eagle, the shape of the orchid, the diversity of species, and all other occasions of wonder in the world of nature. It is hard to believe that something as mindless and mechanical as an algorithm could produce such wonderful things. No matter how impressive the products of an algorithm, the underlying process consists of nothing but a set of individually mindless steps succeeding each other without the help of any intelligent supervision; they are 'automatic' by definition: the workings of an automaton.[14]

Darwin mitigated the ruthlessness of that definition by emphasising the immense time-scapes in which such changes have occurred and by linking them to a process whose very unconsciousness implied a benignity not shown in the conscious machinations of human 'artificial selection'. Artificial selection is a selfish process; natural selection a selfless one: 'Man selects only for his own good; Nature only for that of the being which she tends.'[15] Darwin's imaging of selflessness is ethical: the sustaining action of mother or nurse; Dennett's is of impervious process, selfless because without self, automatic only. What binds them convincingly together is unconsciousness: not Freud's 'unconscious' but a process recuperable only through immense numbers or through vast tracts of time. Strikingly, Dennett brings back in at least the terminology of design and creation when he remarks on the capacity of creatures to form other creatures by the ways in which their predatory demands articulate the contrary form of those that elude them. In that sense, cats may be said to make mice.[16] Like Dawkins, Dennett refuses either a species or an individual perspective on survival, preferring to work at the level of the gene, bent on replicating itself. This insistence on single-purpose survival at the level of the gene certainly clears away

---

[13] See note 4 above.
[14] *Ibid.*, pp. 50–51, 59.
[15] *Origin*, p. 69.
[16] See e.g. Dennett, *Darwin's Dangerous Idea*, p. 511.

some sentiment, but it does not do away with the need to interact or collaborate for the purposes of survival.

Exactly as it did in the nineteenth century, Darwinism has generated profoundly opposed insights and narratives now: on the one side, the deterministic sequences of sociobiology with its emphasis, at the human level, on the constrained choices of any individual whose DNA has already mapped its own trajectory. Whose story is this anyway? Dawkins's metaphor of the selfish gene, like the story of eggs countenancing chickens simply as the medium of egg-production, has a gruelling, mischievous comfort in it.[17] Not much can be changed; the social order is always already implemented by the interactions of genes in the gene-pool, expressed over time as intelligence, gender, even class. That is one extreme story Darwinism offers now. Another story is of the random non-purposive profusion of possibilities genetically encoded, scarcely a one of them to be played out.

A compelling reason for the presence of Darwin in argument and in popular imagination at present has been the accumulating realisation over the past decade of how significant the discovery of DNA is for all our lives and futures. Darwin achieved his advances without knowledge of genetics but DNA has raised anew in a more immediate form many of the controversies crucial in the first wave of reception of *The Origin of Species*, particularly the troubled realisation that humans and animals share common ancestry, and, it is now known, common genetic material. Ruskin's shudder of distaste at the 'filthy heraldries' that link man and crocodile thrills still through the discussions of trans-genic organs.[18] And the biological determinism that some saw in Darwin's taxonomy has become central to the arguments about mapping the human genome. Cloning, a powerful technique with immense future consequences, is at present the contrary of evolution. It replicates; it refuses deviance; it is the strongest form of artificial selection yet invented since it allows humankind to select whole organisms for absolute replication. But already difference is emerging. The cloned creature is born into a new generation. Its conditions vary from those of the mother. On the other hand, it may be born further through its life-cycle since it shares with its mother the stage of life at which cloning took place. As Borges foresaw, to write *Don Quixote* now produces a different text even if it is word for

---

[17] *The Selfish Gene* (London, 1978); *The Blind Watchmaker* (London, 1986).
[18] See discussion on pp. 7–8 and ch. 4, passim.

word identical with the original. And that applies to Dolly the Sheep and her like too.

The title of this book, *Darwin's Plots*, is a double genitive: it indicates both the plots that Darwin grew up with and the plots he generated for others. When I was at work on the project I was always conscious of the degree to which Darwin drew on familiar narrative tropes (such as leaving the garden, or discovering your ancestry was not what you believed). That seemed crucial to understanding how it was possible for him to produce so many stories within his theory that could be teased out, or redesigned, by imaginative writers: the descent of man, the ascent of man, transformation, extinction, the great family, the tree of life, marriage as artificial selection or sexual selection.

I have chosen in this second edition not to alter what I wrote in the body of the 1983 text. This is not because I am fully content with the scope of the analysis I offer there but rather because so much has intervened that were I to begin again I would want to add a good deal more on Darwin's writing outside the *Origin* and to develop at large the insights offered by more recent race and gender analysis. In *Open Fields: Science in Cultural Encounter* (Oxford, 1996) I have engaged with some of these issues, in particular, I have worked with the writing on and after the *Beagle* and explored Darwin's encounters with indigenous peoples. I now view these as being of equal importance for the precipitation of his theories as his encounter with the tortoises and finches of the Galapagos. My discussion in *Darwin's Plots* of *The Descent of Man* is slight and there is now great need for thorough engagement with that book. It is likely that the *Descent*, even more than the *Origin*, was the seedbed for later Victorian writers, such as George Gissing, Grant Allen, H. G. Wells, and for New Woman novelists, like Sarah Grand, Mona Caird, and George Egerton. The *Descent* is also a much less tractable, or attractive, book for the modern reader. It is by far the most culturally dependent of Darwin's works, drawing for its evidence and affirmations on the works of ethnographers, race-theorists, and primatologists of the 1860s, themselves often affected by Darwin. The circle of evidence is therefore sometimes disturbingly untroubled since materials are passed round and back from one field to another, as I suggested in 'Darwin and the Growth of Language Theory' was the case with philology and Darwinian evolution.[19] In *Darwinism and the Linguistic Image: Language, Race, and Natural Theology in the Nineteenth Century* Stephen Alter argues this case at large. He writes:

[19] *Open Fields: Science in Cultural Encounter* (Oxford, 1996, paperback, 1999), ch. 4.

Every age, perhaps, has its special predilections with regard to this kind of cross-disciplinary affinity, its couplings of different phenomena that mutually resonate nonetheless. These seemingly natural metaphors – half-conscious bonds of logic among distinct fields of knowledge – draw upon the aesthetic sensibility of a given time and place.[20]

At the time that I was composing this work the study of science in relation to literature had been developed by only a few earlier pioneers though it is now a highly productive seam at the critical coalface and producing some outstanding work.[21] The aesthetic sensibility of this present time has freed scientific writing from its privileged (and therefore peripheral) autonomy and has emphasised the degree to which scientists work with (and against) the shared metaphors and preferences of the broader community within which they live, work, play and think. This book does not imply that Darwin's work is 'fiction', as some puzzled readers at first assumed. It argues that how Darwin said things was a crucial part of his struggle to think things, not a layer that can be skimmed off without loss. It shows how his non-technical language (which may indeed have imagined a technical readership) allowed a wide public to read his work and appropriate his terms to a variety of meanings (Nature, race, man, struggle, fit, and family would be examples of story-generating words). My argument demonstrates the degree to which narrative and argument share methods; indeed, it enquires what differences can be maintained between narrative and argument.

Were I to begin, wholesale, again I might not now hold to the form I frequently used then of deliberately adopting the Victorian form 'man' as a gender-inclusive term when discussing mid-nineteenth-century controversies. It seemed to me cumbersome (and perhaps misleading) to correct 'man's place in nature' to 'humankind's place', without being able to correct the many assumptions of the mid-nineteenth century with which Huxley's title is loaded. Above all, I did not wish to assume (nor would I still) the condescension of history towards Victorian terms. That condescension has a dangerous capacity to let the present off the hook and to suggest that we are now free of prejudices we can so readily symptomise when we recognise them set back one hundred or so years. I have written more extensively elsewhere about such questions,

---

[20] Stephen G. Alter, *Darwinism and the Linguistic Image* (Baltimore and London, 1999), p. 1.

[21] One of the first and best of the wave is Sally Shuttleworth, *George Eliot and Nineteenth Century Science: The Make Believe of a Beginning* (Cambridge, 1984). See George Levine (ed.), *One Culture: Essays in Science and Literature* (Madison, 1987), *Realism and Representation: Essays on the Problem of Realism in Relation to Science, Literature, and Culture* (Madison, 1993); Elinor Shaffer (ed.), *The Third Culture: Literature and Science* (Berlin, 1998).

particularly in 'Speaking for the Others: Relativism and Authority in Victorian Anthropological Writing'.[22]

Since *Darwin's Plots* appeared feminist writers such as Evelyn Fox Keller[23] have explored some of the ways in which the epistemic contours of scientific activity and writing can be shifted when attributes associated with the feminine are allowed their place. Her work, together with that of Donna Haraway on the history of primatology in the twentieth century, has raised issues that would have been helpful to me at the time. In particular, Haraway's analysis would have allowed me to extend the work on race that I moot here in a rather preliminary form. It is striking that Homi Bhabha's immensely usable idea of 'hybridity' follows on, at a distance, from Darwin's rather anguished discussion of 'Hybridism'.[24] Darwin is troubled principally by the question as to whether hybridism inevitably produces sterility, which suggests that species are fixed natural categories, rather than the moveable varieties he sought. In Bhabha's work hybridity and mimicry allow interchange and shifting power relations between groups where the power hierarchies have previously appeared to be (and have been represented as being) inexorably fixed.

In Darwin I encountered a man thinking within the frame of his society, certainly, but with all the sensory resources of the human, and with an enthusiasm and empathy for other living forms that took him far from any stereotype of the Victorian patriarch. His life may have fallen into conventional patterns but his mind continued to assay materials that ran counter to his society. My understanding of Darwin is of a figure less assured, more deflected by insight, than that presented in so robust a fashion in the major biography *Darwin*, by James Moore and Adrian Desmond.[25] Had Darwin been so at ease with the cultural conditions of his class and nation he could not, I think, have reached the radical insights offered in his theory. I have written at large about these issues in 'Four Bodies on the *Beagle*'.[26] The difference of perception

---

[22] In *Open Fields*.
[23] Evelyn Fox Keller, *Reflections on Gender and Science* (New Haven and London, 1985); Donna Haraway, *Primate Visions: Gender, Race and Nature in the World of Modern Science* (London, 1989). See also Londa Schiebinger, *Nature's Body: Gender in the Making of Modern Science* (Boston, 1993); Marina Benjamin (ed.), *Science and Sensibility: Gender and Scientific Enquiry 1780–1945* (London, 1991).
[24] Homi Bhabha, *The Location of Culture* (London, 1994); *Nation and Narration* (ed.) (London, 1990).
[25] Adrian Desmond and James Moore, *Darwin* (London, 1991). See also Janet Browne, *Charles Darwin*: Volume I, *Voyaging* (London, 1995) for a nuanced account, yet to be completed by a second volume.
[26] *Open Fields*, pp. 13–30.

between my own analyses and those of his biographers is, I think, because I work with the writing, in which hesitation, reach, inhibition, and empathy declare themselves in the syntax as well as the semantics of sentences – and where stories abound and grate upon each other.

The struggle for existence inevitably follows from the high geometrical ratio of increase which is common to all organic beings. This high rate of increase is proved by calculation, – by the rapid increase of many animals and plants during a succession of peculiar seasons, or when naturalised in a new country. More individuals are born than can possibly survive. A grain in the balance will determine which individual shall live and which shall die, – which variety or species shall increase in number, and which shall decrease, or finally become extinct.[27]

The secure 'inevitability' of the first sentence, whose grammatical structure reinforces its argument, begins to jump in the second with its move from proof to general examples. Then the odd 'More individuals are born than can possibly survive' demands that the reader understand 'survive' here as continuance through progeny. Individuals all die. And suddenly the frailty of the process comes home 'a grain in the balance' – and the large leap is made from the individual to variety or species. That leap is permitted by the comma and dash in the middle of the sentence. The swerve is followed by a series of clauses that seems to promise expansion 'which variety or species shall increase in number', but which then closes down upon itself to end the sentence with 'become extinct'. Writing gives phenomenological entry into the uncertainties on which creative thinking draws.

It is the constant movement between reach and correction that produces contradiction in the stories Darwin's writing generates. In the second half of this book I explore ways in which some nineteenth-century novelists who read his work responded to, and resisted, Darwinian insights. George Levine has tackled this question in a different way, placing his emphasis on those writers who did *not* read Darwin (at least in any systematic way we can discover) but who, all the more, could draw freely on the ideas his work had generated and who provided fictional materials for Darwin to work with. Levine's analysis in *Darwin and the Novelists: Patterns of Science in Victorian Fiction* (Cambridge, Mass., and London, 1988) importantly supplements what I offer as well

[27] *Origin*, p. 378.

as engaging with other authors, but there is no inconsonance between the two projects.

Perhaps the most striking phenomenon of recent years has been the assurance with which creative writers have turned to scientific materials for their imaginative work. A. S. Byatt, Peter Carey, Michael Frayn, Tom Stoppard, are just the start of the roll-call. Science always raises more issues than can be answered solely within the terms of scientific enquiry. It suggests, as Darwin so strongly did, questions about chance, about the future, about the very large and the very small, the near and far. Quantum mechanics, as much as Darwinian evolution, has yielded new forms for fiction, as in Jeannette Winterson's *Sexing the Cherry* (1989) and *Gut Symmetries* (1997), which undoes the fixed bounds of living and being dead; and for poetry, as in Jorie Graham's *The Dream of the Unified Field* (1996) which includes poems also from her earlier collection 'Hybrids of Plants and of Ghosts'. What new tales are being unleashed from scientific work now? and what new forms for storytelling? Must there be new grammars for narrative or is Propp's view of fixed folk-tale grammars, based on the analogy with morphology, still viable? Are there stories to be told from places and organisms until now unrecognised? Can first person be induced from ticks, dramatic monologues from mad cows? The answer to that last question is certainly yes, as the poems of Jo Shapcott and Les Murray make clear.[28]

Les Murray, in his poem 'Cell DNA' from the sequence 'Translations of the Natural World' pinpoints the necessary disruption of gene-life, too, as part of evolutionary processes:

> I am the singular
> in free fall.
> I and my doubles
> carry it all:
>
> life's slim volume
> spirally bound.
> It's what I'm about,
> it's what I'm around.
>
> Presence and hungers
> imbue a sap mote
> with the world as they spin it.
> I teach it by rote

---

[28] Jo Shapcott, the mad cow sequence in *Phrase Book* (London, 1992).

but its every command
was once a miscue
that something rose to,
Presence and freedom

re-wording, re-beading
strains on a strand
making I and I more different
than we could stand.[29]

Difference is painful as well as creative ('strains on a strand/making I and I more different/than we could stand); rote action and miscuing are necessary to evolutionary reach. Algorithm and meme alike are caught in Murray's description, voiced from cell DNA.

That feeling for lost, impossible, or discounted voices finds expression also in subaltern stories such as Roger McDonald's novel *Mr. Darwin's Shooter* (1998) which awakens us to the presence of Covington, Darwin's servant. Covington accompanied Darwin on all the revelatory land-journeys from the *Beagle*, collected and tabulated specimens and continued to send Darwin samples until Covington's death – and is nowhere mentioned by name in the *Origin*.

Half of Covington was in its pages – those years when his life was disgorged at Darwin's feet – the bundles of bones and birdskins to be interpreted – the glass jars devotedly sealed – the million gouged eyes – the innumerable notes copied in his own true hand.[30]

McDonald endows Covington with religious belief that runs ecstatically counter to the implications of the theory he has helped to ground. The novel brings home that Darwin was never a singleton. He needed and used the work, information, and insights of many people to do his work and be himself. Jenny Diski, in her novel *Monkey's Uncle* (London, 1994), brilliantly shows Fitzroy at work emotionally and intellectually in Darwin, as well as genetically in his possible descendant Charlotte, the heroine of this story. In a moving long poem 'Darwin in 1881' the American poet Gjertrud Schnackenberg captures the sense of Darwin as Prospero, understanding the chancy games in which sex and universe may be oscillating terms and so many possibilities remain unplayed:

He'd quite by chance beheld the universe:
A disregarded game of chess
Between two love-dazed heirs

[29] Les Murray, *Translations from the Natural World* (London, 1993) p. 41.
[30] Roger McDonald, *Mr. Darwin's Shooter* (London, 1998) p. 367.

Who fiddle with the tiny pairs
Of statues in their hands, while numberless
Abstract unseen
Combining on the silent board remain
Unplayed forever when they leave the game
To turn, themselves, into a king and queen.[31]

At the end of her poem she imagines Darwin wandering the garden on his last night alive and coming at last to bed:

He lies down on the quilt,
He lies down like a fabulous-headed
Fossil in a vanished river-bed,
In ocean drifts, in canyon floors; in silt,
In lime, in deepening blue ice,
In cliffs obscured as clouds gather and float;
He lies down in his boots and overcoat,
And shuts his eyes.

In those last lines sleep, space, and species, ice and eyes, soften into death.

Darwin himself saw that taxonomies always cause trouble with boundaries, that they draw on prior assumptions, that their values tend to form an evidential circle about what matters for categorisation.[32] Darwin never doubts the world is real. But he does doubt our categories for understanding it and indeed questions, while he shares, the categorising zeal of human beings. That unsteadying of plot allows him to continue to generate new debate and insight in an extraordinary variety of fields.

Gillian Beer
August 1999

BOOKS REFERRED TO IN THE PREFACE TO THE SECOND EDITION

Stephen G. Alter, *Darwinism and the Linguistic Image* (Baltimore and London, 1999).
Gillian Beer, *Open Fields: Science in Cultural Encounter* (Oxford, 1996; paperback, 1999).
  'Writing Darwin's Islands: England and the Insular Condition', in Timothy Lenoir (ed.), *Inscribing Science: Scientific Texts and the Materiality of Communication* (Stanford, 1998).

---

[31] Gjertrud Schnackenberg, *The Lamplit Answer* (London, 1986), p. 44.
[32] Harriet Ritvo, *The Platypus and the Mermaid* (Cambridge, Mass., 1997).

Marina Benjamin (ed.), *Science and Sensibility: Gender and Scientific Enquiry 1780–1945* (London, 1991).

Homi Bhabha (ed.), *Nation and Narration* (London, 1990).
The Location of Culture (London, 1994).

Janet Browne, *Charles Darwin: Volume I, Voyaging* (London, 1995).

Frederick Burkhardt; Sydney Smith; David Kohn; William Montgomery, eds. *The Correspondence of Charles Darwin*, 1821–1882, volume I (Cambridge, 1985). The edition has now reached volume XI.

Charles Darwin, *The Origin of Species* ed. Gillian Beer (Oxford, 1996).

Richard Dawkins, *The Selfish Gene* (Oxford, 1976).
The Blind Watchmaker (London, 1986).

Daniel C. Dennett, *Darwin's Dangerous Idea: Evolution and the Meanings of Life* (New York, 1995).

Adrian Desmond and James Moore, *Darwin* (London, 1991).

George Dyson, *Darwin among the Machines* (London, 1997).

Richard Grove, *Green Imperialism: Colonial Expansion, Tropical Island Edens and the Origins of Environmentalism, 1600–1800* (Cambridge, 1995).

Donna Haraway, *Primate Visions: Gender, Race and Nature in the World of Modern Science* (London, 1989).

Evelyn Fox Keller, *Reflections on Gender and Science* (New Haven and London, 1985).

George Levine, *Darwin and the Novelists: Patterns of Science in Victorian Fiction* (Cambridge, Mass., 1988).
(ed.), *One Culture: Essays in Science and Literature* (Madison, 1987).
(ed.) *Realism and Representation: Essays on the Problem of Realism in Relation to Science, Literature, and Culture* (Madison, 1993).

Richard Lewontin, *The Genetic Basis of Evolutionary Change* (New York, 1974).

Roger McDonald, *Mr. Darwin's Shooter* (London, 1998).

Les Murray, *Translations from the Natural World* (London, 1993).

Stephen Pinker, *The Language Instinct* (London, 1995).

Harriet Ritvo, *The Animal Estate: The English and Other Creatures in the Victorian Age* (Cambridge, Mass., 1987).
The Platypus and the Mermaid (Cambridge, Mass., 1997).

Londa Schiebinger, *Nature's Body: Gender in the Making of Modern Science* (Boston, 1993).

Gjertrud Schnackenberg, *The Lamplit Answer* (London, 1986).

Elinor Shaffer, *Erewhons of the Eye: Samuel Butler as Painter, Photographer and Art Critic* (London, 1988).
(ed.), *The Third Culture: Literature and Science* (Berlin, 1998).

Jo Shapcott, *Phrase Book* (London, 1992).

Sally Shuttleworth, *George Eliot and Nineteenth Century Science: The Make Believe of a Beginning* (Cambridge, 1984).

E. O. Wilson, *On Human Nature* (Cambridge, Mass., 1978).
The Diversity of Life (Cambridge, Mass., 1992).
Consilience: the Unity of Knowledge (London, 1998).

Jeanette Winterson, *Sexing the Cherry* (London, 1989).
  Gut Symmetries (London, 1997).
David Worster, *Nature's Economy: a History of Western Ecological Ideas* (Cambridge, 1985).

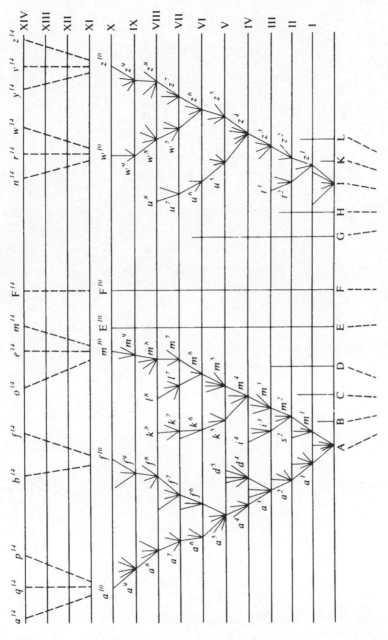

Sea-weed, narrative, tree?

Introduction

I THE REMNANT OF THE MYTHICAL

Most major scientific theories rebuff common sense. They call on evidence beyond the reach of our senses and overturn the observable world. They disturb assumed relationships and shift what has been substantial into metaphor. The earth now only *seems* immovable. Such major theories tax, affront, and exhilarate those who first encounter them, although in fifty years or so they will be taken for granted, part of the apparently common-sense set of beliefs which instructs us that the earth revolves around the sun whatever our eyes may suggest. When it is first advanced, theory is at its most fictive. The awkwardness of fit between the natural world as it is currently perceived and as it is hypothetically imagined holds the theory itself for a time within a provisional scope akin to that of fiction. Throughout the 1850s and well into the 1860s, for example, evolutionary theory was commonly referred to as 'the Development Hypothesis'.

In *The Structure of Scientific Revolutions* Kuhn discusses this phase in the conception and reception of a new scientific idea:

Discovery commences with the awareness of anomaly, i.e. with the recognition that nature has somehow violated the paradigm-induced expectations that govern normal science. It then continues with a more or less extended exploration of the area of anomaly. And it closes only when the paradigm theory has been adjusted so that the anomalous becomes the expected. Assimilating a new sort of fact demands a more than additive adjustment of theory, and until that adjustment is completed – until the scientist has learned to see nature in a different way – the new fact is not quite a scientific fact at all.[1]

A hundred years earlier Claude Bernard in his *Cahier Rouge* had noted that science proceeds by revolution and not by addition pure and simple.[2] This revolution must take place not only in the minds of scientists but in the beliefs of other inhabitants of the same culture if the theory

1

is to reach its full authority – an authority which rests upon an accepted congruity between theory and nature. The willed, half-consciously fictive and incomplete nature of hypothesis is touched on by Mackay in *The Progress of the Intellect* which George Eliot reviewed for the *Westminster Review* in January 1851. She there chose the following passage from his chapter 'The Mediation of Philosophy' as part of an extract to show him at his best. Mackay is arguing about the relationship between myth and science:

A remnant of the mythical lurks in the very sanctuary of science. Forms or theories ever fall short of nature, though they are ever tending to reach a position above nature, and may often be found to include more than the maker of them at the time knew.[3]

In its imaginative consequences for science, literature, society and feeling, *The Origin of Species*[4] is one of the most extraordinary examples of a work which included more than the maker of it at the time knew, despite all that he *did* know.

In this study I shall explore some of the ways in which evolutionary theory has been assimilated and resisted by novelists who, within the subtle enregisterment of narrative, have assayed its powers. With varying degrees of self awareness they have tested the extent to which it can provide a determining fiction by which to read the world. The book is concerned with Victorian novelists living, in relation to evolutionary theory, in the phase when 'a fact is not quite a scientific fact at all' and when 'the remnant of the mythical' is at its most manifest. I shall analyse works by writers as various in their responses as Kingsley, George Eliot and Hardy. But evolutionary ideas are even more influential when they become assumptions embedded in the culture than while they are the subject of controversy. As Barry Barnes writes in *Scientific Knowledge and Sociological Theory*:

A successful model in science frequently moves from the status of an 'as if' theory to a 'real description'. From here it may develop into a cosmology, before eventual disintegration into a mass of techniques and procedures, wherein what were key theoretical conceptions become mere operators, the ontological status of which is scarcely given a thought, (c.f. force, temperature, frequency).[5]

That process of naturalisation is the other major topic of my enquiry. We pay Darwin the homage of our assumptions. Precisely because we live in a culture dominated by evolutionary ideas, it is difficult for us to recognise their imaginative power in our daily readings of the world. We need to do so.

In the earlier chapters of this study I shall analyse some of the problems Darwin faced in precipitating his theory as language. He sought to appropriate and to recast inherited mythologies, discourses, and narrative orders. He was telling a new story, against the grain of the language available to tell it in. And as it was told, the story itself proved not to be single or simple. It was, rather, capable of being extended or reclaimed into a number of conflicting systems.[6]

In speaking of evolutionary theory I take as my focus the work of Darwin, though in the course of my argument I shall give some account of other writers such as Lamarck, Lyell, and Robert Chambers whose earlier writings had contributed to the acceptance of evolutionary ideas.[7] I concentrate on Darwin partly because his appreciation of the means through which change, development, and extinction of species took place was to revolutionise our understanding of natural order (though when his book first came out it was not immediately obvious to all that his work did more than substantiate and give authority to ideas already current). A second reason for focusing sharply on *The Origin of Species* is that it was widely and thoroughly *read* by his contemporaries. Reading *The Origin* is an act which involves you in a narrative experience. The experience may seem to diverse readers to be tragic (as postulated by Jacques Barzun) or comic (as Dwight Culler argues) but it is always subjective and literary.[8]

Related to this question of focus is another, of evidence. Perhaps I can best express it by an analogy. We now live in a post-Freudian age: it is impossible, in our culture, to live a life which is not charged with Freudian assumptions, patterns for apprehending experience, ways of perceiving relationships, even if we have not read a word of Freud, even – to take the case to its extreme – if we have no Freudian terms in either our active or passive vocabulary. Freud sufficiently disrupted all possible past patterns for apprehending experience and his ideas have been so far institutionalised that even those who query his views, or distrust them, find themselves unable to create a world cleansed of the Freudian. This was the nature also of Darwin's influence on the generations which succeeded him. Everyone found themselves living in a Darwinian world in which old assumptions had ceased to *be* assumptions, could be at best beliefs, or myths, or, at worst, detritus of the past. So the question of who read Darwin, or whether a writer had read Darwin, becomes only a fraction of the answer. The related question of whether the reader had read Darwin turns out also to have softer edges than might at first appear. Who had read what does not fix limits. On the face of it, then, a very generous use of evidence would have been possible for this study, which would see it as inevitable that all writers were affected by such theory. This would have permitted me to point out analogies of theme and order in almost anyone I chose.[9] But although I do not believe that this would be an improper enterprise, it seems to me to be in one sense an insufficient one, because it does not take account of the *act of reading* and reaction.

Reading creates uncertainty as well as satisfaction. As Richard Ohmann remarks:

> The very act of predication is an emotional act, with rhythms of its own. To state something is first to create imbalance, curiosity, where previously there was nothing, and then to bring about a new balance. So prose builds on the emotional force of coming to know, of pinning down part of what has previously been formless and resolving the tensions which exist between the human organism and unstructured experience.[10]

One's relationship to ideas depends significantly on whether one has read the works which formulate them. Ideas pass more rapidly into the state of assumptions when they are *unread*. Reading is an essentially question-raising procedure. This is one reason why in this study I have limited close discussion to the work of novelists whom we know to have read Darwin, and usually Lyell, Spencer and Huxley as well. I want to track the difficult flux of excitement, rebuttal, disconfirmation, pursuit, forgetfulness, and analogy-making, which together make up something of the process of assimilation.

In the mid-nineteenth century, scientists still shared a common language with other educated readers and writers of their time. There is nothing hermetic or exclusive in the writing of Lyell or Darwin. Together with other scientific writers such as G. H. Lewes, Claude Bernard, John Tyndall, W. K. Clifford, and even so far as his early work is concerned Clerk Maxwell (writers whose works ranged through psychology, physiology, physics and mathematics), they shared a literary, non-mathematical discourse which was readily available to readers without a scientific training. Their texts could be read very much as literary texts. In our own century scientific ideas tend to reach us by a process of extrapolation and translation. Non-scientists do not expect to be able to follow the mathematical condensations of meaning in scientific journals, and major theories are more often presented as theorems than as discourse. We unselfconsciously use the term 'layman' to describe the relationship of a non-scientist to the body of scientific knowledge. The suggestion of a priestly class and of reserved, hermetic knowledge goes mostly unremarked. In the mid-nineteenth century, however, it was possible for a reader to turn to the primary works of scientists as they appeared, and to respond directly to the arguments advanced. More-over, scientists themselves in their texts drew openly upon literary, his-torical and philosophical material as part of their arguments: Lyell, for example, uses extensively the fifteenth book of Ovid's *Metamorphoses* in his account of proto-geology, Bernard cites Goethe repeatedly, and – as has often been remarked – Darwin's crucial insight into the mech-anism of evolutionary change derived directly from his reading of Malthus's essay *On Population*. What has gone unremarked is that it derived also from his reading of the one book he never left behind during his expeditions from the *Beagle*: *The Poetical Works of John Milton*.[11] The traffic, then, was two-way. Because of the shared discourse not only *ideas* but metaphors, myths, and narrative patterns could move rapidly and freely to and fro between scientists and non-scientists: though not without frequent creative misprision.

The second premise of my argument is that evolutionary theory had particular implications for narrative and for the composition of fiction. Because of its preoccupation with time and with change evolutionary theory has inherent affinities with the problems and processes of nar-rative. 'There is not one great question relating to the former changes of the earth and its inhabitants into which considerations of time do not enter,' wrote Lyell in *The Principles of Geology* (1830, I:302).[12] And although Lyell at this time still believed in the fixity of species his explo-ration of an infinitely extended time-scale for the earth was one of the necessary preconditions of later theory. When Lyell wanted to point out how too short an imagined time-scale had misled geologists into a catastrophist view of the past, he did it by invoking the metaphor of romance time as opposed to historical time:

How fatal every error as to the quantity of time must prove to the introduction of rational views concerning the state of things in former ages, may be con-ceived by supposing that the annals of the civil and military transactions of a great nation were perused under the impression that they occurred in a period of one hundred instead of two thousand years. Such a portion of history would immediately assume the air of a romance; the events would seem devoid of credibility, and inconsistent with the present course of human affairs. A crowd of incidents would follow each other in thick succession. Armies and fleets would appear to be assembled only to be destroyed, and cities built merely to fall in ruins. (I:78–9)

As in *Tristram Shandy*, the pace of record and of event are here fatally at odds. Uncle Toby and Trim must build up and knock down their fortifications within the hour to catch up with the events in France. Geologists, too parsimonious of time, are obliged to imagine a world governed by catastrophic events which prepare for present tranquillity.

Evolutionary theory is first a form of imaginative history. It cannot be experimentally demonstrated sufficiently in any present moment. So it is closer to narrative than to drama. Indeed in the then current state of genetic knowledge many of the processes of inheritance were beyond explanation. The rediscovery of Mendel's experiments took place after Darwin's death. It took a century before the discovery of DNA demonstrated the organism as a structural narrative programmed to enact itself through time.[13] Evolutionary ideas proved crucial to the novel during that century not only at the level of theme but at the level of organisation. At first evolutionism tended to offer a new authority to orderings of narrative which emphasised cause and effect, then, descent and kin. Later again, its eschewing of fore-ordained design (its dysteleology) allowed chance to figure as the only sure determinant. On the other side, the organisation of *The Origin of Species* seems to owe a good deal to the example of one of Darwin's most frequently read authors, Charles Dickens, with its apparently unruly superfluity of material gradually and retrospectively revealing itself as order, its superfecundity of instance serving an argument which can reveal itself only *through* instance and relations.

Evolutionary ideas shifted in very diverse ways the patterns through which we apprehend experience and hence the patterns through which we condense experience in the telling of it. Evolutionism has been so imaginatively powerful precisely because all its indications do not point one way. It is rich in contradictory elements which can serve as a metaphorical basis for more than one reading of experience: to give one summary example – the 'ascent' or the 'descent' of man may follow the same route but the terms suggest very diverse evaluations of the experience. The optimistic 'progressive' reading of development can never expunge that other insistence that extinction is more probable than progress, that the individual life span is never a sufficient register for change or for the accomplishment of desire, an insistence which has led one recent critic to characterise Darwinian theory as a myth of death.[14]

Darwinian theory will not resolve to a single significance nor yield a single pattern. It is essentially multivalent. It renounces a Descartian clarity, or univocality. Darwin's methods of argument and the generative metaphors of *The Origin* lead, as I shall demonstrate later, into profusion and extension. The unused, or uncontrolled, elements in metaphors such as 'the struggle for existence' take on a life of their own. They surpass their status in the text and generate further ideas and ideologies. They include 'more than the maker of them at the time knew'. The world Darwin proposes can be felt as either plenitude or muddle. Darwin was much wounded by Herschel's description of his theory as 'the law of higgledy-piggledy',[15] but the phrase exactly expresses the dismay many Victorians felt at the apparently random – and so, according to their lights, trivialised – energy that Darwin perceived in the natural world.

Darwinian theory takes up elements from older orders and particularly from recurrent mythic themes such as transformation and metamorphosis. It retains the idea of *natura naturans*, or the Great Mother, in its figuring of Nature. It rearranges the elements of creation myths, for example substituting the ocean for the garden but retaining the idea of the 'single progenitor' – though now an uncouth progenitor hard to acknowledge as kin. It foregrounds the concept of kin – and aroused many of the same dreads as fairy-tale in its insistence on the obligations of kinship, and the interdependence between beauty and beast. Many Victorian rejections of evolutionary ideas register a physical shudder. In its early readers one of the lurking fears it conjured was miscegeny – the frog in the bed – or what Ruskin called 'the filthy heraldries which record the relation of humanity to the ascidian and the crocodile'.[16] In its insistence on chance as part of a deterministic order it perturbed in the same mode as *The Arabian Nights* – though more profoundly, because claiming the authority of science not exotic fiction. The pip thrown over the shoulder strikes the Grand Genie and vengeance ensues. Such tales – and *The Arabian Nights* was at the height of its imaginative influence at that period so that, for example, we find George Eliot one evening enjoying 'music, *Arabian Nights*, and Darwin' – rouse some of the same elated dread as the idea of minute random mutations with their uncontrollable consequences.[17] But Darwin's theories did not pleasurably assuage the dreads.

One of the persistent impulses in interpreting evolutionary theory has been to domesticate it, to colonise it with human meaning, to bring man back to the centre of its intent. Novelists, with their particular preoccupation with human behaviour in society, have recast Darwin's ideas in a variety of ways to make them seem to single out man. In *The Origin of Species* (1859) man is a determining absence, for reasons that I shall analyse in the succeeding chapters. In *The Descent of Man* (1871) man in all his varieties is the topic. The first is a work primarily of biology, the second of anthropology: together they form the substantial statement of Darwin's published views on evolution. Darwin's is a theory of descent as well as of adaptation: in *The Origin* he concentrated on the mechanism of 'natural' (that is, non-human and unwilled) 'selection' in creating change. In *The Descent*[18] he concentrates on the powers of sexual selection: this concentration brings back into the discussion the ideas of will and culture which are notably and deliberately excluded in *The Origin*. Women and men became his problem.

The power of Darwin's writing in his culture is best understood when it is seen not as a single origin or 'source', but in its shifting relations to other areas of study. As Darwin's notebooks, reading-lists, library, and annotations all show, he was immensely alive to concurrent work in a range of disciplines, including not only other directly scientific work but history, historiography, race-theory, psychology, and literature. The problems raised by his writing often manifest themselves most acutely when they are transferred into another field. Equally, his work was profoundly affected by common concerns. An ecological rather than a patriarchal model is most appropriate, therefore, in studying his work.

Darwinian theory has, then, an extraordinary hermeneutic potential – the power to yield a great number of significant and various meanings. In the course of this study I shall show how differing individual and cultural needs have produced deeply felt, satisfying, but contradictory interpretations of its elements. It is, therefore, important at the outset to emphasise that it cannot be made to mean *everything*. Disraeli's satire on Chambers's *Vestiges of Creation*, in *Tancred* where it is renamed 'The Revelations of Chaos', could not apply to Darwin.[19] Of 'The Revelations of Chaos' it is said: 'It explains everything, and is written in a very agreeable style.' Darwinian theory, on the contrary, excludes or suppresses certain orderings of experience. It has no place for *stasis*. It debars return. It does not countenance absolute replication (cloning is its contrary), pure invariant cycle, or constant equilibrium. Nor – except for the extinction of particular species – does it allow either interruption or conclusion.

II 'THE SECOND BLOW'

In 'A Difficulty in the Path of Psycho-Analysis' (1917) Freud comments that 'the universal narcissism of men, their self-love, has up to the present suffered three severe blows from the researches of science'. These three blows he names the *cosmological*, associated with Copernican theory, the *biological*, associated with Darwinian theory, and the *psychological*, associated with psychoanalytic theory.

In the course of the development of civilization man acquired a dominating position over his fellow-creatures in the animal kingdom. Not content with this supremacy, however, he began to place a gulf between his nature and theirs. He denied the possession of reason to them, and to himself he attributed an immortal soul, and made claims to a divine descent which permitted him to break the bond of community between him and the animal kingdom . . . We all know that little more than half a century ago the researches of Charles Darwin and his collaborators and forerunners put an end to this presumption on the part of man. Man is not a being different from animals or superior to them; he himself is of animal descent, being more closely related to some species and more distantly to others.[20]

Freud's formulation of man's dilemma is itself mythopoeic. (Joan Riviere's earlier translation further emphasises this by rendering the 'three blows' as the 'three wounds'.) He reserves to himself the position of youngest brother in this trio of giants (Copernicus, Darwin, Freud), inflicting a double blow: 'The third blow, which is psychological in nature, is probably the most wounding':

these two discoveries – that the life of our sexual instincts cannot be wholly tamed, and that mental processes are in themselves unconscious and only reach the ego and come under its control through incomplete and untrustworthy perceptions – these two discoveries amount to a statement that *the ego is not master in its own house.* Together they represent the third blow to man's self-love . . .[21]

Freud's assertion arrests history. The magical number three belies the possibility of a fourth great wound. Comte had used a similar absolutist numerology in his account of human thought and civilisation, an account whose influence was felt throughout the second half of the nineteenth century:[22] first the theological stage, then the metaphysical, and now the positive. This coming to rest in the number three, endowing the present with a special authority and permanence, is evident in many nineteenth-century orderings of knowledge. Claude Bernard described the three phases of the history of medicine, according to a system which clearly draws on Comte, as the theological, the empirical and the scientific. T. H. Huxley, in his lectures on Evolution, asserts, 'There are three hypotheses which may be entertained, and which have been entertained, respecting the past history of life upon the globe.' The first is that:

living beings, such as now exist, have existed from all eternity upon this earth
. . . the second hypothesis . . . I termed the Miltonic hypothesis . . . according
to the third hypothesis, or that of evolution, the existing state of things is the
last term of a long series of states, which, when traced back, would be found to
show no interruption and no breach in the continuity of natural causation.[23]

For Huxley the present state of things is 'the last term' and even Marx,
in whose system eschatology and the future are essential, uses the same
triple ordering of history which in most such systems stills the past into
the present order.

These examples show one of the difficulties on the path of evolutionary theory. It is a theory which does *not* privilege the present, which
sees it as a moving instant in an endless process of change. Yet it has
persistently been recast to make it seem that all the past has been yearning towards the present moment and is satisfied now. Since Freud wrote,
one might argue, quantum physics has dealt another and yet more
radical blow at man's narcissism because it has brought into question
the fixed causal relations, 'the continuity of natural causation' which
underpinned, in particular, nineteenth-century scientific explanation
and, more generally, the activities of human reason.

Freud's formulation, however, pinpoints two particular elements in
mid-nineteenth-century creative experience. One was the absence of
an analytical and denotative vocabulary for describing the activities of
the unconscious and subconscious. This meant that it remained possible to believe that the ego was master in its own house, capable of
choice, command and control. At the same time there was a growing
fascination with the reaches of experience beyond the domain of reason, a fascination which expressed itself in that oceanic richness in the
use of symbol typical of Victorian prose. Symbol and metaphor, as
opposed to analysis, can allow insight without consequences because
perceptions are not stabilised and categorised. They allow us fleetingly
to inhabit contradictory experience without moralising it. The Victorians were free from that rapid awareness of what images signify, which
may, and in a post-Freudian world frequently does, hamper impulse
and expression. Freud himself acknowledged the extent to which he
had been educated towards analysis by Victorian fiction, and although
mid-Victorian writers may not have been fully aware of the approaching Götterdämmerung for autonomous egos, they shared with Freud
much of the same historical experience.

Crucial to that common historical experience was the weight of Darwin's blow. It is hard to overestimate the imaginative turmoil brought

about by evolutionary theory, beginning in England already in the 1830s with the publication of Lyell's *Principles of Geology*, continuing in the 1840s with the publication of Robert Chambers's anonymously published and immensely popular work *Vestiges of the Natural History of Creation*, and concentrated in 1859 by Darwin's long-ruminated and rapidly written argument, *On The Origin of Species By Means of Natural Selection, or the Preservation of Favoured Races in the Struggle For Life*. Alongside the primarily natural-historical discussion, and pressing upon it conceptually, went the theories of the development of knowledge and society articulated by Auguste Comte and Herbert Spencer.[24] And behind this crisis of ideas lay, as Samuel Butler was soon and irascibly to point out,[25] the work of earlier development theorists such as Buffon, Lamarck, and Erasmus Darwin. As always, behind the theoretical culmination there lay also a long history of *glimpsed* half-formulated or locally pursued evolutionist perceptions which have been thoroughly studied by historians of science.[26] The debate between constancy and transmutation of species had been mooted throughout the eighteenth century, and was part of a much older debate about the constancy and transformation of matter which went back to Lucretius. The word 'evolution' itself is comparatively recent.[27] For example, like so much else, it appears in *Tristram Shandy*, where though championed by Uncle Toby it is treated as a nonce word:

'Kingdoms and provinces, and towns and cities, have they not their periods? and when these principles and powers, which at first cemented and put them together, have performed their several evolutions, they fall back'. – Brother Shandy, said my uncle Toby, laying down his pipe at the word *evolutions* – Revolutions. I meant, quoth my father – by heaven! I meant revolutions, brother Toby – evolutions is nonsense. – 'Tis not nonsense – said my uncle Toby.'[28]

During the eighteenth century, when the word was used, it meant the stages through which a living being passes in the course of its development from egg to adult. That is, it gives an account of a single life span and remains within the pale of individual development. The term for this in biology is ontogeny. But evolutionary theory challenged the single life span as a sufficient model for understanding experience. In the 1830s the word evolution was used for the first time to describe the development of the *species* rather than of the individual. For this the biological term is phylogeny. Etienne Geoffroy Saint-Hilaire is credited with its first use in the *Mémoire sur les sauriens de Caen*, 1831; Lyell used it in English in the following year, in the second volume of *Principles of*

Geology. The blurring of the distinction between ontogeny – individual development – and phylogeny – species development – in the single term 'evolution' proved to be one of the most fruitful disturbances of meaning in the literature of the ensuing hundred years, and is a striking example of the multivalency of evolutionary concepts.

The term 'evolution' only gradually acquired dominance. In French the word 'transformisme' for a long time supplied its place. 'Transformisme' emphasises the activity not only of process but of transformation. Transformation was at once the most verifiable and the most magical aspect of evolutionary ideas. Transformation within the single life span presents some of the most amazing observable phenomena of nature. Whereas 'transformisme' need not imply a progressive pattern to experience, the Development Hypothesis did suggest progress and improvement. Transformation might involve either progression or retrogression, and could give almost as much emphasis to the possibilities of degeneration as to those of improvement. What it could not fully include was the idea of extinction, since transformation suggests a constant process more like that of thermodynamics. Indeed it is striking that both theories share the emphasis upon process and transformation despite the divergence of their emphasis when it comes to the matter of order and confusion. Evolutionary theory appeared to propose a more and more complex *ordering*, while the second law of thermodynamics emphasises the tendency of energy systems towards disorder.

Yet in his observation of the reckless powers of individuation Darwin saw the source not only of creativity but of loss. Evolutionary theory emphasised extinction and annihilation equally with transformation – and this was one of its most disturbing elements, one to which gradually accrued a heavier and heavier weight in consciousness.

But despite the diverse emotional implications of its various related ideas, it is its ability to propose a total system for understanding the organisation of the natural world which has been its most powerful influence. The all-inclusiveness of its explanation, stretching through the differing orders of the natural world, seemed to offer a means of understanding without recourse to godhead. It created a system in which there was no need to invoke a source of authority outside the natural order: in which instead of foreknown design, there was inherent purposiveness. Its order welcomed difference, plenitude, multifariousness so that the exigencies of the environment were persistently controverted by the genetic impulse towards variety and by the multiformity of environmental responses as well. Evolutionary theory created a system which could not be resolved into a simple mathematical elegance. Profusion is a necessary component of its explanation. Selection is crucial also but it is a selection relying on hyperproductivity, upon a fertility beyond use or number. So the three elements of its style of explanation – its inclusiveness, its simplicity, its dependence on profusion and variety – did not all incline the same way: they left room for diverse dispositions of its all-encompassing form. This diversity of implication, its spawning of metaphorical applications, helps to account for the rapid assimilation of evolutionary ideas and the speed with which they occur as assumptions, rather than as propositions. The unexamined and diminished use of the evolutionary metaphor can be encountered all around us now and, as Barnes remarks, the ontological status of its key concepts is scarcely given a thought.

The shape and implications of powerful ideas often become fully discernible only when a reaction against them has set in. We have reached such a point, perhaps, with evolutionism. The reaction has been against the displacement of evolutionary concepts into fields of study other than those to which it originally applied, rather than against its importance to biological theory itself though socio-biology and recent genetic theory have raised questions about the accuracy or sufficiency of Darwin's work. During the past hundred years or so evolutionary theory has functioned in our culture like a myth in a period of belief, moving effortlessly to and fro between metaphor and paradigm, feeding an extraordinary range of disciplines beyond its own original biological field. In the later nineteenth century it gave ordering assumptions to the developing subjects of anthropology, sociology and psychology and elements in its ideas have been appropriated to serve as confirming metaphors for beliefs politically at odds with those of Darwin himself, such as social Darwinism, and even – through a displaced eugenic argument – a nightmare acting-out of 'artificial selection' in Nazism.

The concepts of evolutionary theory have shifted the weight of words in common use: words like development, generation, variety, inheritance, individuals, kinship, transformation. They have brought into ordinary speech words like mutation and extinct. One purpose of this study is to restore the elements of debate implicit in words like inheritance in nineteenth-century fiction, to show the fullness of impulse and counterimpulse compressed in vocabulary or skeined out in narrative order without necessarily ever manifesting itself as theme.

Evolutionary and biological patterns are currently posited for a variety of human activities and enquiries, often by way of submerged metaphor: take for example the title of Otto Jespersen's *Language, Its Nature, Development and Origin* or Propp's *Morphology of the Folk-Tale* with its opening claim: 'it is possible to make an examination of the forms of the tale which will be as exact as the morphology of organic formations', or even, a recent title, *The Evolution of National Insurance in England.* In literary theory we find Northrop Frye, in *Fables of Identity*, wishing for a co-ordinating 'principle' for literary criticism which would afford, it seems, something like a theological unity:

> I suggest that what is at present missing from literary criticism is a co-ordinating principle, a central hypothesis which, like the theory of evolution in biology, will see the phenomena it deals with as parts of a whole. Such a principle, though it would retain the centripetal perspective of structural analysis, would try to give the same perspective to other kinds of criticism too.
>
> The first postulate of this hypothesis is the same as that of any science, the assumption of total coherence.[29]

Derrida and Macherey share a fascinated repudiation of 'origins' and of that centripetal search for total coherence which is in itself a tribute to the surviving power of such organisations. The all-inclusiveness of evolutionary theory is the quality that attracts Frye, because it holds out the promise of system. Evolution has within itself the concomitant ideas of development and energy, and has loosely acquired those of improvement and progress.

So despite its tendency to undermine, the evolutionary metaphor has become also a means of confirming our value, suggesting that we inherit the world at its pinnacle of development and are the bearers of a progressive future. The apparent historical determinism of evolutionary ideas loosely applied, moreover, tends to justify society as it now is, as a necessary phase in progress. The idea of development makes it seem that all past has constantly aspired towards becoming our present. One sees this for example in that literary criticism which praises writers of the past for 'an almost modern' understanding of problems, or looks on *emergence* as the process most worth studying. Teleology is restored in such instances in the guise of historical design, a design which reaches its point of satisfaction in the present.

III   PROBLEMS OF KNOWLEDGE

New organisations of knowledge are particularly vexatious when they shift man from the centre of meaning or set him in a universe not

designed to serve his needs. In the mid-nineteenth century Darwinian
theory issued just such a double challenge. It suggested that man was
not fully equipped to understand the history of life on earth and that he
might not be central to that history. He was neither paradigm nor
sovereign. Man's indefatigable zeal in designing explanations of phenomena which would place him at the centre of reference was seen,
indeed, by some of the most creative scientists of the period as the
major stumbling block to the advance of knowledge.

Four hundred years earlier the congruity of man and universe had
been to a scientist such as Paracelsus the deepest order, and vital to all
explanation:

Consider how great and noble man was created, and what greatness must be
attributed to his structure! No brain can fully encompass the structure of man's
body, the extent of his virtues; he can be understood only as an image of the
macrocosm, of the Great Creature. Only then does it become manifest what is
in him. For what is outside is also inside, and what is not outside man is not
inside. The outer and the inner are *one* thing, *one* constellation, *one* influence,
one concordance, *one* duration . . . *one* fruit. (I/8, 160)[30]

The same tradition of explanation underlies the poem 'Man'. For George
Herbert, writing in the seventeenth century, man was the highest inten-
sification of the natural order:

> For Man is ev'ry thing,
> And more: He is a tree, yet bears more fruit;
> A beast, yet is, or should be more:
> Reason and speech we onely bring.

He continues the Paracelsian idea of universal analogy:

> Man is all symmetrie,
> Full of proportions, one limb to another,
> And all to all the world besides:
> Each part may call the furthest, brother:
> For head with foot hath private amities,
> And both with moons and tides.

In a play on the word 'kind' Herbert both emphasises the benign ordering of the natural world in man's favour ('All things unto our flesh are
kinde') and then extends and shifts the balance of implication in the
run-on of sense into the next line:

> All things unto our flesh are kinde
> In their descent and being; to our minde
> In their ascent and cause.

The initial anthropocentric sense of the attentiveness of the world to man extends into a recognition of universal kinship. All things are kin through their descent. The second half of the declaration reemphasises the congruity, the universally knowable quality of natural order 'to our minde'. All things come from the one cause – the mind of God. The speed with which a word like 'kind' can move on its axis in Herbert's compressed and precise language suggests a readiness to acknowledge kinship, but this readiness in turn depends upon a faith that all such interconnection proceeds from God, who places man at the interpretative centre. Though Herbert's lines sound almost proto-evolutionary in their democratic emphasis upon kinship through descent, what Darwin calls the hidden bond of community of descent, his poem celebrates the peculiar fitness and completeness of man for the highest place within a natural hierarchy. Man alone perceives and communicates God's analogical ordering of the world ('reason and speech we onely bring'). Man's unique claims to reason and to speech were also later to become issues of debate.[32]

To Emerson, still, writing in the 1830s, the whole of nature was a metaphor of man's mind. For the theologian Feuerbach in the 1840s the origin of all significance was man. But to the geologist Charles Lyell man's preoccupation with himself had distorted past records of the earth and obscured the laws underlying occurrences:

It is only within the last century and a half, since Hooke first promulgated his views respecting the connexion between geological phenomena and earthquakes, that the permanent changes effected by these convulsions have excited attention. Before that time, the narrative of the historian was almost exclusively confined to the number of human beings who perished, the number of cities laid in ruins, the value of property destroyed, or certain atmospheric appearances which dazzled or terrified the observers. (*Principles of Geology*, II,399)

In *The Origin of Species* Darwin, with an echo of Ecclesiastes, emphasises that man is unfitted by the shortness of his span either to recognise the great extensions of change in the natural world or to effect change himself: 'How fleeting are the wishes and efforts of man! how short his time! and consequently how poor will his products be, compared with those accumulated by nature during whole geological periods' (133). Claude Bernard, the great French physiologist and methodologist, opens his *Introduction a l'étude de la médecine expérimentale* (1865) by pointing out how narrow are the limits of observation within which man's contracted senses permit him to work. Because we do not recognise the constraints of our perceptions we tend constantly to misjudge what we observe.

'Man is not able to observe the phenomena which surround him, except within very narrow limits; most of them naturally evade his senses, and observation alone will not suffice' (my translation). Bernard sees man as essentially proud and metaphysical, expecting the 'ideal creations of his intelligence, which correspond to his feelings, to represent reality as well'. He argues that, on the contrary, 'man does not possess within him the knowledge and the criterion of things outside himself'. According to Bernard's formulation, man is blind to the extent of the *present*, the phenomena by which he is laterally surrounded and which lie just beyond the activity of his unaided senses. Evolutionary theory emphasises human unawareness of the *past* and obliges us to study a world from whose history we are largely absent. We must survey an antiquity in which we have no place. Lyell moreover rebukes us for 'our habitual unconsciousness that our position as observers is essentially unfavourable' (I,81).

Lyell, and later Darwin, demonstrated in their major narratives of geological and natural history that it was possible to have plot without man – both plot previous to man and plot even now regardless of him.

Even now, the waters of lakes, seas, and the great ocean, which teem with life, may be said to have no immediate relation to the human race – to be portions of the terrestrial system of which man has never taken, nor ever can take, possession, so that the greater part of the inhabited surface of the planet remains still as insensible to our presence as before any isle or continent was appointed to be our residence. (I,158)

The living world is neither entirely open to man's observation nor related to him. He has not taken possession of its meaning. He can no longer, like Adam, confidently name his subjects.

Evolutionary theory was both threatening and exhilarating not simply as a result of its novelty but because so many of the problems concerning development were in human terms *old* problems: chance, environment, death, survival. And even, in part, because the solutions it proposed were not entirely new. Darwin's hypotheses gave, as G. H. Lewes put it, 'articulate expression to the thought which had been inarticulate in many minds', though Darwin himself was irritated by the readiness of his contemporaries to claim this after the event.

No work of our time has been so general in its influence. This extent of influence is less due to the fact of its being a masterly work, enriching Science with a great discovery, than to the fact of its being a work which at once clashed against and chimed with the two great conceptions of the world that have ruled, and still rule, the minds of Europe.[33]

Lewes names these two conceptions of the world as the Monistic and the Dualistic. Darwin was, in Lewes's view, on the side of the Monists which 'reduces all phenomena to community, and all knowledge to unity' whereas the Dualistic conception is one which 'in phenomena separates and opposes Force and Matter, Life and Body, and which in knowledge destroys unity by its opposition of Physical and Final causes'. Darwin saw the natural world in terms of an 'inextricable web of affinities' (*The Origin of Species*, ch. XIII, p. 415) but he also distinguished stringently between 'real affinities' and the analogical. The emphasis on community and unity in Lewes's reading of Darwin's views takes up the element of interrelatedness in Darwin's thinking about phenomena. But it does not sufficiently register the *independence* of phenomena one from the other, the extent to which proximity rather than co-operation may be the dynamic of interchange.

In *The Origin* Darwin concentrated on the role of the mechanism of 'natural selection' in producing change. The fitness of an individual organism to its environment increases the chance of survival of individuals with specific characteristics and of those of their descendants who inherit these characteristics. But the environment is not monolithic and stable: it is itself a matrix of possibilities, the outcome of multiple interactions between organisms and within matter. We tend to think of the individual organism as dynamic and the environment as static – but the environment, being composed of so many more varied needs than the individual, is prone to unforeseeable and uncontrollable changes. The everyday does not last forever. Will and endeavour must always be insufficient. They can never control all the multiple energies of life. There is a satisfying irony in the almost simultaneous publication of Darwin's *Origin* and Samuel Smiles's *Self Help*.[34]

Walter Cannon observes that Darwin had no developed vocabulary of self-help. Cannon presents this as a lack – but it is, rather, a measured exclusion.[35] Natural selection contradicts the Lamarckian idea that will and habit can generate improvement. Darwin's thinking was anti-Platonic, was anti-essentialist, 'a philosophy of flux' as Gerard Manley Hopkins observed, when he speaks of 'the ideas so rife now of a continuity without fixed points, not to say *saltus* or breaks.[36] 'Million-fueled, nature's bonfire burns on.' In 'That Nature is a Heraclitean Fire' Hopkins images the profusion and decay, the endless energy of the natural world, and stays it with the image of Resurrection, man's leap. 'Natura non facit saltum' – 'Nature does not make leaps.' For Hopkins the way out of the 'world's wildfire' is the leap of faith. For Darwin, the old conviction that nature does not make leaps opened into some of his most radical insights, leading him away from the idea of the chain of being or the ladder, with its hierarchical ordering of rungs, towards the ecological image of the 'inextricable web of affinities'. These affinities he perceives sometimes as kinship networks, sometimes as tree, sometimes as coral, but never as a single ascent with man making his way upward. The emphasis upon interrelation and on difficulty, upon profusion and death, is visible in the diagram that Darwin presented in *The Origin of Species* compared with the neat triangulate geometry of Chambers's diagram of ascent. There may be a punning cross-play in Darwin's insistence on 'entanglement' in his theory and his metaphor. The primary meaning given to 'evolve' in the 1826 edition of Dr Johnson's dictionary in Darwin's library is 'To unfold: to disentangle'. In his emphasis through the metaphor of the 'entangled bank' on ecological interdependence and 'the inextricable web of affinities' Darwin distinguishes an important fresh emphasis in his own work from other evolutionist theories.

In Lamarck's theory conscious endeavour, as well as reflexive habit, are agents of evolutionary change. So he writes in *Zoological Philosophy* of 'a bird of the waterside':

Now this bird *tries to act in such a way* that its body should not be immersed in the liquid, and hence *makes its best efforts* to stretch and lengthen its legs. The *long-established habit acquired* by this bird and all its race of *continually stretching and lengthening* its legs, results in individuals of this race becoming raised as though on stilts, and *gradually obtaining* long, bare legs, *denuded* of feathers up to the thighs and often higher still. [my italics][37]

Lamarck proposes a world of intelligent desire rationally satisfied. His work also follows the pattern of all stories of how things came to be the way they are: need brings about change or – in more admonitory versions – bad behaviour results in loss and degradation. It is a pattern of story which has been predominant in many cultures. So the robin flew too close to the sun and acquired a red breast, or, ever after the reeds have whispered. He draws on mythic concepts of metamorphosis and transformation and explains them causally. The Just-So stories of Kipling elaborate the same pattern: how the whale got his throat, how the camel got his hump, how the leopard got his spots. *Intention* is the key to Lamarck's concepts. And in this he accords with human wishes and human language. It is extraordinarily difficult to eradicate the language of intention from accounts of evolutionary development. Darwin himself never entirely succeeded. But for him there was a constant awareness that he must try to expunge from language the suggestion that will is a force for change. It was Wallace who most directly answered Lamarck's self-help philosophy, in the *Proceedings of the Linnaean Society*, August 1858:

Neither did the giraffe acquire its long neck by desiring to reach the foliage of the more lofty shrubs, and constantly stretching its neck for that purpose; but because any varieties which occurred among its antetypes with a longer neck than usual at once secured a fresh range of pasture over the same ground as their shorter-necked companions, and on the first scarcity of food were thereby enabled to outlive them. (p. 61)

Genetic variations gave opportunities for further adaptation and fuller colonisation, but they could not be initiated or sustained by an act of will, of stamina, or of desire.

Lamarck's theory was in its way deeply satisfying: it gave primacy to mind – to intention, habit, memory, a reasoned inheritance from generation to generation in which need engendered solution and solutions could be genetically preserved by means of an act of will, rendered independent of consciousness as habit. Curiously and revealingly, Lamarck's account of evolutionary process is *still* the popular one. An intentionalist language keeps creeping into accounts of evolution. Lamarck's theory shifts the source of intention away from an interventionist deity who either created the World at one stroke or who at intervals intervenes to try out a new species. Instead the source of creativity is in the world of species. But intention or will remained the *instrument* of change, in that creatures learn physically to adapt and can in Lamarck's view pass on their acquired physical adaptations to their inheritors.

This reading of the past has no need of the concept of usurpation. It suggests an intelligible and co-operative world, in which succession is inevitably improvement. Whereas Keats in his proto-evolutionary poem *Hyperion* continued the emphasis of the Greek myth upon the need for revolution, upon the casting down of the old in order that 'The first in beauty shall be first in might', Lamarck's theory emphasises continuity and persisting development. In this way it was in accord with the parallel emphasis in geology upon the continuity of laws in nature. Many myths of origin emphasise the concept of degradation – the fall from Paradise, for example – but Lamarck's reading is more optimistic: it gives primacy to intelligent adaptation and intelligent succession. Lamarck tended to give predominance to the present; he did not envisage rapid change. Darwin suggested that the speed of change was probably increasing and might now more rapidly bring about the transformation of species. Darwin put this down partly to the greatly increased complexity of interrelation between species, and between individual species and their natural environment. Lamarck placed less emphasis on competition and more on co-operation than could Darwin. He also gave less account of process and more of composition – that is, he imaged a world apparently more or less stable. As an ordering of the past in relation to present experience Lamarck's vision is attractive and neo-Lamarckian views continue to revive at intervals. Koestler's account of the case of the midwife toad is one of the most recent appraisals of the implications of Lamarckian metaphysics.

Lamarck's theory made room for one element of accretion to which Darwin paid little attention in *The Origin of Species* since he there suppressed the presence of man. This element is the accumulation of culture and inherited knowledge which man has been able to pass down (independent of genetic means) from generation to generation. But to some later writers even that power came to seem cursed. It was in Hardy's mind when he wrote, 'We have reached a degree of intelligence which Nature never contemplated in framing her laws, and for which she consequently has provided no adequate satisfactions.'[38] Or as Conrad's Heyst put it: 'Man on this earth is an unforeseen accident.'[39]

PART I

Darwin's language

CHAPTER 1

'Pleasure like a tragedy':
imagination and the material world

Darwin's early autobiographical fragment, written in August 1838, just before he thoroughly stabilised the implications of his views on 'transmutation', describes his earliest memories. They are of fear, astonishment, the pleasure of collecting and naming – and the pleasures and dangers of storytelling (or lying). The stories he invented in his childhood were designed to impress and astonish himself and others. His passion for fabulation expressed both a desire for power and an attempt to control the paradoxes by which he was surrounded. At the same time he was exhilarated by the intensity of paradox. He was vividly conscious of the substantiality of what he had made up.

I was in those days a very great story-teller . . . I scarcely ever went out walking without saying I had seen a pheasant or some strange bird (natural history taste); these lies, when not detected, I presume excited my attention, as I recollect them vividly, not connected with shame, though some I do, but as something which by having produced a great effect on my mind, gave pleasure like a tragedy. I recollect when I was at Mr. Case's inventing a whole fabric to show how fond I was of speaking the *truth*! My invention is still so vivid in my mind, that I could almost fancy it was true, did not memory of former shame tell me it was false.[1]

The prowess of invention gives him 'pleasure like a tragedy'. This arresting description exactly conveys the *fullness* and the density of his imaginative life: the power of lying, of invention, of telling and not telling, fuels his passion for discovery: 'I distinctly recollect the desire I had of being able to know something about every pebble in front of the hall door', 'I was very fond of gardening, and invented some great falsehoods about being able to colour crocuses as I liked.' The enduring and obdurate sense of the reality of these inventions which accompanies his sense of their absurdity – the surviving hope that lies are a form of truth-discovery – is both wonderfully comic and wonderfully full of insight.

When Darwin was disbelieved as a boy and had to acknowledge his claims false, he felt shame. Only by means of shame did he thoroughly disbelieve. When he reached his theory of natural selection he kept quiet about it. That powerful impulse to long-continued secrecy in which to relish and develop his own imagined story of a past for the life of our planet, that pleasure in invention, thrives still in the activity of mind which endured over twenty years from the early notebooks, through the two sketches, to the incomplete Big Book and the completed *Origin of Species*.[2] The brief sketch quoted above was written at the height of his imaginative powers, while his mind and his notebooks were thronging (but silently) with his as yet unuttered and unorganised story of metamorphosis, transmutation, and selection. It may be that the length of the account of his story-telling or lying, compared with his other memories, registers an elation and a creative disturbance newly felt again in 1838 by the young Darwin, akin to that which he had experienced as a ten-year-old.

Darwin's own later comments emphasised the loss of his aesthetic powers. In the autobiographical account written for his family towards the end of his life, he summarises in a pained and self-denigrating passage his loss of response.

I have said that in one respect my mind has changed during the last 20 or 30 years. Up to the age of thirty, or beyond it, poetry of many kinds, such as the works of Milton, Gray, Byron, Wordsworth, Coleridge and Shelley, gave me great pleasure, and even as a schoolboy I took intense delight in Shakespeare especially in the historical plays. I have also said that formerly Pictures gave me considerable, and music very great delight. But now for many years I cannot endure to read a line of poetry: I have tried lately to read Shakespeare and found it so intolerably dull that it nauseated me. I have also almost lost any taste for pictures or music. – Music generally sets me thinking too energetically on what I have been at work on, instead of giving me pleasure. I retain some taste for fine scenery, but it does not cause me the exquisite delight which it formerly did. My mind seems to have become a kind of machine for grinding general laws out of large collections of facts, but why this should have caused the atrophy of that part of the brain alone, on which the higher tastes depend, I cannot conceive.[3]

This later clouding of his affective powers has been read back by many commentators into far too early a period of his life. A somewhat similar argument is usual concerning his reading of fiction: because in his later life he liked to have novels read aloud to him and preferred those with a happy ending, it is assumed that he was a naïve reader, irresponsive to the range of literary experience.[4]

Darwin's pleasure in an extraordinary range of writing during his earlier life is to be found in his reading-lists for the late 1830s through to the 1850s, now in Cambridge University Library (Notebooks 119, 120, 128). Among his entries from 10 June to 14 November 1840 we find 'Sir Ch. Bell Anatomy of Expression Midsummer N. Dream. Hamlet. Othello. Mansfield Park. Sense and S. Richd 2nd. Poor. Henry IV Northanger Abbey. Simple Story. Johnson's Tour to Hebrides of Boswell. Macaulay Art. on Bacon in Edin. R. Some of Burke's speeches. Some Arabian Nights. Gulliver's Travels. Robinson Crusoe' (Notebook 119). Sir Thomas Browne, Montaigne, Carlyle, and Harriet Martineau are read enthusiastically. In addition the notebooks of the period allude to many writers including Walter Scott, Edmund Spenser, Wordsworth and Byron. It is likely that he consumed rather than analysed. But it would be an error to assume that his reading in literature therefore had any less effect on him. I have examined extensively in an essay elsewhere the interpenetration of Darwin's literary and scientific reading, and the contribution of writers such as Montaigne, Thomas Browne, Scott and Prescott, to the precipitation of his theory, and to his questioning of simple notions of development.[5]

Darwin's ideas profoundly unsettled the received relationships between fiction, metaphor, and the material world. That power of his was nurtured by his omnivorous reading. If we are fully to understand the importance of his reading to the imaginative development of his ideas, we need also to remember the powerful primary reading which preceded this of young adulthood: the immersive reading experienced in childhood and youth.

This unguarded reading is less controlled in its reception, less capable of being held at bay than any later appreciation. It creates shapes for experience, and those shapes endure into the experience we undergo in adult life also. Our projects and expectations draw on early imaginative habits. This gives a particular value to his boyhood enthusiasm for Shakespeare, particularly the history plays. The intimacy and solitariness of his contact with Milton, the one book he never left behind when he set out on his isolated land-journeys from the *Beagle*, also places it in a particular position. The sustenance he drew from such sources has its bearing on the formation of his ideas and on their mythopoeic powers. His literary resources affect, too, his reception of the *implications* of Malthus's ideas. As an example let us examine briefly some ways in which his reading of Shakespeare and Milton may have contributed to his imaginative intellectual development.

He describes himself when a young boy sitting for hours in a window seat avidly reading the history plays. They emphasise the need for stable succession in order to preserve order and government, to preserve, indeed, the idea of the nation and the race. They presented Darwin with one genetic pattern for interpreting the relationship between race and time. The blood succession becomes a means of stemming the tide of time – replication is emphasised and change is accommodated – the dead king is replaced by a live king whose blood succession ensures that no radical alteration has taken place. Each produces 'after his kind'. In kingship the aspect of *restoration* is intensified, and succession becomes not a means of change but a way of standing still. Buckingham seeks to persuade Gloucester of his lineal right and duty of succession:

> Know then, it is your fault that you resign
> The supreme seat, the throne majestical,
> The scepter'd office of your ancestors,
> Your state of fortune and your due of birth,
> The lineal glory of your royal house,
> To the corruption of a blemish'd stock . . .
> This noble isle doth want her proper limbs;
> Her face defaced with scars of infamy,
> Her royal stock graft with ignoble plants . . .
>
> (Richard III: III, 7, 117–22, 124–6)

The imagery of stock and of engrafting which is so powerfully used throughout the history plays lies somewhere between metaphor and substantiality. The fortunes of families, like plants, will be affected and can to some extent be controlled by conscious breeding and by mingling the qualities of specified stock. Darwin's argument in *The Origin of Species* was based from the outset on the same analogy of husbandry: man's agency in the development of particular properties demanded in plants and animals is compared with the activity of nature in selection and preservation of the characteristics most useful to the individuals of the race themselves. Man breeds plants and animals to serve *man's* ends – not particularly to benefit the plants or animals. In contrast, Darwin asserted, natural processes breed always for the good of the individuals of the race concerned.[6] This is a crucial distinction in his argument and again points to the benevolism of his view of nature, despite his full awareness of how harsh life may be to specific individuals.

In the next example we see how Darwin's literary reading helped to form and to articulate the polarities of his thought.

Almost all commentators follow Darwin himself in stressing the importance of reading Malthus for the precipitation in his imagination of his already half-formed notion of natural selection.[7] What has not been sufficiently recognised, however, is the extent to which Darwin transformed the imaginative tone and emotional balance and hence the intellectual potentialities of Malthus's concept. Malthus opens his essay *On Population* with a passage in which celebration and alarm are finely balanced as he describes the energy of fecundity.

It is observed by Dr. Franklin, that there is no bound to the prolific nature of plants or animals, but what is made by their crowding and interfering with each others means of subsistence. Were the face of the earth, he says, vacant of other plants, it might be gradually sowed and overspread with one kind only, as for instance with fennel, and were it empty of other inhabitants, it might in a few ages be replenished from one nation only, as for instance with Englishmen. This is incontrovertibly true. Through the animal and vegetable kingdoms Nature has scattered the seeds of life abroad with the most profuse and liberal hand; but has been comparatively sparing in the room and the nourishment necessary to rear them. The germs of existence contained in this earth, if they could freely develop themselves, would fill millions of worlds in the course of a few 1000 years. Necessity, that imperious, all pervading law of nature, restrains them within the prescribed bounds. The race of plants and the race of animals shrink under this great restrictive law; and man cannot by any efforts of reason escape from it.[8]

Any single species of plant or animal whose propagation went unchecked could rapidly colonise and take over the entire world, leaving no place for any other. Malthus goes on from this to propose that the reproductive energies of man, if not curtailed, must always outstrip the means of providing him with food. To Malthus fecundity was a danger to be suppressed – particularly by draconian measures among the human poor. To Darwin fecundity was a liberating and creative principle, leading to increased variability, increased potential for change and development. Because of the myriad super-productiveness of natural generative process, the range of individuality and of possible mutation is immense. And here it becomes important to remember two books which accompanied him on the voyage of the *Beagle*, when he was imaginatively at his most responsive. One of them was Lyell's *Principles of Geology*. The other, which he says in his *Autobiography*[9] was the one book that he never left behind, taking it with him on the long land expeditions from the *Beagle*, was Milton's poems.[10]

What kinds of imaginative sustenance did Milton offer to Darwin at this intensely formative period? One of the crucial discoveries that came to Darwin as a result of the voyage was that the green control of English landscape with its many man-induced harmonies and its sober beauties could not be considered normative. Beyond England lay other natural landscapes full of tumultuous colour and life. The full range of sense experience fills out and disturbs the narrowly descriptive authority of the scientific collector.

Who when examining in the cabinet of the entomologist the gay exotic butterflies, and singular cicadas, will associate with these lifeless objects, the ceaseless harsh music of the latter, and the lazy flight of the former – the sure accompaniments of the still, glowing noonday of the tropics? It is when the sun has attained its greatest height that such scenes should be viewed: then the dense splendid foliage of the mango hides the ground with its darkest shade, whilst the upper branches are rendered from the profusion of light of the most brilliant green . . . When quietly walking along the shady pathways, and admiring each successive view, I wished to find language to express my ideas. Epithet after epithet was found too weak to convey to those who have not visited the intertropical regions, the sensation of delight which the mind experiences.[11]

Darwin walks the tropical forests with Milton. His intense sense-arousal takes him beyond his own power of language.

The discovery of diversity and of profusion were of equal importance. The rich, even ecstatic, descriptions which Darwin gives of his travels allow some glimpse of the happiness his experiences engendered. His natural world came close to justifying Comus's earlier (and very anti-Malthusian) view of natural superabundance and the prodigal productivity of the earth. Comus, voluptuary and bacchic villain, interprets the abundance of the world as all being provided for the pleasuring of man:

> Wherefore did Nature pour her bounties forth,
> With such a full and unwithdrawing hand,
> Covering the earth with odors, fruits, and flocks,
> Thronging the seas with spawn innumerable,
> But all to please, and sate the curious taste? (710–14)

He claims that not only has man the right to indulge his luxurious appetites but the duty to do so. Else Nature 'would be quite surcharged with her own weight',

> And strangled with her waste fertility;
> Th'earth cumbered, and the winged air darked with plumes;
> The herds would over-multitude their lords . . . (728–31)

Comus's speciously libertarian arguments are countered by the Lady he has imprisoned; she insists that the appearance of over-plenty comes from the imbalance of want and superfluity among men. Instead of a few men engrossing all natural wealth, what is needed is a more even distribution of plenty.

Darwin's preoccupations at this time are with fertility, the mechanisms of increase and generation and the significances of these for the development of nature through time. In Milton's *Comus* the characters assume that man is at the centre of all concern, and at the top of a hierarchy of nature: 'The herds would over-multitude their lords.' The tendency of all Darwin's earlier unpublished work is to displace man from his central position and to look at the organisation of nature from the point of view of other species and orders of life. So, words that in other contexts have a specifically human application, such as 'inhabitants', in his writing apply equally to all species of animal or vegetable life. The debate in *Comus* provided Darwin with a vantage point from which to consider problems formulated by Malthus: problems of increase, profusion and penury.

When Milton reaches the account of the third day of creation in the seventh book of *Paradise Lost* he describes the parting of the earth and the water:

> over all the face of earth
> Main ocean flowed, not idle, but with warm
> Prolific humor soft'ning all her globe,
> Fermenting the great mother to conceive,
> Satiate with genial moisture: when God said,
> 'Be gathered now, ye waters under heav'n,
> Into one place, and let dry land appear.' (278–86)

The imagery of creation in *Paradise Lost* is that of sexual congress and impregnation, a voluptuously loving insistence upon the female nature of the earth:

> the tender Grass, whose verdure clad
> Her Universal Face with pleasant green (315–16)

There is in every line a representation of superabundance, variety, and plenty, 'the Sounds and Seas each Creek and Bay With Frie innumerable swarme'.

In *Paradise Lost* Darwin met the full poetic expression of 'separate creation', of fully formed, full-grown species. Sexuality there expresses itself as lyrical union, rather than as generation, descent. Milton also emphasises the direct birth of life from sea and earth: 'the Ounce, the Libbard, and the Tyger,' all emerge out of the earth:

> The grassie clods now calved, now half appeared
> The tawnie lion, pawing to get free
> His hinder parts . . . (463–5)

The surreal completeness of this issue from primary matter is also the supreme compression of time:

> aire, water, earth,
> By fowl, fish, beast, was flown, was swum, was walked
> Frequent: and of the sixth day yet remain't. (502–4)

Milton's account extends the dreamlike qualities of Genesis – replacing its assurance of plenitude with a fantastically articulated display of specific life.

Darwin was to rejoice in the overturning of the anthropocentric view of the universe which Milton emphasises, yet his language made manifest to Darwin, in its concurrence with his own sense of profusion, density, and articulation of the particular, how much could *survive*, how much could be held in common and in continuity from the past. Milton gave Darwin profound imaginative pleasure – which to Darwin was the means to understanding.

This sense of *continuity* of culture and insight had an emotional and indeed theoretical importance for Darwin. It accorded with the uniformitarianism he had derived from Lyell. 'Natura non facit saltum' – and neither it seems does mind. Darwin was at pains to emphasise the *congruity* of his images with those previous myth-systems rather than iconoclastically to throw them aside.

In Genesis we read:

And out of the ground made the Lord God to grow every tree that is pleasant to the sight, and good for food: the tree of life also in the midst of the garden, and the tree of knowledge of good and evil.

The 'tree of life' is set over against – as well as alongside – 'the tree of knowledge of good and evil'.

In the M notebook one of Darwin's most extended discussions of the imagination at work describes the train of thought most full of pleasure to a botanist:

the botanist might so view plants and animals. – I am sure I remember my pleasure in Kensington Gardens has often been greatly excited by looking at trees at (i.e. as) great compound animals united by wonderful and mysterious manner.

This sense of the resourcefulness of life in trees, their analogical likeness to 'great compound animals', articulates one strand in Darwin's use of the tree image as part of a complex scheme of reference in *The Origin of Species*.

Darwin's problem in relation to the theology of his age is expressed in the image of two contrasted trees – life versus knowledge. In his argument and its expression he found a means of condensing this image so that the two opposed trees could prove to be one.

He knew well that there are still tracts of forbidden knowledge but he did not allow himself to be deflected from the implications of his 'System'. Amid the noble trees of Paradise stood the Tree of Life:

> High eminent, blooming Ambrosial Fruit
> Of vegetable Gold.

In the Notebooks and later in *The Origin* Darwin fastens on the image of the *tree*[12] to express evolutionary organisation. In doing this he rebuts the Lamarckian idea of a chain of progression – and with it the older hierarchical organisation of the 'great chain of being', its ascending orders of existence each working like a substitute, a more earthbound version of its own platonic idea. The idea of the great chain places forms of life in fixed positions which are permanent and immobile. Quintessential to its organisation is the idea of degree.

Darwin needed a metaphor in which degree gives way to change and potential, and in which form changes through time. He did not simply adopt the image of a tree as a similitude or as a polemical counter to other organisations. He *came upon it* as he cast his argument in the form of diagram. This 'materialisation' of the image is important in understanding its force for him. It was substantial, a condensation of real events, rather than a metaphor. Here we come back to the problems he faced in adapting the language available to him (a language so steeped in natural theological suggestions) to a world of material history in which things must find their explanations, their analogies, and their metaphors, within the material order.

The multivocality of Darwin's language reaches its furthest extent in the first edition of *The Origin of Species*. His language is expressive rather than rigorous. He accepts the variability within words, their tendency to dilate and contract across related senses, or to oscillate between significations.[13] He is less interested in singleness than in mobility. In his use of words he is more preoccupied with relations and transformations than with limits. Thus his language practice and his scientific theory coincide.

Once *The Origin* was published Darwin became far more aware of the range of implications carried by this generous semantic practice. It was brought home to him that many of his terms could mean more and other than he could control.[14] He defended his theory in succeeding editions by paring away multiple significations, trying at points of difficulty to make his key terms mean one thing and one thing only, as in the case of Natural Selection. Such labour came hard to him. The exuberantly metaphorical drive of the language of *The Origin* was proper to its topic. The need to establish more parsimonious definitions and to combat misunderstanding may help to account for that dimming of his imaginative powers which he so deeply regretted.

Darwin's discourse is of the kind that George Eliot characterised as expressing 'life'.

Suppose, then, that the effort which has been again and again made to construct a universal language on a rational basis has at length succeeded, and that you have a language which has no uncertainty, no whims of idiom, no cumbrous forms, no fitful shimmer of many-hued significance, no hoary archaisms 'familiar with forgotten years' – a patent de-odorized and non resonant language, which effects the purpose of communication as perfectly and rapidly as algebraic signs. Your language may be a perfect medium of expression to science, but will never express *life*, which is a great deal more than science.[15]

Darwin's is not an austere Descartian style. There are few lean sentences in *The Origin of Species*. According to his son Francis he often laughed at himself 'for the difficulty which he found in writing English, saying, for instance, that if a bad arrangement of a sentence was possible, he should be sure to adopt it'. He felt the problems of obscurity – the over-rapid condensation of argument and insight which dwells at length on inessential features because the deep connections are already so evident to the writer that they scarcely bear reformulation. His son remarks that his style is 'direct and clear'. Though there is some truth in this, the effect does not derive from actual ordering of the sentences, which is often tortuous. Rather it derives from the frequent intervention of the first person and from what Francis Darwin calls the 'courteous and conciliatory tone towards his reader'.[16] 'The tone of such a book as *The Origin* is charming, and almost pathetic . . . The reader is never scorned for any amount of doubt which he may be imagined to feel, and his scepticism is treated with patient respect.'

The book seeks to persuade, not by any attempt to 'force belief' but through a more and more intricate taking in of possible causes of disbelief and the elaboration of doubts. It has in that sense the fullness of a Utopian text, much of whose pleasure comes from the marshalling of insight and detail (a kind of ethnography of his ideal world) rather than from a simply ideological extrapolation from facts. Darwin's description of 'the polity of nature' is thorough and warm, giving an impression of benign fullness even while it points out loss, failure, and struggle.

The need to *please* his readers as well as to unsettle and disturb them is as vital to Darwin as it was to Dickens. Darwin gives to pleasure and to happiness a privileged place in the evidence for his 'view of things' (as he always calls his hypothesis early in his career): 'the happy survive and multiply'. Late in his life he wrote directly about the relationship between happiness and natural selection in his *Autobiography*:

But passing over the endless beautiful adaptations which we everywhere meet with, it may be asked how can the generally beneficent arrangement of the world be accounted for? Some writers indeed are so much impressed with the amount of suffering in the world, that they doubt if we look to all sentient beings, whether there is more of misery or of happiness, – whether the world as a whole is a good or bad one. According to my judgment happiness decidedly prevails, though this would be very difficult to prove. If the truth of this conclusion be granted it harmonises well with the effects which we might expect from natural selection . . . Now an animal may be led to pursue that course of action which is the most beneficial to the species by suffering, such as pain, hunger, thirst and fear, – or by pleasure, as in eating and drinking and in the propagation of the species &c. or by both means combined as in the search for food. But pain or suffering of any kind, if long continued, causes depression and lessens the power of action; yet is well adapted to make a creature guard itself against any great or sudden evil. Pleasurable sensations, on the other hand, may be long continued without any depressing effect; on the contrary they stimulate the whole system to increased action. Hence it has come to pass that most or all sentient beings have been developed in such a manner through natural selection that pleasurable sensations serve as their habitual guides.[17]

In *The Origin* itself the panglossist tendency of this argument is uneasily phrased in a way that indicates an unresolved trouble in his mind about the necessity for the concepts of struggle and extinction in his hypothesis:

When we reflect on this struggle, *we may console ourselves with the full belief,* that the war of nature is not incessant, that no fear is felt, that death is generally prompt, and that the vigorous, the healthy, and the happy survive and multiply. [my italics] (128)

'We may console ourselves' does not quite square with the implication of 'full belief' and he has recourse to biblical allusion to enforce his conclusion: 'survive and multiply'. The belief that the organisation of things tends to produce happiness is to be found in much natural theological writing. Darwin's mature work sought to repudiate natural theological explanations. But he had studied Paley's *Evidences of Christianity* when he was preparing for his B.A. and said that it was the one exercise which was of any value to his general education, and that he felt the same physical thrill of delight when reading Paley's proofs as when reading Euclid. Traces of this influence persist in his tendency to interpret the order of things as benign, though not designed specifically for man.[18]

Throughout his struggle with the language he had inherited Darwin strove to renew the fullness of *things in themselves* and to avoid the platonic scheme which makes of things insufficient substitutes for their own idea. He persistently controverts all attempts to distinguish meaning from matter. For him meaning inheres in activity and in interrelations. It cannot be referred out or back to 'some unknown scheme of creation', which would justify appearance in terms of its prior system.

Darwin's zest for the observable world shapes imaginatively the particular discoveries he can make. It lances him out not only into history but into the material of the present. It warms the random, with its meagreness and insignificance, into profusion. His imagination is liberated by his relish for fertility, reproduction, generation, variety in all the species of life: 'Ribston-pippin or Codlin-apple' (88), heartsease and red clover (125), leaf-eating and bark-feeding insects (133), petrels, auks, grebes and water-ouzels (216), in his favourite pigeons 'pouters, fantails, runts, barbs, dragons, carriers, and tumblers' (424), the Ibla and the Proteolepas (186), crustacea and Mollusca (214) and the webs of dependency between aphids and ants, coral and chalk and the bones of tertiary mammals (299) – 'Even the now inert domain of geology is composed in large measure of the compacted remains of living forms.'

Darwin lives in a doubly profuse world – the plenitude of present life, its potential for both development and death, and the recessional and forgotten multitudes which form the ground of the present:

It is highly important for us to gain some notion, however imperfect, of the lapse of years. During each of these years, over the whole world, the land and the water has been peopled by hosts of living forms. What an infinite number of generations, which the mind cannot grasp, must have succeeded each other in the long roll of years! Now turn to our richest geological museums, and what a paltry display we behold! (297)

That awareness of an unfathomable past whose individualities are wholly lost, and rarely human, is one of the traits in Darwin's writing to which Hardy most sensitively responded. In *Tess of the d'Urbervilles* he describes the milking shed whose wooden posts are 'rubbed to a glossy smoothness by the flanks of infinite cows and calves of bygone years, now passed to an oblivion almost inconceivable in its profundity'.

The evanishing of matter, even the most recalcitrantly enduring, gives a particular poignancy to Darwin's feeling for materiality. His materialism is a sensuously grounded response to the world of forms and life, not an excluding or purely abstracting force. It is the stress between his delight in the individual example and his sense of it as minute and transient when viewed within the extent of evolutionary time which creates the difficult combination of urgency and massiveness in his ideas and his style.

The idea of the individual is established in the first sentence of chapter I of *The Origin*:

When we look to the individuals of the same variety or sub-variety of our older cultivated plants and animals, one of the first points which strikes us, is, that they generally differ much more from each other, than do the individuals of any one species or variety in a state of nature. (71)

The individual is the most specific, the most *material*, evidence and such study guards against a too rapid systematisation which will appear to resolve difficulties by grouping likeness and leaving out unlikeness. Francis Darwin commented that his father had the quickest eye for exceptions of any thinker he knew and Darwin himself considered his recognition of the exception, the anomalous, even in minutest instances, to be one of the characterising strengths of his mind. Such recognition comes from a highly developed response to individuation as well as from an irresistible power of perceiving patterns.

Darwin's romantic materialism which resulted in a desire to substantiate metaphor, to convert analogy into real affinity, should be understood as part of a profound imaginative longing shared by a great number of his contemporaries. Materialism was not simply an abstraction. Its emphasis upon natural forms and upon organisms could comfort as well as disturb. The palpable, the particular, became not only evidence, but ideal. Evolutionary theory suggested that fixed laws no longer implied a fixed universe of matter. Instead everything was subject to irreversible change. Whole species had vanished and even the evidence of their existence had crumbled away. The concept was more absolute than that of Heraclitus: flux suggests change and reassemblage. But the geological and natural historical evidence of nineteenth-century theory suggested irretrievable loss, made tolerable perhaps by the extreme slowness of the process postulated first by Lyell and then by Darwin.

Lyell's central argument in *The Principles of Geology* was that earlier geologists had unwarrantably assumed a discrepancy between previous and present agents of change and had supposed the earth to be now in a 'period of repose' after periods of catastrophe:

Never was there a dogma more calculated to foster indolence, and to blunt the keen edge of curiosity, than this assumption of the discordance between the former and existing causes of change. It produced a state of mind unfavourable in the highest conceivable degree to the candid reception of the evidence of those minute, but incessant mutations, which every part of the earth's surface is undergoing, and by which the condition of its living inhabitants is continually made to vary. (III,3)

Like Darwin whom he so much influenced, he emphasises both congruity of cause and 'those minute, but incessant mutations'. Both concepts are encapsulated for Lyell in the term 'uniformitarian'. So continuity of cause is stressed equally with incessant change.

The individual organism does not evolve in the course of its life. Though it takes part in the evolutionary process, it does so only through generation, not through any happening within its own life cycle. The individual is thus both vehicle and dead end. This Darwinian insight may not yet have been fully articulate for many Victorians (and indeed it has remained one of the least institutionalised of Darwin's ideas). But they clearly felt a new and urgent poignancy in the particular.

At the centre of such uneasiness was the problem of teleology and its relation to materialism.[19] Is there an ultimate or precedent design in the universe and hence in our experience? Or, in an alternative formulation, do we live in a universe where natural objects generate their own laws?

Natural selection and adaptation suggested that there could be no precedent design, since conformity of need between organism and medium was the result of chance congress. Aristotle in the *Physics*, book II, chapter 8 had considered the possibility that 'such things survived, being organized spontaneously in a fitting way; whereas those which grew otherwise perished and continued to perish'. But Aristotle rejected this idea of natural survival: 'Yet it is impossible that this should be the true view. For teeth and other material things either universally or normally come about in a given way; but of not one of the results of chance or spontaneity is this true.' That is, he could not see any inherent causal sequence in such an order and this led him to reject it. The absence of goal here implies absence of order.

The elements of the haphazard lurked in the material of Darwin's theory and Herschel elaborated his reaction that it was 'the law of higgledy-piggledy' through an analogy with literary production. In the 1868 edition of his *Physical Geography of the Globe* he writes:

We can no more accept the principle of arbitrary and casual variation and natural selection as a sufficient account, per se, of the past and present organic world, than we can receive the Laputan method of composing books (pushed à outrance) as a sufficient account of Shakespeare and the Principia.[20]

Herschel still sought 'intelligent direction': the conflict of interpretation between him and Darwin is between the directed and the random play of forces.

The emphasis on fixed laws in nineteenth-century science and philosophy implies orderliness, though not necessarily design. Uniformitarianism suggests continuity, even a kind of permanence, and can be transformed into covenant and stability.

The humanistic core of Lyell's work is its insistence on the power of man's imagination, which allows him to recuperate the staggeringly extended time-scale of the physical world. Though his presence is diminished in the raw time-scale, his is the only source of powerful *interpretation*. Lyell persistently uses the metaphor of decipherment: for example, he writes of the ancient philosophers: 'the ancient history of the globe was to them a sealed book, and although written in characters of the most striking and imposing kind, they were unconscious even of its existence' (1,26). The 'characters' are physical objects: rocks, animals, and plants. The systematisation and comparison between 'distant eras' brings an 'acknowledgment, as it were, that part at least of the ancient memorials of nature were written in a living language' (1,88).

Darwin adapted from Lyell the metaphor of etymology as a representation of descent and change.[21] So language for Darwin has a 'real affinity' with his theory. The physical world provides its own language-system which may be scanned, interpreted, and *read* into full accord with natural order. But 'reading' does not imply only the interpretation of single words and sentences. It implies narrative order and diverse relations between material and period of telling, sujet and fabula.[22]

The world of forms which the geologist inhabits, the slow phantasmagoria of oceans and continents interchanging, rising and falling as if earth were waves, makes for a tranquil elemental view of the universe, in which time implies an extended scale of existence beyond the span of our minds. Lyell's descriptions of the errors of past cosmogonists bring home his sobered awareness of time past. Here a stone moves, there a ridge slides, but the countervailing imagination of man, so limited temporally, can make sense of this process if he thinks structurally. The past can be played at any speed. Lyell chooses to unroll it at a pace which organises it into a knowable and majestic music.

The past of the organic world cannot be similarly shifted in our minds, because here we are dealing with comprehensible time spans – ten years for a dog, a few days for a daisy, hundreds of years for trees and thousands for corals – set against unthinkable millions of years. What Darwin emphasises is relationship – the ordinary chain of generation – the sense of progeny and diversification, of a world in which profusely various forms co-exist, unseen and yet dependent on each other and related to each other by blood or need.

How have all those exquisite adaptations of one part of the organization to another part, and to the conditions of life, and of one distinct organic being to another being, been perfected? We see these beautiful co-adaptations most plainly in the wood-pecker and missletoe; and only a little less plainly in the humblest parasite which clings to the hairs of a quadruped or feathers of a bird . . . in short, we see beautiful adaptations everywhere and in every part of the organic world. (114–15)

The question of congruity between language and physical order is evidently related to teleological issues, just as narrative order brings sharply into focus the question of precedent design. Victorian novelists increasingly seek a role for themselves within the language of the text as observer or experimenter, rather than as designer or god. Omniscience goes, omnipotence is concealed.[23]

The loss of omniscience is felt particularly in fiction where the design of the narrative and the activity of narration would seem to imply an organising power. Writers could no longer easily share the Shaftesburyian ethic that the artist is imitating God – illustrating the benign organisation necessarily justified in shaping our ends. The 'Providential' organisation of fiction becomes a conscious issue: in *Jane Eyre* dreams, omens and portents sustain and guide the heroine. They are messengers from beyond the self. Yet they tally with the self's deepest needs, they endorse the unconscious. The organisation of Dickens's novels shifts from the picaresque, which can include the random events of every day in the onward dynamism of the journey, to a profuse interconnection of events and characters so extreme as to seem to defy any overall meaning. Instead the activity of such novels ranges out towards infinity rather in the manner of medieval ornament.

The preoccupation with materiality in Dickens takes comic and menacing forms. People are seen formulaically, like objects, and objects are endowed with the energy traditionally reserved for organic life: chimneys lour, drainpipes creep. Moreover, Dickens and other novelists such as Elizabeth Gaskell even sought physically to affect their reader: we are to laugh and weep as we read: rictus and wetness. We are to be physically disarranged by the reading experience. Though this may seem a far cry from Darwin's emphasis on substantiation, there is the identical drive towards confirming experience by appeal to the physical and the material, changing language into physical process. We see another form of it in the 'sensation' novel.[24]

The loss of teleological order is sometimes countered in Victorian writing by the speaking voice. An idiosyncratic, often grotesquely individual, yet accessible human voice is suggested syntactically and semantically. This voice has a life of its own; it addresses us. At times it is purely instrumental, expressing the activity of the characters, but at other times it asserts an individuality which goes beyond and runs askance from the events of the novel. This same insistence on the human subject – Darwin as writer writing, observer observing, voice addressing – is characteristic of Darwin's prose.

The common language of scientific prose and literary prose at this period allowed rapid movement of ideas and metaphors to take place. It is clear that in *The Origin* Darwin was writing not only to the confraternity of scientists but with the assumption that his work would be readable by any educated reader. And 'educated reader' here must imply not simply a level of literacy but a level of shared cultural assumption and shared cultural controversy.

Writing rapidly, Darwin drew upon the imaginative orderings and the narrative formulations of his contemporaries, as well as writing *to* them. One particular current intellectual ideal of nineteenth-century European culture intensified the impact of scientific theory as well as affecting its terms; the ideal of *synthesis*, a panoptic scope which sought similarities between remote disciplines (as in Herbert Spencer's *Synthetic Philosophy*) and which analysed such similarities morphologically, as in general systems study today.[25] Another such ideal was that of relations, implicit in organicism, which in prose allowed the rapid transformation of one kind of reference into another – economics into art history into race-theory, say – the kind of organisation which made for energy and obscurity in Carlyle and Ruskin, and which depended for much of its power on a sense of the profusion of the world and its instances. Carlyle, indeed, wrote that Ruskin 'twisted . . . geology into morality, theology, Egyptian mythology, with fiery cuts at political economy'.[26]

Sometimes, as in the Great Exhibition of 1851, profusion and variety become the *topic*, and the ordering principle is purely location. The profusion and variety of the world is brought together in one place to be displayed, controlled, and categorised – an activity which mimics taxonomy but also mimics possession and imperial garnering. The head of the title page of the Official Descriptive Catalogue insisted on another owner: 'The earth is the Lord's and all that therein is: the compass of the world and they that dwell therein.' To quote Goldmann, relations of structure:

often occurring where there is no apparent relation of content, can show us the organizing principle by which a particular view of the world, and from that the coherence of the social group which maintains it, really operates in consciousness.[27]

Darwin's theories profoundly unsettled the organizing principles of much Victorian thinking but it is all the more worth registering, therefore, the extent to which the relations of structures in his work initially share common concerns, and draw on orderings of experience learnt from other writers of the time.[28] The sense that everything is connected, though the connections may be obscured, gave urgency to the enterprise of uncovering such connections. This was a form of plotting crucial to Dickens's work, as we can see, for example, in *Bleak House*, where the fifty-six named – and many more unnamed – characters all turn out to be related by way either of concealed descent (Esther and Lady Dedlock) or of economic dependency ('The dependency of one organic being on another, as of a parasite on its prey, lies generally between beings remote in the scale of nature'). The work demonstrates the terrible redundancy of human kind (Tom All Alone's) and shows all the interconnections, all the family history codified and obfuscated in the arid law-court proceedings of the will which has set Jarndyce v. Jarndyce. As the book proceeds the immense assemblage of apparently contingent characters is ordered and reordered into multiple sets of relations so that we discover that all of them are interdependent. What at first looks like agglomeration proves to be analysable connection.

The unruly superfluity of Darwin's material at first gives an impression of superfecundity without design. Only gradually and retrospectively does the force of the argument emerge from the profusion of example. Such profusion indeed, *is*, as in Dickens, the argument: variability, struggle, the power of generation and of generations, the 'broken and failing groups of organic beings' (435) are exemplified abundantly. In Darwin this takes place through evidences drawn from geology, biology, botany and in a language generatively charged, always dwelling on the particular case, rich in intensitives, expostulation, and case histories ransacked for implications. It is with a sense of both surprise and recognition, I think, that the reader comes to the opening of the final chapter 'Recapitulation and Conclusion' which runs: 'As this whole volume is one long argument, it may be convenient to the reader to have the leading facts and inferences briefly recapitulated.'

It is true that the book is one long argument but it proceeds by a strange intermingling of acquisition, concretion, analogy and prophecy. For a book thematically preoccupied with the past, the present tense is extraordinarily predominant. This reinforces the effect of *discovery*, of being on the brink of finding out, rather than sharing an already formulated and arrested discovery, a 'luminous and orderly presentation'. *The Origin of Species* lives that subjective experience of accomplishing scientific objectivity which Bachelard describes in *La formation de l'esprit scientifique*. 'Vivre et revivre l'instant de l'objectivité, être sans cesse a l'état naissant de l'objectification.'[29] Darwin shares with Carlyle and Dickens that use of the prophetic present which leaves no space between us and the future and poises us on the edge of the unknown.

CHAPTER 2

Fit and misfitting:
anthropomorphism and the natural order

In the Introduction to the 1814 edition of *The Excursion* Wordsworth discussed the philosophical enterprise in which his poem was engaged and set forth his aspirations for man: the hope that the ideal may be 'A simple produce of the common day', by means of 'the discerning intellect of man' 'wedded to this goodly universe'. In the 'wedding' (the unification and harmonising of mind and universe) the outcome is to be a lyrical materialism, a faith that finds its form in the common appearances and daily objects of the world. 'Simple produce' suggests not only what is intellectually produced by the union, but 'daily bread'. And 'common day' is not only ordinary, but brotherly, even universal – that which is held in common. The idea of things held in common, of the extraordinary kinships implicit in the ordinary, is deeply felt by Darwin also, whom we know to have immersed himself in Wordsworth's poem. He sought a kind of inverted Platonism in which ideas find their truest form in substance.

Wordsworth continues to analyse the harmony between mind and universe in a famous passage which he added to the first version of his proposal. In it he sets forth his ideal theme:

> How exquisitely the individual mind
> (And the progressive powers perhaps no less
> Of the whole species) to the external world
> Is fitted; – and how exquisitely, too,
> Theme this but little heard among men,
> The external world is fitted to the mind.[1]

Mind and world have a hoped-for appropriateness to each other – a 'fitness'. The notions of just proportions, exact craftmanship, sexual harmony, healthful mutuality, are all poised within the repeated 'fitted'. The word takes its energy from the muted reference to diverse human concerns rather than from a purely abstract amalgamation of mind and world. Canguilhem points out that the vocabulary of biological science for a long time depended on unregarded metaphors drawn from human tools and mechanisms.[2] Wordsworth's emphasis upon the congruity of the inner and the outer worlds allows harmony and development without the need to insist upon a preordained design.

Charles Bell in *The Hand* assumed, instead, an anthropocentric world – a much more usual religious point of view:

If a man contemplate the common objects around him . . . he will perceive that he is *in the centre of* a magnificent system, and that the strictest relation is established between the intellectual capacities and the material world . . . [my italics][3]

This emphasis upon the natural capacity of the mind to understand appropriately the material world reinforces (as well as assuming) the centrality of man. Its theological basis is given a mythic form in Adam's naming of the animals. Language is anthropomorphic by its nature and anthropocentric in its assumptions. Only somewhat later in the century did it begin frequently to be argued that this anthropocentrism in itself might subvert the truth-telling powers of language and must consciously be resisted.

If the material world is *not* anthropocentric but language is so, the mind cannot be held truly to encompass and analyse the properties of the world that lie about it. Only by giving up the will to dominate the material world and to relate it to our own needs, conditions, and sensibilities will it be possible for us to find a language that gives proper attention to the nature of things. By the 1850s the concept of sympathy, or of accord between inner and outer world, is formulated as the 'pathetic fallacy' by Ruskin. This famous phrase is often stripped of the force with which it describes as a '*fallacy*' the attempt to centre the natural world upon man's sensibility.[4]

Darwin found the constant placing of man at the centre of explanation probably the most exasperating characteristic of providential and natural theological writing. In the D. Transmutation Notebook he notes:

. . . Mayo (Philosophy of Living) quotes Whewell as profound because he says length of days adapted to duration of sleep in man!! whole universe so adapted!!! & not man to Planets. – instance of arrogance!! (D:49)

The reflexive nature of such an explanation of the universe makes it impossible to outgo man's experience and to propose laws which have nothing to do with him. Moreover it diminishes the extent of possibilities and demeans those powers of life which lie beyond man's cognisance: 'We see a particle move one to another, (or conceive it) & that is all we know of attraction, but we cannot see an atom think: they are as incongruous as *blue* & *weight*' (OUN:41).[5]

The sense of incongruity – of the insufficiency of man's reason as an instrument for understanding the material universe – was always with Darwin, though never perhaps more profoundly than during those early creative years at the end of the 1830s when he was struggling with the basic arguments and observations which were to feed the remainder of his life's work.

Darwin displays, categorises, and argues, but does not expect to contain the workings of the world in his mind, or ever fully to understand them. He believed that he had discovered the *mechanism* of evolution but he did not expect to encompass the whole process. Indeed his theory was necessarily hypothetical rather than traditionally inductive. It took a hundred years for Darwin's projections, his 'fictions' or theories, to be thoroughly authenticated empirically. But the accuracy and scope of his observations were such that they carried conviction as scientific explanation long before they could be proved. Nevertheless the hypothetical non-Baconian status of his theory did affect the way in which Darwin conceived and presented it.[6] *The Origin of Species* is in its way a polemical book, a work which drives *through* fiction and observation to achieve a condition beyond fiction. What place is there for humankind in such a narrative?

My method pays close attention to Darwin's language. He did not *invent* laws. He *described* them. Indeed, it was essential to his project that it should be accepted not as invention, but description. His work is, therefore, conditional upon the means of description: that is upon language. And his description is necessarily conditioned by the assumptions and beliefs condensed in the various kinds of discourse active at the time he was writing. Though the events of the natural world are language-free, language controls our apprehension of knowledge, and is itself determined by current historical conditions and by the order implicit in syntax, grammar, and other rhetorical properties such as metaphor, as well as by the selective intensity of individual experience. Even despite the mathematisation of science, discourse can never be expunged from scientific *enquiry*. And nor, perhaps, can narrative. What particular kinds of story did Darwin's theory tell? What plots did it privilege? Did it invent new ones? And how were they received?

If Darwin had been writing in a way which barred access to his work except for equal specialists, his writing would be far less problematic (and far less important in its impact). But because Darwin was writing in a style accessible to a broad readership – and, also, crucially, because such a style was a more usual one for a scientist to adopt than it now would be – his words encompass a broad spectrum of meaning without his analysing them. For scientists working in the same area, words like 'man', like 'race', like 'contrivance', would be severely and effectually contained by the context of published debate using the same terms. But for readers approaching such terminology without an active experimental involvement in day-to-day scientific procedure, the terms could expand their parameters to draw on other shared assumptions. The implicit contractual recognition that one is reading a natural-historical work, not a theological text, not a novel, could be assumed to exercise some powers of exclusion. But the areas of exclusion would be shifting in a culture that set so much store by relations between the different branches of learning and on application to active life. Moreover the diverse discourses of natural theology, aesthetics, technology, housewifery all provide referents for a word like 'contrivance'. So we have no need to assume, as Morse Peckham does in 'Darwinism and Darwinisticism', that his general readers are simply misreading.[7] Neither need we infer that Darwin is offering a single covert sub-text. Nor indeed should we take it for granted that there is an over and under text, or even a main plot and a sub-plot. The manifest and the latent are not fixed levels of text; they shift and change places according to who is reading and when. By this I do not imply a sentimental indeterminacy: Darwin was writing a polemical book, designed to persuade and convince his readers of 'my view of things'. He had a specific end in view, but he also had a very great delight in and respect for the comparative method in evidence. He culled his examples from a whole range of scientific specialisms: geology, botany, physiology, animal husbandry, natural history (about then becoming 'biology'), cell-theory. And he further used analogy and metaphor to elucidate morphological resemblances within the natural order. The conditions of his *thinking*, over the twenty years during which he brooded before publication, made for completeness, thoroughness and an expanding grasp of the implications of his ideas. The conditions of his *writing* made for compression, for imaginative zeal, and for rapid summary.[8]

Darwin faced four major problems in precipitating his theory as language. Two of them were intrinsic to all discourse. First, language is anthropocentric. It places man at the centre of signification. Even symbol is defined by its referential value and the Symbolist movement of the later nineteenth century might therefore be seen as the last humanist enterprise. Symbols, despite their appearance of independence, take their point of reference from human interpretative power and depend upon their own functions of reference to human concerns.

Second, language always includes agency, and agency and intention are frequently impossible to distinguish in language. Darwin's *theory* depended on the idea of production. The natural order produces itself, and through reproduction it produces both its own continuance and its diversity. His theory had no place for an initiating or intervening creator. Nor for an initiating or intervening author. Yet terms like 'selection' and 'preservation' raise the question, 'By whom or what selected or preserved?' And in his own writing Darwin was to discover the difficulty of distinguishing between description and invention.

Third, he faced a more particular problem concerned with the natural historical discourse he inherited. Natural history was still imbued with natural theology, and salient terms such as 'contrivance' and 'design' were freighted with presumptions of godhead and of pre-emptive patterning.[9] Darwin was therefore obliged to dramatise his struggle with natural theological assumptions within a language weighted towards natural theology. He must write against the grain of his discourse.

We can see the problem of escaping from creationist language very exactly in the changes Darwin made through several editions to passages in which the question of originating forces is unavoidable. Sometimes he makes small emendations which shift into a more openly metaphoric, even misfitting, language: 'since the first creature . . . was created' becomes 'since the first organic beings appeared on the stage' (Peckham: 757). In the conclusion one sentence in the first edition runs thus: 'Therefore I should infer from analogy that probably all the organic beings which have ever lived on this earth have descended from some one primordial form, into which life was first breathed.' The passive 'was breathed' evades the problem. In the second edition he briefly and somewhat surprisingly reinstates the Creator. The sentence now ends, 'into which life was first breathed by the Creator'. In the third edition he changes the whole sentence considerably:

Therefore, on the principle of natural selection with divergence of character, it does not seem incredible that, from some such low and intermediate form, both animals and plants may have been developed: and, if we admit this, we must admit that all the organic beings which have ever lived on this earth may have descended from some one primordial form. (Peckham: 753)

The sentence ends without raising the question of the beginning of life itself. It is concerned with descent and it specifies and privileges the explanatory and active powers of 'the principle of natural selection with divergence of character'. As he had earlier written, 'It is so easy to hide our ignorance under such expressions as the "plan of creation", "unity of design", etc, and to think that we have given an explanation when we have only restated a fact' (453). In such examples we see Darwin's persisting struggle to reach explanations which can extend the scope of enquiry, rather than resting within the circle of assumption.

The fourth problem of language that Darwin faced was that of addressing himself towards a general readership as well as to his confraternity of scientists. I have already sketched some of the ways in which such a readership dissolved the limits of words familiar in a natural-historical context.

One of Darwin's own concerns was to demonstrate as far as possible the accord between scientific usage and common speech. His interest in etymology established language-history as a more than metaphorical instance of kinships hidden through descent and dissemination.[10] An aspect of his insistence on congruities, and branchings, was his desire to substantise or substantiate metaphor wherever this could be done. He needs to establish ways in which language may be authenticated by natural order, so that his own discourse and argumentation may be 'naturalised', and so moved beyond dispute: 'Our classifications will come to be, as far as they can be so made, genealogies; and will then truly give what may be called the plan of creation' (456). 'The terms used by naturalists of affinity, relationship, community of type, paternity, morphology, adaptive characters, rudimentary and aborted organs, etc., will cease to be metaphorical, and will have a plain signification' (456). This search for 'plain signification', as for 'one primordial form', is the counter-ideal which leads him into a labyrinth of connection, interrelation, and extension.[11]

The difficulties which Darwin experienced in his writing gave lodgement to interpretation, counter-interpretation, expansion, fracture, and renewals of meaning. His is not a sealed or neutralised text. His language does not close itself off authoritatively nor describe its own circumference. And this is not because Darwin was worsted. He sought to move out beyond the false security of authority or even of the assumption that full knowledge may be reached. The nature of his argument led into expansion, transformation, and redundancy of information. The Darwinian world is *always capable of further description*, and such description generates fresh narratives and fresh metaphors which may supplant the initiating account.

One of the major questions raised by *The Origin* is how far metaphors may overturn the bounds of meaning assigned to them, sometimes even reversing the overt implications of the argument. Seemingly stable terms may come gradually to operate as generative metaphors, revealing inherent heterogeneity of meaning and of ideology. Darwin's use of the concept of 'struggle' is one well-known example to which I shall return. But there are others, less remarked, such as *generation*, which yields the tree, the great family, the lost parent, the 'changing dialect' of life[12] (316). Each of these consequent ideas extends some element in the initiating one of generation, and itself establishes a further range of incipient meanings.

Sometimes we can watch Darwin seeking to contain implications, as in the more directly political example of the master–slave dialectic. Darwin's own revulsion against slavery, inherited through his family's concern with emancipation and reinforced by his own early experiences of slave-owning societies in South America when on the voyage of the *Beagle*, is an element in his insistence that natural selection – unlike the selection of man – is concerned only with the usefulness of characteristics to the organism which possesses them, and not with their usefulness to any other species: 'natural selection can act only through and for the good of each being' (33).

Having seen the genocidal wars waged upon the Indians by the Spaniards in South America, Darwin knew that the concept of 'environment' must include that of the invader. A being may be in accord with its environment until that environment is invaded from without. When Darwin uses a term like 'natives' he directs it within natural-historical terms: 'Man keeps the natives of many climates in one country; he seldom exercises each selected character in some peculiar and fitting manner; he feeds a long and short beaked pigeon on the same food' (132). But in the paragraph before *that*, he introduced the topic through the term 'inhabitant' and then 'native inhabitant' balanced against 'foreigners'.

For as all the inhabitants of each country are struggling together with nicely balanced forces, extremely slight modifications in the structure or habits of one inhabitant would often give it an advantage over others; and still further modifications of the same kind would often still further increase the advantage. No country can be named in which all the native inhabitants are now so perfectly adapted to each other and to the physical conditions under which they live, that none of them could anyhow be improved; for in all countries, the natives have been so far conquered by naturalised productions, that they have allowed foreigners to take firm possession of the land. And as foreigners have thus everywhere beaten some of the natives, we may safely conclude that the natives might have been modified with advantage, so as to have better resisted such intruders. (132)

Since this paragraph opens the discussion, the non-technical range of senses for 'inhabitant', 'native', and 'foreigner' can thrive before the more precise use is established later. Darwin's argument in that initiating discussion allows room for contrary readings: native inhabitants are not fully developed and thus will inevitably be taken over by colonisers; native inhabitants lack perfection only *in that* they do not have the means to resist foreign intruders.

Darwin does not directly resolve the potential contradiction but turns to the metaphor of selective breeding and sets man's handiwork beside that of Nature, denigrating man's procedures in opposition to 'nature's productions' which are far 'truer in character', thus demurring at man's exploitative procedures. But the contrary implication that colonisation is inevitable (or even 'right' in evolutionary terms) also survives, precisely because it is never brought sharply into the focus of attention.

Despite the attacks on Darwin's biological anthropomorphism later it may be his *disregard* of the potential sociological applications of many of his terms which makes them so uninhibitedly available for application. But this position should not be misunderstood. Darwin worked from the assumption that his theories applied to man equally with all other species and not from any separation. So though the absence of specification in his language may be seen as undesigned or unaware, it is based on the assumed congruity of man with all other forms of life.[13]

Among Darwin's contemporaries the question of man's equivalence to other forms of life was of crucial importance. Marx, for example, said that Darwin's work 'serves me as a natural scientific basis for the class-struggle in history'. Of particular importance to Marx was the fact that in Darwin's work, as he saw it, 'not only is the death-blow dealt here for the first time to "teleology" in the natural sciences but its rational meaning is empirically explained'.[14] Marx refers here, presumably, to the explanatory mode which demonstrates that we need not infer a prime mover nor pre-emptive plan since selection and adaptation will sufficiently explain morphological similarities: 'Nothing can be more hopeless than to attempt to explain the similarity of pattern . . . by the

doctrine of final causes' (416). 'In works of natural history rudimentary
or atrophied organs are generally said to be created "for the sake of
symmetry", or in order "to complete the scheme of nature"; but this
seems to me to be no explanation, merely a re-statement of the fact'
(430). Marx, like Darwin, recognised that the avoidance of teleology
tended to give great emphasis to analogies within the natural order.

One outcome of the emphasis on analogy, and equally of the implied
kinship and equivalence between man and other forms of life, was that
Darwin still tends to use an anthropomorphic biology, despite his distrust of anthropocentrism. Plants and animals in this mode of description appear as the dominant term with mankind serving as a means of
explication. However, as Marx also suggests, the effect is to reproduce
in the mode of explanation the structures of relationship in Victorian
society.

Darwin was alert to some of the colonising impulses in his society
and did not seek merely to naturalise or neutralise them by likening
them to events in nature. One striking example of this is his resistance
to the idea that slave-making could be an instinct. But there are other
interactions within his society which he probably did accept as 'natural', at least to the extent that he took them for granted in describing
activities within the natural order of plants and animals.

Though Marx oversimplifies Darwin's use of the 'struggle for existence', his account is valuable for its caustic specification of the anthropomorphic starting point of Darwin's language.[15] Similarly, he exactly
sees how Darwin diverges from Malthus, though he interprets as Darwin's *mis*reading or insufficient reading of Malthus what was in fact
Darwin's determined rereading and riposte to him.

Darwin . . . amuses me when he says he is applying the 'Malthusian' theory
also to plants and animals, as if with Mr Malthus the whole point were not
that he does not apply the theory to plants and animals but only to human
beings – and with geometrical progression – as opposed to plants and animals.
It is remarkable how Darwin recognizes among beasts and plants his English
society with its division of labour, competition, opening-up of new markets,
'inventions', and the Malthusian 'struggle for existence'. It is Hobbes' *bellum
omnium contra omnes*, and one is reminded of Hegel's *Phenomenology*, where civil
society is described as a 'spiritual animal kingdom', while in Darwin the animal
kingdom figures as civil society.[16]

Darwin had initially in the 'Big Book' used the Hobbesian phrase 'the
war of nature' and had quoted Hobbes directly. His later substitution
of the word 'struggle' was an attempt to move away from the human

into a word which lacked the organised force of war and expressed instead the interpenetration of energies.[17] Moreover, in his account of the 'struggle for existence' he insists on using the term in a 'large and metaphorical sense' and he takes trouble to articulate the varying senses in which he uses it, and to grade the degrees of fictive or metaphoric appropriateness the term possesses. One may argue that his trouble went for nothing, since so many of his contemporaries ignored such velleities and approximated 'the struggle for existence' to Spencer's 'survival of the fittest'. Marx's brief critique is striking for the clarity with which he discriminates the social analogy underlying Darwin's description of the natural order. Darwin, however, did take considerable pains – not always successfully – to avoid legitimating current social order by naturalising it.

Man is a determining absence in the argument of *The Origin of Species*. In the first edition he appears only once as the subject of direct enquiry; that appearance is in the Conclusion of the work and is cast in the future tense. The whole paragraph reads:

In the distant future I see open fields for far more important researches. Psychology will be based on a new foundation, that of the necessary acquirement of each mental power and capacity by gradation. Light will be thrown on the origin of man and his history. (458)

The prophetic mode of the last sentence distances into an authoritative but as yet unknown future the matter of the past: origins and history. The vatic opening 'In the distant future I see open fields' retains, in a manner typical of Darwin's style, an allegorical undertow in a word (here 'fields') working within a scientific discourse. (Langland's Piers Plowman at the beginning of his dream saw 'a faire felde full of folke'.) The poetic and scientific senses are fused by means of the double grammatical function of 'open', primarily verbal, ('I see open') but also with an adjectival relationship to 'fields' implied ('open fields'). Any enquiry into the implications for man of Darwin's ideas is held beyond the bounds of present knowledge and beyond the bounds of the text. That holding off is accomplished partly by the visionary style with its literary and biblical references ('a new foundation') and partly by the implicit narrative positioning of Darwin at the end of his work in a role like that of Moses – seeing from afar off the promised land.

The style within which Darwin here makes his direct reference to humankind sustains a vague and noble distance, and thus avoids offence to man's pride. When in 1857 Wallace asked him whether he would discuss man in *The Origin* Darwin replied: 'I think I shall avoid the whole subject, as so surrounded with prejudices; though I fully admit that it is the highest and most interesting problem for the naturalist.' And just after the appearance of *The Origin* he wrote to Jenyns:

With respect to man, I am very far from wishing to obtrude my belief; but I thought it dishonest to quite conceal my opinion. Of course it is open to every one to believe that man appeared by a separate miracle, though I do not myself see the necessity or probability.[18]

So the avoidance of the topic of man is, according to Darwin, tactical in a worldly sense. He feared that he would injure the success of his book if he 'paraded, without giving any evidence, my conviction with respect to his origin'. Yet it is manifest from the reception of the book that the exclusion of any discussion of man did *not* prevent his readers immediately seeing its implications for 'the origin of man and his history'. Many indeed appear simply to have ignored the lack of open reference to man and to have grasped the argument forthwith as centrally concerned with man's descent. In doing this, of course, they were manifesting again precisely the overweening pride which Darwin saw as typical of man's ordering of experience.

However much Darwin may have represented to himself and his correspondents the absence of man from the text as a matter of diplomatic restraint, the exclusion had an immediate polemical effect: it removed man from the centre of attention. An act of will by the reader was required to restore him to his centrality. This transaction in itself problematised the centrality of man to the natural order. The absence of any reference to man as the crowning achievement of the natural and supernatural order made the text subversive: it was – as at some level it must have been known to be – deeply disquieting. Throughout *The Origin* Darwin attempts to subdue the hierarchical nature of man's thought which places himself always at the pinnacle or centre.[19] Even at the celebratory culmination of the work man is not named, not distinguished from the other higher forms of life: 'Thus, from the war of nature, from famine and death, the most exalted object which we are capable of conceiving, namely, the production of the higher animals, directly follows' (459).

When man does appear, it is to serve as the second term in metaphors – for example, illuminating the social behaviour of ants by an ironic glance at man's class organisation, or as an exterminated tribe whose monuments lie beneath the forest trees. He is the 'artificial selector' whose efforts are disparagingly compared with the power and extent of nature's 'natural selection'. And in later editions Darwin makes it clear that man can neither originate nor obliterate selection. He is disqualified from observing the great movements of natural law by the shortness of his life span, and he is recalled in a language like that of Ecclesiastes:

How fleeting are the wishes and efforts of man! how short his time! and consequently how poor will his products be, compared with those accumulated by nature during whole geological periods. Can we wonder then, that nature's productions should be far 'truer' in character than man's productions, that they should be infinitely better adapted to the most complex conditions of life, and should plainly bear the stamp of far higher workmanship? (133)

A reading of his earlier notebooks reveals the exultant pleasure which Darwin felt in restoring man to an equality with other forms of life and in undermining that hubristic separation which man had accorded himself in all previous natural history. He reminds himself in the notebooks not to speak of 'higher' or 'lower' forms of life.

Animals whom we have made our slaves we do not like to consider our equals – (Do not slave-holders wish to make the black man other kind) animals with affections, imitation, fear of death, pain, sorrow for the dead – respect. (B231)

The image of master and slave which Darwin uses suggests the intensity of his distaste for man's tyrannical self-aggrandisement and for the licence which this had led him to feel towards other species. Darwin emphasises the relativism of the value accorded to diverse properties of consciousness:

People often talk of the wonderful event of intellectual man appearing – the appearance of insects with other senses is more wonderful. Its mind more different probably & introduction of man nothing compared to the first thinking being, although hard to draw line. (B207–8)

The ant's brain, he claims, is a more amazing instrument than that of man and though man gives the highest value to reason, a bee would do so to instinct. Nor does Darwin believe that man's power of language distinguishes him from all other species. Adam had the power of naming – and by naming rendered all other forms of life subservient to himself, and to his language and his progeny. In 1861 without naming Darwin, Max Müller responded to the implications of *The Origin of Species* in this way:

There is *one* barrier which no-one has yet ventured to touch – the barrier of language . . . no process of natural selection will ever distill significant words out of the notes of birds or the cries of beasts.[20]

But as early as 16 August 1838 Darwin notes: 'Origin of man now proved. – Metaphysics must flourish. – He who understand baboon would do more towards metaphysics than Locke' (M84). The absence of man from the text of *The Origin* was not a neutral absence nor one resulting from a lack of concern with human psychology.

Despite his decision to exclude man from his discussion, the tendency of Darwin's argument is to range man alongside all other forms of life. The multi-vocal nature of metaphor allows him to express, without insisting on, kinship. Moreover, man is a familiar in *The Origin* though concealed in its interstices. The activities of planting crops and breeding selected animals allow Darwin to transpose and extend these concepts into the idea of 'natural selection'. Genealogy, with its insistence on 'breeding' and 'inheritance', provides another node of meaning between the values and organisation of his own society and those which he infers to be general in the natural order beyond man. The absence of any reference to man as the crowning achievement of the natural and supernatural order made the text disquieting; but the entire absence of man as a point of reference or a point of conclusion would have rendered it nihilistic.

Darwin did not reach so extreme a position, though his insistence on interactions between organism and environment, and his resistance to absolute origins, is expressed both in the multivocality of his metaphors and in his argumentative insistence on metamorphosis. It places him and his work equivocally within the debate between 'freeplay and history' described by Derrida:

Freeplay tries to pass beyond man and humanism, the name man being the name of that being who . . . through the history of all of his history – has dreamed of full presence, the reassuring foundation, the origin and the end of the game.[21]

It is possible that he was freed from some of the difficulties he experienced in expressing the relation of man to the rest of the natural order by his reading of Dickens, whose style insists upon the recalcitrance of objects – their way of mimicking the human order without yielding their own 'haecceitas'. The theme of hidden yet all-pervasive kinship is one which their narratives share. Like Ruskin and Gerard Manley Hopkins, Darwin experiences the thisness of things, which signals both their full presence and their impenetrability, their free play, their resistance to interpretation in terms of man's perceptions and needs, and yet man's profound need to join himself to them, which may be expressed linguistically through metaphor. Is the sub-text of *The Origin* simply unavoidably full of human reference (because cast in human language) or is it knowingly, even strategically, so? And if so, to what ends?

For example, Darwin sought to restore man to his kinship with all other forms of life. In that sense he was bent on an enterprise which seemed to accord with the surface ideals of his society and its literature. He sought the restoration of familial ties, the discovery of a lost inheritance, the restitution of pious memory, a genealogical enterprise.

As it is difficult to show the blood-relationship between the numerous kindred of any ancient and noble family, even by the aid of a genealogical tree, and almost impossible to do this without this aid, we can understand the extraordinary difficulty which naturalists have experienced in describing, without the aid of a diagram, the various affinities which they perceive between the many living and extinct members of the same great natural class. (413)

The factor of irony in such a passage, however, is that all these themes, so familiar in the novels and dramas of the time, are here displaced from the class structure of his society. In wishful Victorian literature, working-class heroes and heroines, inheritors restored to their kingdom, prove usually to have aristocratic blood (as in Disraeli's *Sybil*). A concealed aristocratic lineage lies behind them, just as in terms of Bible myth it does for man – the son of God, cast out of his inheritance by his forbears' sin and restored to it by the intercession of the immediate heir. Instead, in Darwinian myth, the history of man is of a difficult and extensive family network which takes in barnacles as well as bears, an extended family which will never permit the aspiring climber – man – quite to forget his lowly origins. One of the most disquieting aspects of Darwinian theory was that it muddied descent, and brought into question the privileged 'purity' of the 'great family'. In terms of the class organisation of his time this is clearly a deeply unpalatable view. Without his analysing or needing to analyse his reasons, therefore, there seem to have been as good social as there were religious reasons for Darwin to attempt to conceal man in the interstices of his text – or to permit him almost to escape beyond its parameters.

The emphasis upon kinship changed the status of words such as 'inhabitants' or 'beings' into a far more egalitarian form: 'When I view all beings not as special creations, but as the lineal descendants of some few beings which lived long before the first bed of the Silurian system was deposited, they seem to me to become ennobled' (458). Lineage escapes from class and then from kind: 'We possess no pedigrees or armorial bearings; and we have to discover and trace the many diverging lines of descent in our natural genealogies, by characters of any kind which have long been inherited' (456–7). 'Characters' shifts here from heraldic semiology to living characteristics. The utopian drive in Darwin's thinking declares itself in the levelling tendency of his language, which always emphasises those elements in meaning which make for community and equality and undermine the hierarchical and the separatist. Darwin's rejection of special creation leads him to an enhanced evaluation of all life and to an emphasis on deep community. So classification becomes not an end in itself but an arrested moment in a long story. Taxonomy and transformation are set in tension.

Darwin evades any suggestion that the world is now accomplished and has reached its final and highest condition, though he does present the movement of evolution as one of proliferation and enhancement. This final statement of *The Origin* feeds our imaginative sense of continuance and change: 'Whilst this planet has gone cycling on according to the fixed law of gravity from so simple a beginning endless forms most beautiful and most wonderful have been, and are being evolved.' Cycle and fixed, simple and endless, 'have been and are being'. He alternates in the sentence the principles of stasis and of motion, of completion and continuity, and sets them spinning and growing on into the silence which succeeds the conclusion.

The imaginative release into a continuing and undescribed future is remarkable when it is set alongside the positivistic emphasis on *finality* which we find in Comte, a suggestion that the positive and scientific have now achieved mastery and that the world may fully and definitively be described forever. Darwin persistently emphasises physical process, not completed idea.

Darwin's work is not a search for an originator nor for a true beginning. It is, rather, the description of a process of becoming, and such a process does not move constantly in a single direction. As Kuhn says in the Appendix to the second edition of *The Nature of Scientific Revolutions*, 'there are important contexts in which the narrative and the descriptive are inextricably mixed'. The title of Darwin's book signals that this is one of those cases. The usual shortened form *The Origin of Species* disguises the element of narrative in the title and changes 'origin' from a process into a place or substantive. The full title reads, 'On the Origin of Species by means of Natural Selection, or the Preservation of

Favoured Races in the Struggle for Life'. The title is in polemical contrast with Chambers's insistence on *Vestiges of the Natural History of Creation*. Vestiges are remnants, surviving fragments of a primordial creative
act. Darwin's enterprise is history, not cosmogony. 'I have nothing to
do with the origin of the primary mental powers, any more than I have
with that of life itself' (234).

In his book *Beginnings*, Edward Said emphasises that beginning includes 'the intention to continue'. Darwin is concerned with this particular property of beginning. He is interested in initiation, but he is
interested in it not as completed ceremony, rather as indefatigable process. So the emphasis in his title is on *means*, 'by means of Natural
Selection'. 'On the Origin of Species by means of Natural Selection' is
in a very precise sense a narrative, because what it describes cannot be
correctly described except through the medium of time. Neither analysis nor exposition would in itself suffice for what was new in Darwin's
ideas. Categorisation, classification, description, must all be understood
to be implicated in movement, process, and time. Darwin rejected the
idea of a stable or static world, and would not accept equilibrium as a
sufficient description of the relationship between the forces of change
and continuance. He thus avoided the pattern by means of which many
Victorian writers attempted to set limits to change and to assert mod-
eration as an essential natural order.[22]

Darwin came to see that his own sub-title suggested too inert a procedure and made space for a preserver: he changed 'the preservation of
favoured races in the struggle for life' to 'the survival of favoured races
in the struggle for life' in later editions.

The organisation of his narrative emphasises variability rather than
development. The narrative time of the *Origin* is not one that begins at
the beginning but rather in the moment of observation. The first words
are 'When we look' and the first two chapters are concerned with variation: under domestication and under nature. The ordering reinforces
the argument. It suggests two crucial insights.

Originating is an activity, not an authority. And deviation, not truth
to type, is the creative principle.

Darwin's account of the origin of species ranges to and fro through
time in a way that disturbs any simple sequence or chain. Whereas a
simple developmental narrative still using the model of the single life
span might have placed the embryo at the beginning, and a narrative
preoccupied with origins and cosmogony might have started with the
geological record, Darwin places the initiating emphasis in his narrative

on the profusion of individuals, their variability, the diversity of species. Only gradually do the laws emerge from the welter of particularity.

Even then the law of 'Unity of Type' is seen to be secondary to that of 'Conditions of Existence'. So change, environment, the conditional nature of existence, is reinforced by the ordering as well as the argument of his narrative.

The one permanence in which Darwin concurred with other scientists of his time was that of the possibility of achieved and immovable truth, the tracking of 'fixed laws' though those laws primarily described change and motion. The ornamental title page of *Nature* (4 November 1869) shows a globe surrounded by clouds and bears an epigraph from Wordsworth:

> To the solid ground
> Of Nature trusts the mind which builds for aye.

That condensation of the meanings of 'logic' and 'earth' in the word 'ground' was part of the comforting inheritance of Romantic thought in Victorian science which seemed to assure a continuance of natural truth through the action of permanent discoverable laws – what Whewell in Darwin's first epigraph to *The Origin* called 'the establishment of general laws'. Darwin added a quotation from Butler's *Analogy*, in the second and subsequent editions of the *Origin* (Peckham, p. 40, note 13): 'The only distinct meaning of the word "natural" is *stated, fixed*, or *settled*.' Darwin invoked the same idea in his final sentence with its implicitly validating reference to Newton's 'fixed law of gravity' set alongside his own newly discovered law, as we saw earlier.

When we can feel assured that all the individuals of the same species, and all the closely allied species of most genera, have within a not very remote period descended from one parent, and have migrated from some one birthplace; and when we better know the many means of migration, then, by the light which geology now throws, and will continue to throw, on former changes of climate and of the level of the land, we shall surely be enabled to trace in an admirable manner the former migrations of the inhabitants of the whole world. (457)

In this passage writer and reader are held in comradeship by that initiating 'we'; individuality and community are, equally, promised; continuity is assured, affirmation and hope – something rhetorically both beyond and just short of certainty – are expressed; and history and fullest community are conjoined. 'The inhabitants of the whole world' and their migrations include man, without setting him apart.

The whole of animate nature becomes one moving and proliferating family. Words like 'parent' and 'birthplace', so often reserved for human kind, are here set at the service of all living forms.

The levelling of man with other species is not, then, in Darwin's thinking a necessarily punitive enterprise. Only man's own hubris makes him feel it as such. To Darwin the multitudinous fecundity and variety of life had more than enough room for man among all other living beings. Whereas Müller sees 'the great problems of our being, of the true nobility of our blood, of our *descent* from heaven or earth', Darwin emphasises rather the problems of *relationship*. Where then does Darwin place himself within the text and where does he place the reader?

The language of *The Origin* emphasises the element of address. Conversation rather than abstraction is the predominant mode, and the emphasis is upon things individually seen, heard, smelt, touched, tasted. The voiced presence of the observer in the language is a necessary methodological control, supplementing the work's imaginative history. The reader is encouraged to scrutinise and assay: the exotic instances are brought home for us by analogies with our own native landscape and wildlife. These analogies are both loosely illustrative, alerting the reader's own image-making powers, and also, more precisely, furthering the enquiry into the relationship between habit and environment in bringing about variation:

I have often watched a tyrant flycatcher (Saurophagus sulphuratus) in South America, hovering over one spot and then proceeding to another, like a kestrel, and at other times standing stationary on the margin of water, and then dashing like a kingfisher at a fish. In our own country the larger titmouse (Parus major) may be seen climbing branches, almost like a creeper; it often, like a shrike, kills small birds by blows on the head; and I have many times seen and heard it hammering the seeds of the yew on a branch, and thus breaking them like a nuthatch. (215)

The tone of a single man speaking, the presenter of the evidence, the creator of the theory, is a necessary counterpoise to that speculative extension back through time and change which is also crucial to the argument. And the emphasis upon sense experience, particularly colour and touch, means that our medium of experience is not simply necessarily, but warmly, human.

Darwin's delight in the process of discovery and in the material with which he is working, sometimes makes him represent as benign processes which are not necessarily so. It is at this point that disturbances in his language become registrable. His grandfather had written of mountains that they 'Are Mighty Monuments of Past Delight', representing past pleasure and the felicity of organic life. One strain in Darwin's temperament – and indeed one major premise of his theory – emphasised the tendency towards happiness in living creatures. But in his recognition of 'the appetite for joy', to use Hardy's phrase, Darwin saw also the extent of suffering which any individual organism might at any time have to undergo. This was one of his reasons for rejecting the idea of a benign orderer and it brings about a disturbing oscillation between anthropomorphic and abstract senses within a word. A word like 'inhabitant' can liberally expand without strain to denote all denizens of an environment – as indeed, of course, it had done already in the writing of natural history well before Darwin. But a word like 'face' has a strong and specific human sense, that of visage, as well as the sense of 'surface' or 'plane' – and in expressions such as 'the face of a mountain' and particularly 'the face of nature' the human presence is hard to expunge. St John Mivart, writing on instinct and reason, complained of Darwin's 'biological anthropomorphism' by which he meant 'the attribution of human qualities to brutes', for example, 'maternal tenderness'.[23]

In the first edition of *The Origin* both Nature and natural selection have grammatically the function of agents – and, moreover, despite his later exasperation with the issue, Darwin does endow them in his language with conscious activity. If one examines a sentence like the one that occurs on page 219, there is a noticeable difference between the apparently parallel functions (both grammatical and ideological) accorded to variation, generation, and natural selection: 'In living bodies, variation will cause the slight alterations, generation will multiply them almost infinitely, and natural selection will pick out with unerring skill each improvement.' Variation causes, generation multiplies, but natural selection 'picks out with unerring skill'. The implication of an active and external agent is far stronger in the last term. It would be a mistake, though, to dwell upon the animistic qualities of this metaphor in isolation. In part Darwin is suffering simply the recalcitrance of human language, which is permeated with intention.

The passages in which he had personified Nature and natural selection are some of those with which Darwin most often struggled in later editions. One problem he faced was the tendency of readers to personify natural selection and to see it as an active, intentionalist force ('Some have even imagined that natural selection induces variability . . .'), or as representing immanent intention ('others have objected that the term selection implies conscious choice in the animals which become

modified').[24] Darwin's answer is to point out the metaphorical nature of
language in other scientific propositions – and strikingly he points to
terms which had already been taken up and recast in literary language
by Goethe: elective affinities. In the third edition he writes:

In the literal sense of the word, no doubt, natural selection is a misnomer; but
whoever objected to chemists speaking of the elective affinities of the various
elements? – and yet an acid cannot strictly be said to elect the base with which
it will in preference combine. It has been said that I speak of natural selection
as an active power or Deity; but who objects to an author speaking of the
attraction of gravity as ruling the movements of the planets? Everyone knows
what is meant and is implied by such metaphorical expressions; and they are
almost necessary for brevity. So again it is difficult to avoid personifying the
word Nature; but I mean by Nature, only the aggregate action and product of
many natural laws, and by laws the sequence of events as ascertained by us.
With a little familiarity such superficial objections will be forgotten. (Peckham,
165)

His grandfather, Erasmus Darwin, had already noted the speed and
ease with which personification takes place in English. Since English is
an ungendered language one need only add a 'his' or 'hers' to turn a
word into a personification. With personification enters intention. Darwin expands further on the problem of intention which lurks in all
language, drawing as it does upon human experience and human ordering of experience. He notes the latent metaphor in gravity 'ruling' – the
notion of authoritative ordering, and then he appeals to general usage
as his authority, 'every one knows'.

The problem, of course, for the reader was that every one did *not*
know what was meant by natural selection – the term was a neologism
and therefore stood forth with full metaphorical expressiveness and
personifying power. Its force had not been lessened by familiarity.

It may be said that natural selection is daily and hourly scrutinising, throughout the world, every variation, even the slightest; rejecting that which is bad,
preserving and adding up all that is good; silently and insensibly working,
whenever and wherever opportunity offers, at the improvement of each organic
being in relation to its organic and inorganic conditions of life. (133)

In the second edition he varies this to 'It may metaphorically be said'.

The sense of a brooding presence was reinforced by the way in which
he distinguished the gender of nature and natural selection. Nature is
always 'she', whereas natural selection is neuter: the neuter becomes a
form of sex, a sexless force. In the fifth edition he parallels it to the
'survival of the fittest', a natural process, whose terminology he borrows

from Huxley and which falls dangerously in with the Spencerian notion of an accord between moral fitness and the ability to survive. But in the early editions natural selection cannot avoid a personified presence in his text.[25]

In the mythological order of his language natural selection appears as an aspect or avatar of the more general 'Nature', whose maternal ordering is contrasted with the egocentric one of Man. She tends and nurses with scrupulous concern for betterment. The word 'Man' in this polarisation achieves a masculine rather than a fully inclusive use of the word and this effect is reinforced by the working world with which he is associated: a world of inadequate discrimination, lacking refinement of attention.

Man selects only for his own good; Nature only for that of the being which she tends. Every selected character is fully exercised by her; and the being is placed under well-suited conditions of life. Man keeps the natives of many climates in the same country; he seldom exercises each selected character in some peculiar and fitting manner. (132)

In later editions Darwin attempts to deconstruct the mythological personage Nature – sometimes equating her with natural selection, sometimes with the complexity of interpenetrating laws. Are the objections to his use of Nature superficial, as he suggests? Certainly, his usages do not invalidate his attempt to find a non-teleological language. But the struggle he has comes in part from his relations to natural theology, and from the need to expand the material order rather than to leave a metaphysical void. He has to put something in the space left by God. He is determined to avoid a creationist language though even here he has difficulties with passive forms.

Darwin's personification of nature as female was, of course, part of a long tradition. In Ovid's proto-geological account in the *Metamorphoses*, which Lyell cites in the first chapter of *The Principles of Geology*, Deucalion is instructed to throw behind him the bones of his great mother. It is a usage which can be found both in contemporary literature and in other scientific writing of the period: John Tyndall in 1860 remarks, 'In the application of her own principles, Nature often transcends the human imagination.' Hopkins in 'That Nature is a Heraclitean Fire and of the Comfort of the Resurrection' emphasises equally the maternal and the reckless in nature's nature:

> Million-fuelèd, nature's bonfire burns on.
> But quench her bonniest, dearest to her, her clearest-selvèd spark
> Man, how fast his firedint, his mark on mind, is gone!

The effects of personifying nature as female are manifold: but for the purposes of this argument there are two particularly important effects – one is to distinguish Nature from God, the second is to ascribe a benign surveillance to the natural world, 'natura naturans', efficient Nature. Emerson, in his essay on 'Nature', which Darwin read in 1841, spoke of it as the secularity of nature. In a popular work like J. G. Wood's *Nature's Teachings: Human Invention Anticipated by Nature* (London, 1877), science is gendered as female in a way that tends to equate science reassuringly with nature: 'It is, therefore, partially true that science does destroy romance. But, though she destroys, she creates, and she gives infinitely more than she takes away.' In Darwin's use of the word vulnerability and suffering are also emphasised.

Recently, both Gruber and Colp have discussed Darwin's imagery of wedging and wedges.[26] They point out that despite the appearance of the 'wedge' metaphor in the 1838 notebooks, in the 1842 and 1844 essays and in the 'big book' on natural selection, Darwin removed it from *The Origin of Species* after the first edition. Colp speculates on the sexual and unconscious signification of wedging for Darwin; he considers that it 'may have come to symbolise Darwin's assertion of himself in the areas of work, sex, money, and resistance to opposition'. More scrupulously, Gruber writes: 'It would be interesting to know why Darwin dropped it, since it does convey dramatically the way in which variation and struggle continuously disequilibrate the natural order at almost every point in space and time.' This is exact, but, like all Darwin's major metaphors, 'wedging' holds in equipoise contradictory or divergent implications, signifying equally holding, splitting, stabilising and destabilising. Problems inherent in the anthropomorphic tendency of metaphor can be seen in the particular relationship between Darwin's image of wedging and of Nature.

In the chapter on 'The Struggle for Existence' in *The Origin*, Darwin opens with an admission of the sheer imaginative *difficulty* of bearing constantly in mind the struggle for life: 'We behold the face of nature bright with gladness, we often see superabundance of food.' This vivid passage with its open personification of nature, its joy checked by an apprehension of destructiveness ('we do not see, or we forget, that the birds which are idly singing round us mostly live on insects or seeds, and are thus constantly destroying life'), is charged with that imaginative zest, the vitality of shifting forces, which epitomises Darwin's relationship to the natural world. It is followed only two pages later by the following dark passage:

In looking at Nature, it is most necessary to keep the fore-going considerations always in mind – never to forget that every single organic being around us may be said to be striving to the utmost to increase in numbers; that each lives by a struggle at some period of its life; that heavy destruction inevitably falls either on the young or old, during each generation or at recurrent intervals. Lighten any check, mitigate the destruction ever so little, and the number of the species will almost instantaneously increase to any amount. The face of Nature may be compared to a yielding surface, with ten thousand sharp wedges packed close together and driven inwards by incessant blows, sometimes one wedge being struck, and then another with greater force. (119)

The wedge imagery is placed in apposition to Nature – not 'the economy of Nature', nor 'the surface', as he had written in earlier versions, but 'the face of Nature'.

The drive towards actualisation has created an image so grotesque, so disturbingly figurative of violence, in which the barriers between earth and body have so far vanished that the wedge image has become shockingly sadistic in a way that effaces its argumentative usefulness. Emotionally, it does correspond to Darwin's most sombre sense of the individual within the natural order, but the progressive condensations of language over the various versions have here resulted in an image of uncontrollably intense and repellent anthropomorphism. That last sentence of the paragraph is excised in all future editions.

The same doubling of visage and surface – human form and rough ground – introduces Hardy's novel, *The Return of the Native* and anthropomorphic disturbance is one of the ways in which his writing is most keenly affected by Darwin's. The first chapter is entitled 'A Face on which Time makes but Little Impression', and it describes the vast tract of unenclosed wild known as Egdon Heath; 'Haggard Egdon' is a survival, unchanged since the beginning of vegetation. Hardy allows the suggestion of primitive humanity and of landscape to conjoin in words like 'face' and 'dress' which are moved to and fro between an experimental and an impressionistic discourse: 'The face of the heath by its mere complexion added half an hour to evening.'[27]

Here at least were intelligible facts regarding landscape – far-reaching proof productive of genuine satisfaction. The untameable, Ishmaelitish thing that Egdon now was it always had been. Civilization was its enemy; and ever since the beginning of vegetation its soil had worn the same antique brown dress, the natural and invariable garment of the particular formation. (35)

The oscillation between abstraction and presence was there in Darwin's language too, and associated with just this kind of description.

Darwin always retains his sense of possible incongruities between man's powers of appraisal and observation, and the nature of the phenomena which surround him. Indeed his thought moves towards an acceptance not only of incongruities and insufficiencies in man's recognition and understanding of phenomena, but increasingly to an acceptance of incongruity, imperfection, and maladaptation as essential to an understanding of the world as it is and in its coming to be. In the last revised edition of *The Origin* he turns again to the topic of the eye – that most Wordsworthian of the sense organs, and the one which in Paley's argument had most tellingly furnished evidence for benign complexity in the design of man's place in nature. Darwin acknowledges the difficulties to his theory created by the apparent perfection and complexity of the eye as an organ of perception. In the chapter on 'Difficulties on Theory' he opens the section 'Organs of Extreme Perfection and Complication':

To suppose that the eye, with all its inimitable contrivances for adjusting the focus to different distances, for admitting different amounts of light, and for the correction of spherical and chromatic aberration, could have been formed by natural selection, seems, I freely confess, absurd in the highest possible degree. (217)

But he immediately continues 'Yet reason tells me' and continues with a series of conditional clauses each with its own confirming subordinate clause and a retarded main clause whose argument, 'Yet reason tells me that . . . the difficulty of believing can hardly be considered real', counters the tendency of the first sentence.

Yet reason tells me, that if numerous gradations from a perfect and complex eye to one very imperfect and simple, each grade being useful to its possessor, can be shown to exist, if further, the eye does vary ever so slightly, and the variations be inherited, which is certainly the case; and if any variation or modification in the organ be ever useful to an animal under changing conditions of life, then the difficulty of believing that a perfect and complex eye could be formed by natural selection, though insuperable by our imagination, can hardly be considered real. (217)

'Reason' here must traverse the bounds of imagination, and the 'difficulty' of believing is not a 'real' one, but one consequent upon the trammelled quality of our imagination. The sentence uses accumulated speculation to reach a point of release. This appeal to reason as an authority which can take us *beyond* our imaginative limits blurs the distinction between reason and imagination even while it appears to enforce it. Darwin might equally have reversed the two terms, except that imagination is a less authoritative word than reason in scientific argumentation.

He continues with a recoil from history and from cosmogony equally: 'How a nerve comes to be sensitive to light, hardly concerns us more than how life itself first originated.' But of course it *does* concern him, despite his invocation of the Comtist refusal to discuss origins. *How things came to be as they are* is his great argument. 'How they will be' cannot, in the nature of his emphasis on mutation, response, and variety, be described, though that things will *change* is essential to his theory. The level at which he describes events is not that of *how* adaptations take place but rather of what factors favour the survival of certain adaptations. And as so often, having apparently eschewed a line of argument, he nevertheless speculates about further possibilities in the eagerly hypothesising vein on which his son Francis comments: 'but I may remark that several facts make me suspect that any sensitive nerve may be rendered sensitive to light, and likewise to those coarser vibrations of the air which produce sound' (217).

The emphasis of his argument here is on *incongruence* between mind and world: human image-making power cannot suffice to account for the properties of the world beyond the human. He finds himself expounding the theoretical paradox that reason is our most exquisite instrument for understanding the world, that it can take us beyond fact and even beyond imagination and that it yet is insufficient. Maladaptation is part of the nature of both mental and physical world.

This sense of vital *incongruence* is acceptable to Darwin because it chimes in with his expectation that we should find false approximations, insufficient or imperfect adaptations, if his idea of persisting change and adjustment within organisms and species is correct.[28] Origin drops away; formation alone becomes the topic. Plenitude includes the crabbed, crooked and marred; it does not mean unerring perfection. Process is readiness, each moment a matrix of diverse potential, not of fixed and complete forms.

In the first edition the passage on the eye runs: 'Natural selection will not produce absolute perfection, nor do we always meet, *as far as we can judge*, with this high standard under nature' [my italics]. Our standards for judging perfection are only provisionally accepted. The passage continues: 'The correction for the aberration of light is said, on high authority, not to be perfect even in the most perfect organ, the eye.' In the sixth edition he adds:

Helmholtz, whose judgement no one will dispute, after describing in the strongest terms the wonderful powers of the human eye, adds these remarkable words: 'That which we have discovered in the way of inexactness and imperfection in the optical machine and in the image on the retina, is as nothing in comparison with the incongruities which we have just come across in the domain of the sensations. *One might say that nature has taken delight in accumulating contradictions in order to remove all foundation from the theory of a pre-existing harmony between the external and internal worlds.*' [my italics] (Peckham, 373–4)

A personified and humorously sardonic Nature is half-whimsically introduced by Helmholtz, undeterred by all the anti-anthropomorphic criticism levelled at the word. But more important for Darwin is the cancelling of Wordsworthian 'pre-existing harmony' between mind and material world. When such harmony is created it must be through process, by means of according sequences, provisional always in that they are held within time, though capable of incessant renewal.

Helmholtz ends his essay on 'The Recent Progress of the Theory of Vision' (1868), which Darwin is citing here, with a quotation from Goethe's *Faust* which bemourns the breaking up of the world:

The reader may perhaps feel inclined to reproach Science with only knowing how to break up with fruitless criticism the fair world presented to us by our senses, in order to annihilate the fragments.

> Woe! woe!
> Thou hast destroyed
> The beautiful world
> With powerful fist . . .

The passage describes the shattering and fragmentation of lost beauty:

> Wir tragen
> Die Trümmern ins Nichts hinüber.

Helmholtz sympathises with his reader's sense of lost wholeness. When Freud comes to analyse the breakdown of congruity between self and world in paranoia, he turns to the same passage.[29] The loss of confidence in the outer world means that after the catastrophe it must be built again by the self *in its own image*. The removal of all foundation from the theory of a pre-existing harmony between the external and the internal world results in massive compensatory activity within the psyche. The line of descent here – Goethe – Darwin – Helmholtz – back to Darwin – then on to Freud – analyses an increasingly desolate awareness of maladaptation and of the fragility of the human in an incongruous world. It analyses also an increasingly demonic insistence by the self on its sole powers to authenticate a world.

For Darwin himself such desolation is staved off by an implied epistemological fit between material and theory. The blemished or unfulfilled present moment of adaptation may lead into collapse or into accord. 'Unknown laws' must form part of the theory. His metaphoric language, his examining of analogies, register both incomplete fit and significant affinity.

PART II

Darwin's plots

CHAPTER 3

Analogy, metaphor and narrative in The Origin

Arnold wrote to Clough of Keats that Keats did not understand that one 'must begin with an Idea of the world, in order not to be prevailed over by the world's multifariousness'.[1] Darwin is on Keats's side of this argument. He begins with the multifariousness of the world, is even prevailed over by it, and then uses it as both material and idea. Such an attitude in itself goes some way towards resolving the problem of first causes and of teleology. He refuses any precedent 'Idea' of the world from which to begin. This is not to suggest that he refuses theory, or that he believes facts to be authoritatively inert. In a letter to Fawcett in 1861 he made his position clear:

About thirty years ago there was much talk that geologists ought only to observe and not theorise; and I well remember someone saying that at this rate a man might as well go into a gravel-pit and count the pebbles and describe the colours. How odd it is that anyone should not see that all observation must be for or against some view if it is to be of any service.[2]

In his *Reminiscences* of his father Francis Darwin wrote that 'it was as though he were charged with theorising power ready to flow into any channel on the slightest disturbance, so that no fact, however small, could avoid releasing a stream of theory'.[3]

Darwin's copious imagination constantly tried out and extended possibilities, drawing upon the richness of the perceptual world. Because it refused the notion of precedent Idea with its concomitant assumption of preordained Design, his method of description placed great emphasis upon congruities within the multiple materiality of the world. These became the major means of *organising* knowledge as well as being a part of knowledge. At the same time, however, Darwin's theory, in its emphasis on variation and change, was obliged equally to accept the *shifting* energy of congruities. Aristotle in the *Poetics* wrote that metaphor is a sign of genius, 'since a good metaphor implies an intuitive perception

of the similarity in dissimilars'. That perception is crucial in morphological categorisation and in Darwin's genetic history. But Darwin
needed equally to sustain the perception (sometimes harder) of dissimilarities in similars. Deviance, divergence, accidentals, were the material
of sustained change for him.

Analogy and morphology are both concerned with discovering structures common to diverse forms. In the case of analogy this communality
expresses itself by first ranging two patterns of experience alongside
each other, seeking their points of identity, and then using one pattern
to extend the other. There is always a sense of *story* – of sequence – in
analogy, in a way that there need not be in other forms of metaphor.

If allegory is narrative metaphor, analogy is predictive metaphor.[4]
Whereas in allegory the one-to-one correspondence of object and meaning is sustained, in analogy the pleasure and power of the form is felt in
part because it is *precarious*. We experience a sense of trepidation as we
follow the analogy through its various stages lest we are arriving at the
point where the parallels dispart. Disanalogy may collapse the entire
sequence or vitiate it retrospectively. Darwin's aim is to discover analogies which can move beyond the provisional and metaphorical and
prove themselves as 'true affinities'. Analogies may turn out to be homologies. In such a case the parallel narrative patterns reveal actual
identity, and the distance between the two patterns vanishes. Total and
satisfying congruity is achieved.

Whereas in metaphor resistance as well as accord must persist, in
analogy complete resolution is the sought-for end – albeit an end which
can rarely, if ever, be reached.[5] The speculative, argumentatively
extended character of analogy ranges it closer to narrative than to image.
As in hypothesis, the arc of desire seeks to transform the conditional
into the actual. And again as in hypothesis, such a transformation is
seen as changing fiction into a truth. Hypothesis is a provisional truth,
presenting itself provisionally as a fiction, and seeking ultimately to find
confirmation.

In the process of Darwin's thought, one movement is constantly
repeated: the impulse to substantiate metaphor and particularly to find
a real place in the natural order for older mythological expressions. He
has an almost equal satisfaction in alerting us to the mysterious in *fact*
(and here we can see the influence of Carlyle, whose prodigious linguistic energy goes into recuperating the past and reviving the marvel
of the everyday). The grotesque, the beautiful and the wonderful in the
everyday was a major Victorian imaginative theme. The study of 'fact'

was for Dickens and for Carlyle and for Hopkins an exploration of the fantastic. Darwin shared this pleasure in 'making strange', in skimming off the familiar and restoring it, enriched and stabilised. When the word 'fact' occurs in *The Origin of Species* it is usually intensified as 'a truly wonderful fact – the wonder of which we are apt to overlook from familiarity' (170), 'this great fact' (171) or 'such wonderful and well-established facts' (259), 'we cannot hope to explain such facts . . . until we can say' (followed by a series of extraordinarily difficult propositions) (371) or 'We see the full meaning of the wonderful fact, which must have struck every traveller.' It is this fulfilling, bodying forth, and replenishing what has appeared humdrum, inexplicable, or taken for granted, that most characterises Darwin's imaginative enterprise through language.

In Darwin's emphasis upon the 'wonderful', the 'extraordinary' fact, we can recognise traces of Carlyle's 'great fire-heart of man' – the attempt to recuperate the intense physical presence of the past.[6] All these lived, in the body, as we live, not only as language and idea. That strain of Romantic materialism intensifies Darwin's own dependence on physical evidence – we may remember that he cites 'The Book of Wonders' as his first formative reading alongside Shakespeare.

The axis of the factual and the marvellous was balanced curiously for the Victorians. In their use of the word *fact* they often combine the idea of *performance* with that of observation. Fact is deed as much as object, the thing done as much as the thing categorised. Moreover, *fact* in much Victorian writing partakes still of the heroic connotations of its cognate form, feat. The word is strenuous, not inert. In Darwin's usage, fact often has a sense of the thing achieved. It is incontrovertible and yet opens into mystery. The *word* 'fact' authenticates. It is a source, or origin, in some uses of the word: 'Man makes fiction', wrote Kingsley,

he invents stories . . . But out of what does he make them up? Out of a few things in this great world which he has seen, and heard, and felt, just as he makes up his dreams. But who makes truth? Who makes facts? Who, but God?[7]

In such interpretation, facts are God's deeds. But for scientists like Darwin and like Claude Bernard, empiricism also held the dangers of dream. Facts alone are, Bernard, says, 'faits brutals'.[8] For Darwin, concerned with a time register in which all physical objects are transient in the extreme, facts become identified with laws. So 'fact' and theory converge. Time is stayed not by objects but by ideas. 'This grand fact of the grouping of all organic beings seems to me utterly inexplicable on the theory of creation.' 'It is a truly wonderful fact – the wonder of which we are apt to overlook from familiarity – that all animals and all plants throughout all time and space should be related to each other . . .' Fact here is identified with what is novel in his theory as much as with what is known: 'On the view that each species has been independently created, I can see no explanation of this great fact in the classification of all organic beings.' Fact and discovery are condensed. This is a very different attitude to fact from that utilitarian categorising which Dickens mocked in *Hard Times*. It casts a new light on Darwin's remark in 1860: 'I have an old belief that a good observer really means a good theorist.' And it makes all the odder, as Medawar has observed, Darwin's much later contention in the *Autobiography* that he 'worked on true Baconian principles, and without any theory collected facts on a wholesale scale'.[9]

The status of analogy as a part of the process of valid argumentation, rather than simply as an illustrative aid, has been chequered in the history of science. Analogy by its insistence on underlying similarities tends to support the idea of an orderly universe, and indeed in earlier periods, particularly in the sixteenth and seventeenth centuries, the concept of universal analogy was vital to a theological ordering of the visible world. The thorough-goingly analogical organisation of the great chain of being, as Lovejoy has analysed it, makes this clear.[10] By an extension of this argument the phenomena of the world could be seen as a series of infinitely displaceable symbols, all mirroring the other, and all ultimately figuring forth Design. The discovery of similitudes was one of the processes by which the argument for Design was advanced.

The activity of making analogies is essential to human perception as much as to argument. Meaning presupposes analogies. It would not be possible to describe a thing which was totally *sui generis*. We understand the new by reference to the already known. We cannot do without comparison. But analogy in argument can be used not simply as a method of description, a discussion of similarities, but as a means of claiming congruity and imputing pattern and order as the product of a beneficent Designer. In this function it became part of the armoury of Natural Theology. Analogy seemed to provide evidence for a teleological order.

The dangers of analogy as a procedure of argumentation were well understood by theologians as well as by scientists. Its seductively partial applicability, its tendency to suppress all disanalogous elements, means that it can claim more than it proves. It may be used speciously; its applicability may not survive the telling of its story because of the resurgence in memory of all those excluded aspects which cannot be accounted for by the analogical process.

Paley opens *Natural Theology* with an arresting image – arresting partly because its disjunct objects suggest a surrealist landscape.

In crossing a heath, suppose I pitched my foot against a *stone*, and were asked how the stone came to be there, I might possibly answer that, for anything I knew to the contrary, it had lain there for ever; nor would it, perhaps, be very easy to show the absurdity of this answer. But suppose I had found a *watch* upon the ground, and it should be inquired how the watch happened to be in that place, I should hardly think of the answer which I had before given – that for anything I knew, the watch might have always been there. Yet why should not this answer serve for the watch as well as for the stone? Why is it not as admissible in the second case as in the first? For this reason, and for no other – namely, that when we come to inspect the watch, we perceive (what we could not discover in the stone) that its several parts are framed and put together for a purpose.[11]

The scene is, uneasily, both physical and provisional; its scale is unstable, moving rapidly between generality and articulated detail. It is at once authoritative and close to the absurd. Its project is to dramatise absurdity and misappropriated evidence, to rouse resistance, and then to satisfy our sense of congruity so that we accept as much – and more than – his analogy can imply. The process is like that of a riddle – the yoking of unlike objects, the unlocking of shared signification – and like a riddle it gratifies and disappoints. It simultaneously enriches and humbles expectation. Both the bravura and the common sense are important in the learning process created by analogy: the abrupt shifts of scale and the fickle movements between concepts and objects set it always on the edge of fantasy, though claiming for itself a more than metaphorical status, a real presence in the natural order.

Paley's image of the watch lurches towards fantasy later when the course of his argument requires him to propose watches which propagate future generations of watches:

Can it be doubted but that the seed contains a particular organisation? Whether a latent plantule with the means of temporary nutrition, or whatever else it be, it encloses an organisation suited to the germination of a new plant. Has the plant which produced the seed anything more to do with that organisation, than the watch would have had to do with the structure of the watch which was produced in the course of its mechanical movement? I mean – has it anything at all to do with the *contrivance*? The maker and contriver of one watch, when he inserted within it a mechanism suited to the production of another watch, was in truth the maker and contriver of that other watch . . . In producing it by the intervention of a former watch, he was only working by one set of tools instead of another. So it is with the plant, and the seed produced by it. Can any distinction be assigned between the two cases – between the producing watch and the producing plant – both passive, unconscious substances; both, by the organisation which was given to them, producing their like without understanding or design; both, that is, instruments? (39–40)[12]

The fictive nature of analogy is reinvoked to ward off charges of absurdity but as soon as we turn our attention to the fictionality of analogy – its selectivity – then its claim to grounded truth is disturbed.

The shifty, revelatory quality of analogy aligns it to magic. It claims a special virtue at once incandescent and homely for its achieved congruities. A *living*, not simply an imputed, relation between unlikes is claimed by such discourse. The power of analogy to transform the homely into the transcendent or the lesser into the greater intensity draws on a formulation of experience learnt by Christians in the sacraments. Analogy requires transformation and implicitly claims transubstantiation.

The theological use of analogy was given a special reference to congruity with the natural order in Bishop Butler's *The Analogy of Religion Natural and Revealed to the Constitution and Course of Nature*[13] This immensely influential book led many writers to seek analogies between the physical and the ideal world, between natural and revealed religion, but it led others also to seek analogies between the diverse domains of natural order. 'Nature operates by general laws, hard to trace out' (II, iv, 4) writes Butler and he cites the implied laws of heredity, psychology, and politics, pointing out that we ascribe to chance what is actually the result of unknown general laws.

We know indeed several of the general laws of matter: and a great part of the natural behaviour of living agents is reducible to general laws. But we know in a manner nothing, by what laws, storms and tempests, earthquakes, famine, pestilence, become the instruments of destruction to mankind. And the laws, by which persons born into the world at such a time and place are of such capacities, geniuses, tempers; the laws, by which thoughts come into our mind, in a multitude of cases; and by which innumerable things happen, of the greatest influence upon the affairs and state of the world; these laws are so wholly unknown to us, that we call the events which come to pass by them, accidental: though all reasonable men know certainly, that there cannot, in reality, be any such thing as chance, and conclude, that the things which have this appearance are the result of general laws, and may be reduced into them.

This position is the one retained by Darwin, with his insistence that chance is the name we give to as yet unknown laws, and by Freud, with his concept of overdetermination. Similarly, T. H. Huxley in the opening paragraph of 'On the Physical Basis of Life' appropriates the same argument to draw conclusions of a quite different kind from those of Butler. For Butler 'Observation likewise proves the body to be no part of ourselves'; for Huxley 'There is some one kind of matter which is common to all living beings, and . . . their endless diversities are bound together by a physical, as well as an ideal, unity.' Huxley goes on to seek the 'community of faculty', the 'hidden bond' 'underlying all the diversities of vital existence'.

What, truly, can seem to be more obviously different from one another, in faculty, in form, and in substance, than the various kinds of living beings? What community of faculty can there be between the brightly-coloured lichen, which so nearly resembles a mere mineral incrustation of the bare rock on which it grows, and the painter, to whom it is instinct with beauty, or the botanist, whom it feeds with knowledge?[14]

Once *a single order* is proposed – whether it be that of God the Designer, community of descent, or 'a single physical basis of life' – analogy can stabilise. It can take its place as an instrument of perception which allows latent but actual corollaries to become visible. It permits cross-cuts through time and space and askance our habitual categories. Analogy disturbs demarcations and challenges the emphasis on sustained diversity. But because its examples are discrete it is hard to free it from wilfulness. The chosen instances are composed into a contrived pattern. For that reason analogy works best when at the service of universalist world views in which all phenomena are and can be shown to be interrelated.[15]

The emphasis on the congruity between 'natural religion' (or 'natural theology') and 'the constitution of nature' went beyond parable: it drew on the concept of design in the natural world. And beyond design, it had recourse also to the phenomenon of transformation. To take first the concept of design: morphology describes the common structures which organise the diversity of appearances. Paley sees those common structures as implying 'a general plan pursued, yet with such variations in it as are in each case, required by the particular exigency of the subject to which it is applied' (121). He compares, for example, 'feet, wings, and fins':

The Creator, therefore, if we might so speak, had to prepare for different situations, for different difficulties . . . Strip a wing of its feathers, and it bears no obscure resemblance to the fore-leg of a quadruped . . . But fitted up with its furniture of feathers and quills, it becomes a wonderful instrument, more artificial than its first appearance indicates, though that be very striking (132).[16]

The language here describes activity – preparing, stripping, fitting up: the Creator is active, interventionist, accommodating. Both primary plan and diversity of application, argues Paley, manifest intelligence – and he uses the instance of Arkwright's mill to exemplify a similar principle of sound design conformable to diverse needs. Paley's formulation insists, too, upon a prime *consciousness* organising the multiformities of the world, busied and contriving. In his discussion of morphology (415) Darwin separates the 'Natural System' of classification from the idea of a revealed plan of the Creator: 'unless it be specified whether order in time or space, or what else is meant by the plan of the Creator, it seems to me that nothing is thus added to our knowledge' (399).

Darwin proposes a crucial distinction. Instead of superadding the idea of *design* to that of *description*, he adds the idea of *descent* (399). Resemblance, or 'unity of type' is, he goes on to say, 'included under the general name of Morphology':

This is the most interesting department of natural history, and may be said to be its very soul. What can be more curious than that the hand of a man, formed for grasping, that of a mole for digging, the leg of the horse, the paddle of the porpoise, and the wing of the bat, should all be constructed on the same pattern, and should include the same bones, in the same relative positions? (415)

Even in this passage (which Darwin emended in the sixth edition to read somewhat more cautiously, so that the transcendent 'Soul' becomes metaphor: 'This is one of the most interesting departments of natural history, and may almost be said to be its very Soul'), there are vestiges of design and of intentionalist language in the verb 'formed for', which controls the diverse activities, 'grasping', and 'digging', and in the carefully passive interrogative form that they 'should all be constructed on the same pattern'. Such indications are muted but they make it the more essential for Darwin to proceed as he does in the next paragraph to distinguish similarity of pattern both from usefulness and from final causes: 'On the ordinary view of the independent creation of each being, we can only say that so it is – that it has so pleased the Creator to construct each animal and plant.' In the fourth edition he adds bluntly: 'but this is not a scientific explanation'.

The elements of *contrivance* and *consciousness* are essential to natural theological explanation. Paley's leading argument proposed that:

There cannot be design, without a designer; contrivance, without a contriver; order, without choice; arrangement, without anything capable of arranging; subserviency and relation to a purpose, without that which could intend a purpose; means suitable to an end, and executing their office, in accomplishing that end, without the end ever having been contemplated, or the means accommodated to it. (15)

In contrast to Kant, he cannot conceive purposiveness without purpose, or in more Darwinian terms, aptness without intent. For this, among other reasons, *approximation* and *unconsciousness* become important counter terms for Darwin: 'this unconscious process of selection' (148), 'a large amount of change . . . slowly and unconsciously accumulated' (95). Artificial selection works 'methodically and more quickly'; natural selection works 'unconsciously and more slowly, but more efficiently'.

Paley specifically rejected the idea of 'appetencies' – unconscious inclinations which reach unmeditated fulfilments. In an energetic fantasy Paley jokes about the idea that, given a long enough time, propensities can transform matter:

A piece of animated matter, for example, that was endued with a propensity to *fly*, though ever so shapeless, though no other, we will suppose, than a round ball to begin with, would, in a course of ages – if not in a million of years, perhaps in a hundred million of years (for our theorists, having eternity to dispose of, are never sparing in time) – acquire *wings*. (242)

Paley's opposites are design versus habit, and intention versus use.

Darwin agrees with Paley's opposition to the idea of use and habit as the major transforming powers but introduces a third explanation: natural selection. The profound importance of Darwin's idea was in revealing a new dynamic for change and in disclosing a fresh space occupied neither by concepts of design nor of use. The abiding problem for Darwin was how to express it in a language which was imbued with intentionality.[17] The lateral rather than causal organisation of analogy offered him one possibility.

Just as determinism requires that we accept the idea of unconsciousness and oblivion, so Darwinian theory requires that we accept forgetfulness and the vanishing of matter.[18] These are preconditions to its method of explanation. Origins can never fully be regained nor rediscovered. Origins – whether of species, of individual experience, or even of language – are always antecedent to language and consciousness.

Huxley makes clear this connection in the analogy he uses to justify the lack of 'testimonial evidence' for evolution:

I need not say that it is quite hopeless to look for testimonial evidence of evolution. The very nature of the case precludes the possibility of such evidence, for the human race can no more be expected to testify to its own origin, than a child can be tendered as witness to its own birth.[19]

The same emphasis upon lost and unreclaimed origins, upon antecedent oblivion, is found in Freud. As Ernst Bloch comments:

Freud's topology is the most striking model of time oriented around the past, a picture of an apparent movement toward the future whose vital incentives lie buried in early childhood; for such a model comprehension consists in working back to origins. The Freudian unconscious is therefore a no-longer-consciousness, an unconsciousness of a world and a self which have officially, in the eyes of the reality principle, ceased to be.[20]

There is a problem in the word 'unconscious', which by its negative form raises its spectral opposite, 'conscious'. Freud's spatial hierarchy of consciousness with unconsciousness *beneath* must be distinguished from Darwin's 'unconscious' which signifies a permanent organic state quite separate from, and having nothing to do with, consciousness.

Oblivion must be part of the material of *explanation*, just as latency is part of the dynamic of *change* in Darwinian theory. Both give room to unconsciousness, but the unconscious must – for Darwin's purposes – be scrupulously distinguished from intention (or even 'appetency').

Hardy grasped the implications of Darwin's historiography, perhaps without directly associating it with Darwin:

History is rather a stream than a tree. There is nothing organic in its shape, nothing systematic in its development. It flows on like a thunderstorm-rill by a road-side, now a straw turns it this way, now a tiny barrier of sand that. (Spring 1885)[21]

One extreme view of analogy is that it is a rhetorical trick, unstable in its implications and distorting in its procedures, asserting only specious, temporary, or accidental similarities. At the other extreme, it is seen as an instrument of discovery which reveals grounded congruities and makes manifest the actual though concealed coherences of a stable world order. The question of whether the perception of analogies was fickle and momentary or whether there were stable analogies in nature which we could discover and then retain as a means of explanation, was a topic much discussed in the middle of the nineteenth century: Comte's view was austere. He preferred, for example, the term 'gravitation' to 'attraction', because it expresses a fact without any reference to the nature or cause of this occurrence.[22] He inherited consciously from Descartes an emphasis upon the necessary univocality of scientific language and an avoidance of metaphor because of its uncontrollable element. Metaphor creates proliferation of meaning by means of its never thoroughly parallel terms. The fashionable view in the period when Darwin was writing was to deplore the evasions and transferences of metaphor, and to seek a declarative directness for scientific or philosophical language. George Eliot, even, lamented 'That we can so seldom declare what a thing is, except by saying it is something else'.[23] The problem of a stable semantics for science was one of the preoccupations of the British Association in the 1830s and Darwin himself served on a committee on nomenclature.

The role of analogy and metaphor in the formation of scientific theory and in extending the possibilities of hypothesis has been a preoccupation of philosophers and historians of science during the past thirty years and much illuminating work has been achieved in this field. Black, Popper, Canguilhem, Hesse, and Schon's economical and suggestive works on the transposition of concepts, have been supplemented by theorists such as Barry Barnes working on *Scientific Knowledge and Sociological Theory* who have pointed out the extent to which thinking, because metaphor based, is culture bound.[24] There has been a shift away from the kind of work which saw metaphor as decorative and extraneous to the process of thinking. Through the work of writers such as Bloor and Robert M. Young there has also been a movement away from the assumption that science inhabits an absolute domain of its own, exempt from the ideological, and exempt also from the preoccupations of the society which the scientists inhabit. Such work has brought out the importance of 'heuristic fictions'.[25] Despite manifest divergencies the primary procedures of scientific theorising and of the making of fiction have much in common: hypothesising, a reliance upon the future for confirmation, projecting possibilities rather than confirmed data; replotting observed relations of cause and effect or of possibility; observation; perceiving underlying patterns by means of analogy; a pleasure in boldness, a sense of the insufficiency of present understanding, the recognition of a world beyond the compass of our present knowledge.

The usual answer to claims for the essentially imaginative properties of scientific writing and their community with other forms of fiction is *testability*, and what Popper has called 'falsifiability', which makes him give much value to 'unexpectedness'. The element of surprise, including unforeseeable reorderings of known data, new information, formal boldness, are qualities valued in scientific enquiry as in fiction. One pleasure they both offer is enfranchisement: they release us from the loop of the foreknown, they enlarge possibility. On the whole, however, and rightly, scientists resist the collapsing of the distinction between scientific theory which must at some stage – if not immediately – be assayable, and fiction, which can be assayed only subjectively, and cannot be experimentally repeated. Yet this is not a complete distinction – many major scientific theories declare themselves *in advance of* the data needed to confirm them. They foretell, in Polanyi's phrase, 'the coming of yet unknown future manifestations'.[26] In that sense, major scientific theories have the function of prophecy – a function much claimed by the novel which seeks to register emergent forms for consciousness before they are capable of manifesting themselves within a society. The precarious affinities between all modes of creative thinking and reception, (whether the creation of a fiction which convinces readers as knowledge, or of a scientific theory which convinces through its own coherence) need and repay analysis. What is remarkable about the mid- and late nineteenth century is that instead of ignoring or rebutting attempts to set scientific writing and literature side by side, as is sometimes the case in our own time, both novelists and scientists were very much aware of the potentialities released by the congruities of their methods and ends. Clifford, Tyndall, Maxwell, all affirmed the imaginative properties of their work. It is perhaps not surprising that the novelists turned to science for confirmation. But the scientists, too, drew upon literary evidence and models, and were aware of the imaginative nature of their enterprise.

An apparently iconoclastic attitude to the autonomy of science as a mode of thinking and truth perception is seen in this passage from Paul Feyerabend, author of *Against Method*, in his essay 'Problems of Empiricism Part II'.[27]

The inventions and tricks which help a clever man through the jungle of facts, a priori principles, theories, mathematical formulas, methodological rules, pressures from the general public and his 'professional peers' and which enable him to form a coherent picture out of apparent chaos are much more closely related to the spirit of poetry than one would be inclined to think. Indeed, one has the suspicion that the only difference between poets and scientists is that the latter, having lost their sense of style, now try to comfort themselves with the pleasant fiction that they are following rules of a quite different kind which produce a much grander and more important result, namely, the Truth.

Feyerabend casts as 'inventions and tricks' those elements in thought which he sees as 'closely related to the spirit of poetry' and there is a reactive undertow in the passage. Science is assumed to be less grand, less important than it proposes to itself, *because* closer to poetry than it will recognise.

Metaphor is never fully stable. It initiates new meaning but not permanent meaning. Mary Hesse contrasts poetic metaphor, which she interprets as 'striking and unexpected, if not shocking', with the explanatory aim of scientific metaphor.[28] Some kinds of literary metaphor do thrive on wilful distance, but in the long intercommunications typical of narrative, metaphors become part of a continuous truth-discovering process. Indeed, the functions of metaphor which Hesse specifies as scientific are in fact specifically *narrative*, whether that narrative be scientific or novelistic. It may be, as she suggests, that in scientific metaphor all the implications are not simultaneously present, but the power of metaphor in all kinds of narrative depends precisely upon the stretching 'to radically new situations' that she associates peculiarly with scientific metaphor. Whewell described how single words expand in meaning so as to disguise change and accommodate it while it establishes itself.[29] Hesse emphasises the full accord of first and second term in scientific metaphor, but then concludes with an implicitly evolutionist metaphor of expansion, and adaptation which yields a sense of effortful growth rather than of congruity: 'Rationality consists just in the continuous adaptation of our language to our continually expanding world.'

Space, expansion, forecast; these are powers offered by metaphor, whether scientific or literary – and they are powers as important as the correspondence, similitude, and exactness of measure, which we habitually look for. But space, expansion, and forecast are not the same as vagueness. The terms of each metaphor designate that which is left out or left over.

The drive in metaphor towards merging, towards the single domain, is a search for an ideal wholeness which its disjunct nature persistently counters. First and second terms are interactive. But because of the possibility always of *further description*, the drive towards divergence and diversification survives through metaphor, only a little less powerful than the drive towards stable equivalence, and persistently subverting it. The polysemism of metaphor means that it is hard to control its implications: it may be argued, for example, that Darwin's metaphor of the tree is a formal analogy whose function is purely diagrammatic, describing a shape not an experience. Its initial value for Darwin lay undoubtedly in the fact that the diagram *declared* itself as tree, rather than being foreknowingly designed to represent a tree-like shape for descent. On the page, however, it could as well be interpreted by the eye as shrub, branching coral, or seaweed. But Darwin saw not only the explanatory but the mythic potentiality of this diagram, its congruity with past orders of descent, and extended these in a form which is experimental rather than formal at the conclusion of the same chapter 'Natural Selection'. The tree discovered in the diagram is not only Arbor Vitae but the Arbor Scientiae. Darwin establishes so close a connection between representation and actuality that he can claim 'truth' for it. The prose succession imitates the order it describes, branching out into further and further similitudes:

The affinities of all the beings of the same class have sometimes been represented by a great tree. I believe this simile largely speaks the truth. The green and budding twigs may represent existing species; and those produced during each former year may represent the long succession of extinct species. At each period of growth all the growing twigs have tried to branch out on all sides, and to overtop and kill the surrounding twigs and branches, in the same manner as species and groups of species have tried to overmaster other species in the great battle for life. The limbs divided into great branches, and these into lesser and lesser branches, were themselves once, when the tree was small, budding twigs; and this connexion of the former and present buds by ramifying branches may well represent the classification of all extinct and living species in groups subordinate to groups. Of the many twigs which flourished when the tree was a mere bush, only two or three, now grown into great branches, yet survive and bear all the other branches; so with the species which lived during long-past geological periods, very few now have living and modified descendants. From the first growth of the tree, many a limb and branch has decayed and dropped off; and these lost branches of various sizes may represent those whole orders, families, and genera which have now no living representatives, and which are known to us only from having been found in a fossil state. As we here and there see a thin straggling branch springing from a fork low down in a tree, and which by some chance has been favoured and is still alive on its summit, so we occasionally see an animal like the Ornithorhynchus or Lepidosiren, which in some small degree connects by its affinities two large branches of life, and which has apparently been saved from fatal competition by having inhabited a protected station. As buds give rise by growth to fresh buds, and these, if vigorous, branch out and overtop on all sides many a feebler branch, so by generation I believe it has been with the great Tree of Life, which fills with its dead and broken branches the crust of the earth, and covers the surface with its ever branching and beautiful ramifications. (171–2)

The sanguine profusion of comparisons makes for a fantastic comprehensiveness which is both truth-affirming and self-confirming. And so the chapter on 'Natural Selection' ends, with an image that lays claim on a succession of metaphors from deep antiquity.

The aptness of Darwin's simile is from time to time put at risk by its expansion, as in the sentence 'as we here and there see a thin straggling branch' where the grounds of comparison are reached only at the end of the sentence, 'a protected station', and the formal similitude is slight. But the heuristic process for the reader – and, it seems in this passage, for Darwin himself – is in the triumph of making the metaphor, like its topic, grow, develop, change, extend, and finally complete itself. Fulfilment here is given an effect of causality without a complete commitment to it.

The metaphor in this passage extends a process found in the argument from analogous structure elsewhere in the work. Mary Hesse notes:

Extensive use of such homologies and analogies was made in nineteenth-century morphology. It was, however then generally assumed that analogical inference is justified only if co-occurrence of properties indicate some stronger relation between properties which would constitute a causal law linking individuals in a species, or species in a genus. Both common evolutionary ancestry and functional correlation of parts required for viability in similar environments were appealed to, to provide such causal relationships. Causality has been defined here essentially as a matter of more comprehensive correlations over the total evidence, but whatever be the interpretation of causality, the common assumption remains that analogical argument from morphological similarities is possible.[30]

Metaphor depends upon species and upon categorisation. It cannot inhabit an entirely promiscuous world. It is polymorphic, but its energy needs the barriers which it seeks to break down. Therefore it is particularly apt to a work whose project is to describe the means by which species came to be. When Erasmus Darwin was revelling in the profusion of the world, Sade was seeking to break all the barriers which discriminated that profusion: gender, class, bodies and machines. His work demonstrates the extent to which promiscuity takes its power from speciation. Lévi-Strauss insists on the value of categorisation *in itself* and Darwin's work clearly shares the drive towards categorisation, yet because his primary concern is to track back the extraordinary variety of the world towards common ancestry there is a two-direction movement in his thought:

we shall have to treat species in the same manner as those naturalists treat genera, who admit that genera are merely artificial combinations made for convenience. This may not be a cheering prospect; but we shall at least be freed from the vain search for the undiscovered and undiscoverable essence of the term species. (456)[31]

Darwin is anti-essentialist, preoccupied always with clusters of properties whose groupings and relations shift as they yield meaning, and whose meaning depends upon their being part of the physical order. The living organism and the secession of organisms emerge as the result of the shared potentialities of their parts, not as a result of predetermined assemblage. This view is close to Kant's assertion of purposiveness without a governing purpose: *Zweckmässigkeit ohne Zweck*. Categorisation becomes implicated in process, rather than being foreknown or pre-emptive. It is a stage in discovery, not the beginning of discovery, and it is, moreover, always conditional and temporary since it is grounded in history.

It is striking to see the same double process explored in a recent study of metaphor by Donald Schon, first published as *Displacement of Concepts*, and then republished with a more open recognition of one of its own two constitutive metaphors as *Invention and the Evolution of Ideas* (London 1967). Schon argues that there has been throughout history a relatively small body of central metaphors:

No-one can look seriously at the life of metaphors in theories since Plato and fail to be impressed both by how *slight* a change there has been in the roots of our thought and by the unexpected homogeneity of our intellectual space. Nevertheless, there has been evolution. (193)

Schon's emphasis upon the very broad communality and inertness of metaphor would seem to some extent to undermine Barnes's insistence on the culture-bound nature of thought: Barnes writes:

It has been established that the main path of cultural change is laid down by scientists concerned to utilize, extend and develop a metaphor as much as possible. The key forms of thought and argument involved are metaphorical or analogical . . . To show the metaphorical nature of thought is to show the culture-bound nature of thought. (Barnes 1974, 57)

In both examples just cited the emphasis is upon single metaphor and its capacity for expansion and change. This is not to suggest that throughout the work of Schon, in particular, such an emphasis is constant. Schon excellently analyses the emotion of discovery – its dangerousness, its playfulness, the 'oscillations between wrenching pain and unexpected joy'. 'In our culture,' he writes, ' "novelty", "the new", "innovation", "creativity", have taken on highly positive emotive meanings. But we are easier in our minds talking about the new than actually experiencing it.'

Metaphor is a means both of initiating and of controlling novelty. Schon's description of the reader's participation could be aptly extended from scientific discovery to participation in narrative: a sense of powerlessness is generated by a text which will not permit us to 'build up', or select, or fulfil expectation. Too great a freedom for the creator will mean oppression for the reader. Metaphor, both in its residuum of the known and in its heuristic powers, offers a means to recognisable discovery.

Gruber has valuably pointed out that the effect of Darwin's metaphors in *The Origin* derives not only from each of them individually but from the interplay between them. Indeed, the limits to Robert Young's thorough and subtle essay 'Darwin's Metaphor: Does Nature Select?' are indicated in his insistence on one metaphor in isolation, whereas interaction and the formation of significance take place not only within a single metaphor but *between metaphors sustained in narrative*.

If we read metaphor, as Cassirer (1925) does, neither as ornament nor as privileged discourse, but as a fundamental means of initiating discovery, we shall better understand its value as a part of theory for Darwin. If, at the same time, we recognise how much metaphoric activity takes place at a level beneath attention, we shall be better able to specify the cultural presumptions which shape Darwin's creativity, and the responses of his contemporaries – and we shall be enabled to examine the ways in which our own presumptions are conditioned by his. In metaphor's emphasis on selection and, equally, in its redundancy, we have two strains which made it an essential mimetic element in Darwin's rhetoric, as theory. 'Univocity of meaning is ultimately grounded in essence', remarks Paul Ricoeur. We begin to see more clearly why multivocity was crucial to Darwin's discourse.

In *Zoological Philosophy* Lamarck described selection as part of the procedure for acquiring knowledge: his first two named methods concern selecting material:

to bring order among the infinitely numerous and varied objects which he has before him; to distinguish without danger of confusion, among this immense multitude of objects, either groups of those in whom he is interested, or particular individuals among them. (19)

The first chapter is entitled 'On Artificial Devices in Dealing with the Productions of Nature'. Lamarck is here discussing the procedures of argument and discovery such as classification and nomenclature, not husbandry and grafting; but the artificial/natural contrary organised and moralised his argument as it was later to do Darwin's. The dyadic Artificial Selection, Natural Selection, thus drew on an implicit analogy with this earlier epistemology. The idea discovered and the procedures of its discovery turn out to have a very close congruity.[32] Nomenclature and numen accord.

In Lamarck's analysis, the acquisition of knowledge of the natural world depends on the two interdependent principles, of super-fecundity ('the infinitely numerous and *varied* objects', 'this immense multitude of objects') and of selection. He warns man against confusing his *artificial devices* for bringing nature within his understanding and 'the laws and acts of nature herself'. The contrast Lamarck develops between economically motivated research in which man wants 'to turn the productions of nature to his own use' and the disinterested observer, 'interested impartially in all natural productions', offers to Darwin the possibility of a dramatic role for the writer within the procedures of his argument which will approximate more closely to that of Nature, and to the processes of *natural* as opposed to artificial, wilful selection (19–20). When we turn to Darwin's own opening sentences we notice that knowledge is being created now, communally, and is not part of a pre-established order of fact as in Chambers's pre-emptive 'factual' opening. 'It is familiar knowledge that the earth which we inhabit is a globe of somewhat less than 8000 miles in diameter . . .'[33]

For his theory to work Darwin needs the sense of free play, of 'jeu', as much, or even more, than he needs history. In his epistemology argument must emerge out of a plethora of instances because, of its nature, his text must at all costs avoid aligning itself with the procedures of artificial selection, wilful or premature, which a more closely honed or simply sequential argument would require. It is essential for Darwin's *theory* that the multitudinousness and variety of the natural world should flood through his language. His theory deconstructs any formulation which interprets the natural world as commensurate with man's understanding of it. It outgoes his powers of observation and is not co-extensive with his reasoning. Yet in the use of metaphor and analogy he found a means of restoring equivalence without false delimitation.

'Relative similarities', 'graduated differences' – these are the major topics of *The Origin*, but instead of examining them only spatially, in the present moment attainable by the experimental method, Darwin seeks to examine them also through time, through that which is not 'present to our eye'. It is this historical, or proto-historical, element in his work which means that he must give primacy to imagination, to the perception of analogies, and must extend the study of forms fixed in the present moment into a study of their mutability and transience as well as their powers of transformation and of generation. 'No organism wholly soft can be preserved.' Shells and bones will decay and disappear.

The individual becomes the congress of potentialities, and these potentialities play within and surpass the single life span. The relation of individual to species is perhaps *the* radical analogy which Darwin explores in this work. The book opens with this sentence:

When we look to the individuals of the same variety or sub-variety of our older cultivated plants and animals, one of the first points which strikes us is that they generally differ much more from each other, than do the individuals of any one species or variety in a state of nature.

This analogy is tested and explored and to some extent dissolved as the book proceeds. Darwin does not give much credence to any essentialist view of species and therefore distrusts the tendency to see each individual as an avatar of a hidden idea, expressible as species.

The delineation of species tends to take the individual as its model, but such a model is instantly subverted by the fact that no single individual is archetypical – individuals are individual – and the discrepancies between them press upon the bounds of species-description, making it difficult to ascribe limits and conformities. Moreover, Darwin uses behaviour as well as structure and descent in his description of species and therefore immediately finds himself involved in sociological reference. This is one point of entry into his organisation which was to be opened up by George Eliot.

Darwin uses the term analogy in two different ways in *The Origin* – one is technical, distinguishing 'analogical resemblances' from 'real affinities' for purposes of classification. Analogical resemblances are the result of adaptation to the environment; 'real affinities' of descent:

The resemblance of the greyhound and race-horse is hardly more fanciful than the analogies which have been drawn by some authors between very distinct animals. On my view of characters being of real importance for classification, only in so far as they reveal descent, we can clearly understand why analogical or adaptive characters, although of the utmost importance to the welfare of the being, are almost valueless to the systematist. For animals, belonging to two most distinct lines of descent, may readily become adapted to similar conditions and thus assume a close external resemblance; but such resemblances will not reveal – will rather tend to conceal – their blood-relationship to their proper lines of descent. (410)

He then complicates the problem by pointing out that 'the very same characters are analogical when one class or order is compared with another, but give true affinities when the members of the same class or order are compared one with another. True affinity is inheritance from a common ancestor' (410) and the generative organs because 'most remotely related to the habits and food of an animal . . . afford very clear indications of its true affinities' (400 – Darwin is here quoting Owen).

Darwin's distinction establishes the *temporary* quality of such analogical resemblances – they are to do with appearance or adaptation and are thus closer to an observer's fiction than to the irremovable properties of life. But this technical use of the term did not prevent Darwin from appropriating it in argumentation – though it did keep him alert to the provisional quality of such resemblances.

Darwin was seeking to create a story of the world – a fiction – which would not entirely rely upon the scope of man's reason nor upon the infinitesimally small powers of observation he possesses, as they act within the world spread all about him, and as they enclose him through the shortness of his time span. Yet Darwin was not seeking a covertly metaphysical world nor attempting an enthusiasm which would extend the material into a form of mysticism. Throughout his use of metaphor and analogy one can feel the double stress – the attempt to create exact predications and the attempt to press upon the boundaries of the knowable within a human order.

His text is an unusually extensive fiction – one which deliberately extends itself towards the boundaries of the literally *unthinkable*, which displaces the absoluteness of man's power of reason as an instrument for measuring the world. Despite the metaphoric density of his writing, Darwin seems never fully to have raised into consciousness its imaginative and sociological implications. Yet we know that in his notebooks he saw a good way into the implications for man and that he wished to avoid naturalising current social organisations. He saw some of the dangers of 'authorisation'.

It is the element of obscurity, of metaphors whose peripheries remain undescribed, which made *The Origin of Species* so incendiary – and which allowed it to be appropriated by thinkers of so many diverse political persuasions. It encouraged onward thought: it offered itself for metaphorical application and its multiple discourses encouraged further acts of interpretation. The presence of *latent meaning* made *The Origin* suggestive, even unstoppable in its action upon minds.

Darwin *could not* fully formulate all that his ideas might mean, or come to mean, though from edition to edition he sought to steady their implications. He continued to try to establish boundaries between the scientific meaning and the possible application of his work – but the language he had chosen and the story he had unfurled did not allow such rigid delimitation. The whole movement of *The Origin* is towards expansion, not stabilisation. Again the paradox enters: it was the expansion of *material explanation* that he sought, not a metaphysical sweep into the 'inexplicable' language of creation, which he sedulously avoided.

Colin Turbayne in *The Myth of Metaphor* (revised edition, Columbia, 1970, 65) remarks that 'the sciences are riddled with metaphors, but the scientists who use them, for example, Descartes and Newton, do not always admit to their use'. Darwin, on that scale of awareness, was probably unusually conscious that there was a spectrum of fictiveness in his use of metaphor.

The deliberately guarded and consciously metaphoric status that he gives to the phrase 'struggle for existence' which he sometimes varies as 'struggle for life' and even in one instance 'the great battle for life' (127) also expresses his unwillingness to give dominance to a militant or combative order of nature. He sees struggle as essential to the continuity of nature, but he interprets it as interdependence or endurance as much as battle. The egalitarian, horizontal, ordering of his view of the natural world means that he eschews the simplicity of hierarchy. Neither the ladder nor the pyramid is a useful model for him. When he uses the term 'the scale of nature' (124, 126) it is not to sort and distinguish in a vertical order. In nature relations can never be simple (124). There is no single line of ascent and descent, but rather an abstruse lateral range of interconnections.

This complexity of interrelation is another reason why he needs the metaphoric and needs also at times to emphasise its transposed, metaphorical status – its imprecise innumerate relation and application to the phenomenological order it represents. The representation is deliberately limited to that of 'convenience' and does not attempt to present itself as a just, or full, equivalent. One can see this desire to *specify* complexity without appearing to *simplify* that complexity in another related passage. He begins with precise instances and then moves into deliberately vague speculation:

The recent increase of the missel-thrush in parts of Scotland has caused the decrease of the song-thrush . . .

One species of charlock will supplant another, and so in other cases. We can dimly see why the competition should be most severe between allied forms, which fill nearly the same place in the economy of nature; but probably in no one case could we precisely say why one species has been victorious over another in the great battle of life. (127)

'Dimly', 'nearly', 'probably' – the tentative, blurred, half-glimpsed reasons for happening are momentarily stabilised in the vivid martial image of 'why one species has been victorious over another in the great battle of life'. *Of* life, not *for* life – the particle harks back to another sense of struggle: the struggle to survive, not to conquer.

In passages such as this Darwin deliberately sets off against each other the wayward and the iconic elements in metaphor. He insists upon the dark space behind the summary formulation, 'the battle of life'. The chapter ends by encouraging us to try an experiment 'in imagination' (128) and then proving to us that we cannot sufficiently imagine the complexities of relation in nature to succeed in our experiment:

It is good thus to try in our imagination to give any form some advantage over another. Probably in no single instance should we know what to do, so as to succeed. It will convince us of our ignorance on the mutual relations of all organic beings; a conviction as necessary, as it seems to be difficult to acquire. (129)

Again he places more value on the expansion rather than the stabilisation of our sense of the world which surrounds us. This awareness of partial knowledge and imaginative desuetude provides a counter-current to the final sentence of the chapter, which urges itself towards a meliorist belief which it yet never fully shares:

When we reflect on this struggle, *we may console ourselves* with *the full belief,* that the war of nature is not incessant, that no fear is felt, that death is generally prompt, and that the vigorous, the healthy, and the happy survive and multiply. (129)

The form of the sentence is optative, 'we may', not absolute – it is also urgently assertive, its confidence sagging momentarily with that word 'generally', and it comes to rest in the testamental word 'multiply'.

The will to believe in a happy world and the dark flood of insight into suffering which accompanies it is a frequent movement in Darwin's prose. It would be easy to make either an optimistic or a pessimistic selection from *The Origin*. This poignant tension between happiness and pain, a sense simultaneously of the natural world as exquisite and gross, rank and sensitive, constantly subverts the poise of any moralised description of it.

The quagmire of the metaphoric troubles Darwin, yet he needs it – he needs its tendency to suggest more or other than you meant to say, to make the latent actual, to waken sleeping dogs, and equally, he needs its powers of persuasion through lassitude, through our *inattention*. Ideally Darwin would like to restore that which is metaphorically invoked to complete congruity with the material order, so that imagination is verified physically. As I have already suggested, one way to draw all the obscure correspondences of organic being and of description of organic being into a stable order is to discover 'a plain signification' which has previously been speculatively expressed through analogy and metaphor or through mythology. As a result, Darwin's style is characterised by rapid movements between description, myth, hypothesis, and homology such as we observe in this sentence:

If we suppose that the ancient progenitor, the archetype as it may be called, of all mammals, had its limbs constructed on the existing general pattern, for whatever purpose they served, we can at once perceive the plain signification of the homologous construction of the limbs throughout the whole class. (416)

But there was another problem of position and of language for Darwin to solve. It is a difficulty inherent in his text and in its status in our culture. How far did Darwin figure himself as *creating* what he describes? He was producing a text certainly, creating an argument. He seeks in his argument to emphasise production; but he could not rely upon a fully experimental method. He was obliged to work in terms of an imaginative history. He moved outside the protecting terms of Baconian induction into a role more like that of a creative artist; all his creative energy was concentrated on authenticating his account of the way in which species had been formed. The 'great facts' which Darwin perceived were expressed through a profusion of example and through a profusion of metaphor; they demanded an imaginative reordering of experience. *The Origin of Species* was itself a work which could only too readily be cast by its critics as speculative and utopian, fascinated with its own ethnography in the style of Utopias from Thomas More on.

Although the dismissive edge of such criticism may have passed away, there is still a sense in which we hold Darwin *responsible* for his history of the world, as though he had created rather than simply recorded the processes he describes. There is some justice in that too, because the highly individualistic yet culture-bound language of *The Origin* with its terms like 'the struggle for life', 'the great family', and 'natural selection', its ransacking of contemporary ideologies, has had consequences beyond the control or cognisance of the text which engendered them. So Darwin is in a creationist dilemma. He wishes simply to record orders which in no way depend upon him. But because of his highly charged imaginative language and the need to invent fresh terms and to forge new metaphorical connections, he appears to undertake an individual creative act. His text has a progenitive power. He seeks to express the equivalence of man with all other forms of life but the power of his writing and the novelty of his narrative make it appear that Darwin, man's representative, has as much created as described.

CHAPTER 4

Darwinian myths

I GROWTH AND ITS MYTHS

Evolutionary theory brings together two imaginative elements implicit in much nineteenth-century thinking and creativity. One was the fascination with growth expressed also in Natürphilosophie and in Bildungsroman. The other was the concept of transformation. The intellectual interest in märchen, fairy-tale, and myth, which increased as the century went on, was fuelled by these preoccupations, while its methodology was indebted to evolutionary patterns of argument. The work of anthropologists and mythographers such as Müller, Lubbock, Tylor, and Lang was strengthened by reference to the work of Darwin and Spencer, though their responses to Spencer were on the whole a good deal less enthusiastic than to Darwin.

The extraordinary metamorphoses within the natural life cycle of creatures such as frogs and butterflies, as well as the sustained transformation of baby into adult, had long been a subject of marvel. Such transformation now became a preoccupation with theorists of development:

It is a truth of very wide, if not universal, application, that every living creature commences its existence under a form different from, and simpler than, that which it eventually attains.

The oak is a more complex thing than the little rudimentary plant contained in the acorn; the caterpillar is more complex than the egg; the butterfly than the caterpillar; and each of these beings, in passing from its rudimentary to its perfect condition, runs through a series of changes, the sum of which is called its Development. In the higher animals these changes are extremely complicated; but . . . the labours of such men as Von Baer, Rathke, Reichert, Bischoff, and Remak, have almost completely unravelled them, so that the successive stages of development which are exhibited by a Dog, for example, are now as well known to the embryologist as are the steps of the metamorphosis of the silk-worm moth to the school-boy.[1]

The new question formulated for nineteenth-century people by the contemplation of transformation and metamorphosis was this: can transformations within the individual life cycle (ontogeny) act as a valid model for species-mutation (phylogeny)? And, as a subsidiary question, do we see the phases of evolutionary process *recapitulated* in the individual organism?[2]

The rapidity of Darwin's narrative made it difficult for him to render accurately the extreme slowness of the processes he was describing. Ontogeny and phylogeny might therefore be confused in the reader's mind – and even in the syntax of the text.

A passage that became a locus classicus for this kind of attack was the one in the first edition where Darwin described the bear which swam with open mouth like a whale, catching insects in the water.

Even in so extreme a case as this, if the supply of insects were constant, and if better adapted competitors did not already exist in the country, I can see no difficulty in a race of bears being rendered, by natural selection, more and more aquatic in their structure and habits, with larger and larger mouths, till a creature was produced as monstrous as a whale. (215)

As Ellegård remarks, 'anti-Darwinian writers seem to have deliberately played on the ambiguity of "a bear" and "a whale". The word can be used to denote the individual, and to denote the class, or species.'

The image of the swimming bear is so particular, so comic, that even a sympathetic reader will be inclined to indulge the dreamlike image of the bears with larger and larger mouths metamorphosing into something 'very like a whale'. And antagonists like Sedgwick were enabled to mock at the idea: 'Darwin seems to believe that a white bear, by being confined to the slopes floating in the Polar basin, might be turned into a whale.' Darwin omitted this passage in later editions, but the mockery and confusion serve to show one of the ways in which his theory opened out in popular imagination towards fairy-tale: if other intermediate forms could exist, why not mermaids? 'With such a range and plasticity . . . we know not where to stop – centaurs, dryads, and hamadryads . . . (and perhaps) mermaids once filled our seas.'[3]

The idea of massive transformation could also take on a religious meaning:

For if the changes of the lower animals are so wonderful, and so difficult to discover, why should not there be changes in the higher animals far more wonderful, and far more difficult to discover? And may not man, the crown and flower of all things, undergo some change as much more wonderful than all the rest, as the Great Exhibition is more wonderful than a rabbit-burrow?[4]

But the version of transformation which most fascinated Victorian writers was that of recapitulation. It offered the pleasures of miniaturisation and of magical speed. The whole evolutionary process was condensed within the embryo.

Stephen Jay Gould gives a full account of the theory in *Ontogeny and Phylogeny* (1977).

Recapitulation had experimental attractions for serious scientists. Haeckel and Weismann each saw it as the most important discovery consequent upon Darwinian theory.[5] For Weismann, it served as a theoretical tool in his study of the adaptive significance of colour patterns in caterpillars, and for Haeckel it seemed a basic pattern for reading the history of all living forms.

The embryo was held to recapitulate (or condense) the development of the species to which it belonged. It seemingly offered, therefore, visual and experimental evidence for earlier phases of evolutionary development.

This theory was a particular and immensely influential offshoot of the earlier nineteenth-century fascination with growth. The attempt to parallel the phases of the individual life cycle and the phases of species development not only had real experimental interest but also represented another attempt to domesticate evolutionary theory, here by miniaturisation. To understand the forms in which Darwin's ideas permeated the literature of his time it is necessary to supplement the study of his language and narrative with a brief analysis of ideas of growth, some peculiar to nineteenth-century European culture, some common to us all.

II GROWTH AND TRANSFORMATION

Growth is a primary sense experience just beyond the reach of consciousness. We have all grown, within our mothers, and then from babyhood to adulthood. It is an experience none of us quite remembers. Growth is an invisible process, registered only in retrospect. It can therefore be expressed intellectually only as narrative; it has meaning primarily in terms of its own past. It is common to all forms of organic life but the time-scales of its performance are extraordinarily various; mayflies to oaks. The common experience and the shared amnesia concerning the experience give growth a status in consciousness which may be read equally as mysterious or banal. If it lies beyond the reach of consciousness it must lie beyond the reach of language, so that there may be nothing to be said about it. It is prior to narrative, though it is itself narrative in form and can be expressed primarily by the narrative past tense: You *have* grown, I grew. But this same quality of latency in the experience of physical growth makes it a possible metaphor for all invisible process which is nevertheless substantively *there*.

The first equivalence is between mental and psychological growth: the development of the mind and of the individual identity. The two processes are interconnected of course, and the growth of the sensibility, like physical growth, is anterior to language. But the mind may come to a point when it can analyse its own development.

> From early days,
> Beginning not long after that first time
> In which, a Babe, by intercourse of touch,
> I held mute dialogues with my Mother's heart
> I have endeavour'd to display the means
> Whereby this infant sensibility,
> Great birthright of our Being, was in me
> Augmented and sustain'd.[6]

Physical growth retains its autonomous nature, its hermetic power. It can be invoked as a model for understanding a great number of experiences which are registrable only over a long retrospect of time and which are not accessible to any single consciousness during that time. Throughout the past two hundred years this reference to physical growth as a model has been a common procedure, in historiography, sociology, psychology and political theory. There are processes which are inescapable and irreversible: physical growth is one of them. Virginia Woolf comments in 'A Sketch of the Past':

But somehow into that picture must be brought, too, the sense of movement and change. Nothing remained stable long. One must get the feeling of everything approaching and then disappearing, getting large, getting small, passing at different rates of speed past the little creature; one must get the feeling that made her press on, the little creature driven on as she was by growth of her legs and arms, driven without her being able to stop it, or to change it, driven as a plant is driven up out of the earth, up until the stalk grows, the leaf grows, buds swell. That is what is indescribable, that is what makes all the images too static, for no sooner has one said this was so, than it was past and altered.[7]

Here she seizes upon the rapidity, the silently expanding kaleidoscope of childhood growth. The particular organisation implied by evolutionary theory and determinism borrows the idea of irreversible onward sequence from the experience of growth. It can't run backwards, though it may include equally convergence and branching. Nor can it stay still. Recrudescence also is not a concept easily assimilable to evolutionary ideas.

Equivalence is claimed between the creative imagination and natural order by means of the model of growth. The most striking transposition of the model is in organicism which from the late eighteenth century on has provided an immense literature as well as an ideological model for explaining individual development, social relations, the process of a work of art, the process of history, and the relations between diverse types of knowledge within a society.[8] It asserts equivalence between natural and social process, the organic interdependence of all the parts within a whole, as well as the interdependence of a whole and its parts. That is, it is both a holistic and an analytical metaphor. It permits exploration of totalities, and of their elements, without denying either, or giving primacy to either. Organicism is more space than time oriented. It describes an organisation – it provides a *means of studying* development, but it is not necessarily always concerned with growth. Growth and organicism are not interchangeable concepts. Whereas growth is an experience shared by all of us, organicism is an observation transposed from such experience, and then organised into an assertion capable of being moved from field to field of study.

Growth antedates consciousness, and therefore consciousness can never give a full account of it or indeed of itself: first, because the complete cycle of growth cannot be contained within consciousness and second, because consciousness of growth can never be *at any one time* complete. Two essentials in growth are time and movement. Transformation and metamorphosis may take place almost without time. Growth cannot. It is therefore in some measure equivalent to history. In *The Prelude* Wordsworth gives a record of repeated experience repeatedly recalled, an experience which is differentiated from time to time but which is remembered as an amalgam of repeated moments.

> Nor seldom did I lift our cottage latch
> Far earlier, and before the vernal thrush
> Was audible, among the hills I sate,
> Alone, upon some jutting eminence
> At the first hour of morning, when the Vale
> Lay quiet in an utter solitude.
> How shall I trace the history, where seek
> The origin of what I then have felt. (59–60)

If time is the first essential for growth, movement is the second. That movement may well be internal and invisible, proceeding, as it were, outwards. Coleridge caught that power vividly:

I feel an awe . . . I feel it alike, whether I contemplate a single tree or a flower, or meditate on vegetation throughout the world, as one of the great organs of the life of nature. Lo! – with the rising sun it commences its outward life and enters into open communion with all the elements, at once assimilating them to itself and to each other. At the same moment it strikes its roots and unfolds its leaves, absorbs and respires, steams forth its cooling vapour and finer fragrance, and breathes a repairing spirit, at once the food and tone of the atmosphere, into the atmosphere that feeds it. Lo! – at the touch of light how it returns an air akin to light, and yet with the same pulse effectuates its own secret growth, still contracting to fix what expanding it had refined! Lo! – how upholding the ceaseless plastic motion of the parts in the profoundest rest of the whole it becomes the visible organismus of the entire silent or elementary life of nature, and therefore, in incorporating the one extreme becomes the symbol of the other.[9]

One of the resources of both Wordsworth and Coleridge is their awareness of experience at the farthest stretch of sense and their recognition that such experiences are not rare. They reorganise the categories of sense-data to create a condition more like that of divination. I have in mind, for example, the famous passages in *The Prelude* such as the skating scene, the rearing up of the mountain as the boy rows across the lake, the scene when, birdnesting, he clings to the windy buffeted mountain side, or Lucy rolled in earth's diurnal course with rocks and stones and trees. All these scenes use movement as their primary sense experience. Wordsworth releases back into consciousness those moments to do with growth, and with balance and disorientation which tend to be lost to adult awareness, but which are commonly among the most powerful of our childhoods, swings and dizziness among them.

We see perhaps some of the reasons why Wordsworth and Coleridge mattered to Darwin. The emphasis on growth and process rather than on conclusion and confirmation was a releasing element in his intellectual upbringing. It is the essential experience of organic life.

The Prelude is subtitled 'the growth of a poet's mind', and among the first generation of Romantic poets, the primary interest was in the process of growth itself rather than in its confirming conclusion, or anterior purpose. It was neither *Bildungsroman* nor spiritual autobiography. *Bildungsroman* emphasises the full entry of individuality into social bonds – there is a sense always of reduction and appeasement in its conclusion: infantile omnipotence, adolescent hubris, must give way to a chastened acceptance of the reduced scale of the individual within society. Typically, we are disappointed by the ending. In a somewhat similar way, spiritual autobiography tracks by devious pathways the inevitable destination of redemption.

When Mary Shelley came to describe a monster in *Frankenstein* she shows a creature denied the experience of growth. He is fabricated as if he were a machine, but out of organic bits and pieces. There is a gap between concept and material. Though he is a creature capable of undergoing the full cultural development of a man, he is excluded from humanity because he has never partaken of the primary experience of human kind: that of physical growth. He is necessarily hideous. The monster has never been conceived in anything but an intellectual sense. He is the result of external labour, piecing together, and galvanic impulse.

Sex is notably excluded from the book. Frankenstein's bride has been brought up as his sister. And Frankenstein refuses a mate to his monster for fear that they will then enter the natural order and become in that sense uncontrollable. The monster's uncreated mate is the book's determining absence. Frankenstein denies to his monster entry into the natural order through mating and generation. In revenge the monster murders Elizabeth, Frankenstein's bride, on their wedding night before Frankenstein can enter the chamber. The most moving part of the story is that where the monster recounts his own perceptual and cultural development, and his attempt to express human emotions for which he can have no outlet, because there is no possibility of reciprocity.

Mary Shelley, not yet nineteen, had already borne a child. She knew what it felt like to carry a baby within you. In *Frankenstein* she explored the mind's inordinate will towards creativity,[10] a creativity which has no natural bounds, but which has so often sought them, particularly in the Romantic period, in that metaphor which claims a comforting equivalence with the procedures of the natural world for the creative works of man. Literature and the literary imagination have no such intrinsic equivalence with the natural order.

What she shows in Frankenstein's relationship to his monster is a worse degree of artificial selection. In *Frankenstein*, she creates a work which looks bleakly at what lies beyond organic form. It suggests, even, in the figure of the monster made out of men to look like a man, that 'organic form' may itself be no more than a simulacrum of life if it does not allow full recourse to those secret, pre-conscious and beyond consciousness experiences of growth which are the full conditions of creativity.

So basic is the concept of development to our culture and to our adult experience that we forget that it is a *learnt* concept. Evolutionary assumptions of irreversible change have reinforced our observation of individual growth. It is salutary to remind ourselves that the two concepts are not inevitably connected. When our youngest child was a little less than three years old, he would often say: 'When I'm a baby again' or 'Granny a little girl soon' or 'Daddy carry me till Mummy gets bigger' or 'When Mummy's a baby I'll do so-and-so'. The idea of irreversible onward growth and cessation of growth was not yet fixed – perhaps he was trying it out and testing it, but against what seemed to him a natural order in which growth was variable, reversible, spasmodic. Death was the significant absence from his economy.

'Omnia mutantur, nihil interit.' Everything changes, nothing dies. Ovid's assertion in *Metamorphoses* marks one crucial distinction between the idea of metamorphosis and Darwin's theory of evolution. Darwin's theory required extinction. Death was extended from the individual organism to the whole species. Metamorphosis bypasses death. The concept expresses continuance, survival, the essential self transposed but not obliterated by transformation. In some ways, evolutionary theory looks like the older concept of metamorphosis prolonged through time, transformation eked out rather than emblazoned. Both ideas seek to rationalise change but through diverse means.

Metamorphosis turns out to be a concept as crucial to physiology, geology, or botany, as to myth. (Linnaeus published the *Metamorphosis Plantarum* in 1755 and Goethe's *Versuch die Metamorphose der Pflanzen zu Erklären* was published in 1790.) But the concepts of metamorphosis and of transformation were organised in nineteenth-century thinking by that third, crucial, term to which Huxley in the passage quoted at the beginning of this chapter gives the dignity of upper-case: Development. Von Baer in 1828 gave his study the title *Ueber Entwickelungsgeschichte der Thiere* – literally the development story of animals – and his work provides the basis for Spencer's evolutionary theory.

C. H. Waddington comments in 'The Character of Biological Form' that the 'flow of time' is a component of organic forms:

Science is essentially concerned with causal relations; and causal relations cannot be expressed unless there is change. It is therefore in the changes of form – during individual development, during evolution, or under the influence of function – that the biologist is mainly interested.[11]

One might extend that emphasis on *change* to the laws of narrative also. Metamorphosis and development offer two radical orders for narrative: the tension between the two orders and the attempt to make them accord can be observed in the organisation of many Victorian fictions.

Causal relations preoccupy novelists and biologists alike. Dickens particularly exemplifies the problems, both in the energy of concealed interconnection which characterises his narrative order and in the menacing archness of exchanges such as this from *Dombey and Son*:

'My dear Louisa must be careful of that cough,' remarked Miss Tox.

'It's nothing,' returned Mrs. Chick. 'It's merely change of weather. We must expect change.'

'Of weather?' asked Miss Tox, in her simplicity.

'Of everything,' returned Mrs. Chick. 'Of course we must. It's a world of change. Any one would surprise me very much, Lucretia, and would greatly alter my opinion of their understanding, if they attempted to contradict or evade what is so perfectly evident. Change!' exclaimed Mrs. Chick, with severe philosophy. 'Why, my gracious me, what is there that does *not* change! even the silkworm, who I am sure might be supposed not to trouble itself about such subjects, changes into all sorts of unexpected things continually.'

'My Louisa' said the mild Miss Tox, 'is ever happy in her illustrations.'

Metamorphosis emphasises abrupt disconnection, the apparent fissuring of past and present. As Cassirer puts it in *Language and Myth*:

The mythic consciousness does not see human personality as something fixed and unchanging, but conceives every *phase* of a man's life as a new personality, a new self; and this metamorphosis is first of all made manifest in the changes which his name undergoes.[12]

Renaming and redescription initiate change as well as confirming it. But beneath this emphasis on novelty, the metamorphosis of human person, or of plant or rock, relies upon the idea of identity. The name changes but the elements remain constant.

Nothing retains its own form; but Nature, the great renewer, ever makes up forms from other forms. Be sure there's nothing perishes in the whole universe; it does but vary and renew its form. What we call birth is but a beginning to be other than what one was before; and death is but cessation of a former state. Though, perchance, things may shift from there to here and here to there, still do all things in their sum total remain unchanged.[13]

The movement of metamorphosis is lateral as much as developmental. The movement in evolutionary theory is genetic. The same genetic mode of explanation is present in positivism, in the older style of Marxism (the emergence of capitalism from earlier feudal and tribal societies) and in Freud.

In the light of this emphasis upon irreversible growth and succession
we can understand the force of one popular form of Victorian fantasy,
that which disturbs the necessary sequence of growth. So, Alice in
Wonderland grows small again, and then finds herself, and parts of
herself, varying inconveniently in size according to which side of the
mushroom she nibbles.

Comte's developmental ordering of history placed the 'mythological'
tendency near the beginning of human culture and thereby suggested
that it was a phase which had been outgrown and left behind. George
Eliot in *Middlemarch* was to suggest that on the contrary mythologising is
a vital and continuing method of human explanation and experience.[14]
Many Victorian anthropologists, among them notably Tylor, saw the
primary function of myth as proto-scientific, a problem-solving activity.
But mythologising may be as much a way of keeping problems in sus-
pense as of solving them. It makes endurable the contemplation of
irreconcilable contraries. Whewell remarked on the near-impossibility
of sustained attention to two opposing theories at one time.[15] Darwin's
theories not only undermined older orderings but contained *within them*
opposing stories. His heuristic process led in contrary directions. His
theory could be extrapolated to suggest a random and disordered play
of forces, or it could be made to yield the assurance of irreversible
upward growth (his own image of the *tree* emphasised verticality).

Northrop Frye in 'Myth, Fiction, and Displacement' comments on
the 'odd tendency' of myths to 'stick together and build up bigger structures. We have creation myths, fall and flood myths, metamorphosis and
dying-god myths, divine-marriage and hero-ancestry myths, etiological
myths, apocalyptic myths.'[16] Darwinian theory calls on many of these
mythic elements and challenges others by inversion. For example, there
is an 'umgekehrte Erhabene' or 'inverted sublime' in Darwin's treatment of 'divine marriage' and 'hero-ancestry, fall and flood'. Instead of
descent from a lofty deity his mythic history shows the difficult ascent
from swamp, from an unknown progenitor, but asserts the nobility of
this story. It was possible in evolutionary theory to trace a new form
of quest myth, and to transpose the paradise garden from the past to
present: the past consisted of a few simple forms, the present is bur-
geoning and various.

The multiplicity of stories implicit in evolution was *in itself* an element in its power over the cultural imagination: what mattered was not
only the specific stories it told, but the fact that it told many and diverse
ones. Profusion and selection were part of the procedure of reception as

well as being inherent to the theory – and the congruity of reception and theory created confirmation, at a level beneath that of analysis.

For example, whereas the story of man's kinship with all other species had an egalitarian impulse, the story of development tended to restore hierarchy and to place at its apex not only man in general, but contemporary European man in particular – our kind of man, to the Victorians. (I use in such instances the gender dominance that the Victorians – and much of our own society – assume.)

This hierarchy was achieved by reintroducing the model of the single life cycle with its pattern of growth, both physical and intellectual, from childhood through to manhood. Development extends into the idea of progress and bears with it the assumption that control is achieved by and accorded to the fully adult, that the process of cultural change is one of improvement, and that the passage from ape to man can be charted through the degrees of development of diverse races.

A similarly contrasting pair of stories can be traced in the emphasis upon superfecundity and profusion in evolutionary theory, which accorded great value to diversity and to deviation from accepted norms. At the same time the concept of usefulness (even of utilitarianism) in selection gave a counter-emphasis to *compliance*, since the organism must conform to the demands of the environment. Darwin verifies metamorphosis. He offers a new creation myth which challenges the idea of the fall, and makes the tree of life and the tree of knowledge one, and central to meaning. Moreover, his representation of natural order sways between an optimistic and a pessimistic interpretation: it gives room to both comic and tragic vision. To cite Frye's categories: 'in comic vision the *animal* is a world community of domesticated animals' (pigeons, artificial selection). 'In tragic vision the animal world is seen in terms of beasts and birds of prey.'

We behold the face of nature bright with gladness, we often see superabundance of food; we do not see, or we forget, that the birds which are idly singing round us mostly live on insects or seeds, and are thus constantly destroying life; or we forget how largely these songsters, or their eggs, or their nestlings, are destroyed by birds and beasts of prey; we do not always bear in mind, that though food may be now superabundant, it is not so at all seasons of each recurring year. (116)

In comic vision, 'the *vegetable* world is a garden, grove or park, the tree of life or the rose':

Having found a female tree exactly sixty yards from a male tree, I put the stigmas of twenty flowers, taken from different branches, under the microscope, and on all, without exception, there were pollengrains, and on some a profusion of pollen. As the wind had set for several days from the female to the male tree, the pollen could not thus have been carried. The weather had been cold and boisterous, and therefore not favourable to bees, nevertheless every female flower which I examined had been effectually fertilised by the bees, accidentally dusted with pollen, having flown from tree to tree in search of nectar. (140–1)

In tragic vision, 'it is a sinister forest, heath or wilderness, the tree of death'.[17]

What a struggle between the several kinds of trees must here have gone on during long centuries, each annually scattering its seeds by the thousand; what war between insect and insect – between insects, snails, and other animals with birds and beasts of prey – all striving to increase, and all feeding on each other or on the trees or their seeds and seedlings, or on the other plants which first clothed the ground and thus checked the growth of the trees! (126)

Darwin saw the manifold contradictions in the natural world, the interplay of life and death, but organised them also into the controlling powers of opposites, 'artificial selection' and 'natural selection', in which the more powerful was the more benign. To that extent he followed the cultural inheritance of Christianity.

Darwin delighted in variability of life and in his letters records a moment of happiness and release like a vision, in which having slumbered he watches the play of life among the creatures in a grove. At that moment, he cares nothing for knowledge or for origins.[18] It is a moment of pure comic vision. But it is matched at other times by his sense of the painfulness of life preyed upon and the need to find an origin for suffering which will avoid the sadistic figure of a God meting out pain moralistically:

Finally, it may not be a logical deduction, but to my imagination it is far more satisfactory to look at such instincts as the young cuckoo ejecting its foster-brothers, – ants making slaves, – the larvae of ichneumonidae feeding within the live bodies of caterpillars, – not as specially endowed or created instincts, but as small consequences of one general law. (263)

The application of these ideas as something like fable is more thoroughly set forth in *The Descent of Man* than in *The Origin*. In *The Descent* a double, contrary, story is indicated forthwith in the title: – the genealogy of man. 'Descent' may imply his fall from his Adamic myth or his genetic descent (ascent) from his primate forebears. In *The Origin* humanity lurks in the interstices of text, summoned and evaded, kept always out of the centre of attention, glimpsed askance in such a way that the reader must involve himself in a clandestine quest, seeking an anthropocentric signification for a text that extrudes humanity. Or, which makes humanity *serve*, metonymically, simply as a tool for the understanding of other species.

The 'survival of the fittest' seems at first sight one of the few single-direction stories in evolutionary thought – but its tautological structure makes of it a satire on organicism. It is (with a vengeance) as Coleridge said narrative should be, a serpent with its tail in its mouth. The survival of the fittest means simply the survival of those most fitted to survive; this implies not distinction, nor fullest development, but aptness to the current demands of their environment – and these demands may be for deviousness, blueness, aggression, passivity, long arms, or some other random quality. So chance reenters the potentially deterministic organisation of evolutionary narrative.

But Darwin was bent on reemphasising community – the monogenist case proposed again that all species are related and all humanity from a common stock. This had, and was known to have, political bearings: it aligned Darwin where he had wished to stand, firmly against those who would separate other races from the 'Caucasian'.

The idea of a common progenitor gave an egalitarian basis to theories of development, whether of races or of species. It took over into the language of science the implications of myth.

In *Primitive Culture* (1871) Edward Tylor, perhaps the greatest of the early anthropologists, remarks that:

To suppose that theories of a relation between man and the lower mammalia are only a product of advanced science, would be an extreme mistake. Even at low levels of culture, men addicted to speculative philosophy have been led to account for the resemblance between apes and themselves by solutions satisfactory to their own minds, but which we must class as philosophic myths. Among these, stories which embody the thought of an upward change from ape to man, more or less approaching the last-century theory of development, are to be found side by side with others which in the converse way account for apes as degenerate from a previous human state.

Tylor himself uses an evolutionary organisation to explain the phases by which diverse cultures have come to understanding of their surroundings and psychology, though he claimed independence from Darwin and Spencer.[19] The ideas of progression and degeneration are, he says, both part of development theory. He sees myth as a problem-solving activity which draws on the current state of scientific knowledge, and creates 'explanatory stories, produced from that craving to know causes and reasons which ever besets mankind' (354). Tylor cites, as an example of a scientific problem condensed in myths and legends, the question of how fossils of shells and corals found high on mountains could have come there. He points out how the explanatory stories depend upon the apparently more probable solution, whereas the scientific theory goes against the habitual evidence of our sense.

Unlikeliness is as much a property of scientific argument as it is of myth making – or more so. Voltaire had earlier ironically proposed that rather than being proof of the Deluge, shells had been dropped by crusaders on their way to the Holy Land. Tylor says that we recognise such explanatory stories as myth only when 'it is not consistent with our notions to believe them' (355). In such a relativistic reading, myth lodges in the gap between teller and listener.

Tylor summarises the activity of the mythic faculty – 'its force and obstinacy' – as being shown in

the processes of animating and personifying nature, the formation of legend by exaggeration and perversion of fact, the stiffening of metaphor by mistaken realization of words, the conversion of speculative theories and still less substantial fictions into pretended historical events, the passage of myth into miracle-legend, the definition by name and place given to any floating imagination, the adaptation of mythic incident as moral example, and the incessant crystallisation of story into history. (375)

Tylor analyses types of fiction into an evolutionary sequence:

legend, when classified on a sufficient scale, displays a regularity of development which the notion of motiveless fancy quite fails to account for, and which must be attributed to laws of formation. (376)

He sees animism as the primal stage in mythopoeic development.

Although his premise of development leads him to use the customary Victorian expressions such as 'the lower races' and 'savages', his project is the recognition of the 'real culture' and the imaginative energy of peoples throughout the world and throughout history. He brings out caustically the brutal ignorance of so-called advanced races which allows them to mythologise indigenous peoples back into apes and so permits them to hunt and slaughter them.

Thus we can have no difficulty in understanding how savages may seem mere apes to the eyes of men who hunt them like wild beasts in the forests, who can only hear in their language a sort of irrational gurgling and barking, and who fail totally to appreciate the real culture which better acquaintance always shows among the rudest tribes of man. (343)

We recall that Tylor saw *The Water Babies* as a modern myth.

This passage has an affinity with the chilling conclusion to Kingsley's parable of degeneration where the last of the Doasyoulikes is shot by Du Chaillu (who appeared at the British Association meeting in 1861 and caused great popular interest by his accounts of 'gorilla country and habits').[20]

And in the next five hundred years they were all dead and gone, by bad food and wild beasts and hunters; all except one tremendous old fellow with jaws like a jack, who stood full seven feet high; and M Du Chaillu came up to him, and shot him, as he stood roaring and thumping his breast. And he remembered that his ancestors had once been men, and tried to say, 'Am I not a man and a brother?' but had forgotten how to use his tongue; and then he had tried to call for a doctor, but he had forgotten the word for one. So all he said was 'Ubboboo!' and died. (275)

'Am I not a man and a brother?' was inscribed on medallions by Wedgwood during the anti-slavery campaign.

The loss of language is the final phase of degeneration. Whereas Kingsley's legend shows the decay of mankind back into primitivism and thence into animality, Tylor insists on the rational language of the hunted tribes and on the white man's failure to interpret.

The idea of development harboured a paternalistic assumption once it was transferred exclusively to human beings, since it was presumed that the observer was at the summit of development, looking back over a past struggling to reach the present high moment. The European was taken as the type of achieved developmental pre-eminence, and other races studied were seen as further back on the chart of growth. The image of growth was again misplaced from the single life cycle, so that whole races were seen as being part of the 'childhood of man', to be protected, led, and corrected like children.

But the metaphor of European man as the adult parent, and other races as caught somewhere on the scale of childhood and adolescence, was only occasionally glimpsed as implying the future dominance of that second generation.

The struggle between ideas of degeneration and development permeated arguments about language and about myth from the 1850s to the 1870s.

Among mythographers and anthropologists, ideas of evolution and of natural selection were viewed in immediate relation to language – since language was held to be the one crucial distinguishing feature between man and the other animals. In this debate, too, Darwin denied separatism and emphasised animals' powers of communication. The principal difference of method between writers like Tylor and like Max Müller, was that Tylor used ethnological evidence in his appraisal of myth-making, whereas Müller used entirely linguistic evidence. Broadly, Müller was degradationist, Tylor evolutionist in the interpretation of their social materials. Müller, the great Sanskrit scholar, was profoundly influential in his analysis of myths and in his discussion of the organisation and roots of language. In Tylor's classification of myths one of the most striking categories is 'the stiffening of metaphor by the mistaken realization of words'. This category seems clearly to be based on Müller's representation of the relationship of myth to thought.

In *The Cornhill Magazine* in 1877 Henry Hewlett set out six different current theories of the meaning and nature of myth. These are the aetiological (myths are explanatory stories); the etymological (myths are based on misunderstood words); the euhemerist (myths are stories about real people retrospectively fictionalised); the poetic (myths are purely fanciful tales); the 'physical' (myths are rationalisations of phenomena); the allegorical (myths are encoded revelations of the wisdom of the ancients). Robert Ackerman[21] points out that Hewlett did not directly categorise E. B. Tylor's theory of animism, announced in *Primitive Culture*, 1871 (that myths arise out of the habit of ancient peoples of attributing life to all objects).

R. A. Proctor wrote in *Myths and Marvels of Astronomy* (London, 1884):

The expression 'astronomical myth' has recently been used, on the title page of a translation from the French, as synonymous with false systems of astronomy. It is not, however, in that sense that I here use it. The history of astronomy presents the records of some rather perplexing observations, not confirmed by later researches, but yet not easily to be explained away or accounted for. Such observations Humboldt described as belonging to the myths of an uncritical period; and it is in that sense that I employ the term 'astronomical myth' in this essay.

Observations which *make* problems, rather than solve them: these are the source of myths as Proctor understands them. The emphasis in much Victorian mythography was on the *problem-solving* function of myths. But here Proctor intelligently grasps the *explanation-resisting* quality of myth also. It is at the point of difficulty between resistance and explanation that many Victorian imaginative uses of Darwinism are located.

Müller, like Darwin, sought common origins. In his case, what he studied were common origins as expressed in the 'roots' of Indo-Germanic tongues. In his study of language he starts from two premises: first, 'the one great barrier between the brute and man is *Language!*' (340); second, that there is 'a common origin of language'. Like Darwin, Müller was a monogenist, believing in the common stock of all the races of the world:

I have been accused of having been biased in my researches by an implicit belief in the common origin of mankind. I do not deny that I hold this belief, and if it wanted confirmation, that confirmation has been supplied by Darwin's book 'On the Origin of Species' . . . But I defy my adversaries to point out one single passage where I have mixed up scientific with theological arguments.

His approximation of his law to that of Darwin is the more striking because of the uncertainty of his attitude to 'Natural Selection', or as he renamed it 'Natural Elimination' – placing the emphasis on the failure of the weaker or less apt to survive, and on extinction and loss. Sometimes he praises the law for its universal applicability, at others he completely denies it: 'It is a well known fact, which recent researches have not shaken, that nature is incapable of progress or improvement . . . The hexagonal cells of the bee are not more regular in the nineteenth century than at any earlier period' (31). He seems gradually to have changed his mind in the course of writing the lectures about the importance of Darwin's work, and he came to do this because the model fitted so well his own researches. He was won over by his view that Darwin offered a new 'tool of thought', a new linguistic access to hitherto unbroached resources of thought.[22]

We want an idea that is to exclude caprice as well as necessity – that is to include individual exertion as well as general co-operation – an idea applicable neither to the unconscious building of bees nor to the conscious architecture of human beings, yet combining within itself both these operations, and raising them to a new and higher conception. You will guess both the idea and the word, if I add that it is likewise to explain the extinction of fossil kingdoms and the origin of new species – it is the idea of *Natural Selection* that was wanted, and being wanted it was found, and being found it was named. It is a new category – a new engine of thought; and if naturalists are proud to affix their names to a new species which they discover, Mr. Darwin may be prouder, for his name will remain affixed to a new idea, a new genus of thought.[23]

'Natural selection' is a term in its first state of meaning. And this, for Müller, is of the utmost importance, since, according to his theory, myth rapidly intervenes and degenerates language. Language is subject to the deterioration of metaphor and myth.

The belief in the power of myth to corrupt the relationship between language and thought is the idea of Müller's that most caught the imagination of his contemporaries and which underlay his own system of mythological analysis, solar mythology. He deeply suspects the tendency of language to usurp mental space as if it were an entity:

Ether is a myth – a quality changed into a substance – an abstraction, useful, no doubt, for the purpose of physical speculation, but intended rather to make the present horizon of our knowledge than to represent anything which we can grasp either with our senses or with our reason. As long as it is used in that sense, as an algebraic x, as an unknown quantity, it can do no harm – as little as to speak of the Dawn as Erinys, or of Heaven as Zeus. The mischief begins when language forgets itself, and makes us mistake the word for the thing, the Quality for the Substance, the Nomen for the Numen. (579)

The animus which Müller himself shows against myth, 'the disease of language', suggests that he has unconsciously converted it into a heroic adversary, very much on the principles he deplores. The history of ideas for him is a Titanic battle between thought and language, with metaphor as the agent of decomposition.

Whenever any word . . . is used without a clear conception of the steps that led from its original to its metaphorical meaning, there is a danger of mythology; whenever these steps are forgotten and artificial steps put in their places, we have mythology, or, if I may say so, diseased language . . . yet through the rank and poisonous vegetation of mythic phraseology we may always catch a glimpse of that original stem round which it creeps and winds itself. (358)

To Müller, surviving folk-tales, märchen and legends are the detritus of lost high myth systems. In Indo-Germanic roots he found evidence of the immovable foundations of language and valued them therefore with the veneration reserved to origins. Like Darwin, he felt the pull of the 'few forms or one' though, like him, he was preoccupied with the many varieties which such forms had generated.

III   TRANSFORMATION, RETROGRESSION, EXTINCTION: DARWINIAN ROMANCE

Darwin's theories, with their emphasis on superabundance and extreme fecundity, reached out towards the grotesque. Nature was seen less as husbanding than as spending. Hyperproductivity authenticated the fantastic. In the following argument I shall illustrate some of the ways in which works of fantasy in the Victorian period fastened on problems *within* Darwinian ideas or on problems *revealed by* evolutionary theory in relation to older world orders. Writers could expand areas of difficulty while remaining secure within the provisionality of fantasy.

In *Orlando* (1928) Virginia Woolf characterises the Victorian age by rank profusion, prodigious growth, as well as by fulminating clouds: in a bravura passage she captures its oppressive fertility. Using hyperbole to mimic hyperbole she suggests the melancholy Romanticism, both rampant and dampened, of Victorian culture. Her memoir writer 'Eusebius Chubb' is overcome by this fertility:

Innumerable leaves creaked and glistened above his head. He seemed to himself 'to crush the mould of a million more under his feet'. Thick smoke exuded from a damp bonfire at the end of the garden. He reflected that no fire on earth could ever hope to consume that vast vegetable encumbrance. Wherever he looked, vegetation was rampant. Cucumbers 'came scrolloping across the grass to his feet'. Giant cauliflowers towered deck above deck till they rivalled, to his disordered imagination, the elm trees themselves. Hens laid incessantly eggs of no special tint. Then, remembering with a sigh his own fecundity and his poor wife Jane, now in the throes of her fifteenth confinement indoors, how, he asked himself, could he blame the fowls?

Thus, she comments, 'through this alarming fertility' the British Empire came into existence 'for twins abounded'; 'and thus . . . sentences swelled, adjectives multiplied, lyrics became epics, and little trifles that had been essays a column long were now encyclopaedias in ten or twenty volumes'.[24] Darwin's 300-page *The Origin of Species*, as 'abstract' for his longer work, appears in this light as a triumph of compression.

The lush and menacing superfecundity of the earth and of living beings could appal as much as reassure. The argument about measure and the unmeasured is crucial to Victorian sensibility.

R. H. Hutton, reviewing Arnold's *Essays in Criticism*, comments on Arnold's love of measure, and contrasts it with 'that rampancy of insatiable unmeasured longing with which the intellect stands on no terms'. Darwin's theory of development depended to a large extent upon that 'rampancy of insatiable unmeasured longing', on the unassuageable passion of the sexes for each other, on the vigour of survival, on the profusion of production and on the insurgency of growth. To that extent his is a daemonic theory, emphasising drive, deviance and the will to power. It is not a theory which readily accords with ideas of measure or reason.

Tennyson was dismayed by the same problem:

An omnipotent Creator who could make such a painful world is to me sometimes as hard to believe in as blind matter behind everything. The lavish profusion too in the natural world appals me, from the growths of the tropical forest to the capacity of man to multiply, the torrent of babies.[25]

To Darwin, in contrast, the tropical forest was the fullest type of natural beauty and the 'torrent of babies' simply a part of the general fructifying capacities of the natural order.

Whereas Malthus sought to curb and curtail human hyperproductivity, Darwin speaks of 'slow-breeding man'. In Kingsley's *The Water Babies* the shoals of babies are all the neglected, the unwanted, the superfluous, for which society found no love or use. They have returned to a foetal existence in the sea, relishing an oceanic abundance, as well as being chastened by the two moralistic sisters, the voluptuously maternal Mrs Doasyouwouldbedoneby and the hard-witted and censorious Mrs Bedonebyasyoudid.

Kingsley emphasised the fullness of the deeps, the play of life beyond use or number.[26] The terms of his allegory raise by implication a curious question present also in Darwin's theories. When did sexual distinction enter the economy of life?

In Darwin's own account of the primordial ancestor we hear always of 'one parent', an ungendered progenitor closely approximated to 'Nature'. His account of change and development (of the out-flaring and continuity of life on the earth, as well as its extinction) is an account of procreative energies. Indeed, evolutionary process relies on sexual division. But he never until *The Descent of Man* greatly emphasised sexual drive and choice. It is true that in chapter IV of *The Origin* he discusses sexual selection, which he describes as 'a struggle between the males for possession of the females' and of females (as in the case of bantams) 'selecting, during thousands of generations, the most melodious or beautiful males' (136–7). But the discussion occupies only two pages in a major account of natural selection to which at this stage in his thinking, he clearly gives prime importance. So the emphasis in Darwin's account is always upon productivity rather than on congress; on generation rather than on sexual desire. He is describing an entire economy of nature in which production may take many forms, and he inherits the romantic lyricism of his grandfather's work on *The Loves of the Plants*, without developing it further.[27] Nevertheless, style and theory both are lyrical and effusive, rather than sceptical and parsimonious.

His writing emphasises clutter and profusion. It relies on a nature which surges onward in hectic fecundity, a system both estranged and voluptuous in its relations to humanity. The organism – or the body – becomes the medium of transformation; engendering becomes the means of creating change. The physical is prolonged through generations. In the methodology of life proposed by Darwin, production, growth and decay are all equally needed for the continuance of life on earth.

The realisation that when organic form and life have gone the detritus of life becomes the ballast of the earth appealed to many Victorian writers as it had to Erasmus Darwin. Instead of the *memento mori* of the seventeenth-century skull, the geologist's hammer uncovers the surviving forms of the past. G. H. Lewes in *Studies in Animal Life* (London 1862) contrives to find reassurance in this image:

Our very mother-earth is formed of the debris of life. Plants and animals which have been, build up its solid fabric. Ages ago these tiny architects secreted the tiny shells, which were their palaces; from the ruins of these palaces were built our Parthenons, our St Peters and our Louvres. So revolves the luminous orb of Life! Generations follow generations; and the Present becomes the matrix of the Future, as the Past was of the Present; the Life of one epoch forming the Prelude to a higher Life.[28]

This rather grandiose reading of the death cycle (all marble, no clunch) reinforces itself with Vico's image of cycle and spiral – an upward series of revolutions.

Exact responses and discrete relationships are necessary to the survival of the individual, for the continuance of the species, and even more for its adaptation to new conditions. But superabundance and waste are the primary conditions of such survival, and diversity is the medium of development. Darwin shared with Mill an emphasis on the creativity of *diversity*. Mill cites Darwin's much-loved Wilhelm von Humboldt at the beginning of *On Liberty*: 'The grand leading principle . . . is the absolute and essential importance of human development in its richest diversity.'[29] Remove the word 'human' and you have Darwin's enlarged and salient emphasis too.

The value of diversity is the new emphasis enforced by Darwin's thinking. Praise of hyperproductivity goes back much further. In Bernard Silvester's *Cosmographia* in the twelfth century, for example, we find:

> Cum morte invicti pugnant genialibus armis,
> naturam reparant perpetuantque genus.
> Non mortale mori, non quod cadit esse caducum,
> non a stirpe hominem deperiisse sinunt.

(The unconquerable armies of procreation fight with death, renew nature, and perpetuate the species. They do not permit what is dying to die, what is falling to fall, nor do they allow mankind to perish from its stalk.)[30]

When Spenser described the Garden of Adonis in the third Book of *The Faerie Queene* he offered a world of cycle and of endless renewal: all plants, flowers, living beings pass forth out of the garden and 'returne backe' by the hinder gate. They take part in a replenishing cycle of fecundity:

Infinite shapes of creatures there are bred,
And uncouth formes, which none yet ever knew,
And every sort is in a sundry bed
Set by it selfe, and ranckt in comely rew:
Some fit for reasonable soules t'indew,
Some made for beasts, some made for birds to weare,
And all the fruitfull spawne of fishes hew
In endlesse rancks along enraunged were,
That seem'd the *Ocean* could not containe them there.[31]

Yet the stock is never lessened 'but still remaines in everlasting store,/ As it at first created was of yore'.

Despite the cyclic nature of life, time in Spenser implies nihilistic destruction, because it implies the destruction of the individual. But in the Mutabilitie cantos he moves further towards the centre of the problem: Adonis is 'eterne in mutabilitie', and 'by succession made perpetuall'. Nature says that 'all things'

by their change their being doe dilate;
And turning to themselves at length againe,
Doe worke their own perfection so by fate.[32]

Things through desire of change find constantly their own perfected form.

Mutability, to be bearable, must not include the idea of irreversible mutation. That was the new fear which natural selection enforced. In cycle or flux things may rediscover a persisting form, but not in mutation. In any transferred reading of evolutionary theory in human terms individualism is set under a new and almost intolerable tension by Darwin's emphasis on variability. All deviation, each individual, is potentially valuable as bearing the possibility of mutation and change. Yet many must founder and be squandered, leaving no mark nor consequence. At best, they may be recuperated as part of the unhistoric past: 'and that things are not so ill with you and me as they might have been, is half owing to the number who lived faithfully a hidden life, and rest in unvisited tombs'. (*Middlemarch*, Finale)

Evolutionary theory implied a new myth of the past: instead of the garden at the beginning, there was the sea and the swamp. Instead of man, emptiness – or the empire of molluscs. There was no way back to a previous paradise: the primordial was comfortless. Instead of fixed and perfect species, it showed forms in flux, and the earth in constant motion, drawing continents apart. This consciousness of the fluent, of the physical world as endless onward process, extended to an often pained awareness of human beings as slight elements within unstoppable motion and transformation. Nostalgia was disallowed, since no unrecapturable perfection preceded man's history. Ascent was also flight – a flight from the primitive and the barbaric which could never quite be left behind.

Lying behind diversity in Darwinian theory slumbers the form of some remote progenitor, irrecoverable because precedent to history or anterior to consciousness. That idea of 'the single form' becomes itself a new and powerful source of nostalgia. In this period we see the determination to liberate science and philosophy from the idea of origins, from the study of final causes. But although history, not cosmogony, is the typical narrative form, its drive is always backwards. The activity of describing development may be history, but it seeks always to reach further back into the past, further and further towards the comforting limits of initiation. Freud's enterprise is the analytical form of this obsession, in relation to the individual, but we find it before him in the preoccupation with 'roots' (of language or of species).[33] So although Darwinian theory brought in its wake heterogeneous enquiry yet a monistic ideal persists, as one can see in this passage from Edward Carpenter's *Civilisation: Its Cause and Cure* (1889) in an essay entitled 'The Science of the Future: a Forecast':

So with the doctrine of Evolution as applied to the whole organic kingdom up to man. Like the doctrine of leaf-metamorphosis it obliterates distinctions . . . There is a continuous variation from the mollusc to the man – all the lines of distinction run and waver – classes and species cease to exist – and Science, instead of many, sees only *one* thing. What then is that one thing? Is it a mollusc, or is it a man, or what is it? Are we to say that man may be looked upon as a variation of a mollusc or an amoeba, or that the amoeba may be looked on as a variation of man? . . . There is no answer to be given. And thus it is that *the appearance of the doctrine of Evolution is the signal of the destruction of Science* (in the ordinary acceptation of the word). For Evolution is the successive obliteration of the arbitrary distinctions and landmarks which by their existence *constitute* Science, and as soon as Evolution covers the whole ground of Nature inorganic and organic (as before long it will do) – the whole of Nature runs and wavers before the eye of Science, the latter recognises that its distinctions *are* arbitrary, and turns upon and destroys itself.[34]

Carpenter grasps the simultaneity of form implicit in evolutionary theory, but that is a less common reading than the emphasis on distance from beginnings. Faced with so absent a beginning and so bleak and prodigious an extension of time it is not surprising that many of Darwin's first readers favoured the counter-form of evolutionary myth: that of growth, ascent, and development towards complexity. Viewed in that light evolutionary theory can become a new form of quest myth, promising continuing exploration and creating the future as a prize, since the future now exists only in terms of changes within the natural order.

Before Darwin, the recognition of geological time was already transforming consciousness and giving a new power to the sea and sea-inhabitants. Lyell commented in the first volume of *Principles of Geology* that the sea was a living reminder of the narrowness of man's dominion in space as well as in time:

Even now, the waters of lakes, seas, and the great ocean, which teem with life, may be said to have no immediate relation to the human race – to be portions of the terrestrial system of which man has never taken, nor ever can take, possession, so that the greater part of the inhabited surface of the planet remains still as insensible to our presence, as before any isle or continent was appointed to be our residence.[35]

Not only is the teeming life of the sea regardless of human meaning but it is, according to Erasmus Darwin, specifically the *fons et origo* of human life. Erasmus Darwin's dictum 'Omnia ex Conchis' (All from Oysters) continued to irritate and disturb later generations. They found it particularly offensive to figure themselves as the descendants of such mute and grudging organisms as shellfish. Darwin, having spent several years of his life in the concentrated study of cirripedes, the parasitic crustacea, which 'coat the rocks all over the world in infinite numbers' (298) did not share this hubris.

The fascination with marine biology and with the inhabitants of the sea which thrived particularly in the 1850s and early 1860s drew on a sense of natural beneficence, or prodigal creation, as the rhetoric of Gosse, Kingsley, and Lewes's seaside studies all testify.

As so often in analysing the movements of mind in relation to evolutionary ideas one can observe the impulse to naturalise the new theories back into creationist language, while at the same time disturbance is registered. In Kingsley, the beneficence and the disturbance draw on the idea of recapitulation. Extinction becomes a class parable; the aristocratic old gair-fowl refuses to grow new-fangled wings and perishes absurdly and grandly on her solitary rock.

Tom came up to her very humbly, and made his bow; and the first thing she said was –

'Have you wings? Can you fly?'

'Oh dear, no, ma'am; I should not think of such a thing,' said cunning little Tom.

'Then I shall have great pleasure in talking to you, my dear. It is quite refreshing nowadays to see anything without wings. They must all have wings, forsooth, now, every new upstart sort of bird, and fly. What can they want with flying, and raising themselves above their proper station in life? In the days of my ancestors no birds ever thought of having wings, and did very well without; and now they all laugh at me because I keep to the good old fashion.' (287)[36]

And if 'species are produced and exterminated by slowly acting and still existing causes' (*The Origin of Species*: 457), then Mrs Bedonebyasyoudid points out:

Folks say now that I can make beasts into men, by circumstance, and selection, and competition, and so forth . . . But let them recollect this, that there are two sides to every question, and a downhill as well as an uphill road; and, if I can turn beasts into men, I can, by the same laws of circumstance, and selection, and competition, turn men into beasts. (276–7)

One level of Kingsley's fantasy persistingly reveals the social models implicit in Darwin's work, the procedures (which Marx satirically noted) whereby the natural order in Darwin's formulation reproduces the forms of Victorian society: division of labour, competition, family structures. But there is an element of criticism in Darwin's appropriation of his society's forms. Kingsley, like Darwin, enjoys the enlargement of kinship – the great family which must, in human terms, include the chimney-boy and the scientist, and which moralises the connections between plants, animals, and human life.

More remarkable is Kingsley's pressure upon the point of difficulty in Darwin's appropriation of Malthusian ideas. So much of Darwin's theoretical writing inclines towards enlargement and levelling, that there is an unresolved disturbance in the Malthusian emphasis upon the plethora of humankind. Darwin changed the implications of Malthusian theory by emphasising the creative need for hyperproductivity. Like Darwin, Kingsley perceived profusion as benign rather than threatening. He challenges the Malthusian social doctrine by releasing Tom from the impoverished, excluded status forced on him by his society and makes his death by drowning an entry into a new evolutionary stream. The river flows into the sea and Tom is back at the beginning of the life process, living in the primal element among the throngs of the deep.

Paley, Darwin, and Kingsley all take particular delight in the processes of transformation, though the ideological patterns that they perceive vary profoundly.

And after all, how, or in what sense, is it true that animals produce their *like*? A butterfly, with a proboscis instead of a mouth, with four wings and six legs, produces a hairy caterpillar, with jaws and teeth, and fourteen feet. A frog produces a tadpole. A black beetle, with gauze wings and a crusty covering, produces a white, smooth, soft worm; an ephemeron-fly, a cod-bait maggot. These, by a progress through different stages of life, and action, and enjoyment (and in each state provided with implements and organs appropriated to the temporary nature which they bear), arrive at last at the form and fashion of the parent animal.[37]

Two things are immediately striking about Paley's description of life cycle: one is the emphasis upon enjoyment and the second is the insistence that transformation and divergence are stages in a journey whose goal is replication. Coming to be like the parent form is in both senses the end of life. The progress through several metamorphoses towards identity implies also *identification* with the parent type. Achieved likeness, not achieved divergence, is the ideal: 'not less calculated to subserve to the gratification of our sense of the beautiful, than to provide against too wide a departure from that order of creation which its great Author has from the beginning instituted'. This is a very important traditional model, in which cycle is at the service of identity, and the diverse needs of diverse life phases are parts of a cycle which comes to rest in the finality of adult form. The model depends upon the single life cycle though it implies that succession also is a search for replication and likeness, rather than for change. In *Bildungsroman* similarly the growing ego learns to accommodate itself to, and internalise, the patterns of its society.

Paley expresses *pleasure* in transformation through sensuous immediacy, particularly the tactile contrasts of 'A black beetle, with gauze wings and a crusty covering, produces a white, smooth, soft worm'. Textures are set side by side and invite tactile response without any intervening hierarchy or physical rejection. In the preceding sentence he insists on the fairy-tale unlikeness of butterfly and caterpillar – six legs, for example, become fourteen feet. The element of play and admiration in Paley's discourse survives in Darwin's description. Disputing the argument that all development within the life cycle is towards complexity, he writes:

The embryo in the course of development generally rises in organisation: I use this expression, though I am aware that it is hardly possible to define clearly what is meant by the organisation being higher or lower. But no one probably will dispute that the butterfly is higher than the caterpillar. In some cases, however, the mature animal is generally considered as lower in the scale than the larva, as with certain parasitic crustaceans. To refer once again to cirripedes: the larvae in the first stage have three pairs of legs, a very simple single eye, and a prosbosciformed mouth, with which they feed largely, for they increase much in size. In the second stage, answering to the chrysalis stage of butterflies, they have six pairs of beautifully constructed natatory legs, a pair of magnificent compound eyes, and extremely complex antennae; but they have a closed and imperfect mouth, and cannot feed: their function at this stage is, to search by their well-developed organs of sense, and to reach by their active powers of swimming, a proper place on which to become attached and to undergo their final metamorphosis. When this is completed they are fixed for life: their legs are now converted into prehensile organs; they again obtain a well-constructed mouth; but they have no antennae, and their two eyes are now reconverted into a minute, single, and very simple eye-spot. In this last and complete state, cirripedes may be considered as either more highly or more lowly organised than they were in the larval condition. (420–1)

'Six pairs of beautifully constructed natatory legs, a pair of compound eyes and extremely complex antennae': Darwin's children laughed at the enthusiasm of this description and told him that it sounded like an advertisement. Certainly, in such passages, Darwin draws unselfconsciously on the older language of design and contrivance, 'six pairs of beautifully constructed natatory legs'. But unlike Paley who emphasised 'the temporary nature' of the states of life Darwin in the preceding paragraph emphasises that 'the adaptation of the larva to its conditions of life is just as perfect and as beautiful as in the adult animal'.

So, in his analysis, '*the period of activity*' is likely to be the period at which the highest and most beautiful organisations are achieved, rather than necessarily during the period of adult form. The period of exploration is given greatest value wherever it occurs in the life cycle. At the other extreme, he instances larvae which become 'complemental males': 'in the latter, the development has assuredly been retrograde; for the male is a mere sack, which lives for a short time, and is destitute of mouth, stomach, or other organ of importance, excepting for reproduction'. In Darwin's account the 'final metamorphosis' after which the cirripedes 'are fixed for life' is a movement of retraction and loss: 'their two eyes are now reconverted into a minute, single, and very simple eye-spot'. The movements of transformation as Darwin describes them involve loss as well as gain, degradation as well as achievement.

This property of Darwin's discourse – new knowledge and theory sheltering within an older discourse and then appearing 'in new habiliments' – allowed writers such as Charles Kingsley and Margaret Gatty

to appropriate his analyses and apply them in ways which fancifully
moralise the connections between evolutionary ideas, social theory and
Christian teaching. Kingsley presents metamorphosis as social comedy:
the shabby genteel fly goes on a spree in a scene based on Darwin's
analysis of 'complemental males'. As so often Kingsley creates a volatile
mixture of mordant observation and condescension, as well as a constant reviving of pleasure where judgement has seemed imminent:

'And what will become of your wife?'
'Oh! she is a very plain stupid creature, and that's the truth; and thinks
about nothing but eggs. If she chooses to come, why she may; and if not, why
I go without her; – and here I go.'
And, as he spoke, he turned quite pale, and then quite white.
'Why, you're ill!' said Tom. But he did not answer.
'You're dead,' said Tom, looking at him as he stood on his knee as white as
a ghost.
'No I ain't!' answered a little squeaking voice over his head. 'This is me up
here, in my ball-dress: and that's my skin . . .'
. . . For the little rogue had jumped clean out of his own skin, and left it
standing on Tom's knee, eyes, wings, legs, tail, exactly as if it had been alive.
'Ha, ha!' he said, and he jerked and skipped up and down, never stopping
an instant, just as if he had St Vitus's dance. 'Ain't I a pretty fellow now?'
And so he was; for his body was white, and his tail orange, and his eyes all
the colours of a peacock's tail. And what was the oddest of all, the whisks at the
end of his tail had grown five times as long as they were before.
'Ah!' said he, 'now I will see the gay world. My living won't cost me much,
for I have no mouth, you see, and no inside; so I can never be hungry nor have
the stomach-ache neither.' (115–16)

But like Darwin, Kingsley moves away from the Paleyian model, in
which the young, through all its transformations, strives *backwards* to
become the parent type. He offers instead the value of change, mutation, the new beginning – and this is part both of his Darwinian and of
his socialist thinking.

In *The Water Babies* Kingsley makes the fantasy a critique of social
realism. So far as social realism goes, Tom is one of the Malthusian
mass, rapidly consumed and abandoned by society. He is a boy chimney-
sweep oppressed by a brutal master. Kingsley uses a double structure as
he had in *Alton Locke*. The boy is drowned and finds himself back at the
beginning of the cycle of creation. The child's animistic conception of
the world here actually releases him out into an earlier phase of evolutionary growth, whereas in his earlier book the experience of evolution
is a hallucinatory dream.[38]

In *Fraser's Magazine* a dozen years earlier Kingsley had spoken out for the rich imaginative needs of children which were denied

in the last generation – and, alas! in this also – little or no proper care has been taken of the love for all which is romantic, marvellous, heroic, which exists in every ingenuous child . . . Protestantism had nothing to do with the imagination – in fact, it was a question whether reasonable people had any; whether the devil was not the original maker of that troublesome faculty in man, woman, and child.[39]

He wants to read the world with the transforming eye of childhood to which everything is equally miraculous and unsurprising.[40] In *The Water Babies* the scientist-giant longs for one hour as a baby again but with full consciousness, because he would know everything then and be at rest. And as the narrator remarks while he expounds the natural history of water babies: 'Am I in earnest? Oh dear no! Don't you know that this is a fairy tale, and all fun and pretence; and that you are not to believe one word of it, even if it is true?'

The primary fairy-tale is told with marvellous spontaneity: little black Tom, the sweep's climbing boy, thrives and suffers in a world where touch and sight and smell are all alert.

They passed through the pitmen's village, all shut up and silent now; and through the turnpike; and then they were out in the real country, and plodding along the black dusty road, between black slag walls, with no sound but the groaning and thumping of the pit-engine in the next field. But soon the road grew white, and the walls likewise; and at the wall's foot grew long grass and gay flowers, all drenched with dew. (11)

and

Out of a low cave of rock, at the foot of a limestone crag, the great fountain rose, quelling, and bubbling, and gurgling, so clear that you could not tell where the water ended and the air began; and ran away under the road, a stream large enough to turn a mill; among blue geranium, and golden globe-flower, and wild raspberry, and the bird-cherry with its tassels of snow. (14–15)

Watched over always by 'the Irishwoman' soot-blackened Tom comes down the wrong chimney in the great house into a little girl's bedroom, is hunted off the estate like an animal, slides down a great cliff and comes to an old dame's schoolroom. Feverish and hallucinated he wanders out of the outhouse where he is laid to sleep and, driven by the need 'I must be clean', he steps down into the river. He

went on to the bank of the brook, and lay down on the grass, and looked into the clear clear limestone water, with every pebble at the bottom bright and clean, while the little silver trout dashed about in fright at the sight of his black face; and he dipped his hand in and found it so cool, cool, cool; and he said, 'I will be a fish; I will swim in the water; I must be clean, I must be clean'.

So he pulled off all his clothes in such haste that he tore some of them, which was easy enough with such ragged old things. And he put his poor hot sore feet into the water; and then his legs; and the further he went in, the more the church bells rang in his head. (63)

Of course, he is drowned, though it was not until I read the book as an adult that I recognised that, for the limpid telling makes us feel only his need and fulfilment: a cool, green sleep.[41] Indeed the point is also that he is *not* drowned, but released from the ordinary cycle of human development, allowed to grow anew. Now he has gills; he is a water baby, swimming in an all-encompassing element. The foetal imagery is open. The book as a whole has an oceanic richness typical of just pre-Freudian storytelling, in which all the elements of primal experience are present without interpretation.

This is a distressful book as well as a rancorously funny one. It is surcharged with all the troubles of the day, intellectual as well as religious and political. Some of the episodes have a savage cruelty: the fight between the lobster and the otter, the crows pecking the Quaker vegetarian crow to death. Some make us wince: Tom picking open the caddis before her transformation is complete: 'But when Tom spoke to her she could not answer; for her mouth and face were tight tied up in a new night-cap of neat pink skin.' Everything is presented through powerful sense-experience. Kingsley draws particularly on touch and taste.

Kingsley is writing as a partisan in defence of children: not only little climbing boys, though the book's publication did help to hasten the long battle to prevent the use of boys in this way. He presents Grimes as a blockish stupid man and as the book goes on he tracks this same imaginative stultification into most areas of the adult world: he proposes a heavy tax on words over four syllables, 'as heterodoxy, spontaneity, spiritualism, spuriosity'. Even the scientists, for whom the book shows so much reverent affection, will not accept the limits of their knowledge. The Professor quickly drops Tom back into the sea, having just told Ellie that there are no such things as water babies. But, Kingsley reminds the child reader:

You must not talk about 'ain't' and 'can't' when you speak of this great wonderful world round you, of which the wisest man knows only the very smallest corner, and is, as the great Sir Isaac Newton said, only a child picking up pebbles on the shore of a boundless ocean. (78–9)

Kingsley, seeking for a way of preserving religious meaning in a world saturated with cruelty and beauty, found it through the idea of transformation implicit in and newly authenticated by evolutionary theory. Kingsley was a friend of Charles Lyell; he corresponded with Darwin and Huxley, and in the evolutionary debate he came down on their side against his friend Philip Gosse, who saw the implanted fossils as God's test of our faith. His involvement with Darwin's theories in their first reception created the disturbance out of which *The Water Babies* came with extraordinary spontaneity.

Darwinian theory with its emphasis on random mutation rebuffed common sense and appearance: Darwin felt as strongly as others the staggering unlikeliness of so precise an instrument as the eye being evolved by random mutation. Kingsley seized on the restoration of the *wonderful* in Darwinian theory: 'Don't fancy that anything is too wonderful to be true.' He wrote in a letter to Maurice in 1863 that the scientists 'find that now they have got rid of an interfering God – a master-magician, as I call it – they have to choose between the absolute empire of accidents, and a living, immanent, everworking God'.[42]

In his version of evolutionary theory Kingsley emphasises the idea of transformation within the life cycle, like efts, caddis, salmon and dragonflies.

... under a bank he saw a very ugly dirty creature sitting, about half as big as himself; which had six legs, and a big stomach, and a most ridiculous head with two great eyes and a face just like a donkey's. (106–7)

At the end of its transformation

It grew strong and firm; the most lovely colours began to show on its body, blue and yellow and black, spots and bars and rings; out of its back rose four great wings of bright brown gauze; and its eyes grew so large that they filled all its head, and shone like ten thousand diamonds. (108–9)

Kingsley presents evolutionary ideas as a series of social fables, like the aesthetical Doasyoulikes gradually retrogressing by a process of natural selection from high leisure culture to gorillas. But beyond these individual tales there is the emphasis on the prodigality of creation, the thronging lower world of the deep sea, and in the midst of this bountiful creativity, the responsibility of the individual to transform himself. Mother Carey, who haunts the book in many aspects as Irishwoman, Mrs Doasyouwouldbedoneby and Mrs Bedonebyasyoudid, is discovered at the end of Tom's quest sitting on a white marble throne in the pool where the good whales go.

And from the foot of the throne there swum away, out and out into the sea, millions of new-born creatures, of more shapes and colours than man ever dreamed. And they were Mother Carey's children, whom she makes out of the sea-water all day long.

He expected, of course – like some grown people who ought to know better – to find her snipping, piecing, fitting, stitching, cobbling, basting, filing, planing, hammering, turning, polishing, moulding, measuring, chiselling, clipping, and so forth, as men do when they go to work to make anything.

But, instead of that, she sat quite still with her chin upon her hand, looking down into the sea with two great grand blue eyes, as blue as the sea itself. (313)

and

'I heard, ma'am, that you were always making new beasts out of old.'

'So people fancy. But I am not going to trouble myself to make things, my little dear. I sit here and make them make themselves.'

'You are a clever fairy, indeed,' thought Tom. And he was quite right. (315)

Instead of an interventionist masculine God, she offers an entirely 'female' principle of creativity: a sustaining and inactive presence which expresses godhead through fecundity.

As Kingsley saw it, Darwin's emphasis on the creativeness of the random, the marvellous unlikeliness and reality of metamorphosis (its 'plain signification', as Darwin called it), liberated a whole area of thought out of fairy-tale and into actuality. When, at the end of the book, Tom is restored to life, having 'done the thing he did not like' and completed his quest, he grows into

a great man of science, and can plan railroads, and steam-engines, and electric telegraphs, and rifled guns, and so forth; and knows everything about everything, except why a hen's egg don't turn into a crocodile, and two or three other little things which no one will know till the coming of the Cocqcigrues. And all this from what he learnt when he was a water-baby, under the sea. (385)

The orphaned Tom returns to the womb, swimming with gills in the sea, until he has reached the point of development where it is possible for him to be reborn and to have a future *quite different from* that permitted to boy-sweeps in Victorian England. And that is both the satirical and the evolutionary point of Kingsley's organisation of his tale.

Kingsley, in his images of extinction, of degeneration, and of recapitulation and development, mythologises Darwinian theory with remarkable insight. One of the first reviews of *The Water Babies* was in the third issue of the newly founded *Anthropological Review* (1863). Kingsley was an Honorary Fellow of the Anthropological Society of London.[43]

The review commented that 'great changes in the thoughts of mankind have often been distinguished by the publication of poetical or satirical effusions'. In its unguarded and unanalytic response to Darwin's ideas and rhetoric, Kingsley's work represents the first phase of assimilation. He grasped much of what was fresh in Darwin's ideas while at the same time retaining a creationist view of experience.

Darwin cited a letter from Kingsley in the third edition of *The Origin* (1861):

A celebrated author and divine has written to me that 'he has gradually learnt to see that it is just as noble a conception of the Deity to believe that He created a few original forms capable of self-development into other needful forms, as to believe that He required a fresh act of creation to supply the voids caused by the action of His laws.[44]

Darwin was attacked by critics as various in their own beliefs as Morley and Mivart for the anthropomorphism of some of his procedures. Huxley opened his essay 'Man's Place in Nature' with a paragraph which claimed a prescient function for legend, tradition, and myth:

Ancient traditions, when tested by the severe processes of modern investigation, commonly enough fade away into mere dreams: but it is singular how often the dream turns out to have been a half-waking one, presaging a reality. Ovid foreshadowed the discoveries of the geologist: the Atlantis was an imagination, but Columbus found a western world: and though the quaint forms of Centaurs and Satyrs have an existence only in the realms of Art, creatures approaching man more nearly than they in essential structure, and yet as thoroughly brutal as the goat's or horse's half of the mythical compound, are now not only known, but notorious.[45]

These essays are contemporaneous with Kingsley's work (the first three were published in January 1863) and were preoccupied with 'the relations of man to the lower animals'. The 'man-apes' of Huxley's enquiry are paralleled in Kingsley's work by the retrograded 'Doasyoulikes' who finally pass back over the great divide between man and 'brute' and lose the power of speech and 'mope and sulk in the dark forests, never hearing each other's voice, till they have forgotten almost what speech is like'.

Huxley concurred with writers such as Müller in fixing speech as the Rubicon between man and beasts:[46]

Our reverence for the nobility of manhood will not be lessened by the knowledge that Man is, in substance and in structure, one with the brutes; for he alone possesses the marvellous endowment of intelligible and rational speech, whereby, in the secular period of his existence, he has slowly accumulated and organized the experience which is almost wholly lost with the cessation of every individual life in other animals.[47]

The double issue of man's language and of his place in nature was at the centre of mythography and anthropology in the 1860s and 1870s – and they were bound up with the conflict between degradationist and evolutionist views. Such discussion occupies the space left by the suppression of man in the argument of *The Origin*.

The ideas of development and of retrogression or degeneration were complementary in many minds. Darwin's argument, with its emphasis on the drive towards individuation and divergence, lessened the force of replication, but it did not admit of a foreknown perfection towards which organisms were moving. That was the method of artificial not natural selection. 'In man's methodical selection, a breeder selects for some definite object, and free intercrossing will wholly stop his work' (*Origin of Species*, 148). The shared premise of writers as various as von Baer, Humboldt, Comte, Spencer and Darwin was that development implied increasing complexity (though Darwin insisted that complexity was not the uniform consequence of development). The consequences of complexity are hard to foresee and harder to control. Spencer wrote in *Principles of Psychology* that his arguments rely on

a tacit adhesion to the development hypothesis – the hypothesis that Life in its multitudinous and infinitely-varied embodiments, has arisen out of the lowest and simplest beginnings and by steps as gradual as those which evolve a homogeneous microscopic germ into a complex organism.[48]

As the *Anthropological Review* commented, 'great changes in the thoughts of mankind' often result in 'satirical effusions'. Margaret Gatty's *Parables from Nature*[49] (second series) wittily satirise ideas of development and degeneration, as well as astutely capturing that speculative, conditional element in Darwin's syntax which makes denial difficult. 'Inferior Animals' adopts the rooks' point of view – and to their spokesman, man is self-evidently a degenerated rook.[50] The rook takes up the proper anthropological topic of the need to study *origins*:

'The origin, therefore, of these creatures – these men – whom we equally fear and dislike, is decidedly the most useful of all subjects of study . . . Their treatment of us, and our feelings to them, can never be placed on a proper footing, until we know something of the nature of the people themselves.'

Then the rook moves into a quasi-Darwinian syntax of conditionals:

'My friends, man is not our superior, was never so, for he is neither more nor less than a degenerated brother of our own race! Yes, I venture confidently to look back thousands on thousands of generations, and I see that *men* were once *rooks*! Like us they were covered in feathers, like us lived in trees, flew instead of walking, roosted instead of squatting in stone boxes, and were happy and contented as we are now!

'This is a bold proposition, and I do not ask you to assent to it at once. But if on testing it in various ways, you are forced to admit that by it you are able to explain things hitherto inexplicable, and to account for things otherwise unaccountable, though ocular proof cannot be had, then I insist that you cannot reasonably reject my solution without offering me a better one in exchange. *If things are not so, how are they?* is the ground I stand upon. For remember we have already laid down the maxim that every thing *ought* to be and *can* be explained.'

One remembers similar shifts in *The Origin*, for example:

Natural selection *may modify and adapt* the larva of an insect to a score of contingencies, wholly different from those which concern the mature insect. These modifications *will no doubt affect*, through the laws of correlation, the structure of the adult; . . . So, conversely, modifications in the adult *will probably often affect* the structure of the larva . . . A structure used only once in an animal's whole life, if of high importance to it, *might be modified* to any extent by natural selection. [my italics] (135)

Mrs Gatty's attack is on the assumption of full explanation within the natural order, and also on that vastly extended time-scale which makes everything possible. 'But heap ages upon ages, and other ages upon them in a succession to which the century-lives of our grandfathers are a tiny fraction of time, and what then? Anything is possible in the course of such a period.'[51] Paley had made a similar objection to arguments about appetency. Gatty goes on to satirise Darwin's claim of enormous numbers of unused facts behind *The Origin* and his acceptance of his friends' researches. So she performs a double pastiche – of Darwin's methods of argumentation and of the concealed anthropocentrism of much development theory, an anthropocentrism which – it should be noted – itself lies behind many of the attacks on Darwin's anthropomorphism. As Huxley remarked: 'Is mother-love vile because a hen shows it, or fidelity base because dogs possess it?'[52]

Many Victorians were fascinated by transformation and the limits of metamorphosis. Mrs Gatty also includes in the first series a tale called 'Transformation' about a caterpillar which cannot believe that it will one day be a butterfly. The stories of Ondine and of the Ugly Duckling are two of the best known of these stories – and both tales seem to have held a particularly poignant interest for George Eliot. Precisely accompanying the belief in determinism was an enhanced recognition of complex possibilities which may be figured as conversion, transformation, or metamorphosis – or reversion.

Until Darwin's insistence on natural selection and extinction it had been possible to imagine a return to the larger-scale world of prehistory. Lyell, like Buckle later, ascribed to changes in *climate* the changes in species, and it is therefore possible for him to speculate on the summer of the 'Great Year':

Then might those genera of animals return, of which the memorials are preserved in the ancient rocks of our continents. The huge iguanodon might reappear in the woods, and the ichthysaur in the sea, while the pterodactyle might flit again through umbrageous groves of tree-ferns. Coral reefs might be prolonged beyond the arctic circle, where the whale and the narwal now abound. Turtles might deposit their eggs in the sand of the sea beach, where now the walrus sleeps, and where the seal is drifted on the ice-floe.[53]

In Lyell's thought along with this sense of possible reversal went a sense of the *temporariness* of man and of the present order of the world – but when he imagined change he tended to imagine it as relapse or return. 'A relapse would take place to the ancient state of things, the domesticated animal, for example, recovering in a few generations its wild instinct, and the garden-flower and fruit-tree reverting to the likeness of the parent-stock.' Relapse suggests simplification – the reversion to an earlier likeness.

Fifty years later in *After London* (1885) Richard Jefferies projects a natural order simplified, its few species of plants and animals described in a discourse which is both taxonomic and liturgical. The title of Part I, 'The Relapse into Barbarism', is belied by the assuaging pastoralism of the first paragraph with its recourse to the comforts of oral tradition: 'The old men say their fathers told them', of pre-lapsarian primal spring, 'It became green everywhere in the first spring, after London ended', of simplification 'so that all the country looked alike'.[54]

The Great Forest

The old men say their fathers told them that soon after the fields were left to themselves a change began to be visible. It became green everywhere in the first spring, after London ended, so that all the country looked alike. (1)

The menace of 'all looking alike' is realised in the succeeding chapters: the brambles advance: 'Starting from all sides at once, these brambles and briars in the course of about twenty years met in the centre of the largest fields.' Of cats: 'After a while the several varieties disappeared, and left but one wild kind.' There are two kinds of cattle, four kinds of wild pig, three of sheep, two of horses. Each of these kinds is described with graceful thoroughness, a sturdy taxonomic sobriety gives a sense of order for as long as no human beings appear on the scene. Lost history is mingled with categorial description:

From the horses that were in use among the ancients the two wild species now found are known to have descended, a fact confirmed by their evident resemblance to the horses we still retain. The largest wild horse is almost black, or inclined to a dark colour, somewhat less in size than our present waggon horses, but of the same heavy make. It is, however, much swifter, on account of having enjoyed liberty for so long.

. . . Tradition says that in the olden times there were horses of a slender build whose speed out-stripped the wind, but of the breed of these famous racers not one is left. Whether they were too delicate to withstand exposure, or whether the wild dogs hunted them down is uncertain, but they are quite gone. (12–13)

The work is haunted by extinction, by the throttling power of a few dominant species, and the loss of varieties in the wild state. The opening lines of *The Origin of Species* had called attention to the greater differences between individuals under cultivation than in a wild state:

When we look to the individuals of the same variety or sub-variety of our older cultivated plants and animals, one of the first points which strikes us, is, that they generally differ much more from each other, than do the individuals of any one species or variety in a state of nature. When we reflect on the vast diversity of the plants and animals which have been cultivated, and which have varied during all ages under the most different climates and treatment, I think we are driven to conclude that this greater variability is simply due to our domestic productions having been raised under conditions of life not so uniform as, and somewhat different from, those to which the parent-species have been exposed under nature. (71)

Reversion to 'wild England' implies the obliteration of many varieties and species by the despotic power of a few rank forms. In the same way the society is marked by tyranny, oppression, and enslavement. At the core of the country lies 'the vast stagnant swamp' which covers all that is left of London:

Thus the low-lying parts of the mighty city of London became swamps, and the higher grounds were clad with bushes. The very largest of the buildings fell in, and there was nothing visible but trees and hawthorns on the upper lands, and willows, flags, reeds, and rushes on the lower. These crumbling ruins still more choked the stream, and almost, if not quite, turned it back. If any water ooze past, it is not perceptible, and there is no channel through to the salt ocean. It is a vast stagnant swamp, which no man dare enter, since death would be his inevitable fate.

There exhales from this oozy mass so fatal a vapour that no animal can endure it. The black water bears a greenish-brown floating scum, which for ever bubbles up from the putrid mud of the bottom. When the wind collects the miasma, and, as it were, presses it together, it becomes visible as a low cloud which hangs over the place. The cloud does not advance beyond the limit of the marsh, seeming to stay there by some constant attraction; and well it is for us that it does not, since at such times when the vapour is thickest, the very wildfowl leave the reeds, and fly from the poison. There are no fishes, neither can eels exist in the mud, nor even newts. It is dead. (37)

The real subject of Jefferies's dark fantasy is extinction. Instead of creating abundance, the resurgence of nature has obliterated life. The noxious gases on the lake drive the birds to a false migration, leaving their nests with eggs and young behind them; the corrupted water of the swamp as well as its land is composed 'of the mouldered bodies of millions of men who had passed away in the centuries during which the city existed'. The heavy rolling waves which pursue Felix are the product of their gases in 'vast conduits, sewers, and tunnels' meeting with 'the ascending tide'. Water here has become foetid with corruption, a whole civilisation collapsed and lost. And the same theme of extinction, preying, and brutal colonisation by a few coarse species, is repeated in the genocidal wars which take place in the book beween bush-men, gypsies, and shepherds, as well as in the rapacious, treacherous atmosphere of the quasi-feudal king's court. The writing is extraordinarily direct and extraordinarily dark: the promise of perfection and of continued growth towards complexity which buoys up the conclusion to *The Origin of Species* is here curdled. Darwin's prophecy of knowledge of the past is ironised:

When we better know the many means of migration, then, by the light which geology now throws, and will continue to throw, on former changes of climate and of the level of the land, we shall surely be enabled to trace in an admirable manner the former migrations of the inhabitants of the whole world. (*Origin*, 457)

In Jefferies' work, glimpsed darkly through surmises and traditions, the level of the land changed indeed, and migrations have certainly ensued:

the people crowded on board all the ships to escape starvation, and sailed away, and were no more heard of.

It has, too, been said that the earth, from some attractive power exercised by the passage of an enormous dark body through space, became tilted or inclined to its orbit more than before, and that this, while it lasted, altered the flow of the magnetic currents, which, in an imperceptible manner, influence the minds of man. Hitherto the stream of human life had directed itself to the westward, but when this reversal of magnetism occurred, a general desire arose to return to the east. (16)

The call of those Aryan sources was strong in Müller's mythography. *After London* suggests that the search for the first home of man, for the lost high culture, may be a delusion whose powerful other aspect is the degeneration of the present world.[55] Jefferies's work condenses fears which in the 1870s and 1880s intensified in the wake of Darwinian controversy: fears that decadence may be an energy as strong as development, and extinction a fate more probable than progress.

PART III

Responses: George Eliot and Thomas Hardy

CHAPTER 5

George Eliot: Middlemarch

I THE VITAL INFLUENCE

George Eliot was often taken to task by contemporary reviewers for the persistent scientific allusions in her works. Henry James, indeed, complained that '*Middlemarch* is too often an echo of Messrs. Darwin and Huxley'.[1] And R. H. Hutton objected to her use of the word 'dynamic' in the opening sentences of *Daniel Deronda* as being pedantically over-scientific: 'Was she beautiful or not beautiful? and what was the secret of form or expression which gave the dynamic quality to her glance?'[2] The surprise that any modern reader is likely to feel at Hutton's particular objection should alert us to the degree to which language that has now lost its scientific bearing still bore a freight of controversy and assertion for George Eliot and her first readers. If, in the light of James's remark, one turns to the Prelude to *Middlemarch* words that may now read as flat generality renew their powers of controversy.[3] The concluding paragraph asserts ironically the problems of treating the social lot of women:

if there were one level of feminine incompetence as strict as the ability to count three and no more, the social lot of women might be treated with scientific certitude. Meanwhile the indefiniteness remains, and the limits of variation are really much wider than any one would imagine from the sameness of women's coiffure and the favourite love-stories in prose and verse. (1;1:2–3)

To take up only one of several possible words from that passage: 'variation'. 'The limits of variation' are part of the controversy about species and about how far it is possible to describe species through their characteristics. They are part also of that argument about whether resemblances of appearance and use could count as 'real affinities' or as 'analogical or adaptive resemblances' – resemblances brought about, that is, by a common response to the pressures of environment. Although the example that Darwin uses is remote from George Eliot's, the argument follows the same course: 'The resemblance, in the shape of the body and in the fin-like anterior limbs, between the dugong, which is a pachydermatous animal, and the whale, and between both these mammals and fishes, is analogical' (410). Response to environment can make very diverse creatures look and behave alike: 'the limits of variation are really much wider than any one would imagine from the sameness of women's coiffure'.

Within each species, in Darwin's argument, *variation* is the key to evolutionary development. Diversification, not truth to type, is the creative principle, as he emphasises throughout the first chapter of *The Origin of Species* whose title is 'Variation Under Domestication'. George Eliot takes the word 'variation', in which so much current controversy is moving, and applies it to 'the social lot of women': 'variation under domestication' is for them a difficult endeavour. So her use of the phrase 'limits of variation' is a polemical signal which harbinges much for the 'domestic epic' she is about to present.

Some of her critics appreciated this weighting of words with the fullest concerns of the time – those concerns in which emotion and intellect are not kept apart but most completely imply each other. Colvin commented in these terms on her use of medical knowledge and imagery in *Middlemarch*,[4] and Edward Dowden, in particular, seized upon the implications for language of the turmoil of scientific ideas and hypotheses current in the period:

She has actually employed in a work of fiction such words as 'dynamic' and 'natural selection', at which the critic picks up his delicate ears and shies . . . Language, the instrument of literary art, is an instrument of ever-extending range, and the truest pedantry, in an age when the air is saturated with scientific thought, would be to reject those accessions to language which are the special gain of the time. Insensibility to the contemporary movement in science is itself essentially unliterary . . . The cultured imagination is affected by it, as the imagination of Spenser's time was affected by his use of the neoclassical mythology of the Renaissance.[5]

The comparison with Spenser is particularly just and telling. The acquired cultural language of science, like that of neo-classical allusion, offers a controlled range of imaginative consequences shared by writer and first readers.[6] It offers an imaginative shift in the valency of words, new spaces for experience to occupy in language, confirmation of some kinds of vocabulary, increased prowess of punning, in which diverse senses are held in equipoise within the surveillance of consciousness. These effects register a moment when a particular discourse has reached its fullest range. It can then suggest new bearings for experiences which had earlier seemed quite separate from each other.[7] At such moments of transposition emotion can find its full extent in language.

One can find specific sources in scientific writing of the time for certain famous passages in *Middlemarch*: for example the imaginative reach of Lydgate's scientific exploration:

But these kinds of inspiration Lydgate regarded as rather vulgar and vinous compared with the imagination that reveals subtle actions inaccessible by any sort of lens, but tracked in that outer darkness through long pathways of neces-sary sequence by the inward light which is the last refinement of Energy, capable of bathing even the ethereal atoms in its ideally illuminated space. (1:16:249)

G. H. Lewes quotes the following passage from John Tyndall in *Problems of Life and Mind*:

Indeed the domain of the senses in Nature is almost infinitely small in compar-ison with the vast region accessible to thought which lies beyond them. From a few observations of a comet when it comes within the range of his telescope, an astronomer can calculate its path in regions which no telescope can reach; and in like manner, by means of data furnished in the narrow world of the senses, we can make ourselves at home in other and wider worlds, which can be traversed by the intellect alone.[8]

The complex of ideas (intellect outgoing instruments, heat and en-ergy as images of the productive and transforming powers, the vastness and plurality of the worlds beyond the reach of unaided sense) is shared by the two writers.

Like Tyndall, George Eliot emphasises the congruity between all the various processes of the imagination: the novelist's and the scientist's enterprise is fired by the same prescience, the same willingness to ex-plore the significance even of that which can be registered neither by instruments nor by the unaided senses; the same willingness to use and to outgo evidence. At the end of his Rede lecture, Tyndall remarks that

It is thought by some that natural science has a deadening influence on the imagination . . . But the experience of the last hour must, I think, have con-vinced you, that the study of natural sciences goes hand in hand with the culture of the imagination. Throughout the greater part of this discourse we have been sustained by this faculty. We have been picturing atoms and mol-ecules and vibrations and waves which eye has never seen nor ear heard, and which can only be discerned by the exercise of imagination.[9]

The imagery of transcendence, of the invisible world, is one which George Eliot shares. The microscope and the telescope, by making realisable the plurality of worlds, scales, and existences beyond the reach of our particular sense organisation were a powerful antidote to that form of positivism which refused to acknowledge possibilities beyond the present and apparent world. They were permitting factors in that particular strain of Romantic materialism – a sense of the clustering mystery of a material universe – which is dominant in both the scientific writing and the literature of the period. Far from eschewing mystification, the extension of possibility through scientific instruments and scientific hypothesis-making actually gave at this time a fresh authority to the speculative and even to the fictive. Projects cannot rest in the present – they rely upon extension and futurity.

Perhaps better known as an example of George Eliot's 'scientific' discourse is the close parallel between her famous passage on the limits of sensibility in chapter 20 and T. H. Huxley's essay 'The Physical Basis of Life,' published in *The Fortnightly Review*, February 1869, which illustrates the dullness of human senses in this way:

the wonderful noonday silence of a tropical forest is, after all, due only to the dullness of our hearing; and could our ears catch the murmur of those tiny Maelstroms, as they whirl in the innumerable myriads of living cells which constitute each tree, we should be stunned, as with the roar of a great city.[10]

In *Middlemarch* we read:

That element of tragedy which lies in the very fact of frequency, has not yet wrought itself into the coarse emotion of mankind; and perhaps our frames could hardly bear much of it. If we had a keen vision and feeling of all ordinary human life, it would be like hearing the grass grow and the squirrel's heart beat, and we should die of that roar which lies on the other side of silence. (1.20:297–8)

In that same essay, 'The Physical Basis of Life', Huxley draws attention to the religious panic experienced by many in the face of material explanations, and compares it to Max Müller's explanation of 'solar myth'.

The consciousness of this great truth weighs like a nightmare, I believe, upon many of the best minds of these days. They watch what they conceive to be the progress of materialism, in such fear and powerless anger as a savage feels, when, during an eclipse, the great shadow creeps over the face of the sun. The advancing tide of matter threatens to drown their souls; the tightening grasp of law impedes their freedom; they are alarmed lest man's moral nature be debased by the increase of his wisdom.[11]

He claims that far from demeaning the world, scientific materialism *extends* the range of connectedness within the natural order, even while it inhibits 'spirit and spontaneity'.

To come closer to home (and to destabilise the question of priority) consider this passage from G. H. Lewes's[12] series of articles for the *Fortnightly Review* in 1868 on 'Mr. Darwin's Hypotheses':

Let us for a moment glance at the resemblances and diversities observable in all organisms. All have a *common basis*, all being constructed out of the same fundamental elements: carbon, hydrogen, nitrogen and oxygen . . . Beside this community of *Substance* we must now place a community of *History*.[13]

Lewes's argument draws upon the work particularly of Claude Bernard, which has succeeded that of Bichat (Lydgate's mentor):

That great Frenchman first carried out the conception that living bodies, fundamentally considered, are not associations or organs which can be understood by studying them first apart, and then as it were federally; but must be regarded as consisting of certain primary webs or tissues, out of which the various organs – brain, heart, lungs, and so on – are compacted . . . This great seer did not go beyond the consideration of the tissues as ultimate facts in the living organism, marking the limit of anatomical analysis; but it was open to another mind to say, have not these structures some common basis from which they have all started, as your sarsnet, gauze, net, satin and velvet from the raw cocoon? (*Middlemarch* 1:15:223–4)

The phrase *common basis*, which Lewes italicises, is used again for the *Middlemarch* passage in a very similar context and in the light of Lewes's analysis of the several 'organogens', we understand more precisely why Lydgate's question 'What was the primitive tissue?' does not put the problem 'quite in the way required by the awaiting answer'.

There is not one 'primitive tissue', just as there is not one 'key to all mythologies'. Lewes diverged from Darwin's history on one major point: the idea of the single progenitor. He postulated instead that 'the earth at the dawn of Life was like a vast germinal membrane, every diversified point producing its own vital form'. This emphasis upon plurality, rather than upon singleness, is crucial to the developing argument of *Middlemarch* which, with all its overtly taxonomic ordering, has as its particular deep counter-enterprise the establishment of individual diversity beneath ascribed typologies: 'the favourite love-stories in prose and verse'.

Middlemarch is a work that draws attention to its own organisation; the naming of the individual books emphasises categorisation ('Waiting for Death', 'Two Temptations', 'Three Love Problems'). But the process of reading leads into divergence and variability. Even while we are observing how closely human beings conform in the taxonomy of events we learn how differently they feel and think. For Dorothea and Casaubon waiting for death means something very different from what it means for Mary Garth and Featherstone. The *relations* are different. The distances between people are different. Lydgate, here at one with the project of the book, 'longed to demonstrate the more intimate relations of living structure' (1:15:225). In this double emphasis on conformity and variability George Eliot intensifies older literary organisations by means of recent scientific theory. In Darwinian theory, variability is the creative principle, but the type makes it possible for us to track common ancestry and common kinship. It makes it possible also for us to assess the degree to which common environment bends creatures unlike each other to look alike.

In the Victorian period the Romantic search for the 'One Life' had been set back in time and become a search for origins. In *Middlemarch* 'relations' and 'origins' are set in a particular historical sequence: 'Beside this community of Substance we must now place a community of History.' In George Eliot's later novels we have an imagination permeated by scientific ideas and speculations, an imagination which can achieve what Wordsworth looked towards in the second Preface to the Lyrical Ballads.[14] Incarnation summarises all that is most difficult for her and rewarding to her as a novelist. As Dowden implies George Eliot both registered and extended the imaginative and emotional implications that current scientific discovery and practice carried for her culture. She draws on the 'vital influence of the period' so that she responds to shared anxieties, moves within shared controversies, and creates a reader alert equally to the scientific potential of everyday language and to the everyday potential of scientific terminology: as in that word 'dynamic' or as in the almost obliterated scientific reference implicit in Dowden's own phrase 'vital influence'. This communality and novelty of system and of enquiry is essential to her project.

In indicating specific parallels and sources which draw on the writing of scientists, it is important to emphasise that this is not a matter simply of discrete passages which struck her attention (though clearly some did that). Rather, it is an engagement with the controversies and enquiries of which those texts are themselves a part. Within all these controversies two precepts are persistently presented, criticised, celebrated: 'The power of nature is the power of motion', and 'Evolution is the universal process.' The two principles are understood as inter-extensive. The universality of both laws and their preoccupation not with replication but with change are seen as mutually confirmatory. Both laws carry within them many of the properties expressed particularly by narrative: extension of time: sequence; shifting relations; complex movement from one phase to another. The two laws diverge in one important way – movement does not necessarily imply transformation or change. Evolution does.[15] In *Middlemarch* the historical aspect of both laws is expressed: individuals are trapped in the determined pace of successive historical moments. Particularly in *Daniel Deronda* George Eliot springs the argument of the book on the contradiction between untransformed extension and irreversible change and development.

In the preface to *Roderick Hudson*, published in the same year as *Daniel Deronda* (1876), Henry James recognised the problems for the artist because 'Really, universally, relations stop nowhere' but he interpreted his duty as being not to reproduce this process but, 'by a geometry of his own', to interfere with it and find a satisfying means of enclosing 'the continuity of things' which is 'the whole matter with him'.

Really, universally, relations stop nowhere, and the exquisite problem of the artist is eternally but to draw, by a geometry of his own, the circle within which they shall happily appear to do so. He is in the perpetual predicament that the continuity of things is the whole matter with him.

Even in James's vocabulary there is an underlying assumption that it is the scientific level which represents enduring actuality: 'really, universally'. The artist must create by means of a counter-fiction which will contain that which is truly not to be contained. Through the geometric image of the circle or the round framing eye of microscope or telescope, a readable focus is achieved and enquiry can be both initiated and brought to a conclusion.[16]

In *Middlemarch* George Eliot distinguished her enterprise from that of 'the great historian' Fielding with his 'copious remarks and digressions'.

We belated historians must not linger after his example . . . I at least have so much to do in unravelling certain human lots, and seeing how they were woven and interwoven, that all the light I can command must be concentrated on this particular web, and not dispersed over that tempting range of relevancies called the universe. (I:15:214)

The problems of a system of thought which promises 'no vestiges of a beginning . . . no prospect of an end', in the geologist Hutton's phrase, are being borne in on writers from the mid-nineteenth century on. In *The Mill on the Floss* George Eliot wrote in 1861: 'In natural science, I have understood, there is nothing petty to the mind that has a large vision of relations, as to which every single object suggests a vast sum of conditions. It is surely the same with the observation of human life.'[17] In the late novels however this infinite implication or infinite extension is perceived as at once alluring and yet artistically and existentially threatening.

Dowden's comments were written with the long retrospect of George Eliot's career behind them, but her assimilation of scientific theory and particularly of Darwin's ideas had been gradual and sometimes troubled.

When George Eliot first began reading Darwin's *The Origin of Species* immediately after it appeared in November 1859 she wrote in her Journal: 'We began Darwin's work on The Origin of Species tonight. It seems not to be well written: though full of interesting matter, it is not impressive, from want of luminous and orderly presentation', and in a letter two days later she says that it is 'an elaborate exposition of the evidence in favour of the Development Theory, and so, makes an epoch'.[18]

It seems at first sight a curiously inadequate reaction to a book whose theories were to leave man wandering in a thronged, strifeful world of nature which offered him no peculiarly endowed place. And of course George Eliot's reaction was soon to change – but those first impressions are nevertheless revealing. Initially she was misled by her very familiarity with contemporary debate: she had read Lamarck and commissioned an article on his work for *The Westminster Review* in the early 1850s. Lamarck had suggested a theory of development which relied on learning: each generation learnt to cope with its environment and handed on the fruits of its learning as acquired characteristics to its successors. And she had read Chambers's inaccurate but influential popularisation of evolutionary ideas, *The Vestiges of Creation*. She admired the work of Lyell whose expansion of the geological time-scale had provided a necessary precondition for evolutionary ideas. She was familiar with Herbert Spencer's evolutionary thought in the 1850s. At first she simply sees Darwin as summarising such ideas and giving them the weight of his scientific standing: she does not perceive the novelty of what he is doing. She does not grasp his insight into the major *mechanism* of evolutionary change: that of natural selection – a process which depends on the individual *happening* to accord with the needs of the environment and so surviving, and on minute random mutations which better fit the individual and his particular descendants for the world in which they live until that world changes and the advantage passes elsewhere. It is an idea so much at variance with George Eliot's own morality that it is not surprising that she did not immediately grasp its implications.

Whenever she refers directly to the idea of natural selection, that faintly facetious orotund style appears, to which she is driven by ideas that cause her deep disquiet and which she yet cannot repudiate:

Pray, if you fall in love ascertain first that the *objet aimé* is without encumbrances. If not let him find some poor governess who is well broken in and without prospects. I have no patience with these widowers who are always expecting women to take compassion on them, and never themselves take compassion on women really forlorn. They must always have the best, forsooth – are always good enough for the best to accept. This is the fine principle of Natural Selection, they will say. I admit it, but it is also the Selection of conceited gentlemen.[19]

The same harsh awkward tone is heard in *Daniel Deronda*:

It was impossible to be jealous of Juliet Fenn, a girl as middling as mid-day market in everything but her archery and her plainness, in which last she was noticeably like her father: underhung and with receding brow resembling that of the more intelligent fishes. (Surely, considering the importance which is given to such an accident in female offspring, marriageable men, or what the new English calls 'intending bridegrooms', should look at themselves dispassionately in the glass, since their natural selection of a mate prettier than themselves is not certain to bar the effect of their own ugliness.)[20]

More chilling is one of her very late works, her essay 'Shadows of the Coming Race', published in *The Impressions of Theophrastus Such* in 1879, which has a perturbingly prophetic potential still:

... there rises a fearful vision of the human race evolving machinery which will by-and-by throw itself fatally out of work ... one sees that the process of natural selection must drive men altogether out of the field ... Thus the feebler race, whose corporeal adjustments happened to be accompanied with a maniacal consciousness which imagined itself moving its mover, will have vanished, as all less adapted existences do before fittest ... Thus this planet may be filled with beings who will be blind and deaf as the inmost rock, yet will execute changes as delicate and complicated as those of human language and all the intricate web of what we call its effects, without sensitive impression, without sensitive impulse: there may be, let us say, mute orations, mute rhapsodies, mute discussions, and no consciousness there even to enjoy the silence.[21]

'Changes as delicate and complicated as those of human language and all the intricate web of what we call its effects' – is here assimilated to human language and its effects.

It is only retrospectively that it becomes clear how much of Darwin's argument has found expression in narrative through parallelisms and description and George Eliot had not yet absorbed this when she initially commented on his lack of 'luminous and orderly presentation'.[22]

In George Eliot's two late and greatest novels, *Middlemarch* and *Daniel Deronda*, written during the period of the late 1860s and the 1870s, Darwin's insights, and the difficulties raised by those insights, move into the substance of the novels' project. She has by then fully assimilated the implications of evolutionary ideas. Lewes's 1868 articles on Darwin acted as a catalyst.

II   STRUCTURE AND HYPOTHESIS

In a letter of 1873 George Eliot emphasised the extend to which meaning is expressed through *form* in her fiction. She wrote in reply to an editor wishing to make a selection of 'wise and witting sayings' from her work:

Unless my readers are more moved towards the ends I seek by my works as wholes than by an assemblage of extracts, my writings are a mistake. I have always exercised a severe watch against anything that could be called preaching, and if I have ever allowed myself in dissertation or in dialogue [anything] which is not part of the *structure* of my books, I have there sinned against my own laws.[23]

Her insistence on structure as the bearer of signification and on congruity between semantics and form draws upon scientific procedures of the time as well as on Coleridge's concept of 'significant form'. George Eliot opens *Middlemarch* by presenting it as a series of experiments designed to study 'the history of man': 'how the mysterious mixture behaves under the varying experiments of Time'. 'Experiments', Claude Bernard points out, are to be distinguished from observations because of the more active, organising, even disruptive, role of the experimenter. The experimenter disturbs the conditions he observes:

Where then, you will ask, is the difference between observer and experimenter? It is here: we give the name observer to the man who applies methods of investigation, whether simple or complex, to the study of phenomena which he does not vary, which he therefore gathers as nature offers them. We give the name experimenter to the man who applies methods of investigation, whether simple or complex, so as to make natural phenomena vary, or so as to alter them with some purpose or other, present themselves in circumstances or conditions in which nature does not show them.[24]

In the organisation of *Middlemarch* George Eliot creates a series of structural comparisons – a series of likenesses which make sharp appreciation of divergence possible. But in the very multiplicity of interconnection she simultaneously offers a critique of any attempt at unifactorial description of human behaviour under varying conditions.

To us now, the word 'experimental' in relation to art (experimental novel, experimental theatre, for example) suggests a free-ranging, exploratory, innovatory project often lacking or avoiding any determined conclusion. For Victorian writers, the new methodological emphasis on 'experimental' (i.e. experiment-based) science meant that the word suggested careful controls, precise articulation of differences, an empirical rather than a metaphysical approach to evidence. That was, of course, what Zola meant by *Le roman expérimental,* with its open reference to Claude Bernard's concept of *La médecine expérimentale.* In approaching *Middlemarch* we may expect to find the scientific and medical concerns of the text expressed not only at the level of theme, character, and opinion, but in the structural order. Whether we work with the grain of the work or against it, we shall find the analogy with scientific procedures essential.

In such a situation the analogy of fiction with science may work in counterfacing ways: one direction is towards mystery and expansion. As old Mr Brooke in *Middlemarch* succinctly and absurdly puts it: 'I went into science a great deal myself at one time, but I saw it would not do. *It leads to everything*', (1:2:21) [my italics]. Another direction leads towards fixing and proving – and here the parallels between plot and scientific hypotheses emerge as crucial.

Fiction in the second half of the nineteenth century was particularly seeking sources of authoritative organisation which could substitute for the god-like omnipotence and omniscience open to the theistic narrator. At the beginning of this period science had escaped for a time its collusion with the magical, the world of occult knowledge, which in the work of Renaissance scientists such as John Dee had ranged it closer to fiction. Experimental procedures in biology and physiology claimed objectivity. Workers such as Bichat (in whose tracks Lydgate in *Middlemarch* is following) and, later, Bernard, emphasised repetition, testing and recording. These elements distinguished scientific method in a tonic way from the procedures of fiction, which cannot submit itself in its totality to the tests of repetition.

Within the organisation of the novels the scientific emphasis upon repetition and comparison is taken up into the almost taxonomic ordering of, say, *La Bête humaine* or *Middlemarch* with their emphasis upon speciation and variability through the use of related examples. But both novels go beyond taxonomy into a study of process and relations. That is, they move away from the models of Cuvier and Bichat to those of Darwin and Bernard, away from structure, to function and to history. The movement in scientific thinking was from description to narration: time becomes an inherent part of theory. This brings the objective insights of the scientist into accord with the procedure of the fiction writer and offers another kind of authentication.

Lyell's epigraph to the first edition of *Principles of Geology* is from Playfair's *Illustrations of the Huttonian Theory* and begins: 'Amid all the revolutions of the globe the economy of Nature has been uniform, and her laws are the only things that have resisted the general movement.'[25] This belief in the presence of permanent yet hidden laws of nature provides the drive towards discovery in the work of George Eliot, and Zola. They seek to track and uncover natural laws. This pursuit is the deepest level of plot in their fictions. The fixity of the laws uncovered, moreover, serves to confirm the fictions which disclose them.

At the same time, their vehement fascination with individuality makes for a painful play of energies between the scrupulous disclosures of law and the passionate unanswerable needs of human beings. The writer's authority is drawn from this task of tracking and revealing the primary fixed laws of nature – with which his fiction proves to accord – but his creativity is absorbed in people. The emphasis on fixed laws has a compelling significance precisely because it was the last fixed thing remaining in 'the theatre of reiterated change'. The novelist therefore has newly to explore an organisation in which man's experience is traversed by laws which take no account of his presence. Writers are forced to question the assumption that because man's reason can *discover* natural laws, those laws are part of an order of rationality centring upon man. In a writer like George Eliot, the systems proposed by current scientific thinking are consciously appropriated. The *methods* of scientists become the methods of employment and scientific theories suggest new organisations for fiction.

In the later nineteenth century the theme of incongruities between natural law and individual need, one of the oldest in literature, achieved a new saliency because it concurred with the most advanced propositions of science. Deterministic organisations of plot in science and in fiction emphasised always the inevitable sacrifice of the individual, but this organisation fuelled outrage rather than acquiescence. The gap between individuality and significant plot began to widen.

Plot must appear to have an equivalence with ulterior organisation beyond the control, and to some extent the knowledge, of the single psyche. It can never be generated solely out of the subjective individual. Even in plots of paranoia the paranoiac believes in the 'other' as the maker of plots, however much the reader may uneasily strive towards a counter-interpretation. The paranoiac is both self and other. Plot in nineteenth-century fiction is a radical form of interpretation: it fixes the relations between phenomena. It projects the future and then gives real form to its own predictions. It is to that extent self-verifying: its solutions confirm the validity of the clues proposed.

Such plot assumes that what is hidden may be uncovered, and that what lies beyond the peripheries of present knowledge may be encompassed and brought within the account by its completion. In this particular sense it shares the nature of hypothesis, which by its causal narrative seeks ultimately to convert its own status from that of idea to truth. Plot does this by provoking in the reader multiple hypotheses. From among these a confirming sequence is selected which offers a complete solution to the puzzles its clues have proposed. Scientific hypotheses in this period might seek to confirm themselves either through experimental practice, as did Bernard, or through analogy and history, as Darwin was driven to do.

George Eliot used the images of history and of experimentation in the opening sentence of *Middlemarch*. 'Who that cares much to know the history of man, and how the mysterious mixture behaves under the varying experiments of Time . . .' Implicit in 'the history of man' is the parallel 'natural history'. In her second clause she suggests that the novelist's ranging command of time gives him a particular experimental instrument capable, as Bernard insisted such instruments should be, of extending the limits of our unaided observation.

Time in experimentation is strictly controlled. There is a convergence of evidence and observation marked out *in time*. Hypothesis and possibility, though preceding and succeeding the experimental process, must, Bernard insists, be set aside during the period of experimentation. In *Problems of Life and Mind* G. H. Lewes commented on the problems of controlling the speculative urge towards certainty:

In our eagerness for an explanation we readily accept conjectures as truths. *The anticipatory rush of Thought prefigures qualities and foresees consequences*; instead of pausing to ascertain whether our anticipations do or do not correspond with fact, we proceed to argue, to act on them as if this mental vision were final.[26] [my italics]

One of the methods by which in *Middlemarch* George Eliot controls speculation and its implicit drive towards finality, is persistingly *to set alongside.* By this means, lateral as well as causal relations are emphasised. She interrupts the movement towards resolution by revealing further and further affinities of event and feeling between characters who have no close personal relationship to each other. At the same time, however, the discovery which this method increasingly reveals is the extent of diversity within the order of apparently-like incident and personality.

As Lewes remarked, following Darwin: 'Let us never forget that Species have no existence. Only individuals exist, and these all vary more or less from each other.'[27] He follows this remark by quoting Darwin's tree of life passage. Darwin had emphasised that it was vain to seek any special universalist authority for the idea of species. Common language often registers real differences of identity too easily ignored by systematists: 'It is quite possible that forms now generally acknowledged to be merely varieties may hereafter be thought worthy of specific names, as with the primrose and cowslip; and in this case scientific and common language will come into accordance.' Darwin always welcomed such 'accordance' because its emphasis on the concrete and the particular offered a way out of essentialism:

In short, we shall have to treat species in the same manner as those naturalists treat genera, who admit that genera are merely artificial combinations made for convenience. This may not be a cheering prospect; but we shall at least be freed from the vain search for the undiscovered and undiscoverable essence of the term species. (456)

Within *Middlemarch* the argument about taxonomy and morphology, about diversity of example and structural systematics, is carried on most openly and simply between Lydgate and Farebrother, though not simply judged. Lydgate does not appreciate Farebrother's collection of insects and his 'new species':

'I fancy,' says Farebrother, 'I have made an exhaustive study of the entomology of this district. I am going on both with the fauna and flora; but I have at least done my insects well. We are singularly rich in orthoptera: I don't know whether – Ah! you have got hold of that glass jar – you are looking into that instead of my drawers. You don't really care about these things?'
'Not by the side of this lovely anencephalous monster. I have never had time to give myself much to natural history. I was early bitten with an interest in structure, and it is what lies most directly in my profession.' (1:17:261–2)

Natural history concentrates on variety, and physiology on structure, it seems here. But the same problems about community of type are expressed in the work's own organisation and in Casaubon's search for 'the key to all mythologies' – a key which gives him no access to the lived world. His systematics enervate. The work of fiction must avoid the lure of typology.

In his *Introduction to Experimental Medicine*, 1865, Bernard sets out the developing experimental method which made physiology for the first time *the* basis of medical theory and practice. His argument is anti-vitalist. He is concerned primarily with describing and establishing procedures for enquiry. He contends that experimental science is concerned to consider in any phenomenon solely the specific conditions which are necessary for its production: 'En effet, la science expérimentale ne considére dans un phénomène que les seules conditions définies qui sont nécessaire à sa production' (II:I:sec.VI).[28] In G. H. Lewes's copy of the *Introduction* this is the first passage marked. Bernard goes on to specify two particular dangers to science: an excess of particularity, and an excess of generality which creates an ideal science out of touch with reality. These dangers are particularly salient for medicine, with the emphasis on the individual case. He distinguishes his practice from that of thinkers concerned with the 'milieu cosmique'. As a practitioner of medicine and a physiologist his emphasis is on the 'milieu intérieur', a term which Bernard invented.

When George Eliot wrote *Middlemarch*, she chose as the man most deeply beset by the intellectual and emotional problems of the novel's time of setting a young doctor, Lydgate, engaged in both research and pastoral care. Lydgate is working at the end of the 1820s, following Bichat, and he seeks the underlying unity beneath the diversity of matter. In his medical practice he rejects bromides and authority in favour of experimental diagnosis. In the novel Lydgate goes astray because he does not use the full powers of his imagination on 'the complexities of love and marriage' as he does on his study of pathology:

Many men have been praised as vividly imaginative on the strength of their profuseness in indifferent drawing or cheap narration:– reports of very poor talk going on in distant orbs; or portraits of Lucifer coming down on his bad errands as a large ugly man with bat's wings and spurts of phosphorescence; or exaggerations of wantonness that seem to reflect life in a diseased dream. But these kinds of inspiration Lydgate regarded as rather vulgar and vinous compared with the imagination that reveals subtle actions inaccessible by any sort of lens, but tracked in that outer darkness through long pathways of necessary sequence by the inward light which is the last refinement of Energy, capable of bathing even the ethereal atoms in its ideally illuminated space. (1:16:249)

'Necessary sequence' is controlled by the reasoning imagination and there is an emphasis upon the liberty of reason first to use, and then to outgo, observation. George Eliot's vocabulary here moves towards the transcendental ('ethereal atoms', 'ideally illuminated space'), while the extraordinarily extended sequence of connectives (with, that, by, but, through, of, by, which) expresses thought moving onward and inward, drawing upon an ever fuller series of relations. The paragraph opens with a reference to narration. At the end, having moved within the guise of Lydgate's musings, the accord between scientific imagination, healer's imagination, and that of the novelist is consummated by a shift into the description applicable equally to the enterprise of scientist and novelist:

He for his part had tossed away all cheap inventions where ignorance finds itself able and at ease: *he was enamoured of that arduous invention which is the very eye of research, provisionally framing its object and correcting it to more and more exactness of relation*; he wanted to pierce the obscurity of those minute processes which prepared human misery and joy, those invisible thoroughfares which are the first lurking-places of anguish, mania, and crime, that delicate poise and transition which determine the growth of happy or unhappy consciousness. (1:16:249–50) [my italics]

Momentarily the word 'relation' can express what to her is the node of its meanings: narration and relations.

Multiple analogy creates a web of interconnections in *Middlemarch*. George Eliot's intellectual characters are preoccupied with sources: 'the primitive tissue', 'the key to all mythologies', but the text is organised in terms of variability. *Middlemarch* creates an experimental situation by its use of structural analogy and by its 'provisional framing', which draws the focus ever more sharply, shifting and refocusing where necessary, testing situations through diverse consciousnesses, repudiating the subjectivity of the single point of view. The apparent congruities set out in the book's titles (Waiting for Death, Three Love Problems, The Dead Hand, Two Temptations) disguises dissimilarities which take us beyond structure into function. In a world which no longer consisted of fixed species a struggle had begun to be manifest between external form and potential meaning: 'she was undergoing a metamorphosis', she writes of Dorothea, 'in which memory would not adjust itself to the stirring of new organs'. Relationships become the organising principle of all life and in *Middlemarch* this is emphasised in repudiation of any search for origins or even of succession. *Middlemarch* is a single work preoccupied with the 'web of affinities', setting out relations in a particular space and time. This allows a sense that everything is knowable and even that it may finally become known.

G. H. Lewes had some reservations about the universalist tendencies of Darwin's arguments on natural selection and the single progenitor. He wrote in 1868 to Darwin: 'While I think every unbiassed naturalist whose rational organs are not rudimentary must admit your principle, I am disposed to think that many organic details are the simple consequences of organic combination and are irrespective of advantage.' Lewes here seizes upon the implicitly purposive – or socialised – elements in Darwin's analysis. In the same way he perceives the implicitly theistic basis of the idea of the 'single progenitor'. In the discussion of the 'limitations of knowledge' in *Problems of Life and Mind* his own single acknowledged 'universal' was the invariability of a thing so long as the conditions which produce it are unaltered, and he decries 'the metempirical uniformity of Nature'. (6:39)

In the course of *Middlemarch* the reader similarly learns to be chary of any 'metempirical uniformity', whether of event, consequence, or feeling. Epistemologically, this experience is produced by means of the systematic laying alongside or collocation of apparently similar happenings. Equally, variation within the structure of personality is shown (as in the case of Rosamond) not to imply conversion or transformation. In the first paragraph of the Finale inconsistency is emphasised. The writing repudiates the favourite image of spun fabric – at least in its suggestion of evenness: 'For the fragment of a life, however typical, is not the sample of an even web: promises may not be kept, and an ardent outset may be followed by declension; latent powers may find their long-awaited opportunity; a past error may urge a grand retrieval' (3:455).

Declension and outcropping, the enactment or withering of potentialities, all take place in time, in the medium of history. The amplitude of the present is withered into summary past and in this work the reader is the medium of over-determination. The foreclosed future is held in the gap between the characters' time-experience and our surveying backward interpretation from the vantage point of forty years (or now, a hundred and fifty years). Patterns have become apparent, and have faded. The claims of 'growing good' are brought to the test. The setting alongside of our time and their time provides another control by means of which we recognise 'experimentally' common factors and divergences. The imagery of interconnection and of necessary sequence apparently conflicts with that of divergence and incongruity. But George Eliot – in common with other writers of the time – used a metaphor and a metaphoric form which could accommodate these conflicting models: *the web*, itself a product as much of strain and conflict as of supple interconnection.

III   THE WEB OF AFFINITIES

The two major and interconnected problems on which Darwin wrote which fascinated George Eliot were those of *relations* and of *origins*. These preoccupations control her late novels as both theme and structure. The interdependence of the two ideas is expressed in *The Origin of Species* in the metaphor of 'the inextricable web of affinities'. In his discussion of descent and morphology Darwin writes:

We can clearly see how it is that all living and extinct forms can be grouped together in one great system; and how the several members of each class are connected together by the most complex and radiating lines of affinities. We shall never, probably, disentangle the inextricable web of affinities between the members of any one class; but when we have a distinct object in view, and do not look to some unknown plan of creation, we may hope to make sure but slow progress. (415)

Darwin's metaphor is striking, not for its novelty, but because it combines in a peculiarly Victorian manner two models of 'the web' and adds a third, which further complicates the explanatory and imaginative possibilities of the image. 'The several members of each class are connected together by the most complex and radiating lines of affinities' – the spatial pattern suggests a spider's web. 'We shall never, probably, disentangle the inextricable web of affinities between the members of any one class' – the suggestion is now of woven fabric. There is also the further space-free suggestion of chemical affinities, unsettling the space-bound order of the web. But the degrees of relatedness suggest, further, the 'table of affinities' by which sexual relations between kin are tabooed and this introduction of the family connections needs further discussion.

For us now, the spider's web is probably the predominant association of the word 'web'. But for Victorian people, woven fabric seems to have been the predominant reference. Web imagery is to be found everywhere in Victorian writing. It is as common among scientists and philosophers as it is among poets and novelists. Mill wrote in the *System of Logic* that 'the regularity which exists in nature is a web composed of distinct threads', and G. H. Lewes in *Foundations of a Creed*:

Out of the general web of Existence certain threads may be detached and rewoven into a special group – the Subject – and this sentient group will in so far be different from the larger group, the Object; but whatever different arrangement the threads may take on, they are always threads of the original web, they are not different threads.[29]

The absence of transformation is important in both these citations. Threads remain themselves, though part of a total fabric. When Tyndall seeks expression for endless movement he achieves it through an implicit metaphor which draws simultaneously on the concepts of wave and web – the process of weaving is foregrounded here, rather than the achieved fabric.

Darkness might then be defined as ether at rest; light as ether in motion. But in reality the ether is never at rest, for in the absence of light-waves we have heat waves always speeding through it. In the spaces of the universe both classes of undulations incessantly commingle. Here the waves issuing from uncounted centres cross, coincide, oppose and pass through each other, without confusion or ultimate extinction. The waves from the zenith do not jostle out of existence those from the horizon, and every star is seen across the entanglement of wave motions produced by all other stars. [The waves of interstellar ether] mingle in space without disorder, each being endowed with an individuality as indestructible as if it alone had disturbed the universal repose.[30]

Spider, fabric, human tissue: Alexander Bain in *Mind and Body* describes the nerves thus: 'They are a set of silvery threads, or cords of various sizes, ramifying from centres to all parts of the body, including both sense surfaces and muscles.'[31] The webs of bodily order – veins, nerves, tissues – allow the metaphor of the web to move into the intimate ordering of life. Tissue and cloth are contiguous images. So are web and tree: 'threads . . . ramifying'. The web could intimate the 'milieu intérieur' – the relations within bodily and mental experience as much as the interconnections of society.

Hardy, for example, wrote in his diary on 4 March 1886: 'The human race to be shown as one great network or tissue which quivers in every part when one point is shaken, like a spider's web if touched.'

The web as woven cloth expressed also the process of coming to knowledge. Descartes had already used it as an image of heurism.[32] Tennyson's Lady of Shalott works on the reverse side of her weaving and sees the pattern gradually emerging only through the mirror, through which she also sees the world beyond. This narrative element in the image had a particular usefulness for George Eliot. The web exists not only as interconnection in space but as succession in time. This was the aspect of the image emphasised by Darwin in his genealogical ordering.

Several connections implicit in the Victorian apprehension of the image do not seem self-evident to us now. One is family and kin; the other is the idea of origins.

Robert Chambers quotes Herschel on bodies in space. Again 'true affinities' are distinguished from mere analogies by means of the web image (as in the Darwin passage already quoted). Herschel writes:

When we contemplate the constituents of the planetary system from the point of view which this relation affords us, it is no longer mere analogy which strikes us, no longer a general resemblance among them, as individuals independent of each other, and circulating about the sun, each according to its own peculiar nature, and connected with it by its own peculiar tie. The resemblance is now perceived to be a true *family likeness*; they are bound up in one chain – interwoven in one web of mutual relation and harmonious agreement.[33]

'One web of mutual relation': Herschel's space-ordered family becomes Darwin's sequences of descent. The suggestion of family harmony in Herschel's description is given a genetic actuality by Darwin. In his most developed and climactic discussion of classification the 'web of affinities' expresses equally the interconnections of kinship and the energies of descent. In the immediately preceding passage Darwin has called on the image of the tree: 'In a tree we can specify this or that branch', and on the image of family descent: 'the many descendants from one dominant parent-species'. 'I believe,' he writes, 'this element of descent is the hidden bond of connexion which naturalists have sought under the term of the Natural System.'

The web is a different shape from the chain, and this formal property of the image has great importance for Darwin: 'The several subordinate groups in any class *cannot be ranked in a single file*, but seem rather to be clustered round points' (171) (my italics). Sequence is so ramified and diversified, so devious, that it presents itself in the form of web or cycle rather than pure onward procedure.

Darwin twice elsewhere develops the image of 'entanglement' in relation to the web: 'Plants and animals, most remote in the scale of nature, are bound together by a web of complex relations.' In the next paragraph he writes: 'When we look at the plants and bushes clothing an entangled bank, we are tempted to attribute their proportional numbers and kinds to what we call chance.' But: 'What a struggle between the different kinds of trees' . . . 'what war between insect and insect' has brought about this proportioning? (125–6.) In Darwin's first passage on the 'entangled bank' confusion and struggle are emphasised, the claustrophobic interconnections of like and of unlike. When he takes up the image again in the Conclusion, profusion and harmonious contiguity replace conflict:

It is interesting to contemplate an entangled bank, clothed with many plants of many kinds, with birds singing on the bushes, with various insects flitting about, and with worms crawling through the damp earth, and to reflect that these elaborately constructed forms, so different from each other, and dependent on each other in so complex a manner, have all been produced by laws acting around us. (459)

The emphasis in these final affirmative pages is on the delicate richness and variety of life, on complex interdependency, ecological interpretation, weaving together an aesthetic fullness.

The cluster of common contiguous metaphors (tree, family, web, labyrinth) was given a new meaning by his theory. No single one of the metaphors was peculiar to Darwin. But in his argument the gap between metaphor and actuality was closed up, the fictive became substantive. Fictional insights were confirmed as physical event. The web is not a hierarchical model. It can express horizontality and extension, but it does not fix places, as on the rungs of a ladder or 'in single file'. Yet an important emphasis in the idea of the web is fixed patterns and achieved limits.[34] That tendency of the image is taken up by Darwin immediately after his description of 'the inextricable web of affinities' in his discussion of morphology:

What can be more curious than that the hand of a man, formed for grasping, that of a mole for digging, the leg of the horse, the paddle of the porpoise, and the wing of the bat, should all be constructed on the same pattern, and should include the same bones, in the same relative positions? (415)

Undeviating patterns and their diverse uses raise problems which are the novelist's province. George Eliot's awareness of the varying powers of the web image are expressed in the successive, and very diverse, references in chapter XV of *Middlemarch*. In the well-known passage that opens the chapter she compares her own practice with that of Fielding, the 'great historian, as he insisted on calling himself':

We belated historians must not linger after his example, I at least have so much to do in unravelling certain human lots, and seeing how they were woven and interwoven, that all the light I can command must be concentrated on this particular web, and not dispersed over that tempting range of relevancies called the universe. (1:15:214)

The web is not co-extensive with the universe. The weaver poring over the fabric needs a concentrated light. Indeed, (as in the round eye of the microscope) it is the light which concentrates and which creates an effect of wholeness.

Next the narrative alludes to the web of the human body and its contiguous image, the labyrinth, which will become of such importance later in *Middlemarch*. The connection of evolutionary theory and labyrinth was already established, for example, in an article by Julia Wedgwood (Darwin's niece)[35] in *Macmillan's Magazine* in 1861. We read:

> The infinitude of small deviations from the parent type . . . may be regarded as a labyrinth laid out by the hands of the Creator, through which he furnishes a clue to a higher state of being, in the principle which rewards every step in the right direction.

The *Middlemarch* passage describes the awakening of Lydgate's scientific interests:

> The page he opened on was under the heading of Anatomy, and the first passage that drew his eyes was on the valves of the heart. He was not much acquainted with valves of any sort, but he knew that *valvae* were folding-doors, and through this crevice came a sudden light startling him with his first vivid notion of finely-adjusted mechanism in the human frame. A liberal education had of course left him free to read the indecent passages in the school classics, but beyond a general sense of secrecy and obscenity in connection with his internal structure, had left his imagination quite unbiassed, so that for anything he knew his brains lay in small bags at his temples, and he had no more thought of representing to himself how his blood circulated than how paper served instead of gold. But the moment of vocation had come, and before he got down from his chair, the world was made new to him by a presentiment of endless processes filling the vast spaces planked out of his sight by that wordy ignorance which he had supposed to be knowledge. From that hour Lydgate felt the growth of an intellectual passion. (1:15:217–18)

The 'presentiment of endless processes filling the vast spaces', the circulation of the blood, the *valvae* through which 'a sudden light comes', all these interpenetrating metaphors express the process of coming to knowledge. And the imagery reaches its issue in the concept of 'primary webs or tissues' which Bichat has established (1:15:128). Lydgate's speculation adds to the consideration of tissues the question, again, of origins: 'some common basis' of 'the raw cocoon'.

> Of this sequence to Bichat's work, already vibrating along many currents of the European mind, Lydgate was enamoured; he longed to demonstrate the more intimate relations of living structure and help to define men's thought more accurately after the true order . . . What was the primitive tissue? In that way Lydgate put the question – not quite in the way required by the awaiting answer; but such missing of the right word befalls many seekers. (1:15:225)

The various threads from which are woven 'sarsnet, gauze, net, satin, and velvet' have one basis. The image of the spider's web stirs again in 'the vibration along many currents'. Lydgate's work is to demonstrate 'the more intimate relations of living structure'. Relations, and origins, are both implicit in the one metaphor. This organisation is taken over into that of the book itself, so that its enterprise is preoccupied both with morphological likeness and with variation.

In *Middlemarch* George Eliot seeks out ways beyond the single consciousness. She creates a sense of inclusiveness and extension. Nothing is end-stopped. Multiplicity is developed through the open relation created between narrator and reader, through participation in the immanent worlds of others and through the unlimited worlds of ideas. When she uses the image of the microscope in *Middlemarch* there is no suggestion of condescension to ways of being more minute in scale: rather there is a recognition of the multiple unseen worlds by which we are surrounded and which new methods of perception may reveal without reducing the mystery inherent in the fact of multiplicity. Simultaneity of experiences is the equivalent in the novelist's art, and *Middlemarch* is enriched by a sense of multiple latent relations which are permitted to remain latent.

Significant repetition and variation is an essential principle in the structure of *Middlemarch*. Science and mythology create within the work ways beyond the single into a shared, anonymous, and therefore more deeply creative knowledge. Myth, in particular, offers the continuity of collective insight against the anomie of the solitary perceiver. It is with the uses of myth as a means of enriching the concept of 'relations' that I shall be chiefly concerned in the argument that follows.

Middlemarch the book is something different from Middlemarch the town. It is worth emphasising this simple primary distinction because the inhabitants of Middlemarch within the book are so confident that Middlemarch is not only in the Midlands but in the Middle of the world; the book's expansiveness creates an effect of size for the town, so that Paris, Rome, and London look thin and small by comparison. But we as readers are made also to recognise its mediocrity. George Eliot, or Marian Evans, after all, escaped from Middlemarch. The narrator's business in the novel is to remind us of worlds intellectual, aesthetic, spiritual, which do not naturally flourish in the provinces. Not only the individual selves but the collective social self of Middlemarch is framed and placed. She creates a double time within the novel – the 'now' of herself and her first readers and the 'now-then' of the late 1820s. The intellectual concerns of the people and period within the novel are carefully dated and set in relation to her own time. This relation is often ironic, as in her treatment of the Reform Bill, sometimes prophetic, as in the imagery drawn from the development of the microscope, and occasionally a fusing of the values of several times, as in the opening sentence of chapter 1 which makes of Dorothea a genuinely pre-Raphaelite Madonna.

The typical concern of the intellectual characters in the book is with visions of unity, but a unity which seeks to resolve the extraordinary diversities of the world back into a single answer: the key to all mythologies, the primitive tissue, allegorical painting (Ladislaw mocks Naumann: 'I do *not* think that all the universe is straining towards the obscure significance of your pictures' (1:19:290). Casaubon and Dorothea, for different reasons, are distressed by the miscellaneity of Rome, where the remains of different cultures are all topographically jostling each other, apparently without hierarchy of meaning:

She had been led through the best galleries, had been taken to the chief points of view, had been shown the grandest ruins and the most glorious churches, and she had ended by oftenest choosing to drive out to the Campagna where she could feel alone with the earth and sky, away from the oppressive masquerade of ages, in which her own life too seemed to become a masque with enigmatical costumes. (1:20:295)

Much later in the book, at the great crisis of her life, that earth and sky are peopled in the dawn with impersonal permanent figures, characteristic of human destiny in their ordinariness and their mystery: 'On the road there was a man with a bundle on his back and a woman carrying her baby; in the field she could see figures moving – perhaps the shepherd with his dog' (3:80:392). In that image of the family (though we are not certain that it is a family) and of the possible shepherd there are echoes of Christian mythology – but it is here diffused and brought down to earth. These are valuable figures because, simply, they are human figures each pursuing their own concerns: 'she felt the largeness of the world and the manifold wakings of men to labour and endurance'. The numinous must express itself in this book solely through the human.

Myths – the religious and proto-scientific perceptions of differing cultures – survive because they tell stories about human or quasi-human figures which satisfy the need for recurrence. Cultures are defined by their myths but myths outlive the culture which produced them. Casaubon's dry collation of myth, arranged according to the authenticity of their 'period', is set against George Eliot's own rich, manifold, free-ranging invocation of diverse mythologies within the book. Casaubon cannot accept the protean nature of myth because renewal and embodiment are beyond his imaginative grasp. Dorothea may be a poem to Ladislaw; she is never, in any sense, myth to Casaubon.

Casaubon is in a sense judged by myth. (The original bearer of his name, the seventeenth-century Casaubon, had written a treatise *against* John Dee, the Elizabethan necromantic scientist who believed he had discovered the key to the universe.) The acquisitive sensibility tabulates, collects, and reduces; the creative sensibility has the responsibility not only of perceiving but of making connections. In Dorothea knowledge and feeling actively generate each other. So she can learn; he must withdraw from learning. We see this particularly clearly in their attitude to art and Christian legend.

Instead of the desolate privacy of the Romantic ego, or the moral types of neo-classicism, George Eliot is seeking communal insights. In *Middlemarch* the narrator weaves into commentary, dialogue, and metaphor, allusions to a great number of mythological systems: classical myth, folk-tale and theatre, Troubadour romance and courtly love, the Arabian Nights, hagiography, mythography, the Brothers Grimm's collections, Christian legend and martyrology. Most of them are unemphatically placed, not seeming to demand a contextual alertness from the reader. But if we explore the context the allusions always yield insights into the accord between any individual's experience and the lived world of remote others.

So, for example, a little earlier in the scene between Ladislaw and Dorothea where he tells her that she is a poem, he has accused her of wanting to be a martyr:

I suspect that you have some false belief in the virtues of misery, and want to make your life a martyrdom . . . You talk as if you had never known any youth. It is monstrous – as if you had had a vision of Hades in your childhood, like the boy in the legend. You have been brought up in some of those horrible notions that choose the sweetest woman to devour – like Minotaurs. (1:22:336–7)

Ladislaw's verbal energy readily shifts dead metaphor into myth: (monstrous becomes Minotaur). The labyrinth of ideas and beliefs harbours monsters. Before pursuing the Minotaur, however, that other, less familiar, allusion is worth pondering. Who was the boy in the legend? and how does he relate to the idea of martyrdom? The answer seems to be that he was Anskar, a ninth-century missionary to Scandinavia, whose boyhood vision was a promise of his own eventual martyrdom. In the event, he died in his bed, finally full of faith in God's purpose: his martyrdom was *not to be a martyr*.[36] This curiously Jamesian tale lies buried beneath that allusion of Ladislaw's. Its beautiful appropriateness to Dorothea's problems and fate is complete but latent. It is an extraordinary example of the 'inextricable web of affinities' recorded in *Middlemarch* and of the labyrinthine sub-text of allusions which are never brought to the surface.

George Eliot uses diverse mythological structures simultaneously; in particular the lives of the saints and classical myth. She was indebted particularly to Anna Jameson for her full realisation of the value of 'Christian legends or fairy tales'. George Eliot knew Mrs Jameson personally. She used her *Legends of the Monastic Orders* (1850) and *Legends of the Madonna* (1852) while she was writing *Romola*. And *Sacred and Legendary Art* (1848) has particular significance for *Middlemarch*. Anna Jameson's main contention in that book is that in the mythology of the saints we have a visual and symbolic system equivalent in complexity and in intensity to classical myth. She contrasts the knowledge of classical myth with the general ignorance of the symbolism of medieval Christian legend in a way likely to discomfit the modern reader:

Who ever confounds Venus with a Minerva, or a Vestal with an Amazon; or would endure an undraped Juno, or a beardless Jupiter? . . . but . . . We learn to know St Francis by his brown habit and shaven crown and wasted ardent features: but how do we distinguish him from St Anthony, or St Dominick?[37]

George Eliot takes up Mrs Jameson's point quite directly at the beginning of chapter 19 where she is discussing the coming of Romanticism and the deliberately religious, symbolic art of the Nazarenes (whom many art-historians see as the precursors of the Pre-Raphaelite movement).

Travellers did not often carry full information on Christian art either in their heads or their pockets; and even the most brilliant English critic of the day [Hazlitt] mistook the flower-flushed tomb of the ascended Virgin for an ornamental vase due to the painter's fancy. (1:19:287)

She expects her readers of the 1870s to register the start of a movement which opened a system of symbolism vital to the sensibility of their own time. What seems decorative and discrete to the ignorant eye is part of a far-ranging, implicit system of meaning: that had been Mrs Jameson's central point too.

In the very next paragraph George Eliot presents 'a young man whose hair . . . was abundant and curly . . . who had just turned his back on the Belvedere Torso in the Vatican'. The Apollonian figure is, of course, Will Ladislaw. Then, beside 'the reclining Ariadne, then called the Cleopatra', the two men see 'a breathing, blooming girl whose form, not shamed by the Ariadne, was clad in Quakerish grey drapery . . .' (1:19:288). In the description of Dorothea the double-time system enters: the knowledge that the figure is Ariadne, who can offer a means of disentangling the labyrinth, is historically beyond the reach of the characters, but is invoked by George Eliot as part of the shared world-knowledge of herself and her reader. Ladislaw, the bringer of cultural tidings, as so often, is given a midway status; it is he who two chapters later brings into the open the idea of Dorothea 'brought up in some of the horrible notions that choose the sweetest women to devour – like Minotaurs'. To Naumann she is 'antique form animated by Christian sentiment – a sort of Christian Antigone – sensuous force controlled by spiritual passion' (1:19:290). But if she is related in terms of classical myth to Ariadne she is also Dorothea. She cannot become a St Theresa. Who then was St Dorothea? The answer is to be found in the second volume of Mrs Jameson's work. St Dorothea was both a martyr and a spiritual bride.

She was then led forth to death; and, as she went, a young man, a lawyer of the city named Theophilus, who had been present when she was first brought before the governor, called to her mockingly: 'Ha! fair maiden, goest thou to join thy bridegroom? Send me, I pray thee, of the fruits and flowers of that same garden of which thou hast spoken: I would fain taste of them!' And Dorothea looking on him inclined her head with a gentle smile, and said: 'Thy request, O Theophilus, is granted!' Whereat he laughed aloud with his companions; but she went on cheerfully to death. When she came to the place of execution, she knelt down and prayed: and suddenly appeared at her side a beautiful boy, with hair bright as sunbeams:

A smooth-faced glorious thing,
With thousand blessings dancing in his eyes.

In his hand he held a basket containing three apples, and three fresh-gathered and fragrant roses. She said to him: 'Carry these to Theophilus; say that Dorothea hath sent them, and that I go before him to the garden whence they came, and await him there.' With these words she bent her neck and received the death-stroke.

Meantime the angel (for it was an angel) went to seek Theophilus; and found him still laughing in merry mood over the idea of the promised gift. The angel placed before him the basket of celestial fruit and flowers, saying: 'Dorothea sends thee this,' and vanished. What words can express the wonder of Theophilus?[38]

The 'beautiful boy, with hair bright as sunbeams,' bringer of fruit and flowers, seems a familiar figure. Within the novel Ladislaw fitfully appropriates images of sunlight, issuing perhaps not only from Apollo but from St Dorothea's 'smooth-faced glorious' angel. Müller's solar myth and Jameson's saint's tale reinforce Ladislaw's sunny brightness, the little ripple in his nose which is a preparation for metamorphosis. The way his hair seems to shake out light is set in contrast (perhaps too easy contrast) with the Saturnian presence of Mr Casaubon, even with Casaubon's own idealised description of himself at the beginning of the book: 'My mind is something like the ghost of an ancient, wandering about the world and trying mentally to construct it as it used to be, in spite of ruin and confusing changes' (1:2:23).

These fugitive references give no guarantees of human perfection, but they do enlarge the scale of reference for the fallible present-day which Ladislaw represents. Casaubon cannot grasp the ongoing nature of experience, or of knowledge. Imprisoned in his tractate on the Egyptian mysteries, he is incapable of perceiving any relation between the present world and his work. Not only is he ignorant of German scholarship on mythology (which would include the Brothers Grimm's work on folk myth as well as on linguistics), but he is ignorant of the significance of Christian iconography:

Dorothea felt that she was getting quite new notions as to the significance of Madonnas seated under inexplicable canopied thrones with the simple country as a background, and of saints with architectural models in their hands, or knives accidentally wedged in their skulls. Some things which had seemed monstrous to her were gathering intelligibility and even a natural meaning; but all this was apparently a branch of knowledge in which Mr Casaubon had not interested himself. (1:22:327–8)

The suggestion is that he thinks it beneath his attention, just as, in a poignant passage, he dismisses the Cupid and Psyche myth as a 'fable . . . probably the romantic invention of a literary period', which 'cannot, I think, be reckoned as a genuine mythical product' (1:20:302). The beating of wings, the castle of Amor, night flesh, the travails of Psyche to come again to Love – all these lie outside his imaginative experience. He tabulates; he does not inhabit myth. His method is acquisitive, not radiating. He sees 'the world's ages as a set of box-like partitions without vital connection' (1:22:325). He is disquieted by the multiplicity of myth: the ways in which differing systems refract meaning at diverse angles, the sense of revelation and yet of incomplete relevance which George Eliot herself explores in her suffusing of experience with mythical analogues, analogues which emphasise variability while accepting the morphological 'Soul' of common patterns.

In contrast to the scientific or artistic imagination which is capable ultimately of 'bathing even the ethereal atoms in its ideally illuminated space' Mr Casaubon has lost the sense of mystery which for George Eliot lies in connections and relations. 'Lost among small closets and winding stairs' he cannot recognise the Ariadne who could deliver him out into sunlight. In his 'bitter manuscript remarks on other men's notions about the solar deities, he had become indifferent to the sunlight' (1:20:303).

At the beginning of the 1870s Max Müller's interpretation of myth in terms of solar symbolism was the dominant intellectual reading. George Eliot invokes the system herself within the novel in her treatment of Ladislaw and in the hindsight knowledge with which she judges Casaubon, but she does not allow it to dominate her created world. The scientific imagery ranges far forward beyond any research that Lydgate succeeds in accomplishing. The variety of myth and legend within the book embraces a free-ranging lateral world of meaning beyond Mr Casaubon's awareness. Most important of all, she uses these immanent worlds to indicate that any single interpretation of experience will mislead. The self, to be valid, must stand as pars pro toto. The single focus contains; the one candle makes for introspective vision.

Your pier-glass or extensive surface of polished steel made to be rubbed by a house-maid, will be minutely and multitudinously scratched in all directions; but place now against it a lighted candle as a centre of illumination, and lo! the scratches will seem to arrange themselves in a fine series of concentric circles round that little sun. It is demonstrable that the scratches are going everywhere impartially, and it is only your candle which produces the flattering illusion of a concentric arrangement, its light falling with an exclusive optical selection. These things are a parable. (1:27:403)

The maze is what matters. The recurrent imagery of the web suggests simultaneously entanglement and creative order – and beyond them both, the web of human veins and tissues: human being.

The labyrinth, the web, the tree, the microscope: the contiguity of these concepts is significant for *Middlemarch*. But George Eliot needs also a sense of disparity and unrelatedness which cannot be expressed by any of these means. Much earlier, in a letter, she had used the web as an image of impassive uniformity and unvarying process from which she needed to escape: 'If one is to have the freedom to write out of one's own varying unfolding self, and not to be a machine always grinding out the same material or spinning the same sort of web, one cannot always write for the same public.'[39] In the Finale to *Middlemarch* the writing repudiates the evenness of spun fabric as a sufficient image of the potentialities of human life: 'the fragment of a life, however typical, is not the sample of an even web'.

The web is not co-terminous with life: it is not, either, identical with organicism. The shears as well as the spinning haunt the metaphor from its oldest use. In this final section of her book the imagery of the web is hauntingly suggested but never reconstituted. At the beginning of the final paragraph its powers are fugitively recollected and then given up:

Her finely-touched spirit had still its fine issues, though they were not widely visible. Her full nature, like that river of which Cyrus broke the strength, spent itself in channels which had no great name on the earth. (3: Finale: 465)

'Finely-touched' suggests the tremor of a spider's web as well as of musical instrument, and that parallelism of 'finely-touched', 'fine issues', with the four insistent preceding 't's just stirs the suggestion of 'tissues' to extend the parallelism. Then the image changes to that of the nameless river, spent in many channels: the irrigating version of the labyrinth.

CHAPTER 6

George Eliot: Daniel Deronda *and the idea of a future life*

Daniel Deronda is a novel haunted by the future, that purest and most taxing realm of fiction. For the first time in George Eliot's work the dependence of the future on the past is brought into question. Earlier in her career she had found a meta-religious security in the 'great concept of universal sequence', 'the gradual reduction of all phenomena within the sphere of established law, which carries as a consequence the rejection of the miraculous'.[1] Causal sequence had been the organising principle both of her morality and of her practice as a novelist.

In *Daniel Deronda* causal sequence is disturbed and pressed upon by resurgence, synchronicity, the miraculous, the hermeneutic, and by unassuageable human need. In the uniformitarian ordering of *Middlemarch* events, however seemingly catastrophic, are prepared for by the slight incipient movements, crumblings, pressures, erosions, and siltages observable to an immeasurably patient eye, whether it be that of Uriel in the sun 'watching the progress of planetary history' (as she writes in *Middlemarch*) or that of the novelist exempted from the partiality and subjectivity of her personages. The outcome, though melancholy in tone, is reassuring to the reader in that it creates an infinitely knowable world. Our discoveries keep pace with the increasing insight into relations and connections that the work offers us – though the sequences of *Middlemarch* do not share that optimistic sense of a development preparing for man's betterment which we remember from her earliest essays: 'Every past phase of human development is part of that education of the race in which we are sharing; every mistake, every absurdity into which poor human nature has fallen, may be looked on as an experiment of which we may reap the benefit.' The progressive nature of experimental discovery is assumed in that metaphor of 1851 where she goes on to a specifically geological image: 'A correct generalization gives significance to the smallest detail, just as the great inductions of

169

geology demonstrate in every pebble the working of laws by which the earth has become adapted for the habitation of man.'[2]

In *Middlemarch* generalisation still comforts, both because it increases significance and because it sets bounds. The book's organisation emphasises congruity as well as variability among the characters. Sequence and analogy enrich our sense of the kinship of human lots even while they register what constricts and determines.[3] As a result the book is ramifying, but not entropic: there is no sense of chaos nor of redundancy. All noise may be retrieved as information.

In *Daniel Deronda* descent and extension are the ordering principles – and simultaneously its unsolvable problems. The publication of Darwin's *The Descent of Man and Selection in Relation to Sex* in 1871 shifted the focus of evolutionary debate on to man's specific inheritance and future. Darwin set out the objects of his work as being 'to consider, firstly, whether man, like every other species, is descended from some pre-existing form; secondly, the manner of his development; and thirdly, the value of the differences between the so-called races of man'.[4] Descent, development, and race are central to *Daniel Deronda*. Sexual selection and the socio-economic elements in genetic choice are part of the book's polemic –

> 1st. Gent. What women should be? Sir, consult the taste
> Of marriageable men. This planet's store
> In iron, cotton, wool, or chemicals –
> All matter rendered to our plastic skill,
> Is wrought in shapes responsive to demand:
> The market's pulse makes index high or low,
> By rule sublime. Our daughters must be wives,
> And to be wives must be what men will choose:
> Men's taste is women's test. You mark the phrase?
> 'Tis good, I think? – the sense well winged and poised
> With t's and s's.
>
> (Epigraph to chapter 10)[5]

The constraints on sexual selection were part of Darwin's polemic, too. He cites approvingly the 'Grecian poet, Theognis' of 550 BC who saw 'that wealth often checks the proper action of sexual selection' and quotes John Hookham Frere's translation:

> But in the daily matches that we make,
> The price is everything: for money's sake,
> Men marry: women are in marriage given . . . [6]

This topic of the marriage market they share also with novelists from Richardson's *Clarissa* on, but in *Daniel Deronda* questions of pairing and of relations between the sexes do not have an exclusively genetic or eugenic meaning: 'I am not sure that I want to be an ancestor,' said Deronda, 'It doesn't seem to me the rarest sort of origination' (1:15:242).

George Eliot's first original work was to have been a book entitled *The Idea of a Future Life.*[7] The book remained unwritten. But its concerns were never abandoned, although the solution of individual immortality was very early given up. Discussing Butler's *Analogy* in 1842 she remarks with a mixture of asperity and nostalgia:

It is no small sacrifice to part with the assurance that life and immortality have been brought to light, and to be reduced to the condition of the great spirits of old who looked yearningly to the horizon of their earthly career wondering what lay beyond: but I cannot think the conviction that immortality is man's destiny indispensable to the production of elevated and heroic virtue and the sublimest resignation.

Earlier still, she had been deeply impressed by Isaac Taylor's *The Physical Theory of Another Life* (1836), which granted her a paroxysm of escape: 'the rapture this precious book caused me, as intense as that of any school girl over her first novel'.[8] The images of reconcilement, individual expansion and knowledge which Taylor offered, gave her an ecstatic experience of enfranchisement like that of first entry into fiction. Indeed 'the future Life' is the absolute form of fiction, whether it be the idea of personal immortality or the hypothetical, multiple predictions of daily life, or that sense of futurity intensified by evolutionary theory which is preoccupied with the future of life on this earth.

The book on 'the further life' would always have been premature, since the topic continued to preoccupy George Eliot throughout her working life and found its intensest form in *Daniel Deronda*. While she was at work directly on 'the future life', one of the first books she read was William Warburton's *The Divine Legation of Moses Demonstrated on the Principles of a Religious Deist, from the Omission of the Doctrine of a Future State of Rewards and Punishments in the Jewish Dispensation* (1738–41).[9]

Her loss of belief in *individual* survival perhaps intensified her fascination with survival and development for the race, the culture, and for mind. The evolution of mind was a typical preoccupation of the 1870s in particular. The idea of the future life for George Eliot was very early secularised. As a result, concepts of descent, of necessary sequence (the particular working out of general laws), of change and transformation on this earth (within individuals as well as through the succession of cultures) all had an acute emotional and intellectual force. Moreover, the problem of the future of the earth itself – its survival or decay – was much under discussion among astronomers and physicists of the period.

But there was another kind of futurity which pressed hard upon the working novelist. As always for George Eliot, technical problems are deeply intermelded with emotional and moral problems and charged with the same intellectual intensity. The problem which presented itself with compelling complexity was that of the future within a fiction. George Henry Lewes said of the process of evolution that 'it makes the implicit explicit'. Equally, it revealed the manifold potentialities of the world, not all of which could be realised. The double emphasis on transformation and on redundancy – on sequences of development and accretion alongside possibilities lost, energies wasting away – foregrounded the future. At the same time, evolutionary theory brought with it a sense of being responsible for the shaping of the future, which was celebrated in Francis Galton's work and could express itself as eugenics, as social planning.[10] Darwin's latter emphasis on sexual selection meant that a new shaping influence was accorded to ideas and values, the action of the individual or communal will, as opposed to the apparent randomness of natural selection. In the controversy on 'plurality of worlds' – an argument which had been significant since the seventeenth century – the question was again brought to the fore: is the future life *in the future*? The question of multiple inhabitable worlds, which was given a cosmic scale by Fontanelle, could also be realised as a question of individual identities.[11] There was a clear answer to the question 'Are we the only ones?' when applied to multiple individual experience: 'No'. In her late work, as we have seen in *Middlemarch*, George Eliot became increasingly fascinated with synchronicity and plurality.

The novel as a form is particularly dependent on the future for its pleasures. The reader reads *on*. Only a few novels (for example, Marquez's *Autumn of the Patriarch*) risk the saturating pleasures of endless replication and textual expansion. The novel in general relies upon the drive of anxiety and hope, on the pleasures of prediction and hypothesis. Yet within the text the future is covertly converted into retrospect. The future we are about to read has already been inscribed by author and experienced by characters. Language is reified as book. In George Eliot's work, up to and including *Middlemarch*, retrospect was made to be a part of the book's topic. The idea of the future foregrounds the insufficiency of determinism. We cannot fully know, nor groundedly predict. The present and the past together do not form a sufficient authority: interpretation is always baulked of certainty. The problem that George Eliot faced (particularly acute as a result of her earlier closeness to positivism and her persisting acceptance of determinism) was this: how to liberate the future into its proper and powerful state of indeterminacy and yet make it part of the story.

The future is, properly, *indescribable*, but in novels it tends to be implicitly under control, because contained within the book's compass. Yet it is also clear that past and future are not 'box-like partitions': coming to *know* is the point of conversion at which other people's pasts may become our future. In *Daniel Deronda* past and future are dubiously intercalated: the order of telling and the order of experience are confused and can never thoroughly be rearranged. The work brings to the centre of our attention the idea of a future life.

In all George Eliot's previous novels time is end-stopped. The future is suggested through progeny. We have the genre-painting image of Dinah, Adam, and their children outside the cottage door at the end of *Adam Bede*, Tessa's children in *Romola*, Dorothea's more mistily suggested in *Middlemarch*. At the end of *Daniel Deronda* no new generation has been born. Daniel has been incarnated as Mordecai's dream successor, a succession and progeny of race and culture. Gwendolen is childless. In *Middlemarch* the emphasis was upon the power of life continuing beyond the individual. For the individual the renunciation of *will*, of brooding and determined control over events, is hard and inevitable. This expresses itself thematically in a fascination with Wills and bequests – those frail and often stultifying attempts to subdue the future to our purposes. Casaubon and Featherstone callouse the future with the grip of their dead hands. But inevitably their attempts fail because they cannot encompass all the future's multiformity.

The action of the will and of sexual selection become major topics in George Eliot's late work. So does the idea of prediction. 'Prediction' was a preoccupation among scientific writers in the 1870s. W. K. Clifford in 'Of the Aims and Instruments of Scientific Thought', his address to the British Association in 1872, emphasised prediction and the extent to which we can rely on past uniformities. Clifford says that all new reasoning in the sciences, from biology to sociology, must rely on the scientific law of evolution. But he claims that 'We have no right to conclude . . . that the order of events is always capable of being explained.'[12]

In *Daniel Deronda* cause and effect and prediction are brought into the focus of our attention. There is no longer (as in her earlier work) a critical, unwritten gap of time between material and author. The period of George Eliot's own adult life is significantly absent from her previous novels, but in this work she re-enters history without the melancholy safety of hindsight. *Daniel Deronda* is set in the near present; there is no reserved space for the knowing reader. Determinism is no longer confirmed by a stably retrospective structure.

The work brings into question the sufficiency of *descent* as an ordering of experience. So descent is no longer implied in that primary reader/text relationship, as it had earlier been in *Middlemarch*. We are granted no privileged vantage point in history. This is a different kind of 'Experiment in time' from that of *Middlemarch*: 'even strictly-measuring Science could hardly have got on without that forecasting ardour which feels the agitations of discovery beforehand, and has a faith in its preconception that surmounts many failures of experiment' (2:41:358).

In a passage which George Eliot quotes in her Notebook 707 from Comte he speaks, somewhat unexpectedly, of 'the illusion of causality'. Much of *Daniel Deronda*'s activity is spent in establishing new relations between apparent causes and apparent effects. George Eliot never lost her sense of the unstayable quality of deeds. They travel like sound waves. But here she explores also the influence of the unperformed: the impulse given no expression, the sealed thought, the sequestered passion. Do these undischarged, half-conscious forces shape the future too? Fantasies create lateral empires or prisons for the self-existences insistently present, though unacted. And our conjectures about the uncommunicated life of others – our acts of interpretation or surmise – become a part of our own future behaviour. 'No chemical process shows a more wonderful activity than the transforming influence of the thoughts we imagine to be going on in another' (2:35:222).

The book abounds in questions, and the interrogative is the form of speech which most invokes the future. Indeed questions require the future – the satisfactions of reply – if they are to accomplish a completed sense. Questions breed suppositions, possibilities, the sense of imminent change. Interpretation and forecasting are activities in which (without habitually bringing the activity to consciousness) we spend much of our waking lives. In this book not only the characters but the readers are forced into a preternaturally heightened awareness of our habitual dependency on prophecy. Certain words (and others like them) occur persistently: prediction, presentiment, forecasting, preparation, foreboding, foretaste, provision, prevision, anxiety, 'phantom of the future', 'ugly visions', hints, conjecture, calculation, dread.

In *Middlemarch* the reader is constantly guided through a historicised and interpreted world in which cause and effect are clearly discriminated and set in succession, in which likeness and unlikeness are laid alongside each other for our sympathetic yet authoritative survey, and in which everything is presented finally as knowable and explicable. *Daniel Deronda* sets us in a vertiginous relationship to the future. Causes can no longer be authoritatively ascribed to events: multiple possibility and prediction are offered within the text and very frequently we are more jostled by possibilities than invited to select. The sense of the unknowable is very strong. It is there in the ellipses of time, in the spaces between chapters which disjoin continuities instead of knitting them up, and in the lack of information, for example, about Grandcourt's past. Presentiment, prolepsis, the phenomenological unwary leaps of consciousness from one expected result to another are replicated in the reader. The moment-by-moment activities of confirmation and disconfirmation in which our minds habitually seethe and select are here brought to the level of consciousness and contemplation. The reader must feed the book's occluded images of evil with his own dreads, rather as he must do in Coleridge's unfinished *Christabel*. George Eliot is no longer writing an autonomous novel which includes its own origin and conclusion and thereby stabilises them.[13] There is a vertiginous alternation between synchronicity and sequence and the one cannot readily be distinguished from the other.

Much of the book is preoccupied with thoughts – passionate thoughts which can for the most part find no pathway into action. Here the biological model of generation and incarnation presents only a partial answer. In this clandestine mental world of sequestered experience analogies with physics, astronomy and acoustics mean most. In her notebook 711 she quotes from Clerk Maxwell's address to the Mathematics and Physics section of the 1870 British Association for the Advancement of Science meeting:

Ring vortices – : If a whirling ring be once generated in uniform, frictionless incompressible fluid, *it will go on for ever, always consisting of the same portions of the fluid first set going*, & because its elasticity causes it to rebound when touched, it could never be divided nor destroyed.[14] (f. 67)

The idea of endlessness, the *absence* of transformation, is a severe emotional and intellectual strain in this work.

Daniel Deronda opens with an epigraph which places the fictions of science alongside those of poetry and emphasises the insufficiency of each. The paragraph initiates the novel by questioning the concept of beginning even as it enacts it: 'Men can do nothing without the make-believe of a beginning.' Are beginnings to be identified with origins? Is it possible to search out the primal repose of the original? Is there a necessary connection between the idea of the source and the idea of development – or is this habitual connection itself ideological and polemical? These are some of the questions which the process of the book will enregister and which are implicit in the language of these first statements. These questions were crucial throughout the 1870s, deriving much of their emotional and intellectual saliency from Darwin's ideas and the responses they aroused.

Men can do nothing without the make-believe of a beginning. Even Science, the strict measurer, is obliged to start with a make-believe unit, and must fix on a point in the stars' unceasing journey when his sidereal clock shall pretend that time is at Nought. His less accurate grandmother Poetry has always been understood to start in the middle; but on reflection it appears that her proceeding is not very different from his: since Science, too, reckons backwards as well as forwards, divides his unit into billions, and with his clock-finger at Nought really sets off *in medias res*. No retrospect will take us to the true beginning; and whether our prologue be in heaven or on earth, it is but a fraction of that all-presupposing fact with which our story sets out. (Epigraph)

In December 1874 R. A. Proctor published an essay on 'The Past and Future of Our Earth' in *The Contemporary Review* in which, through primarily astronomical and evolutionist evidence, he considered the probable beginnings of the world and its future.[15] George Eliot had already read and made notes from Proctor's earlier article 'Gambling Superstitions' and used ideas and information from it in the opening scene of the novel. Her epigraph shows clearly that she had read and absorbed the implications of this second article. Proctor points out that Science 'shows us that there can be no conceivable limits to space or time' and 'in so far as she presents personal infinity to us at all, presents it as an inconceivable, like . . . other inconceivable infinities'. Though 'so far as Science is concerned, the idea of a personal God is inconceivable', yet 'Science no more disproves the existence of infinite personal power or wisdom than she disproves the existence of infinite material energy (which on the contrary must be regarded as probable) or the existence of infinite space or time (which must be regarded as certain)' (74–5).

Proctor goes on to discuss the origin of the solar system and its 'process of evolution'. At every stage his argument emphasises the illimitable vastness of past and future; in discussing the stages through which the solar system must have passed, he ends by saying that we reach the point where 'speculation helps us as little as it does in attempting to trace the evolution of living creatures across the gap which separates the earliest forms of life from the beginning itself of life upon the earth' . . . 'we cannot hope to determine the real beginning of this earth's history' (76). This was Darwin's point.

His essay concludes:

It has been said that progression necessarily implies a beginning and an end; but this is not so where the progression relates to absolute space or time . . . Progression implies only relative beginning and relative ending . . . The end, seemingly so remote, to which our earth is tending, the end infinitely more remote to which the solar system is tending, the end of our galaxy, the end of systems of such galaxies as ours – all these endings (each one of which presents itself in turn to our conceptions as the end of the universe itself) are but the beginnings of eras comparable with themselves, even as the beginnings to which we severally trace back the history of our planet, of the planetary system, and of galaxies of such systems, are but the endings of prior conditions which have followed each other in infinite succession. (91–2)

Daniel Deronda shares some of the preoccupations of George Eliot's notebook 707 where, for example, she summarises material from C. D. Ginsburg's *The Kabbalah* (1865): 'Many primordial worlds destroyed, not containing the human form until the present world created' (f. 19), and annotates Comte's account of the 'Influence of the various stages of astronomy on the development of thought' (f. 75) as well as discussing the development and possible thermal death of our solar system. 'Men, like planets, have both a visible and an invisible history', she writes later in *Daniel Deronda*.

Proctor emphasises that the 'real beginning' is irrecoverable: 'no retrospect will take us to the true beginning' (Epigraph). In her initiating epigraph George Eliot parallels in an allusive and condensed form his emphasis upon the relativism of beginnings and endings, their ways of becoming each other. She suggests that Science must start 'with a make-believe unit' and Science's 'less accurate grandmother Poetry has always been understood to start in the middle'.

Claude Bernard remarked that

possessing absolute truth matters little to the man of science, so long as he is certain about the relations of phenomena to one another. Indeed, our mind is so limited that we can know neither the beginning nor the end of things; but we can grasp the middle, i.e., what surrounds us closely.[16]

Bernard's formulation emphasises both time and space: 'what surrounds us closely'. We are 'in medias res' but this does not endow us with the power of interpreting or knowing absolutely. The literary concept of 'in medias res', however, assumes centrality for the subject. The subject is placed at the fullest point, over which is described the arc of the past into the future. By locating itself 'in medias res' the subject can encompass its own antecedents and enact its own futurity. But George Eliot's epigraph makes it clear that we cannot sufficiently imply either past or future. All that can be recuperated is 'make-believe', a pretence that time is 'at Nought', a philosophy of 'as if'.[17] In *The Act of Reading* Iser remarks: 'For all the given material that goes to make up a mental image, it is only the fictive element that can establish the consistency necessary to endow it with the appearance of reality, for consistency is not a given quality of reality.'[18]

From the outset in *Daniel Deronda* George Eliot implies the precarious nature of consistency and insists upon our recognising the plurality of fictions. Darwin had emphasised in *The Origin of Species* the randomness of mutation, the dysteleological abundance of possibilities. Natural selection, as Ernst Mayr remarks, 'rewards past events, that is the production of successful recombinations of genes, but it does not plan for the future'.[19] Francis Galton's eugenic theories were an attempt to apply evolutionary theory to the future and Darwin's own emphasis in *The Descent of Man* upon acts of choice and will in sexual selection (however circumscribed by society's pressures) brought into the foreground questions of inheritance. These issues have an important part in the novel and bind the Jewish and the English characters. But the other equal emphasis is upon the multiplicity of possibilities, on coincidence as a creative force, on the absorbing unpredictability of what is to come.

Prophecy and divination, whose effect depends upon our *surprise* when they are confirmed, pay homage to the uncontrollable multiformity of the future. In this novel George Eliot surveys the range of prescience – from that dependence on luck or 'system' which Gwendolen shows in the gambling scene at the beginning, to Mordecai's fulfilled confidence in the enactment of proleptic imagery. And the book moves into that central problem focused by Darwinian theory: is there a foreknown or an ultimate plan? Is teleology itself a fiction? – do we self-protectively interpret as providence that which is chance? This question must have particularly difficult implications for the writer of narrative which is so preoccupied with past and future, and for the prescient novelist who, when he has veiled his omniscience, finds it difficult to be rid of his omnipotence. In *Daniel Deronda* the problem of the author as originator, which was never satisfactorily solved in *Middlemarch*, is edged into the open.

The first page of the book is problematic, cryptic. Eliot makes the epigraph exemplify its own assertion. Instead of allowing it the authority of the narrator's introduction she places it marginally, an apparently optional part of the text which we are tacitly licensed to skip. But if we skip it and turn to the main text we are without introduction, immediately plunged into a provisional, interrogatory sentence: 'Was she beautiful or not beautiful?' in which neither subject nor thinker is known to us. The epigraph is a secondary beginning – but its presence makes the opening of the main text also only problematically a beginning. For of course this preliminary paragraph *is* a necessary prologue to the significance of the text and does encapsulate its problems. We need to read it – we need the make-believe of a beginning. By the teasing formal relationships of these first paragraphs George Eliot signals from the outset that the source of authoritative statement is to be problematised. In the epigraph the direct authority of narrator is withdrawn and an assumed impersonality is substituted without a source; in the first sentences of text, interrogation is placed doubtfully between narrator and character's consciousness, and between full consciousness and the meditative speculations of an attention not yet fully focused on its object.

Instead of the coherence of uniformitarian sequence what is emphasised is faulture and slippage, the difficulty of interpretation, the inevitable incompleteness of knowledge. Beginning, the irretrievable initiation whether of consciousness, event or world, is the topic of this opening. What Edward Said in *Beginnings* calls 'beginning intention' – the promise or at least the project to continue – remains a major force in the book's argument and unfolding.[20] It ends with beginning – a beginning which it was not possible for writer or first readers to discriminate as fiction or history: is the Zionist state a mirage?

In *Middlemarch*, as we have seen, the characters seek roots, keys, original tissues – a return to some single source which will unify the diversity of the present and the past. The narrative activity, however, is preoccupied with *relations*, and emphasises those diversities which the characters in their Platonic urgency seek to transcribe back into singleness and into Idea. In *Daniel Deronda* this controversy enters further into the book's emotional and narrative order.

The fixing and staying implicit in the idea of *the beginning* (as opposed to the idea of *beginning*) goes against laws of motion and evolution. Comte identified movement with existence, and George Eliot cited in her note-book for *Daniel Deronda* a passage from his General Introduction which has its bearing on the problems of private and public life, and of inher-itance, broached in the novel. Comte is warning against giving too high an authority to the retrospective:

The historical spirit has a natural tendency to make us disdain sentiment from constantly dwelling on results without taking account of intentions. It might thus so far misunderstand its true mission as to procure a sort of systematic sanction for those most mischievous corrupters of society who think to mag-nify the importance of public life by disparaging that of private life. But all these intellectual dangers are at an end the moment we found social dynamics in accordance with their true nature; that is to say, by making movement uniformly dependent on Existence, as in the other sciences. (f. 84)

At the end of chapter 11 of the novel there is a space in the text followed by two concluding paragraphs which justify the novel's insistence on the playing out of private lives amidst more notable public events:

Could there be a slenderer, more insignificant thread in human history than this consciousness of a girl, busy with her small inferences of the way in which she could make her life pleasant? – in a time, too, when ideas were with fresh vigour making armies of themselves, and the universal kinship was declaring itself fiercely: when women on the other side of the world would not mourn for the husbands and sons who died bravely in a common cause, and men stinted of bread on our side of the world heard of that willing loss and were patient: a time when the soul of man was waking to pulses which had for centuries been beating in him unfelt, until their full sum made a new life of terror or of joy.

What in the midst of that mighty drama are girls and their blind visions? They are the Yea or Nay of that good for which men are enduring and fighting. In these delicate vessels is borne onward through the ages the treasure of human affections. (1:11:181–2)

Gwendolen's story also, like that of the Zionist state, is still to come, a matrix of fictions, not yet fixed and diminished by the retrospect of history. Comte, Eddington, Clerk Maxwell, Clausius, Darwin, Helmholtz, all in their diverse fields of social theory, physics, evolutionary and genetic theory, acoustics, and astronomy, at this period emphasised the unstayable and ever-extending movement of all phenomena. This movement may be expressed as succession, as sound waves, as the stars' unceasing journey, as the transmission of stories, as heat, as the instabil-ity of species.

Movement, however, is not uni-directional: nor does it necessarily imply either a centripetal or a centrifugal force alone. In this it differs from the customary concept of time, which moves from past to present to future. This concept of irreversible time had gained power from the emphasis in *The Origin of Species* on transformation and on extinction. The theme, ordering and dialogue of *Daniel Deronda* all explore and question the genealogical view of time as descent and succession and bring into debate its adequacy as complete explanation.

In notebook 707 George Eliot quotes Comte's Definition of Humanity: 'The continuous whole formed by the Beings which *converge*' (f. 82). Convergence creates one form of identity which does not require a study of beginnings and it is an important organising principle of the novel which generates its own metaphysics: Deronda, in particular, is gifted with the power of convergence, of meeting with others at their needed moment. But convergence also displays more sinister characteristics in the ordering of the novel: 'Meeting Streams' tracks the coming together of Grandcourt and Gwendolen as well as of Deronda and Mirah.

Streams meet and flow together outward to the sea, not back to any source. But as the opening of the novel recognises, men need the idea of a beginning and in this novel many of the characters must seek their origins. Both Daniel Deronda and Mirah are in quest of their lost mothers and the matrilineal inheritance of Judaism gives a particular meaning to this search. For Daniel, the rediscovery of his mother assures his future, though her coldness to him debars him from any return to a knowable source. In this they contrast with Gwendolen who is preoccupied with possibility, with the future. She *has* her mother and for her as for the other major characters, including the Meyricks, the mother is the well-spring of emotion.

The novel condenses much significant anxiety from the shared preoccupations of the time. In the 1870s the search for origins, the enquiry into their nature and into their relationship to development had become an intellectual obsession. Both Comte and Darwin had earlier eschewed the study of absolute origins in favour of process and transformation. In chapter 6 of *The Origin of Species*, 'Difficulties on Theory', Darwin remarks: 'How a nerve comes to be sensitive to light, hardly concerns us more than how life itself first originated' (217). Such statements had a polemical force in placing the development of species late in the history of the development of life on earth. But the paradoxical relationship between Darwin's title, which suggests a starting point, and his argument, which evades discussion of primal origins, substituting history for cosmogony, aroused interest not only in process but in those unrecorded and perhaps irretrievable beginnings.

In the twenty years which span the novel's historical time-setting and its composition the word 'origins' is everywhere. A glance at the new psychological and philosophical journal *Mind* which appeared in 1876, the year in which *Daniel Deronda* was published, shows the frequency of the word as a means of placing an argument. In the third number, July, for example, we find Helmholtz on 'The Origin and Meaning of Geometrical Axioms', Flint on 'Associationism and the Origin of Moral Ideas', Max Müller on 'The Original Intention of Collective and Abstract Terms'. The word has become a sine qua non of intellectual discussion and covers an inner debate about whether our proper study should be cosmogony – how things were in the beginning – or descent – how things came to be as they are now. That debate brought in its wake the further speculation: how will things be? So when George Eliot was making notes on Croll's article on 'The Probable Origin and Age of the Sun' with its discussion of combustion and of thermal death, or reading Pictet's *Origines des races aryennes* she was doing so within a complicated series of interrelated enquiries and controversies. Her interest in the origin of the Aryan races was not simply part of a 'background' study for what is often called the Jewish half of *Daniel Deronda*. Indeed, to conceive of Jews and English entirely in dualistic terms misses the point that what she is exploring in the novel is not polarity but common sources: the common culture, story, and genetic inheritance of which the Jews and the English are two particularly strongly interconnected expressions, which raises questions of transmission.

A major problematic in this novel is the question of typology – can there be new movements, new stories? Is it possible to rupture the links of descent and to set out anew? – (as Daniel Deronda's mother has attempted to do) – or is genetic inheritance what most determines us? – (as Daniel's history might suggest). Can fiction propose fresh possibilities? or will it find itself inevitably retelling the old stories to avoid the captious novelty which in the book is associated with Gwendolen's willful maiden dreams (of flight exploration and predominance), the ephemeral expressions of a profound need:

'What should you like to do?' said Rex, quite guilelessly, and in real anxiety.

'Oh, I don't know! – go to the North Pole, or ride steeplechases, or go to be a queen in the East like Lady Hester Stanhope,' said Gwendolen, flightily. Her words were born on her lips, but she would have been at a loss to give an answer of deeper origin.

'You don't mean you would never be married.'

'No, I didn't say that. Only when I married, I should not do as other women do.' (1,7:99)

One question vehemently explored in the course of the book is whether there can be new plots for stories about women. It is a question indicated by the epigraph to chapter 31:

> A wild dedication of yourselves
> To unpath'd waters, undream'd shores – Shakespeare

Notebook 707 reminds us of earlier stories about Gwendolen:

> Gwen is considered as the British Venus . . . Gwendolen, or the Lady of the bow, or perhaps from Gwendal, white browed, was, it seems, an ancient British Goddess, probably the moon.

She is thus the British equivalent to Diana, archer and moon-goddess, figure of virginity.

> Gwendolen is made by the Brut, and by Geoffrey of Monmouth the daughter of Corineus, Duke of Cornwall, and wife of Locrine, son of the original Brutus. He deserted her for Estrild, a fair German captive, and she made war upon him, in the course of which he was killed, and Estrild and her daughter Sabre, or Avern, made prisoners; whereupon the jealous and revengeful queen caused both to be drowned in the river, thenceforth called Sabrina or Severn, in Welsh, Havern. (ff.10–11)

Not quite Gwendolen's story, though drowning and vengeance have a place in her history as well, as does the destructive force of the deserted woman. But the Arthurian references in the name (she is also 'the mother of Caradoc Vreichfras, the excellent Sr Cradocke of the Round Table' and 'a beauty of Arthur's Court') suggest a buried history, half myth, half racial recollection, moving beneath the surface of the text. Whereas in *Romola* all the encyclopaedic knowledge is ranged on the surface of the work, in *Daniel Deronda* the equivalences between myth-systems, languages, and races, are allusively implied and form part of an argument which is conducted for the most part covertly, expressed almost as much through structures as through semantics. It is an argument which draws upon material that has been set in quite new relationships by evolutionary theory. Earlier analyses read differently in the wake of Darwin's writing.

A related debate concerning homogeneity and heterogeneity as that within the study of race is present also in the study of language and of myths. In the late eighteenth century Herder in his *Abhandlung über den Ursprung der Sprache* had maintained that original language was redundant and complex and that as it developed it had become simpler. This view contrasts sharply with that of Max Müller who, following Grimm, emphasised the beauty of roots.[21] His own theory of myths insisted upon the single reference system: all myths are 'solar' myths and have to do with interpreting the phenomena of climate. The insistence on the sun in mythography is replicated at that time in astronomy. In the 1870s many besides Darwin were disturbed by Helmholtz's theory of the inevitable future death of the sun as a result of its cooling down.[22] Solar myth is not only a categorising of the past, it is active in people's anxieties in the 1860s and 1870s. We see it at work in the measured reassurance which Proctor provides concerning the long future life span of the earth. The same problematic is present in *Daniel Deronda* both in its astronomical imagery and in its projective organisation, which struggles to present past and future in terms of familial descent but suggests persistently the hazard and the hazardousness of the unknown future.

At the period that George Eliot was preparing and writing *Daniel Deronda* the nature of the interconnection of myth-systems was a burning issue. Are the interconnections the result of transmission? Are they – and this possibility is coming only gradually to consciousness – the outcome of typological needs of the human imagination? Is there a morphology of the unconscious yet to be discovered, as insistent and inescapable as that of physical organic life? 'What can be more curious than that the hand of a man, formed for grasping, that of a mole for digging, the leg of a horse, the paddle of the porpoise, and the wing of the bat, should all be constructed on the same pattern, and should include the same bones, in the same relative positions', asks Darwin in the section on Morphology in the chapter on Classification in *The Origin*. George Eliot in her notebook records ancient Egyptian variants of the Cinderella story.

Darwinian organisations of experience underpin a great many structuralist analyses. In 1928, for example, Vladímir Propp opens *The Morphology of the Folktale* with these words:

The word 'morphology' means the study of forms. In botany, the term 'morphology' means the study of the component parts of a plant, of their relationship to each other and to the whole – in other words, the study of a plant's structure.

But what about a 'morphology of the folktale'? Scarcely anyone has thought about the possibility of such a concept.

Nevertheless, it is possible to make an examination of the forms of the tale which will be as exact as the morphology of organic formations . . .

I feel that in its present form this study is accessible to every fancier of the tale, provided he is willing to follow the writer into the labyrinth of the tale's multiformity, which in the end will become apparent to him as an amazing uniformity.

The problem of typology – of the inalienable symbols of the unconscious – was to be explored by Freud very soon after the publication of *Daniel Deronda.*

When George Eliot was working towards *Daniel Deronda* she was studying a range of texts, all of which have some bearing on the problems of cultural evolution and race as well as on the question of *humanity* as opposed to nationhood or ethnic origin. She turns again to Comte's *Positive Polity* which in the early 1870s had been freshly translated by Frederic Harrison and others. Among her extensive quotations from Comte are observations such as these:

The conception of Fatherland, at one time co-extensive with that of Home, is now in danger of being swallowed up in that of humanity (f.96). Comte says in *Positive Polity* (I,333): 'We regard Humanity as composed essentially of the dead; these alone being fully amenable to our judgment . . . If the living are admitted it is, except in rare instances, only provisionally.'

George Eliot comments: 'If our duties are towards "Humanity" how are the living and those who are to come to be excluded?' The emphasis upon Humanity as including not only the present but 'those who are to come' is a key concept in *Daniel Deronda*:

a man steeped in poverty and obscurity, weakened by disease, consciously within the shadow of advancing death, but living an intense life in an invisible past and future, careless of his personal lot, except for its possibly making some obstruction to a conceived good which he would never share except as a brief inward vision – a day afar off, whose sun would never warm him, but into which he threw his soul's desire, with a passion often wanting to the personal motives of healthy youth. It was something more than a grandiose transfiguration of the parental love that toils, renounces, endures, resists the suicidal promptings of despair – all because of the little ones, whose future becomes present to the yearning gaze of anxiety. (2:42:388–9)

Music, mystics, myths, etymology, and the evolution of mind are the major topics of this preparatory notebook. Medieval music, the work of Palestrina (who at this period was a renewed influence in liturgical music, as Bruckner's work demonstrates) and Gregorian chant are all touched on and she gives long accounts from Hullah's history of music. The emphasis upon early music is remarkable, just as, among writers, is the number of medieval texts she cites: not only Chaucer, but, tellingly, the 'Ayenbite of Inwit, or remorse of Conscience XIVth Century' – a work that has much to do with the emotional climax of *Daniel Deronda*: Gwendolen's suffering after Grandcourt's death and the repressed and unwilling remorse of Daniel's mother, the great musician who has sacrificed all else to her career. In her notebooks George Eliot cites Gnostic mystics alongside Thomas à Kempis and points out the Buddhist equivalent to the Grail legend: 'This Patra is the Holy Grail of Buddhism. German scholars have traced in the romances of the Grail remarkable indications of Oriental origin.' She quotes from Yule's *Marco Polo* and continues the citation to demonstrate its Indian source and its meaning: 'When it has disappeared from Earth the Law gradually perishes, and violence and wickedness more and more prevail.' Just as Gregorian chant is related to the ancient chant of the synagogue and to Vedic chant, so the 'Matter of Britain' is related to Buddhist and to Asiatic lore. This gives a greater significance to the considerable Arthurian and Celtic material in the notebook. The name Gwendolen, of whose origins and sombre narrative she gives an account, has meaning not only in terms of Arthurian allusion but exists, like the Cabbalistic material, as the small point above ground that indicated a system of connections between a variety of legendary orders including equally the Norse, the Judaic, the Arabic, the Indian: 'Alexandrian philosophy, derived from India'.

George Eliot commented to Harriet Beecher Stowe on the 'spirit of arrogance and contemptuous dictatorialness' with which the English treated not only the Jews but all 'oriental peoples' with whom they came in contact.

There is nothing I should care more to do, if it were possible, than to rouse the imagination of men and women to a vision of human claims in those races of their fellow-men who most differ from them in customs and beliefs. But towards the Hebrews we western people who have been reared in Christianity, have a peculiar debt and, whether we acknowledge it or not, a peculiar thoroughness of fellowship in religious and moral sentiment. Can anything be more disgusting than to hear people called 'educated' making small jokes about eating ham, and showing themselves empty of any real knowledge as to the relation of their own social and religious life to the history of the people they think themselves witty in insulting? They hardly know that Christ was a Jew. And I find men educated at Rugby supposing that Christ spoke Greek. To my feeling, this deadness to the history which has prepared half our world for us, this inability to find interest in any form of life that is not clad in the same coattails and flounces as our own, lies very close to the worst kind of irreligion. The best that can be said of it is, that it is a sign of the intellectual narrowness – in plain English, the stupidity, which is still the average mark of our culture.[23]

This passage has been often quoted as evidence of George Eliot's sympathy for the Jews. What has been less often remarked is her emphasis upon the related historical cultures of English, Jews, and Oriental people. British insularity makes for meagreness of national culture, not its enrichment. The emphasis throughout the book is on stultification, on the failure of the British to perceive their connections with other races and cultures:

We English are a miscellaneous people, and any chance fifty of us will present many varieties of animal architecture or facial ornament; but it must be admitted that our prevailing expression is not that of a lively, impassioned race, preoccupied with the ideal and carrying the real as a mere make-weight. (1:10:149)

English exploration and diaspora take always the form of dominance through colony and empire. Their journeying is always unreceptive, their repose a kind of annulment:

This handsome, fair-skinned English couple manifesting the usual eccentricity of their nation, both of them proud, pale, and calm, without a smile on their faces, moving like creatures who were fulfilling a supernatural destiny. (3:54:207)

All this is most directly figured in Grandcourt, of course, the inheritor of an uncle's estate:

Mr Deronda was a familiar figure regarded with friendliness; but if he had been the heir, it would have been regretted that his face was not as unmistakably English as Sir Hugo's.

Grandcourt's appearance when he came up with Lady Mallinger was not impeached with foreignness: still the satisfaction in it was not complete. It would have been a matter of congratulation if one who had the luck to inherit two old family estates had had more hair, a fresher colour, and a look of greater animation; but that fine families dwindled off into females, and estates ran together into the single heirship of a mealy-complexioned male, was a tendency in things which seemed to be accounted for by a citation of other instances. It was agreed that Mr Grandcourt could never be taken for anything but what he was – a born gentleman; and that, in fact, he looked like an heir. (2:36:251–2)

The dwindling energy of England is related directly to the insistence on descent through the male line. The troubles of Gwendolen's mother, similarly, come from having a family of daughters whose only hope of salvation is to marry well. Grandcourt's cast-off mistress, Mrs Glasher, has a son who is debarred from inheritance by illegitimacy. By widening the significance of 'breeding' in this book George Eliot brings the old theme of the English gentleman into greatly extended intellectual relations. Daniel, whose 'breeding' makes him an English gentleman

by virtue of Sir Hugo Mallinger's upbringing, discovers his true inheritance through his Jewish past and through his *matrilineal* succession to
Judaic culture. But he does not cease to be an Englishman. Like Klesmer,
who is 'a felicitous combination of the German, the Sclave, and the
Semite' (1:5:65). Deronda is enriched by the multiple past, both genetic
and cultural. The past here is no longer a matter of one or two generations in a local community, but of transformation from the primary
forms of life and, particularly, problems of transmission. How are races
and cultures interconnected and how do they change? Is transformation necessarily for the better? Are past, present, and future on a stable
continuum? Are there stable limits to enquiry?

In a typical movement of mind, these questions, which are given
their abstract expression in her notebooks and in earlier articles such as
that on 'The Influence of Rationalism', find their form in this book
through the individual human lots of people 'in a corner of Wessex'
and are communicated as emotion more often than as idea.

In the absence of any profound research into psychological functions or into
the mysteries of inheritance, in the absence of any comprehensive view of
man's historical development and the dependence of one age on another, a
mind at all rich in sensibilities must always have had an indefinite uneasiness
in an undistinguishing attack on the coercive influence of tradition.[24]

In *Daniel Deronda* she explores 'the mysteries of inheritance' and both
the coercive and the liberating influence of tradition. She explores sometimes openly, as in the wide-ranging discussion at the Hand and Banner; sometimes through event, as in the inheritance of the diamonds;
sometimes through feeling, as in the passionate resistance of Gwendolen
to courtship and of the Princess Halm-Eberstein to motherhood; sometimes through narrative order, as in the evading of a predominant time
sequence which will carry the authority of cause and effect.

In her notes she sets down quotations and observations which set out
'the mysteries of inheritance' through etymology – the shifts of meaning into metaphor, then into substance, the selection of aspects of a
word's significance, the succession and transformation of senses. Language as a principle of survival and transformation becomes central to
Daniel Deronda in the Cabbalistic tradition, which allows Mordecai to
interpret the written prophecies into the present of his relationship
with Daniel. In the passionate conversations between Deronda and
Gwendolen energy is converted into direct speech. The articulations of
the written word, of conversation, of narrative, even of thought, are
acts of connection in a milieu where much is unuttered, impenetrable,

enigmatic. But George Eliot now also links the attempt to describe with 'stupidity', because of the difficulty of sufficiently registering 'differences'. She underlines emphatically in her notebook the remark, ' "*Truth is always particular, though language is commonly general.*" Austin' (f.107). Words may blank out the particular. Descent, whether of single words, of stories, of individuals, does not show any simple linear progression. Transformation and separation are energies in language as strong as community, and so they are in story and in genetic order. Among the possibilities of major discovery that she proposes doubtfully in *Daniel Deronda* is that man may go 'eastward and discover a new key to language telling a new story of races'.

The fascination with race is for many Victorian writers essentially a fascination with class. Race and class raise the same questions of descent, genealogy, mobility, the possibility of development and transformation. The genealogical metaphor had been adopted by Darwin in heraldic terms in *The Origin of Species*. Thackeray in an early essay shows how ideas of race and class condense: 'The inhabitants of our own nation are more remote, less known about than the remote and the exotic.' Dickens angrily shows the failure of sympathy for the near-at-hand, by contrast for the exotically primitive, in the figure of Mrs Jellyby in *Bleak House*.

The emphasis upon categorisation and fixity of species in Linnaeus's work was implicitly carried over into the examination of races. Much was written on 'hybrids'. It tended to be assumed that races were durable, despite crossings. Though capable of analysis into sub-varieties, the diverse races were ranged in a hierarchy, and that hierarchy was unalterable because based on physical characteristics rather than on environmental conditions.

In the debate about races the Jews were a peculiar difficulty – a wandering tribe, and an Asiatic one, but not complying with all the characteristics ascribed to 'Homo asiaticus', genetically exclusive, bearing a culture intact through vicissitudes. In some ways they ideally represented the concept of the stable racial group. Indeed they were cited by Paul Broca in one of the Anthropological Society's first publications as evidence against evolutionary ideas and for the polygenist views of separate races:

The monogenists have objected that the period of distant colonies is too recent; that the observations tending to establish the permanence of human types date scarcely from three or four centuries, and that this lapse of time is

insufficient to produce a transformation of races, and that such a transformation has been produced gradually during the long series of centuries elapsed,
according to some from the creation of man, and according to others since the
Deluge.

But the study of Egyptian paintings has shown, that on the one hand the
principal types of the human genus existed then, 2,500 years at least before
Jesus Christ, as they exist at this day.

Again, the Jewish race, scattered for more than eighteen centuries in the
most different climates, is everywhere the same now as it was in Egypt at the
time of the Pharaohs.[25]

Equally, they could be called in as evidence, in both Darwinian and
biblical terms, for the survival of favoured races in the struggle for life.
Their loss of a homeland meant that they raised in an acute form the
whole question of the relationship between nationality and race – and
between race and culture. They could clearly not be seen as one of the
less developed races – they resisted extinction, and had not been obliterated by genocide, scattering or intermarriage. They were an old and
chosen (or 'favoured') people, who survived culturally by a hermeneutic
process – through interpretation and reinterpretation – rather than
through transformation.

It is in this context that the most open debate of intellectual issues
within the book should be read. The club of 'Philosophers' – 'poor men
given to thought' – are said by Mordecai to be faint likenesses of 'the
great Transmitters . . . who laboured with their hands for scant bread,
but preserved and enlarged for us the heritage of memory and saved
the soul of Israel alive as a seed among the tombs' (2:42:370). George
Eliot glances derisively at the concept of separate physical races in setting the scene: 'pure English blood (if leech or lancet can furnish us
with the precise product) did not declare itself predominantly in the
party' (2:42:372).

The subject under discussion at the club is transformation and development: must it be revolutionary? Can it be accretive? Will it always be
progressive and turned towards the good?[26] The argument opens with
a quotation from Shelley's description of the avalanche in 'Prometheus
Unbound':

> As thought by thought is piled, till some great truth
> Is loosened, and the nations echo round. (2:42:371)

The comparison with geological process was a frequent analogy in the
nineteenth century for the coming both of scientific discovery and of
social revolution. Ernest Jones uses it for its revolutionary significance

in his poems addressed to working men and Müller in its scientific bearing. Placed as it is in this scene, at the head of discussion, it proposes a particular kind of relation between past and future – slow accretive past, present rapidly overtaken by event, and dislodged tumultuously into future.

The conversation at the Hand and Banner is concerned with the interlocking of the ideas of succession, development and progress, 'the causes of social change' and 'the transforming power of ideas'. They discuss the unconscious dissemination of ideas, moving freely through practical, scientific and political analogies:

'Lilly saying this, we went off on the causes of social changes, and when you came in I was going upon the power of ideas, which I hold to be the main transforming cause.' (2:42:374)

'But if you take ready mixing as your test of power,' said Pash, 'some of the least practical ideas beat everything. They spread without being understood, and enter into the language without being thought of.'

'They may act by changing the distribution of gases,' said Marrables; 'instruments are getting so fine now, men may come to register the spread of a theory by observed changes in the atmosphere and corresponding changes in the nerves.'

'Yes,' said Pash, his dark face lighting up rather impishly, 'there is the idea of nationalities; I daresay the wild asses are snuffing it, and getting more gregarious.' (2:42:376)

Pash's witticism condenses the problem of ideological and evolutionary change. He imagines the solitary wild asses getting wind of changes in ideas about nationality and consequently changing their habits in a Lamarckian effort to survive. He links the need for the idea of nationality with states of oppression, with 'backward nations'. In Europe nationalism is bound to die out: 'The whole current of progress is setting against it.' With this, the discussion reaches its central problem; is change necessarily progress?

'Change and progress are merged in the idea of development. The laws of development are being discovered, and changes taking place according to them are necessarily progressive; that is to say, if we have any notion of progress or improvement opposed to them, the notion is a mistake.'

'I really can't see how you arrive at that sort of certitude about changes by calling them development,' said Deronda. 'There will still remain the degrees of inevitableness in relation to our own will and acts, and the degrees of wisdom in hastening or retarding; there will still remain the danger of mistaking a tendency which should be resisted for an inevitable law that we must adjust ourselves to.' (2:42:377)

What, if any, is the role of the will and of resistance? Mordecai introduces the crucial idea of *recrudescence*: 'Revive the organic centre' (388).

The power of return and renewal is one of the elements of mythological ordering least allowed for in evolutionary theory. True, Darwin admitted the concept of paedomorphosis – of attributes which die out before adulthood, but recur in future generations. He said also that it was not from among the most 'advanced' and specialised forms that great evolutionary advances would necessarily come, and in the 1860s he admitted the possible reappearance of long dormant characteristics. But the idea of return, of supping from a feast forever fresh, of the everlasting fountain, of regeneration through reinterpretation not new texts, were mythological images which the arboreal, onward, accretive imagery of evolutionism found no place for. 'They are a standstill people.' Mordecai counters that they bring ever fresh *interpretation*:

The spirit is alive, let us make it a lasting habitation – lasting because movable – so that it may be carried from generation to generation, and our sons unborn may be rich in the things that have been, and possess a hope built on an unchangeable foundation. (2:42:386)

The teleology that Mordecai appeals to is that of kinship – of Darwin's explanatory 'hidden bond of descent, bonds that bind and consecrate change as a dependent growth – yea, consecrate it with kinship: the past becomes my parent, and the future stretches towards me the appealing arms of children'. But the image of the family or tribe is generalised by Miller in monogenist terms which do away with exclusive Jewish claims, 'We're all related through Adam . . . And I suppose we don't want any men to be maltreated, white, black, brown or yellow' (383). He resists the Jews' special claims to virtue and achievement. The narrator suggests that Mordecai has got beyond the familial metaphor, though it is not quite clear how, and the argument ends with a vehement discussion of restoration, the return to the homeland and the literal fulfilment of prophecies. The weight of rationalist argument among the other Jews there is against the hermeneutical tradition. They see the search for Palestine as a discredited superstition. Deronda, however, sets it alongside other achieved nationalist movements such as that of Mazzini in Italy.

Mordecai ends by claiming that the strongest principle of growth lies in human choice: 'The divine principle of our race is action, choice, resolved memory' (2:42:396).

George Eliot gives great weight and space to this vehement debate, just as she does to the impassioned arguments between Deronda and his mother. Such scenes are rare in this novel, much of which has to do with clandestine feeling, its characters absorbed in the buzz of unspoken obsession. So the sheer bulk and intellectual panache of these scenes give them importance. Their function is to confirm openly the pressure of ideas which are covertly tracked and counter-tracked elsewhere in the novel as movements of feeling. The relationship of will and choice to change, the confusion between change and necessary progress, are issues much of whose intensity comes from their urgent testing of evolutionary ideas in their possible application to human life.

Of course, these ideas did not find their single source in Darwin. George Eliot was reading Hegel already in the 1840s, John Oxenford's article on Schopenhauer and Fichte which first made Schopenhauer a subject of debate in England had appeared in the *Westminster* while she was acting editor,[27] and she read Lamarck and Spencer in the 1850s. But in the 1870s, and in the anthropological context that she gave her book, with its challenging relativism and its pessimism about the possibility of advance in English national life, she was working within a current debate about race and culture sparked off by *The Descent of Man*. The debate about men and women's relations, which is examined in my next chapter, is her own response to Darwin's views on Sexual Selection.

The optimistic reading of evolutionary ideas insisted on the future development of mind and assumed that man's physical evolution was complete. This implied that control and development could be brought about by acts of choice. But although much of the surface of the book's argument seems to lead in this direction, there is a counter-surge beneath.

The practice of the novel is indeed more daring than the discussion at the club might suggest. The book is preoccupied with sudden turns of fortune: Gwendolen's loss of her money and the double crash of her family's fortunes; Mrs Glasher's message to her (many of these turns of fortune take epistolary form, with letters functioning like messengers or avengers from Greek tragedy); Daniel's discovery of his birth; and Grandcourt's drowning. Many of these events the reader has half foreseen but he has not foreseen *enough* – the actual occurrences are more radical, more traumatic, more absolute than he has dared or wished to predict. Consequently there is an *effect* of revolution in the work although nowhere an open argument for revolution.[28] The plotting no longer confirms a gradualist world of uniformitarian accretion and dislimning. The way event persistently exceeds prediction creates a sense of extremity. That sense is generated also by the presence of lateral wishes and possibilities moving freely within consciousness and thickening the atmosphere with undischarged possibilities which do not cease to exist though they are not enacted. Dysteleological series of events occur out of the multiple wishes of the characters, neither confirming nor according fully with them. Countering this fitful, precipitous, relativistic order, in which the present always seems slight within its compounding of futures, is the natural teleology of descent. Genetic descent and genealogical time seem to offer a stable succession which cannot be dislodged by individual desire. Yet there is in this book none of that power of fecundity which Zola established as the answer to death – there is only the frantic darkness of individual need or the unbroachable order of genetic succession.

Answering the question with which *Daniel Deronda* opens: 'Was she beautiful or not beautiful?' will take up much of the book. It opens also with something which is not quite an encounter between Daniel and Gwendolen. But Daniel's urgent attentiveness to Gwendolen's behaviour and fortunes convinces us as readers of an inevitable relationship between them yet to come. This conviction is borne out by the book's activity. The initial encounter and the hard fight for predominance and for redemption which is expressed in Deronda's redemption of Gwendolen's necklace also gives a priority to their relationship over that of Deronda and Mirah. In *narrative* time Gwendolen has prior claims. In *chronological* time Daniel has already a year earlier involved himself with Mirah's fate. But for the reader the relationship between Gwendolen and Deronda can never be dislodged from its primacy despite this later information, because we *knew them first*. So in the descent of the text, in which incident follows incident sometimes sequentially, sometimes because it falls ready for telling at that point, the relationship between Gwendolen and Deronda appears to be the original one. Moreover the sequence of the narrative confers prior rights on their relationship over that between Gwendolen and Grandcourt. This narrative authority is set against the authority of chronology or of social ties and brings into consciousness another kind of generation and descent: that of the text and its ordering. This ordering does not rely upon cause and effect, nor upon moral discrimination, but poises itself exactly at the point where chance and intention intersect. We *happen* to hear about them first. But we happen to hear it first because the author chose to tell it that way.

In the reader's reception of the tale ever after, Daniel and Gwendolen appear as the progenitors out of whose encounter the whole future is to issue. So the generative activity of narrative sequence which can include breaks, jumps, reversals of time, reminds us that there are other authoritative orderings besides that of descent – or of cause and effect.

Aristotle in his *Physics* identified time with movement, representing it as the quantifiable aspect of motion, and emphasising therefore its negative and evanescent qualities:

Some of it is past and no longer exists, and the rest is future and does not yet exist; and time, whether limitless or any given length of time we take, is entirely made up of the no-longer and not yet; how can we conceive of that which is composed of non-existents sharing in existence in any way.[29]

Such a conception of time empties the present of its authority, making it simply a one-dimensional passageway from non-existence to non-existence. In *Daniel Deronda*, the present is thick with precedent, encumbered with the past and also implicating itself in multiple futures. But the model employed is not solely that of genetic or biological time. It is also that of imaginative *reach*, which can move in many directions and can include space and prophecy, revival, or revolution. 'This, too, is probable, according to that saying of Agathon: "It is a part of probability that many improbable things will happen." (Aristotle: *Poetics*)' (2:61:351). So runs the epigraph to chapter 41 in which Deronda broods on Mordecai's prophetic spirit:

'this question of the family likeness among the heirs of enthusiasm, whether prophets or dreamers of dreams, whether the "Great benefactors of mankind, deliverers", or the devotees of phantasmal discovery – from the first believer in his own unmanifested inspiration, down to the last inventor of an ideal machine that will achieve perpetual motion.' The kinship of human passion, the sameness of mortal scenery, inevitably fill fact with burlesque and parody. (2:41:354)

Morphology and typology will take us only so far along the path to interpretation. Deviance and new possibility are disguised within similar forms and structures. So in this book George Eliot draws upon a spatial model of time as well as on the arboreal order of descent. And much of the book's own difficulty is in judging whether one or other of them should have predominance.

CHAPTER 7

Descent and sexual selection: women in narrative

During the 1870s and 1880s some of the further implications of evolutionary theory became apparent, particularly the social and psychological implications of Darwin's theories and their bearing on relations between men and women. One crucial and recurrent metaphor in *The Origin* is the heraldic record of great families: 'all true classification is genealogical' (404). Succession and inheritance form the 'hidden bond' which knits all nature past and present together, just as succession and inheritance organise society and sustain hegemony. Darwin emphasised the egalitarian potential of succession within the natural order: 'We have no written pedigrees; we have to make our community of descent by resemblances of any kind' (408). Variations in nature are not within the control of will; they are random and unwilled and may happen to advantage or disadvantage an individual and his progeny in any particular environment.

But in his two major works of the 1870s, *The Descent of Man* (1871) and *The Expression of the Emotions in Man and Animals* (1872), Darwin brought humankind openly into the evolutionary debate and emphasised not only natural – that is, unwilled – selection, but also *sexual selection*. Both the individual will and the internalised values of a community play their part in the processes of sexual selection.

The intersection of evolutionary theory and social, psychological and medical theory therefore became newly important. The bonds between biology and sociology are drawn close in the concept of sexual selection. It began to be asked what emotions, values, and reflex actions help the individual and the race to survive. Did transmitted qualities make specific the character of diverse cultures and races? What was the role of women, whose progenitive powers physically transmitted the race? How did relations between men and women subserve generation and development?

In *The Descent of Man* Darwin, citing Schopenhauer, relates 'love-intrigues' to the future of the race.

With mankind, especially with savages, many causes interfere with the action of sexual selection as far as the bodily frame is concerned. Civilised men are largely attracted by the mental charms of women, by their wealth, and especially by their social position; for men rarely marry into a much lower rank. The men who succeed in obtaining the more beautiful women will not have a better chance of leaving a long line of descendants than other men with plainer wives, save the few who bequeath their fortunes according to primogeniture. With respect to the opposite form of selection, namely, of the more attractive men by the women, although in civilised nations women have free or almost free choice, which is not the case with barbarous races, yet their choice is largely influenced by the social position and wealth of the men; and the success of the latter in life depends much on their intellectual powers and energy, or on the fruits of these same powers in their forefathers. No excuse is needed for treating this subject in some detail; for, as the German philosopher Schopenhauer remarks, 'the final aim of all love intrigues, be they comic or tragic, is really of more importance than all other ends in human life. What it all turns upon is nothing less than the composition of the next generation . . . It is not the weal or woe of any one individual, but that of the human race to come, which is here at stake.' (893)

Despite his suggestion in this passage that 'in civilised nations women have free or almost free choice', he makes it explicit elsewhere throughout *The Descent* that, in contrast to all other species (where the *female* most commonly holds the power of selection), among humankind the male dominates choice. This reversal creates crucial difficulties: 'Man is more powerful in body and mind than woman, and in the savage state he keeps her in a far more abject state of bondage than does the male of any other animal: therefore it is not surprising that he should have gained the power of selection' (911). Again, though he pays homage to the 'mental charms' of women, he gives primacy to beauty: even the chapter in which these words appear is subtitled 'On the effects of the continued selection of women according to a different standard of beauty in each race'.

The emphasis on *beauty* in the concept of sexual selection opened the debate into the domain of aesthetics as well. In *Mind* 5 (1880) Grant Allen wrote an important article on 'Aesthetic Evolution in Man' which draws heavily on *The Descent* and particularly on the idea of sexual selection. He asserts that the 'theory of sexual selection . . . [is] of the first importance for the aesthetic philosopher' and that 'the beauty of woman and of the human form is now and must always remain the central standard of beauty for all humanity' (449). His concept of beauty brings to the fore the idea of eugenics: 'The beautiful for every kind must similarly be . . . the healthy, the normal, the strong, the perfect, and the parentally sound', otherwise 'the race or kind must be on the high-road to extinction'.

In the light of such emphasis on 'fundamental typical beauty, the beauty which consists in full realisation of the normal specific type', one begins more fully to understand the intensity of Hardy's apparently drab praise of Tess of the d'Urberville's as 'an almost standard woman', and to feel the urgency of the opening words of *Daniel Deronda*: 'Was she beautiful or not beautiful?' George Eliot's febrile individualistic Gwendolen, with her distaste for sexual wooing, her dread of entering the world of descent, is expressive of many disturbances entering thought in the 1870s. She possesses the second type of beauty, not normative but diverging towards vivid extremes which Grant Allen specifies.

In *Pathology of Mind* (an edition revised in 1879 from the 1867 *Physiology and Pathology of Mind*) Henry Maudsley set out an evolutionist theory of madness, whose brutal progressivism, though paying homage to Darwin, is in fact closer to Spencer's assumption of a parallel between moral and physical fitness to survive. But Maudsley was also a brilliant observer of the specific conditions which produced madness, and his analysis of the biological, educational, and social determinants which produced in young women more mental disorder than young men of the same age sheds light on the problems faced by women who were to be selected according to the criteria of the culture they inhabited:

Girls are more liable to suffer at this period, I think, than youths; and it is not difficult to understand why. In the first place, the affective life is more developed in proportion to the intellect in the female than in the male sex, and the influence of the reproductive organs upon mind more powerful; secondly, the range of activity of women is so limited, and their available paths of work in life so few, compared with those which men have in the present social arrangements, that they have not, like men, vicarious outlets for feeling in a variety of healthy aims and pursuits; in the third place, social feelings sanction tacitly for the one sex an illicit indulgence which is utterly forbidden to the other; and, lastly, the function of menstruation, which begins at puberty in women, brings with it periodical disturbances of the mental tone which border closely on disease in some cases, while the irregularities and suppressions to which it is liable from a variety of mental and bodily causes may affect the mind seriously at any time. (450)

So topics traditional to the novel – courtship, sensibility, the making of matches, women's beauty, men's dominance, *inheritance* in all its forms – became charged with new difficulty in the wake of the publication of *The Descent of Man*. As so often with Darwin, his writing intensified and unsettled long-used themes and turned them into new problems. For George Eliot subtly, and for Thomas Hardy more frankly, the contradictions, social, psychological, and biological in the man/woman relationship and its identification with genetic succession became crucial to their rereading of traditional fictional topics. Rewriting and resisting are as important as assimilating in creating fictional energy and their relationship to Darwin's work fed both charges. Darwin's reversal of the common order in making man the selector drew attention to the social constituents in human descent as opposed to other species. In *The Descent* Darwin drew on ancient Greek literature to reinforce his argument. Deploring the action of wealth in influencing selection, he quotes from Hookham Frere's translation of Theognis: of 'kine and horses' we choose

> Of a sound stock, without defect or vice.
> But in the daily matches that we make,
> The price is everything: for money's sake,
> Men marry: women are in marriage given.

For Darwin love-intrigues and the marriage market involve the future of the human race. It is this brooding on generation and extinction beyond the lot of the individual which freights such topics with new weight and new resistances. The transfer from ontogeny to phylogeny, the paralleling of individual development to species-development, proves again to be an imaginative resource extraordinarily rich in tragic potential.

Both George Eliot and Hardy emphasise the discordance between a woman's individuality and her progenerative role. In *Tess* the dairymaids, diverse individuals yet alight, all, with desire for Angel Clare are described thus:

The air of the sleeping-chamber seemed to palpitate with the hopeless passion of the girls. They writhed feverishly under the oppressiveness of an emotion thrust on them by cruel Nature's law – an emotion which they had neither expected nor desired . . . The differences which distinguished them as individuals were abstracted by this passion, and each was but portion of one organism called sex. (174)

In *Tess* Hardy plays upon the concept of atavism. Tess, bucolic descendant of a noble county family, retains some of the lineaments of her ancestors, though her *beauty*, Hardy urges, comes from her mother's peasant stock and thus from those who survive outside the park-gates. Darwin's image of the great family is here reappraised, moving back and forth between old notions of social hierarchy and Hardy's post-Darwinian insistence that beauty of body and disposition, as exemplified in Tess, provide the only true 'standard.'

When the antiquarian vicar disastrously initiates the whole sequence of events by revealing to Tess's drunken father that he comes of noble stock, Durbeyfield naturally enquires: 'Where do we d'Urberville's live?' The vicar replies: 'You don't live anywhere. You are extinct – as a county family . . . that is, gone down, gone under.' Hegemony counts as extinct those who have not survived in power. The proper action of sexual selection, undistorted by social pressures and the male dominance peculiar to humankind, would result in the union of Angel and Tess. The social emphasis on virginity, Hardy suggests, cannot be naturalised: 'She had been made to break an accepted social law, but no law known in the environment in which she fancied herself such an anomaly' (114). Hardy's passionate depiction of Tess's purity and fitness runs directly counter to the punitive tautology which exalts the survivors as necessarily those proper to survive. He suggests that it may be, at least among women and the poor, that those fit for their environment must be less perfect than those who go under, and that sexual selection according to the oppressive criteria of current society will set us, in Grant Allen's words, 'on the high-road to extinction'.

Patrick Geddes and J. Arthur Thomson commented in *The Evolution of Sex* (London, 1889):

From the earliest ages philosophers have contended that woman is but an undeveloped man; Darwin's theory of sexual selection presupposes a superiority and an entail in the male line; for Spencer, the development of woman is early arrested by procreative functions. In short, Darwin's man is as it were an evolved woman, and Spencer's woman an arrested man.

The idea of sexual selection made for a complex confusion of biological and social determinants in descent, transmission, and sex-roles. Maudsley argues that the 'affective' and 'reproductive' elements in woman's make-up are necessarily stronger than in man's. Darwin says: 'It is generally admitted that with woman the powers of intuition, of rapid perception, and perhaps of imitation, are more strongly marked than in man; but some, at least, of these faculties are characteristic of the lower races, and therefore of a past and lower state of civilisation' (858). Both of them, however, acknowledge that women's education currently reinforces what they see as natural properties.

The intersection of evolutionary theory and psychological theory therefore became newly important. It was important because it began to be asked what *emotions* and what reflex actions help the individual and the race to survive. Did transmitted qualities make specific the character of diverse cultures? James Sully in *Sensation and Intuition* (1874) emphasised the interdependence of evolutionary and psychological study since, if Spencer and Darwin were right, and

these processes of hereditary transmission have been going on through countless generations of the human race, every infant now born into the world receives along with its primitive nervous organization a very decided and powerful moral bent, whether it be as a predisposition to certain modes of conception, or as an instinctive force of emotional susceptibility in particular directions.[1]

He cites Spencer on infant fears and Darwin on rudimentary conscience in animals as examples of feelings which exemplify the accretion of experience through generations and species, emphasises the need to understand 'the conditions which determine the effects of men's conduct on their fellow-men', and suggests that a complete account of 'political measures might probably involve a recognition of the phenomena of transmitted impulses and habits'.

In *Daniel Deronda* George Eliot condensed with peculiar intensity many of the emotional and intellectual problems current in the 1870s, and liberated into the work half-formulated dreads. Anxiety is the generative emotion of the work, shared by the reader in the more-than-usually conscious task of multiple prediction and by the characters in their attempts to control past and future.

The reader is caught into a predicament in which his usual prophetic and speculative activity within the novel – his task of hypothesising – has itself become a topic of the fiction and one which is impregnated with dread as well as irony. The reader participates in a hermeneutic task – but one in which the text interpreted is full of lacunae, and written (to use a metaphor common throughout the book) in alien languages or in one of which we are not native speakers.[2]

However this is to concentrate on one emotional arc of the novel's indications. For Mordecai also ardently seizes upon the future as sustenance even though that future inevitably will bring his own death soon. His emotional life is concentrated in the will to discover for himself a spiritual successor who can transform his visions into actions. In his searching for a 'second soul' he hopes to 'realise the long-conceived type' (2:38:307). The making real, the incarnating of a type is pictured by him as part of a world of growth: 'The thoughts of his heart . . .

seemed to him . . . too closely inwoven with the growth of things not to
have a further destiny' (2:38:299). The organicist metaphor here is made
to close the gap between mind and body – between culture and race.
Mind is given primacy – it imagines what the body achieves.

Mordecai and Gwendolen both have in the novel experiences of
second sight. George Eliot was impatient of the fashionable occult manifestations of spiritualism, and she and Lewes left an exhibition by a
medium attended by the Darwin family. But George Eliot was impatient only of the interventionist triviality of spiritualist manifestations.
She fixed to *Daniel Deronda* a prescient epigraph which emphasises how
through dread even more than through desire we seize the future into
present action. Her feeling for the Greek concept of Nemesis, most
open in *Felix Holt*, was not only based on her recognition of inexorable
consequences to deeds, but on the *chanciness* of consequences, the
phantasmagoric outflaring of need and dread into acts which confirm
their own predictions: or, at a lower emotional temperature, the sense
that 'a great deal of what passes for likelihood in the world is simply the
reflex of a wish' (1:9:143).[3] Gwendolen is scornful of those determining
patterns which make all stories fall into typologies. She seeks to make a
new story for herself, not satisfied with the traditional one that ends in
marriage: 'Clairvoyantes are often wrong: they foresee what is likely. I
am not fond of what is likely; it is always dull. I do what is unlikely'
(1:7:98). Despite the irony with which her desire is placed in language
and in the events of the novel it nevertheless accords with the work's
own problematic: habit, descent, and new futures.

Accomplishments had ceased to have the exciting quality of promising any
pre-eminence to her; and as for fascinated gentlemen – adorers who might
hover round her with languishment, and diversify married life with the romantic stir of mystery, passion, and danger which her French reading had given
her some girlish notions of – they presented themselves to her imagination
with the fatal circumstance that, instead of fascinating her in return, they were
clad in her own weariness and disgust . . . to solace ourselves with imagining
any course beforehand, there must be some foretaste of pleasure in the shape
of appetite; and Gwendolen's appetite had sickened. Let her wander over the
possibilities of her life as she would, as uncertain shadow dogged her. Her
confidence in herself and her destiny had turned into remorse and dread; she
trusted neither herself nor her future. (2:35:233–4)

Is it possible to write a new story? Does the emphasis in mythography
on common interpretation, and the similarities between myth systems,
imply that the human mind throughout the world knows only a very
few tales and can hope only to vary their surface? There is a clear line

of descent from Max Müller through Cassirer into the work of Lévi-Strauss in their emphasis upon the ultimate fixity of narrative species.

In this her last novel George Eliot seeks ways beyond this fixity. She is hard up against the edge of the future – that uncontrollable period beyond her own death – 'a day afar off, whose sun would never warm him, but into which he threw his soul's desire', as she says of Mordecai. Gwendolen is entrapped in her society's suitable story for a young lady. Her hysteric and predictive fantasies fracture the progressive account which should come to rest in a satisfactory marriage.

In *Daniel Deronda* we are baulked at the book's two climaxes of sure interpretation and of certainty – after Grandcourt's death, and with Daniel Deronda's journey to the East. In each case George Eliot allows the story its full novelty through refusing to offer us an accomplished history. We must speculate, inwards, and forwards. This is crucial to the significance of the third, possibly new, story – one which we are never told: that of Gwendolen's future life.

George Eliot's resistance to the 'barren mystery of the One' here takes the form of fixing her eyes on the unknowable complexities of the future, the escape from history. Despite her political gradualism in this work she is contemplating a time which, like space, is not all set in one direction. One arc of the book's desire drives on into the unknown, accepts the barren as sometimes preferable to descent, refuses to see present culture or present nationhood as absolute, knows that stories are precious and can say new things not yet admitted to a culture. Can fiction restore to the female the power of selection which, Darwin held, men had taken over? And can the woman writing, shape new future stories?

Can one escape from one's genetic and cultural inheritance – from the genealogical imperative? Daniel's story might suggest that it is impossible, except that he *chooses* his cultural identity with the Jews. Descent here marries with will. Gwendolen, on the other hand, survives her marriage, does not bear children to a hated husband, and so avoids becoming a part of that genealogical world of succession which trans-forms personal choice into kinship and knits the individual into the world of descent and transmitted values. At the end of the book she remains, isolated, unpredictable, entering the indeterminate future, in which not all choices are constrained and mapped. Hers may or may not prove to be the world of fruit and seed. It may as readily be the world of single identity, untransformed by submission to sexual selec-tion. She has for the present survived the marriage market where her beauty and her resistance to slavery equally made her sought by a man who favoured mastery. At the end of this text she makes her last assertion of will, in a form which frees Deronda and in its mingled tenses imagines into reality that which has not yet been attained: 'You must not grieve any more for me. It is better – it shall be better with me because I have known you' (3:70:407).

This bleak but tonic liberty for Gwendolen survives precisely because it abuts the book's conclusion. She has come through plot and out of plot into the indeterminacy of that which succeeds the text. The life of passion had begun negatively in her. She has feared solitude. The fierce negativity which has haunted her personality at last finds its creative form in this unshaped space, in which she is both alone and unknown: 'I shall live. I mean to live.' Instead of any movement towards fulfilment, there is the satisfied estrangement of the reader.

'The unripe grape, the ripe, and the dried. All things are changes, not into nothing, but into that which is not at present' (Marcus Aurelius, Epigraph to chapter 57 (3:57:234)). The book concludes with this emphasis on transformation, 'into that which is not at present'. Gwendolen's hysteric fears have had to do with the dread of annihilation of the person, with death as much as sex. Yet she accepts with a greater realism than Deronda the absoluteness of their parting. The book's conclusion includes death – the grave and dignified departure of Mordecai, a little conveniently placed just before Daniel and Mirah set out on their journey to the East.

There is an attempt at the end to exorcise the dread of the future, of what may come, which has been a covert energy throughout the text. The future is transfigured in a long light of pilgrimage for Daniel as he sets out to restore a political existence to his people 'making them a nation again, giving them a national centre, such as the English have, though they too are scattered over the face of the globe' (3:69:398). This curiously placed reference to the empire and its equation with the diaspora is charged with unstable ironies. In one sense the preoccupation with the homeland is a continuation simply of that emphasis upon the congruity between the self and its surroundings, the need of harmonious accord between self and surroundings which she proposed in:

Pity that Offendene was not the home of Miss Harleth's childhood, or endeared to her by family memories! A human life, I think should be well rooted in some spot of a native land, where it may get the love of tender kinship for the face of earth, for the labours men go forth to, for the sounds and accents that haunt it, for whatever will give that early home a familiar unmistakable difference amidst the future widening of knowledge. (1:3:26)

In part it has to do with a belief in the relation between medium and organism in which the organism must be stunted or distorted by exile.

Deronda's people have survived as a cultural entity because of their emphasis upon exclusion and genetic purity, even to the extent that only descent through the mother is sufficient confirmation of genetic inheritance.

In George Eliot's last three novels, *Felix Holt, Middlemarch* and *Daniel Deronda*, questions of descent, inheritance, and succession become dominant. In *Daniel Deronda* 'transmission' is an important term: 'the Masters who handed down the thought of our race – the great Transmitters' (2:41:370). Gwendolen's individual consciousness and its place in the process of inheritance propose problems which bear upon those of race, kinship, and unconscious accumulated impulse: 'pulses which had for centuries been beating in him unheard, until their full sum made a new life of terror or of joy'. Or, in Sully's language, 'a predisposition to certain modes of conception, or an instinctive force of emotional susceptibility in certain directions'.

'In these delicate vessels is borne onward through the ages the treasure of human affections.' The role of women both as vessels of continuity – bearing children, handing on the inheritance of the race – and as representing what men in a specific culture most desire, was foregrounded by Darwin's new emphasis on sexual selection. Because women must accommodate themselves to men's values if they are to be selected in the marriage market and achieve their expected status as wives and mothers, the bearers of the dominant culture, women represent a critique of that culture. George Eliot saw how readily sexual selection could become an instrument of oppression in the service of a patriarchal order.

> The market's pulse makes index high or low.
> By rule sublime. Our daughters must be wives,
> And to be wives must be what men will choose. (1:10:44)

Breeding, in this novel, has connotations not only of class but of race. Exclusion from hegemony may be the result of illegitimacy, or gender, or race. Klesmer, says Mr Arrowpoint, 'won't do at the head of estates. He has a deuced foreign look.' Lady Mallinger's troop of daughters are, she thinks, 'the emblazonment of herself as the infelicitous wife who had produced nothing but daughters, little better than no children, poor dear things, except for her own fondness and for Sir Hugo's wonderful goodness to them' (2:36:252). Because Lady Mallinger has no son, Grandcourt will inherit the estate. Because Daniel Deronda is 'nephew', reputed illegitimate son, to Sir Hugo he cannot inherit either. Grandcourt's mistress Mrs Glasher has four children whose faces are 'almost perfect reductions of her own' – the father is absent even from their appearance. Illegitimacy here literally emphasises succession through the mother. It is to displace the single boy among them that Grandcourt wants an heir from his marriage with Gwendolen. Her triumph, therefore, must be her barrenness.

In a letter George Eliot wrote: 'As a mere fact of zoological evolution, women seem to me to have the worse share in existence. But for that very reason I would the more contend that in moral evolution we have "an art that does mend nature".'[4]

What precisely does she mean here? Not, I think, anything like Darwin's view in *The Descent of Man* that women are parallel on the scale of development with a less developed race, inevitably lagging behind European manhood. Rather, in that term 'mere zoological evolution' I think she is referring to women's function of childbearing, their status as vessels, which she separates from moral evolution. What are the qualities particular to women's experience which she sees as furnishing 'the art that does mend nature'? Many of them are articulated throughout her novels – the capacity to endure, to sustain suffering, to survive lovingly. But in *Daniel Deronda*, and to some extent in *Felix Holt*, she also premises the power of fear – the capacity for dread – as a particular condition of women's experience and potentiality. And she presents the 'large discourse of imaginative fears' not simply as curtailing action but as liberating experience.

Fear is of all emotions that which most takes its life from the future – whether that future be a year, half a lifetime, or a second away. It is Gwendolen's most typical emotion and is strongly related to her love of predominance. I reach at this point the moment where the three terms of my argument come together: problems of descent, of the idea of the mother, and of – to use Kierkegaard's title – *The Concept of Dread*. The 'insistent penetration of suppressed experience', 'the infusion of dread' is seen in *Daniel Deronda* as part of the special condition and the particular power of women.

When Deronda first encounters Mirah, he rescues her from suicide by drowning – which in the ironic premonitory style of this book's ordering offers a benign version of that late demonic scene in which Grandcourt drowns. The chapter ends as he wonders where to take her:

Then there occurred to him the beautiful story Plutarch somewhere tells of the Delphic women: how when the Maenads, outworn with their torch-lit wanderings, lay down to sleep in the market-place, the matrons came and stood silently round them to keep guard over their slumbers; then, when they waked, ministered to them tenderly and saw them safely to their own borders. (1:17:291)

The circle of watching matrons around the orgiastic maenads slumbering and exhausted, provides indeed an arresting image for women's wholeness of identity. The next chapter opens with an epigraph:

> Life is a various mother: now she dons
> Her plumes and brilliants, climbs the marble stairs
> With head aloft, nor ever turns her eyes
> On lackeys who attend her; now she dwells
> Grim-clad up darksome alleys, breathes hot gin,
> And screams in pauper riot.
> > But to these
> She came a frugal matron, neat and deft,
> With cheerful morning thoughts and quick device
> To find the much in little. (1:18:293)

Frozen or screaming – these, equally with the frugal matron, are possibilities for motherhood.

Gwendolen is beset with 'vague, ever-visiting dread of some horrible calamity', partly as a result of her experience of enforced passivity despite a longing for mastery. Partly she is beset also because her power of love is focused only on her mother, and partly because she has broken her bond – not her word only, but her bond of womanhood with women such as her mother – by marrying Grandcourt despite her promise to Mrs Glasher not to do so. Maenad and matron are set at odds.

In the first part of the book there is a disjunction between acting and action which is highly stylised. Gwendolen collects the costumes before she thinks what scenes to put them in; they perform tableaux instead of plays (1:6:75); she imagines herself as a rival to Rachel before she has ever set foot on the stage. And she appears as the statue of Hermione, the wronged mother whose return to life will restore love and knit up kinship, in what the narration calls 'an imitation of acting'. The scene is blasted and liberated at its conclusion by her release not into solemnly renewed life, but into prophetic hysteria as she sees the panel slide open to reveal the dead face and the figure fleeing. At this stage it appears that the only form for action is that of prophecy, describing some emblematic form of the possible future.

Mothers and their functions are ambiguously seen in George Eliot's late novels. In novels such as *The Mill on the Floss* and *Romola* the father is the repository of emotion, the longed-for origin (a dream that turns to nightmare in the relations of Tito and his step-father). In *Daniel Deronda* mothers are the well-spring of being, the quest objects, and fathers are unregrettedly absent. Much of the plot of *Daniel Deronda* is generated out of Mirah and Deronda's seeking of their lost mothers and Gwendolen's exclusive emotional relationship with her mother.

Darwin's emphasis upon the single progenitor had, as Lewes pointed out in his 1868 *Fortnightly* articles, certainly theistic and possibly patriarchal remnants of ideas in it. As we saw earlier, Lewes preferred the idea of a germinal membrane covering all the earth. And Mathilde Blind, George Eliot's first biographer, followed this hint in the orgiastic imagery of life's beginning in her poem *The Ascent of Man*, where 'Life built herself a myriad forms'.[5] In *Daniel Deronda*, a work so preoccupied with origins and yet so distrustful of fixed beginnings, the mother (often half obliterated, never to be restored, yet powerful) is the matrix.

In her notes for *Daniel Deronda* George Eliot summarised the following passage from the Cabbalah:

In its original state each soul is androgynous – separated into male and female when it descends to earth . . . It sometimes however happens that it is the isolation of the soul which is the source of her weakness, she requires help to pass through her probation. In that case she chooses a companion soul of better fortune or more strength. The stronger of the two then becomes as it were the mother; she carries the sickly one in her bosom and nurses her as a woman her child. (f.112)

Perhaps part of the complex relationship between Deronda and Gwendolen – almost equally therapeutic and erotic, his passivity receiving her energy and sustaining it – derives from its unpatriarchal nature. Despite his mentorship, Deronda has an almost maternal relation to her.

Grandcourt, on the other hand, is compared to those denizens of the natural world which express no emotion and which are beyond the scope of Darwin's study in *The Expression of the Emotions in Man and Animals* (from which George Eliot took notes as she worked on *Daniel Deronda*).

Already, in seven short weeks, which seemed half her life, her husband had gained a *mastery* which she could no more resist than she could have resisted the benumbing effect from the touch of a torpedo. *Gwendolen's will had seemed imperious in its small girlish sway; but it was the will of a creature with a large discourse of imaginative fears*: a shadow would have been enough to relax its hold. And she had found a will like that of a crab or a boa-constrictor which goes on pinching or crushing without alarm at thunder. [my italics] (2:35:223)

Grandcourt is like the crab or boa-constrictor whose will functions reflexively. Gwendolen, on the other hand, lives in a clandestine tumult of feeling and projection. To Grandcourt she is interesting because she can be subjected, and because she can provide him with an heir.

One of the fairy-tale elements in George Eliot's own practice as a novelist is the way in which her women in unhappy marriages rarely have children: Romola, Dorothea, Gwendolen all remain childless despite the evident potency of Tito and Grandcourt. They are absolved from taking part in the pattern of descent, and in *Daniel Deronda* particularly this brings into question the assumption that women derive their status from their genetic role.

It is an assumption which is openly challenged and painfully endured within the book's economy by Daniel's mother, the great opera singer who has given away her child in order to be free for her 'myriad' lives. And this is where one of the most dazzling and subversive ironies of the text emerges. Deronda has always feared that when Mirah finds her mother she will be in some way tawdry or wrecked, and he winces at 'other possible realities about that mother'. Mirah never finds her mother, but Deronda himself is given the clue to his parentage by a letter from his own 'unknown mother' and, relieved of his chagrined half-belief that he is Sir Hugo Malinger's natural son, sets out on a journey back to the mother whom he hopes will come anew into his life, offering affection and renewal. The language which describes his receipt of the letter allows for no outpouring. All is curtailed, 'colourless', 'in reserve', 'reticence', 'not to anticipate', 'checked further surmise' (3:49:110). The novel has offered very few forward clues about what awaits Deronda at this reunion. True, we foresee that he may be a Jew. What we do not foresee is why he has lost his Jewish inheritance. His mother's acts have been the most stupendous acts of will described within the novel.

The importance of the Princess Halm-Eberstein within the ordering of the novel is undeniable. As far as plot goes, her revelation of his Jewishness releases a completely new set of possibilities for Deronda which wonderfully concur with his desires – bringing him a mission, love, a reasoned mythology, and a personal history in the chest of papers.[6]

What is more puzzling is her relation to the work's dominant ideology. She has cast aside all the ties which society, kin, and religion sought to impose on her in order to follow her stupendous career as a great opera singer:

> I wanted to live out the life that was in me, and not to be hampered with other lives. You wonder what I was. I was no princess then . . . No princess in this tame life that I live in now. I was a great singer, and I acted as well as I sang. All the rest were poor beside me. Men followed me from one country to another. I was living a myriad lives in one. I did not want a child. (3:54:123)

She has given the two-year-old Deronda away to be educated as an Englishman rather than have him brought up in what she sees as the trap of Jewishness: 'I relieved you from the bondage of having been born a Jew.' She expects no affection from him: 'I have not the foolish notion that you can love me merely because I am your mother, when you have never seen or heard of me all your life' (3:51:123). Deronda asks her the crucial question: 'How could you choose my birthright for me?' She answers:

> Every woman is supposed to have the same set of motives, or else to be a monster. I am not a monster, but I have not felt exactly what other women feel – or say they feel, for fear of being thought unlike others. When you reproach me in your heart for sending you away from me, you mean that I ought to say I felt about you as other women say they feel about their children. I did not feel that. I was glad to be freed from you. But I did well for you, and I gave you your father's fortune. (3:51:127)

Deronda's father, his mother's first cousin, is an eponymous, self-abnegating man who has given himself up to his wife and served her faithfully. Deronda's shock and anger mediate the interview for us and assert the princess to have been wrong in her choices – not to be a mother, to give him up to a society which has little spiritual distinction. But what she advances is a thrillingly sustained argument for the right of a woman to vary in motives, passions, needs, and not to subserve always the assumptions of society or the demands of race and inheritance: the stories of her culture.

It is an argument which is worsted practically by Deronda's wish to attach himself to his cultural inheritance, both because of his spiritual relationship with Mordecai and because it allows him to marry Mirah. And the confrontation has been brought about by her need for magical punishment – she has broken taboos and needs the assurance of self-revenge as she approaches death. She in her turn has been trapped. Believing her voice to have gone she married for security and is now the distinguished mother of a numerous family, who do not know of Deronda's existence. Her condition has a predictive force – representing one possible outcome or (perhaps more exactly) one *impossible* outcome for Gwendolen. The princess has her own greatness as an artist to sustain her in her right to make choices, whereas Gwendolen's predicament is that she has will without authority, rebellion without speculation. She enters the feminist challenge to her prescribed lot without any sort of theoretical or practical *consciousness*. She is eventually liberated by her frantic unconscious.

Of course marriage was social promotion; she could not look forward to a single life; but promotions have sometimes to be taken with bitter herbs – a peerage will not quite do instead of leadership to the man who meant to lead; and this delicate-limbed sylph of twenty meant to lead. For such passions dwell in feminine breasts also. In Gwendolen's, however, they dwelt among strictly feminine furniture, and had no disturbing reference to the advancement of learning or the balance of the constitution. (1:4:52–3)

Though to *have* a mother may be a good thing, then, George Eliot suggests that to *be* a mother may not. Her own life and her role as artist had taught her a good deal about the role of step-mother: a figure notably absent from her fiction. In *Felix Holt* Mrs Transome lives a sequestered imaginative life of dread, stemming to some extent from having borne a son to a man not her husband, but also surcharged with a sense of how frail is the hold of individuality in maternal emotion – how much of the self is submerged or excluded.

It is a fact perhaps kept a little too much in the background, that mothers have a self larger than their maternity, and that when their sons have become taller than themselves, and are gone from them to college or into the world, there are wide spaces of their time which are not filled with praying for their boys, reading old letters, and envying yet blessing those who are attending to their shirt-buttons. Mrs Transome was certainly not one of those bland, adoring, and gently tearful women. After sharing the common dream that when a beautiful man-child was born to her, her cup of happiness would be full, she had travelled through long years apart from that child to find herself at last in the presence of a son of whom she was afraid, who was utterly unmanageable by her, and to whose sentiments in any given case she possessed no key. (1:8:166–7)

Mrs Transome represents George Eliot's first major exploration of the particular quality of dread which she associates with woman's experience and with enforced passivity:

No-one divined what was hidden under that outward life – a woman's keen sensibility and dread, which lay screened behind her petty habits and narrow notions, as some quivering thing with eyes and throbbing heart may lie crouched behind withered rubbish. (1:1:43)

This brings us back to the concept of mastery – and of fear. The epigraph to chapter 9 of *Felix Holt* runs thus:

> A woman, naturally born to fears – *King John*
>
> Methinks
> Some unborn sorrow, ripe in fortune's womb,
> Is coming towards me; and my inward soul
> With nothing trembles – *King Richard II*

Incommensurate or irrational fear – hysteria – has been traditionally associated with women and particularly with pregnancy. So King Lear cries out:

> O, how this mother swells up toward my heart!
> Hysterica passio, down, thou climbing sorrow,
> Thy element's below!

The connection had by no means been abandoned by Victorian medical theory. For example W. B. Carpenter in *Principles of Mental Physiology with their Applications to the Training and Discipline of the Mind and the Study of its Morbid Conditions* (1874) has no entry for women or female in the index or for their particular conditions. But when he discusses hysteria and 'general exaltation of sensibility' he shifts from the masculine gender he uses elsewhere to describe the patient, and instead refers to 'she' and 'her'. Having slipped naturally into the feminine for this description he adds a footnote:

This condition is by no means peculiar to Females; although, from the *greater impressibility of the Nervous system and the lower development of Volitional power*, by which the sex is ordinarily characterised, it is more common among them than in males. [my italics]

The idea of the 'Volitional power' in women refers to their less developed *control* rather than to their less developed emotion, it seems. The treatment he suggests is to deflect attention. The powers he claims to have observed in the patient are remarkable:

Attention is so fixed upon her own bodily state, that the most trivial impressions are magnified into severe pains; while there is often such an extraordinary acuteness to sounds, that she overhears a conversation carried on in an undertone in an adjoining room, or (as in a case known to the Writer) in a room on the second floor beneath. (700)

We remember Mrs Transome looking at her son and the man neither he nor we then know to be his father: 'So Mrs Transome was not observing the two men; rather her hands were cold and her whole person shaken by their presence; she seemed to hear and see what they said and did with preternatural acuteness' (1:2:53).

Darwin's later work had suggested that fear was the most primitive emotion, immediately connected to survival. It was an emotion necessary in primitive states but to be controlled and subdued in the state of civilisation. It is always associated with the unwilled and unconscious levels of personality. George Eliot herself, reviewing Lecky's *Influence of Rationalism* in 1865, had written (in a passage where it is not easy to be certain how far these are her own views, how far a summary of Lecky):

Fear is earlier born than hope, lays a stronger grasp on man's system than any other passion, and remains master of a larger group of involuntary actions. A chief aspect of man's moral development is the slow subduing of fear by the gradual growth of intelligence, and its suppression as a motive by the presence of impulses less animally selfish.[8]

The passage continues in a way that clarifies the relationship between animal and religious dread: 'So that in relation to invisible Power, fear at last ceases to exist save in that interfusion with higher faculties which we call awe.' Fear is a response to danger, but also to oppression. In *Daniel Deronda* fear is raised into consciousness and becomes for Gwendolen in particular a mode of heightened apprehension, which can include prescience and freedom as well as the obliterative terror with which she receives Lydia's diamonds, pallid, shrieking, spellbound.

Her 'large discourse of imaginative fears' opens her to alarm, dread, and multiplicity. It sets her at a disadvantage in relation to Grandcourt's mean will but at the same time opens her to possibilities beyond the range of his interest, offering her a vertiginous freedom which often takes on the aspect of nightmare.

There is a close congruity between the description of Gwendolen's hatred and fear (emotion which dare not express itself) and Darwin's description in the section on Fear in *The Expression of the Emotions*. The same image of slave and master, oppressor and oppressed, colonial dominion, controls in both:

Few individuals, however, can long reflect about a hated person, without feeling and exhibiting signs of indignation or rage. But if the offending person be quite insignificant, we experience merely disdain or contempt. If, on the other hand, he is all-powerful, then hatred passes into terror, as when a slave thinks about a cruel master, or a savage about a bloodthirsty malignant deity. (Darwin)[9]

And the intensest form of hatred is that rooted in fear, which compels to silence and drives vehemence into a constructive vindictiveness, an imaginary annihilation of the detested object, something like the hidden rites of vengeance with which the persecuted have made a dark vent for their rage, and soothed their suffering into dumbness. Such hidden rites went on in the secrecy of Gwendolen's mind, but not with soothing effect – rather with the effect of a struggling terror. (George Eliot) (3:54:195)

Whereas Carpenter relied on deflecting the attention to mitigate the symptoms of hysteria, and Darwin and Sully held that emotion if unexpressed experiences attrition, in *Daniel Deronda* fear becomes a tool of consciousness, not something to be suppressed. Daniel advises Gwendolen to hold on to her fear – and his advice emphasises not only carefulness and retrenchment but fear as a means of perception and apprehension: 'Take your fear as a safeguard. It is like quickness of hearing. It may make consequences passionately present to you. Try to take hold of your sensibility, and use it as if it were a faculty, like vision' (2:36:268).

Gwendolen's remorse and her resistance to Grandcourt oblige her to dread bearing a child which will become simply a piece in the game of inheritance, and will transmit Grandcourt's dominance:

Some unhappy wives are soothed by the possibility that they may become mothers; but Gwendolen felt that to desire a child for herself would have been a consenting to the completion of the injury she had been guilty of. She was reduced to dread lest she should become a mother. It was not the image of a new sweetly-budding life that came as a vision of deliverance from the monotony of distaste: it was an image of another sort. In the irritable, fluctuating stages of despair, gleams of hope came in the form of some possible accident. To dwell on the benignity of accident was a refuge from worse temptation. (3:54:194–5)

Passivity and silence may be means of insurrection and Mirah – in interpreting another of those stories and parables which are so important in this text – makes it clear that vehement selfhood can be expressed through self-immolation.

'And yet,' said Mordecai, rather insistently, 'women are specially framed for the love which feels possession in renouncing, and is thus a fit image of what I mean. Somewhere in the later *Midrash*, I think, is the story of a Jewish maiden who loved a Gentile king so well, that this was what she did: – She entered into prison and changed clothes with the woman who was beloved by the king, that she might deliver that woman from death by dying in her stead, and leave the king to be happy in his love which was not for her. This is the surpassing love, that loses self in the object of love.'

'No, Ezra, no,' said Mirah, with low-toned intensity, 'that was not it. She wanted the king when she was dead to know what she had done, and feel that she was better than the other. It was her strong self, wanting to conquer, that made her die.' (3:61:290)

Women seek power and mastery, but within the *argument* of the book are permitted to achieve it only as instrumentality or negation. The powers of Catherine Arrowsmith and Mirah are those of the executant, subdued to their instrument. Gwendolen achieves mastery briefly and circumscribedly as an archer, safe in her Diana chastity, but she loses it immediately in marriage. The active phase of hysteria and fear in Gwendolen is replaced by the confinement and subjection of terror – her mind remains active, ranging; her presence is reified; her mind is racing:

Why could she not rebel, and defy him? She longed to do it. But she might as well have tried to defy the texture of her nerves and the palpitation of her heart. Her husband had a ghostly army at his back, that could close round her wherever she might turn. She sat in her splendid attire, like a white image of helplessness, and he seemed to gratify himself with looking at her. She could not even make a passionate exclamation, or throw up her arms, as she would have done in her maiden days. The sense of his scorn kept her still. (2:36:260–1)

It is this induced passivity which in the end liberates her – those imprisoned and sequestered fantasies are suddenly seen outside her. She does not act. She is frozen and does not throw the rope. Grandcourt drowns.

Fear's intensity and its febrile visionary quality are sympathetically realised by Darwin in his description of a mad woman in chapter 12 on Fear in *The Expression of the Emotions*, but are curiously absent from most Victorian psychological descriptions of it. It is to Kierkegaard that we must turn to find a writer in affinity with George Eliot here. Dread in Kierkegaard's analysis draws on 'the egoistic infinity of possibility'; 'woman is more in dread than man' (55) because more sensuous than man, with a life culminating in procreation. 'Dread is constantly to be understood as oriented towards freedom' (59–60). 'He who is educated by dread is educated by possibility, and only the man who is educated by possibility is educated in accordance with his infinity' (139–40).[10] Dread allows the play of possibility to those who appear circumscribed.

In a passage which recalls the tonic irony of her early essay, 'Silly Novels by lady Novelists', we read:

Gwendolen was as inwardly rebellious against the restraints of family conditions, and as ready to look through obligations into her own fundamental want of feeling for them, as if she had been sustained by the boldest speculations;

but she really had no such speculations, and would at once have marked herself off from any sort of theoretical or practically reforming women by satirising them. She rejoiced to feel herself exceptional; but her horizon was that of the genteel romance where the heroine's soul poured out in her journal is full of vague power, originality, and general rebellion, while her life moves strictly in the sphere of fashion; and if she wanders into a swamp, the pathos lies partly, so to speak, in her having on her satin shoes. Here is a restraint which nature and society have provided on the pursuit of striking adventure; so that a soul burning with a sense of what the universe is not, and ready to take all existence as fuel, is nevertheless held captive by the ordinary wirework of social forms and does nothing particular. (1:6:74)

So her lack, her negative vision 'a soul burning with a sense of what the universe is not', must take the form of distance, and her integrity must be frigid. Gwendolen is more often correct when she repulses, wrong when she receives. And she is at the mercy of her own unconscious or half-consciousness. Predictive fantasies seize upon her with the same power that they do Mordecai.

The thought of his dying would not subsist; it turned as with a dream-change into the terror that she should die with his throttling fingers on her neck avenging that thought. Fantasies moved within her like ghosts, making no break in her more acknowledged consciousness and finding no obstruction in it: dark rays doing their work invisibly in the broad light. (3:48:94)

In both cases events confirm dream, but in Gwendolen's case there is no extension, only obsession. There is a similar contrast in their relationship to chance: Gwendolen in gambling is seeking a system of personal teleology, in which the world will succumb to the mastery of her need. Mordecai waits, and hopes for the coming of his unknown inheritor. Descent – 'transmission' – may be a matter of spiritual affinity, not of incarnation. The peaceable images of Daniel rowing downstream suggest an equilibrium of control and quiescence. The state of mind is privileged; it accords with natural process and allows him to arrive at the needed place at the needed time. It is a psychologised version of determinism which allows the individual apparently to produce the solution to the problem he arrives at. The effect is of desire assuaged before it is known, a continuity of present and future which sets no strain between them. In this novel such continuity is associated only with Daniel. George Eliot uses the double sense of channels: the channels worn through the land by water and the then current physiological sense of the channels worn through the brain by ideas, which account for the power of memory and habit. The difference between drifting and rowing has frequently come to represent within her books the difference between half-conscious acquiescence in unconscious forces and the activity of the will resisting and attempting to govern such energies.

The sea surrounds Gwendolen's hopes and fears, suggesting, like the astronomical imagery, illimitable space following its own time and laws. Lyell and Darwin both emphasised the sea as a present reminder of how narrow is man's dominion. Here chapter 9 of the first book 'The Spoiled Child' opens with the ominous epigraph:

> I'll tell thee, Berthold, what men's hopes are like:
> A silly child that, quivering with joy,
> Would cast its little mimic fishing-line
> Baited with loadstone for a bowl of toys
> In the salt ocean. (1:9:130)

Despite the boats that track the imperial diaspora across its surface the sea belittles all man's attempts at power. In this book it is linked with the unchartable future. The sea became for post-evolutionary novelists the necessary element against which to measure the human. It comes to represent the unconscious in which there is no narrative. Virginia Woolf and Conrad both seek through it to express that which is beyond the human, and so impervious to the commands of language. The sea is the aboriginal, unchanging element out of which evolving forms have emerged but within which primal forms remain, and its tides forever renew, change and remain. It is upon this element that Grandcourt sets out on his vengeful yachting holiday.

The imagery of drowning has occurred more than once in the earlier part of the book. Daniel, having bid Gwendolen, 'Take your fear as a safeguard', watches her reaction: 'It was as if he saw her drowning while his limbs were bound' (2:36:269). But it has not been an obsessional recurring imagery as that of looking-glass, windows, opaque glass, reflections, have been. Such images freeze and replicate the present, offering no issue out into the future: Gwendolen's mirror-images multiply without variety or progression. The sea is its own place, not constrained to symbol. Struggling with her murderous fantasies within her constricted space, locked with her hated husband aboard the yacht: 'Inarticulate prayers, no more definite than a cry, often swept out from her into the vast silence, unbroken except by her husband's breathing or the plash of the wave or the creaking of the masts.' And in their last sail in the small boat which Grandcourt so skilfully – but not sufficiently skilfully – handles, we are given no direct account of events after the end of the chapter in which Grandcourt says: 'I shall put about.' Just before that

Gwendolen fantasises desperately that 'we shall go on always like the Flying Dutchman' (3:54:209) – after that everything becomes part of that provisional, half-fantasy world of surmise and confession. Could Grandcourt swim? We never know for certain. How long did she hold the rope? Did she take the rope with her when she leapt in after him?

The book's typical form of interrogation is now taken over by the reader – and no absolute answers are provided. In this introspected order, no sufficient knowledge ever comes. The barriers between desire and event have fallen: 'I know nothing – I only know that I saw my wish outside me.' That denial of knowledge is part of the distraught, yet active and intense, questioning of the relation of present to future and of the relation of present to present – since other people's present consciousness creates the future activity of interpretation. There are no stable barriers between tenses either.

The preoccupation with origins in this book turns out to be an exploration which can never recover its own beginnings. Cosmogonies may seem to give assurance – how did things begin? Descent is the only plan that can be tracked in a dysteleological world, what Darwin called 'the chain of ordinary generation'. The individual must live *as if* he were undetermined in order to survive – and it is at least shown that nothing can be securely prophesied. This time in contrast to *The Mill on the Floss* the woman has not drowned. She is taken to the edge of plot, out of the marriage market, out of the ordering of inheritance. This is as far as her freedom can go – but for a George Eliot novel, it is a long way.

Daniel in a muted prophetic conclusion is to set out for the East 'to become better acquainted with the condition of my race in various countries there' with the purpose of 'restoring a political existence to my people'. We do not see him embark, but of course the ending of the novel with its Zionist prospect reads very differently for us from the way it read to its first readers. To them it read like improbable dreams, to us as dangerous reality. This is an extraordinary instance of the enacted future rushing in between text and reader, transforming what is prophetic, surmiseful, quixotic, into what has come about: political, fraught with suffering and explosive in our own world a hundred years on. It is appropriate in a text so obsessed with futurity that its own conclusion should be disrupted by it. Whereas *War and Peace* constantly interrupts itself to point out the historical necessity of what appears as spontaneous individualistic action and feeling, *Daniel Deronda* emphasises the range of dread and desire compressed in the single event – it emphasises also the elements of experience which survive *unexpressed*, alluring or daemonic, only occasionally exorcised in happening. Emotions more often evade any such impacting, so that choice and event begin to share the qualities of the random. No single future can be inferred from the present, yet we all live by prediction.

Whereas in *Middlemarch* the reader's hypothesising role is subdued as we watch the experiments proposed in the Prologue acted out before us, in *Daniel Deronda* the reader's hypothesising power is an essential property of the text. The thickening, barely provisional counter-plots of possibility which we are persistently encouraged to project are the matter out of which events occur. The sequestered information which throbs through each individual presence and is mostly withheld, not acted upon, scarcely recognisable to any but the one who knows his or her own conscious and latent thoughts, the throng of fantasies which suffer no transformation into event, makes up the particular texture of this book.

Incarnation is not inevitable; the speculative infinity of astronomical enquiry is closer to the book's project. It is a novel about that which does not occur: Gwendolen does not kill Grandcourt nor does she marry Deronda. Neither Deronda nor Mirah reach a longed-for reunion of affection with their mothers. Grandcourt does not conceive an heir by Gwendolen. So much are these *desires* conceived as having the force of *acts* within the book that the plot is a wilful and conscious form of negation: its power comes from not telling the stories we anticipate hearing, and, at the end, not telling the story. In her notebook George Eliot cites several instances of the creative spirit making a thing come to pass. And we know from her letter to Harriet Beecher Stowe that she would have wished to change things. In this work change cannot be expressed through the metaphor of descent that she has adopted – though sexual selection is one of the topics of the work. It must figure itself as disruption and incompleteness, however much the book's enterprise strives towards unity.

CHAPTER 8

Finding a scale for the human: plot and writing in Hardy's novels

In *The Expression of the Emotions* Darwin describes fear as a primary emotion whose manner of expression has barely changed over millions of years:

We may likewise infer that fear was expressed from an extremely remote period, in almost the same manner as it now is by man; namely, by trembling, the erection of the hair, cold perspiration, pallor, widely opened eyes, the relaxation of most of the muscles, and by the whole body cowering downwards or held motionless.[1]

Fear is, in the Victorian anthropological sense, a 'survival'. Like certain primitive tribes, this primitive emotion survives into the modern world unchanged. Like them, it represents the primal conditions of man and allows us to observe those conditions still at work. Moreover, it occupies the same place in the metaphor of development as do 'primitive' peoples: fear is an emotion to be controlled, suppressed, outgrown. Reason is cast as an adult emotion, just as western European man is an 'adult' on the scale of development. So, like primitive peoples, fear is to be kept under control. Yet like them, it is still there, not fully left behind, nor entirely dominated. In the arc of development, fear is perceived, disturbingly, as at the base. It retains its insurgent power and is liable – like mutiny – to break out.

The *effort* of empire can be seen in the later-nineteenth-century preoccupation with fear, in a culture which set so much store by courage, or 'pluck'. It is a preoccupation which then fuels much Edwardian writing, particularly Conrad's works. For example, in *Lord Jim* the atavistic emotion of fear leads Jim to jump overboard, abandoning ship and passengers. His attempt to redeem this failure of nerve takes him at last to the position of wise counsellor of a 'primitive' people. In *Heart of Darkness* terror of what will be found at the centre of man's emotions takes the form of a journey into the Amazon jungle and of empire over 'primitive' tribes, a journey of self-destruction. In both cases fear of fear is the initiating emotion.

220

Fear is caused by those who *undergo* fear: servants, animals, women, subject races. Saki in his brief story *Laura* brilliantly condenses the various categories: Laura returns to haunt her friend's husband, as women, otter, and black Nubian servant boy. Children, servants, hunted prey, black races, and women all generate dread here. The fear they feel in the face of the master give them power to terrify that same master.

In *Daniel Deronda*, George Eliot suggested that 'mastering' fear was no answer. It must be entered and used 'like a faculty'. Hardy wrote in his Journal: 'Courage has been idealized: why not fear? which is a higher consciousness and based on a deeper insight.'[2] He here inverts the expected value placed on fear, while in his attribution of a 'deeper insight' he suggests its power in the natural order.

In a journal entry in January 1888 Hardy writes: 'Apprehension is a great element in imagination. It is a semi-madness, which sees enemies etc., in inanimate objects.' His next entry, a week later, continues:

A 'sensation-novel' is possible in which the sensation is not casualty, but evolution; not physical but psychical . . . whereas in the physical the adventure itself is the subject of interest, the psychical results being passed over as commonplace, in the psychical the casualty or adventure is held to be no intrinsic interest, but the effect upon the faculties is the important matter to be depicted.[3]

The emphasis here upon the interconnections between 'sensation' and 'evolution', between apprehension and animism, may lead us a long way into the particular nature of Hardy's creativity. Hardy analysed what he saw as a creative kinship between primitive culture and 'highest imaginative genius' in terms of animism. The analysis comes to him with the relish of a fresh notion when Edward Clodd, first president of the British Folklore Society and Darwinist, explained it in terms of cultural development and 'survivals':

December 18. Mr E. Clodd this morning gives an excellently neat answer to my question why the superstitions of a remote Asiatic and a Dorset labourer are the same: 'The attitude of man', he says, 'at corresponding levels of culture, before like phenomena, is pretty much the same, your Dorset peasants representing the persistence of the barbaric idea which confuses persons and things, and founds wide generalizations on the slenderest analogies.' (This 'barbaric idea which confuses persons and things' is, by the way, also common to the highest imaginative genius – that of the poet.)[4]

The double sense of apprehension is crucial for Hardy. It includes both the sense of fear and of awakening – and these senses are not opposed or disconnected. Though terror may be an obliterative experience, fear makes keen. It awakens thought and sensation. The self becomes alert, ready, yet passive. And this is very much the situation created in the reader by the contradiction of plot and writing in Hardy's work. We are filled with intolerable apprehensions of what future events may bring, while yet the text in process awakens us to sensation full of perceptual pleasure. It is a state Hardy describes often as part of the experience of his characters. For example Tess, exhausted, listens to the other women working. She 'lay in a state of percipience, without volition, and *the rustle of the straw and the cutting of the ears by the others had the weight of bodily touches*'[5] [my italics]. Touch and hearing lie peculiarly close in his economy of the senses. They are particularly associated with alert passivity.

Hardy acknowledged Darwin always as a major intellectual influence in his work and his way of seeing.[6] Much has been written on the connection and there have been excellent studies of individual novels. In this argument I want to explore a more general question to do with the relationship of plot and writing. Most commentators have emphasised the point of connection between Hardy and Darwin in terms of pessimism, a sense that the laws of life are themselves flawed. That Hardy did feel this is undeniable. One notices the implicit cultural evolutionism of a passage like this:

The truth seems to be that a long line of disillusive centuries has permanently displaced the Hellenic idea of life, or whatever it may be called. What the Greeks only suspected we know well; what their Aeschylus imagined our nursery children feel. That old-fashioned revelling in the general situation grows less and less possible as we uncover the defects of natural laws, and see the quandary that man is in by their operation (185).[7]

Aeschylus's imagining has become (by means of evolutionary development) children's feeling. The human quandary is caused by laws themselves defective, and which take no account of us.

A woeful fact – that the human race is too extremely developed for its corporeal conditions, the nerves being evolved to an activity abnormal in such an environment. Even the higher animals are in excess in this respect. It may be questioned if Nature, or what we call Nature, so far back as when she crossed the line from invertebrates to vertebrates, did not exceed her mission. This planet does not supply the materials for happiness to higher existences. Other planets may, though one can hardly see how.[8]

But although he felt the burden of evolution this was by no means all that he felt or all that he makes us feel as a consequence of his familiarity with Darwin's work. Though the individual may be of small consequence in the long sequence of succession and generation, yet Hardy in his emplotment opposes this perception and does so by adopting again the single life span as his scale. Whereas George Eliot's novels, and Dickens's novels, tend to include death, rather than end with death, Hardy's texts pay homage to human scale by ceasing as the hero or heroine dies. The single life span is no longer an absolute but polemical. That is one formal expression of his humanism. It opposes evolutionary meliorism or pessimism by making the single generation carry the freight of signification.

Plot in Hardy is almost always tragic or malign: it involves the overthrow of the individual either by the inevitability of death or by the machinations (or disregard) of 'crass casualty'. Deterministic systems are placed under great stress: a succession of ghost plots is present. The persistently almost-attained happy alternatives are never quite obliterated by the actual terrible events. The reader is pained by the sense of multiple possibilities, only one of which can occur and be thus verified in time, space, and actuality. The belief in fixed laws is a sustaining element in George Eliot's sense of the moral nature of plot. Fecundity for Zola is life's answer to death. But each of these elements becomes for Hardy part of an ulterior plot, beyond the control of humankind. Near the beginning of *Tess of the D'Urbervilles* Hardy comments sardonically: 'Some people would like to know whence the poet whose philosophy is in these days deemed as profound and trustworthy as his song is breezy and pure, gets his authority for speaking of "Nature's holy plan".' Darwin had sought to share Wordsworth's testamental language in his image of 'Natural Selection', which identified nature with benign planning and makes of natural selection a more correct form than man's merely artificial selection.[9] Hardy reads such plans as plot; plot becomes malign and entrapping, because it is designed without the needs of individual life in mind. Human variety is oppressed by the needs which generate plot. Angel Clare begins to free himself from his class-bound assumptions of working people's uniformity:

Without any objective change whatever, variety had taken the place of monotonousness. His host and his host's household, his men and his maids, as they became intimately known to Clare, began to differentiate themselves as in a chemical process. The thought of Pascal's was brought home to him: 'A mesure qu'on a plus d'esprit, on trouve qu'il y a plus d'hommes originaux. Les gens du commun ne trouvent pas de différence entre les hommes.' The typical and unvarying Hodge ceased to exist. He had been disintegrated into a number of varied fellow-creatures – beings of many minds, beings infinite in difference.

But even as he becomes aware of fellow creatures 'infinite in difference', the action of his sexual presence is producing uniformity, as the dairy-maids writhe in the power of their own unasked-for sexuality, 'an emotion thrust on them by cruel Nature's law'.[10]

In reading Hardy's work we often find a triple level of plot generated: the anxiously scheming and predictive plot of the characters' making; the optative plot of the commentary, which often takes the form 'Why did nobody' or 'had somebody . . .', and the absolute plot of blind interaction and 'Nature's laws'. These laws cannot be comprehended within a single order. In Hardy's novels all scales are absolute, but multiple. So he includes many time-scales, from the geological time of Egdon Heath to the world of the ephemerons. The idea that nature is adapted to man is expressive of morbid states of mind in *Tess of the D'Urbervilles* so that 'at times her whimsical fancy would intensify natural processes around her until they seemed part of her own story'. This way lies the plot of paranoia where exterior, interior, and ulterior fuse so that the question of the source of the plot (in the clinic of the head, in the chaos of the universe) cannot be redeemed.

The emphasis upon systems more extensive than the life span of the individual and little according to his needs is essential to Hardy's insight. Much of the grandeur of his fiction comes from his acceptance of people's independence and self-assertion – doomed and curtailed persistently, but recuperating. But further underlying that emphasis upon the individual is the paradox that even those recuperative energies are there primarily to serve the longer needs of the race and are part of a procreative energy designed to combat extinction, not the death of any individual.

Alongside the emphasis on apprehension and anxiety, on inevitable overthrow long foreseen, persistingly evaded, there is, however, another prevailing sensation in Hardy's work equally strongly related to his understanding of Darwin. It is that of happiness. Alongside the doomed sense of weighted past and incipient conclusion, goes a sense of plenitude, an 'appetite for joy'. This finds expression – as it must if at all – in the moment-by-moment fullness of the text. In 'Song of Myself' Whitman (who is quoted in *Tess*) wrote:

> I have heard what the talkers were talking, the talk of the beginning
> > and the end,
> But I do not talk of the beginning or the end.
> There was never any more inception than there is now,
> Nor any more youth and age than there is now,

And will never be any more perfection than there is now,
Nor any more heaven or hell than there is now.
Urge and urge and urge,
Always the procreant urge of the world.

At each moment the world is complete, though urged onwards always by procreation. Whitman's is a powerful alternative to that form of evolutionary thinking which sets the past aspiring to become present, and the present imagining a more satisfying future. Whitman's sense of the world's fullness is yet linked to that 'appetite for joy' which Hardy saw as charging life equally with rapture and disaster. Sexual joy is always dangerous, not only because of the possibility of loss, but because it is linked to *generation*, the law which rides like a juggernaut over and through individual identity and individual life spans.

She clasped his neck, and for the first time Clare learnt what an impassioned woman's kisses were like upon the lips of one whom she loved with all her heart and soul, as Tess loved him. 'There – now do you believe?' she asked, flushed, and wiping her eyes.
'Yes. I never really doubted – never, never!'
So they drove on through the gloom, forming one bundle inside the sailcloth, the horse going as he would, and the rain driving against them. She had consented. She might as well have agreed at first. The 'appetite for joy' which pervades all creation, that tremendous force which sways humanity to its purpose, as the tide sways the helpless weed, was not to be controlled by vague lucubrations over the social rubric. (*Tess*: 218)

The impassioned moment is seized through touch and temperature, the most intimately present of sense-experience. Then the language turns aside, first into the imagery of the sea and of motion (still perpetuating the bodily experience of the lovers). The sense of power and of helplessness change into the jarring abstraction of the 'vague lucubrations over the social rubric', facetiously orotund. The reader must work for meaning, instead of being immersed in meaning – and the sense and sound alike rebuff readers, and distance lovers.

Hardy comments on another natural drive, separate from that of procreation although often associated with it: 'the determination to enjoy': 'Thought of the determination to enjoy. We see it in all nature, from the leaf on the tree to the titled lady at the ball . . . Like pent-up water it will find a chink of possibility somewhere' (August 1888).[11] In 'The Dorsetshire Labourer' (1883) he sees the refusal to believe in happiness among 'the labouring classes' as a class-bound condescension and satirises such views:

Misery and fever lurk in his cottage, while to paraphrase the words of a recent writer on the labouring classes, in his future there are only the workshop and the grave. He hardly dares to think at all. He has few thoughts of joy, and little hope of rest.

In contrast, Hardy asserts, a real observer would discover a diversity of character, life and moods.

He would have learnt that wherever a mode of supporting life is neither noxious nor absolutely inadequate, there springs up happiness, and will spring up happiness, of some sort or other. Indeed, it is among such communities as these that happiness will find her last refuge on earth, since it is among them that a perfect insight into the conditions of existence will be longest postponed.[12]

Again, the creative contradiction is set out. 'There springs up happiness' as against 'the conditions of existence': sensations against laws; writing against narrative. In a comparison of George Eliot and Hardy, one of their earlier critics, Oliver Elton, defined the difference between them thus:

While exhaustively describing life, she is apt to miss the spirit of life itself. Its unashamed passion, its careless gaiety, the intoxication of sunshine – so far as she understands these things, she leaves us with the feeling that she rather distrusts them.[13]

Hardy's work, in contrast, is characterised by these qualities. He does not distrust passion, gaiety and sunshine but he records how through event and time they are threatened, thwarted, undermined. And how for each organism, and through writing, they are recuperated.

He describes not only the 'fearful joy', the 'killing joy' of sexual arousal, but placable, unnoticed happiness, something so 'matter of course' that no one comments on it. So only Eustacia sets out to *act* in the Mummers' play; the rest go through the motions in a way which Hardy thoroughly naturalises by means of the metaphor of mushrooms:

The remainder of the play ended: the Saracen's head was cut off, and Saint George stood as victor. Nobody commented, any more than they would have commented on the fact of mushrooms coming in autumn or snowdrops in spring. They took the piece as phlegmatically as did the actors themselves. It was a phase of cheerfulness which was, as a matter of course, to be passed through every Christmas; and there was no more to be said. (*Return*: 157)

Metaphor in the following passage is slight and is used only laterally, comparing one natural form to another ('almost feline' . . . 'toads made noises like very young ducks') until the last phrase 'their drone coming and going like the sound of a gong'. The propinquity of the human here barely disturbs the animate.

The month of March arrived, and the heath showed its first faint signs of awakening from winter trance. The awakening was almost feline in its stealthiness. The pool outside the bank by Eustacia's dwelling, which seemed as dead and desolate as ever to an observer who moved and made noises in his observation, would gradually disclose a state of great animation when silently watched awhile. A timid animal world had come to life for the season. Little tadpoles and efts began to bubble up through the water, and to race along beneath it; toads made noises like very young ducks, and advanced to the margin in twos and threes; overhead, bumble-bees flew hither and thither in the thickening light, their drone coming and going like the sound of a gong. (*Return*: 207)

The same comedy of propinquity and complementarity is present in most of the descriptions which release pleasure, the human presence delicately stopping and completing the whole:

When Elizabeth-Jane opened the hinged casement next morning the mellow air brought in the feel of imminent autumn almost as distinctly as if she had been in the remotest hamlet. Casterbridge was the complement of the rural life around; not its urban opposite. Bees and butterflies in the cornfields at the top of the town, who desired to get to the meads at the bottom, took no circuitous course, but flew straight down High Street without any apparent consciousness that they were traversing strange latitudes. And in autumn airy spheres of thistledown floated into the same street, lodged upon the shop fronts, blew into drains, and innumerable tawny and yellow leaves skimmed along the pavement, and stole through people's doorways into their passages with a hesitating scratch on the floor, like the skirts of timid visitors.[14]

The problem and the poignancy of narrative for Hardy was the gap between sensation and recall: 'Today has length, breadth, thickness, colour, smell, voice. As soon as it becomes *yesterday* it is a thin layer among many layers, without substance, colour, or articulate sound' (27 January 1897).[15]

His writing seeks the palpable. It is in the present moment that human knowledge is realised and human happiness is experienced. The present is part of the material order as the past can no longer be. Hardy, in fact, shares that Romantic materialism which we have already dwelt on in Darwin's writing.

Observation is charged with sensory power. In both writers the material world is described simultaneously in terms which may lend themselves to an optimistic or pessimistic interpretation, but which function *as terms* through the pleasures of observation. The rapid changes of scale and distance shift the writing between tabulation, recurrence, the single instance, diversity recorded, the historical sense of physical life experienced again and again.

With respect to plants, it has long been known what enormous ranges many fresh-water and even marsh-species have . . . I think favourable means of dispersal explain this fact . . . Wading birds, which frequent the muddy edges of ponds, if suddenly flushed, would be the most likely to have muddy feet. Birds of this order I can show are the greatest wanderers, and are occasionally found on the most remote and barren islands in the open ocean; they would not be likely to alight on the surface of the sea, so that the dirt would not be washed off their feet; when making land, they would be sure to fly to their natural fresh-water haunts. I do not believe that botanists are aware how charged the mud of ponds is with seeds . . . I took in February three table-spoonfuls of mud from three different points, beneath water, on the edge of a little pond; this mud when dry weighed only $6\frac{3}{4}$ ounces; I kept it covered up in my study for six months, pulling up and counting each plant as it grew; the plants were of many kinds, and were altogether 537 in number; and yet the viscid mud was all contained in a breakfast cup! Considering these facts, I think it would be an inexplicable circumstance if water-birds did not transport the seeds of fresh-water plants to vast distances, and if consequently the range of these plants was not very great. (376–7)

Darwin's provisional explanation takes the form of description with a strongly imagined participation in the flight of the wading birds with their muddy feet, their sudden flight, their powers of wandering, their avoidance of the sea and seeking for fresh water. Then the perspective changes suddenly from ranging mind's-eye to the experimental observer, with his pleasure in 'pulling up and counting each plant as it grew' and the precise largesse of the number 537. Darwin combines the domestic object of the breakfast cup of mud and the free space of the ocean-ranging birds to reach a conclusion cast in negatives which delay – and reinforce – its inevitability.

'Herons and other birds, century after century, have gone on daily devouring fish; they then take flight and go to other waters, or are blown across the sea.' Darwin's writing represents the pleasurability of physical process; it registers the felicity, as well as the difficulty, of life's multiple scales and sensations. His evidence is not experimental solely, but imaginative, relying on a felt and learnt identification with alien forms of life.

His range of reference, his sense of lateral experience, finds a new place for man within the natural order, unnamed among many creatures in 'the entangled bank'. Yet his writing also amplifies that image by granting to the human observer the power simultaneously to observe and identify with all other forms of life: the kicking ostrich, the worm 'crawling through the damp earth', 'how much the fruit of the different kinds of gooseberries differ in size, colour, shape, and hairiness', 'humble-bees' which alone can reach the nectar of the purple clover.

He is 'humbly recording diverse readings' of the phenomena of life, and that, Hardy declares, is the 'road to a true philosophy of life'. What Hardy wrote in justification of *Poems of the Past and Present* in 1902 has its application also to the textuality of his novels: 'Unadjusted impressions have their value, and the road to a true philosophy of life seems to lie in humbly recording diverse readings of its phenomena as they are forced upon us by chance and change.'[16] Hardy and Darwin concur in that chance and change are not intermitting conditions in their work. Rather, they are the permanent medium of experience and thus of language. But both of them also insist on repetition as a basic organisation for all experience within the natural order. Heron, ants, plants, exist juxtaposed in the same intensity of physical recall, focused by the strain and the release of fitting them close to the human.

When the nest is slightly disturbed, the slaves occasionally come out, and like their masters are much agitated and defend the nest: when the nest is much disturbed and the larvae and pupae are exposed, the slaves work energetically with their masters in carrying them away to a place of safety . . . During the months of June and July, I have watched for many hours several nests in Surrey and Sussex, and never saw a slave either leave or enter a nest. (214–15, Darwin)

In front of her a colony of ants had established a thoroughfare across the way, where they toiled a never-ending and heavy-laden throng . . . She remembered that this bustle of ants had been in progress for years at the same spot – doubtless those of the old times were the ancestors of these which walked there now. She leant back to obtain more thorough rest, and the soft eastern portion of the sky was as great a relief to her eyes as the thyme was to her head. While she looked a heron arose on that side of the sky and flew on with his face towards the sun. He had come dripping wet from some pool in the valleys, and as he flew the edges and lining of his wings, his thighs, and his breast were so caught by the bright sunbeams that he appeared as if formed of burnished silver. (296, Hardy)

Hardy's writing is characterised by creative vacillation, by a shiftiness which survives the determinations of plot. Life is devious and resource-ful, constantly reassembling about new possibilities which lie just off the path of the obliterative energies of event.[17] Happiness and hap form the two poles in his work.

Happiness here does not share in the powers of narrative. Indeed it is almost always at odds with narrative, because it is at odds with succession. Happiness is, rather, constellatory, 'a series of impressions' at most. His sentences cull material from quite diverse worlds, and contradictory discourses, making no attempt to homogenise the varying densities into one stream: 'He might have been an Arab, or an automaton; he would have been like a red-sandstone statue but for the motion of his arm with the dice-box' (243).

The sloping pathways by which spectators had ascended to their seats were pathways yet. But the whole was grown over with grass, which now, at the end of summer, was bearded with withered bents that formed waves under the brush of the wind, returning to the attentive ear Aeolian modulations, and detaining for moments the flying globes of thistledown. (*Mayor*: 99)

Hardy's associative ear sets 'Arab' and 'automaton' alongside each other, while the sense of each word demands a completely different contextuality from the reader. Time and dimensions shift. Similarly the dialect word 'bents' and its modifier 'withered' gather an auditory pattern composed of 'w's 'r's and 'b's: 'was bearded with withered bents that formed waves under the brush of the wind'. Then that pattern peters out and instead we have the classical-scientific discourse of 'Aeolian modulations' (with its own strong auditory resolves of 'm', 'l' and 'n' which are carried forward into 'moments' . . . 'flying globes', 'thistledown'). The reconciling pleasures of the ear sustain but do not disguise the semantic leaps.

   Hardy like Darwin places himself in his texts as observer, traveller, a conditional presence capable of seeing things from multiple distances and diverse perspectives almost in the same moment.

A traveller who should walk and observe any of these visitants as Venn observed them now could feel himself to be in direct communication with regions unknown to man. Here in front of him was a wild mallard – just arrived from the home of the north wind. The creature brought within him an amplitude of Northern knowledge. Glacial catastrophes, snow-storm episodes, glittering auroral effects, Polaris in the zenith, Franklin underfoot, – the category of his commonplaces was wonderful. But the bird, like many other philosophers, seemed as he looked at the reddleman to think that a present moment of comfortable reality was worth a decade of memories. (*Return*: 109)

They eye of the writing moves far and near, not so much dwelling in multiple minds, as in George Eliot, as creating a shifting space and changing scales. Ear and touch become identified.

Throughout the blowing of these plaintive November winds that note bore a great resemblance to the ruins of human song which remain to the throat of fourscore and ten. It was a worn whisper, dry and papery, and it brushed so distinctly across the ear that, by the accustomed, the material minutiae in which it originated could be realized as by touch. It was the united products of infinitesimal vegetable causes, and these were neither stems, leaves, fruit, blades, prickles, lichen, nor moss.

They were the mummied heath-bells of the past summer, originally tender and purple, now washed colourless by Michaelmas rains, and dried to dead skins by October suns. So low was an individual sound from these that a combination of hundreds only just emerged from silence, and the myriads of the whole declivity reached the woman's ear but as a shrivelled and intermittent recitative. Yet scarcely a single accent among the many afloat to-night could have such power to impress a listener with thoughts of its origin. One inwardly saw the infinity of those combined multitudes; and perceived that each of the tiny trumpets was seized on, entered, scoured and emerged from by the wind as thoroughly as if it were as vast as a crater. (*Return*: 78)

This vacillation of memory and material, near and far, of tactile and abstract makes for a kind of liberty for the reader, even though an unstable liberty. It is something to set against the dogged interpenetration of event by which his plots overdetermine outcome. We always sustain until the last moment a passionate sense of possible happiness: he sustains hope by different levels of plot, liberty by multiple perspectives. And the drive of his plots is so crushing precisely because of the full sense of *life* elated in us by the range of sense perceptions which are evoked through his writing. The intricate affinity of touch and sound keeps the reader alert and close. Looking back on a novel by Hardy many readers are afflicted and aghast. But he is also one of the most popular and widely read of writers: we enter his works not only to be chagrined and thwarted, but also sustained by the moment-by-moment plenitude of experience offered us. Traumatised by conclusion, the reader in retrospect almost forgets the bounty of text. Forgetting and having are both crucial in Hardy.

Derrida's contraries of play and history are again helpful here. The text in process is at present occurring and need not have reference to the absent origin. It permits a sense of free play for the reader. But the mega-plot may also be borne in micro-form within a single sentence, so that we have in much of Hardy's writing *both* the 'broken immediateness' (l'immediatété rompue) which Derrida associates with Rousseau, *and* what he casts as Nietzschean: 'the joyous affirmation of the free play of the world'.[18]

Two elements of Darwin's theory had a peculiarly personal significance in Hardy's writing – and they were elements which pointed in differing directions, forming a contradiction where Hardy could work.

The first element was Darwin's insistence on 'normative felicity': despite the suffering in the natural world, survival depended on a deep association of life and pleasurability.

Darwin's other emphasis was upon imperfect adaptation.[19] Although the individual organism is guided by pleasurability and 'well being', the process of development by means of accumulated variations has not assured complete congruity between need and adaptation.

Maladaptation, 'the FAILURE OF THINGS to be what they are meant to be', obsesses Hardy.[20] In the light of this emphasis his apparently lacklustre praise of Tess as 'an almost standard woman' can be properly read as superlative, a part of that argument about the significance of individual and species which preoccupied Darwin too. But the 'almost' is also important – its force is insensitive rather than demurring. 'New Year's thought. A perception of the FAILURE OF THINGS to be what they are meant to be, lends them, in place of the intended interest, a new and greater interest of an unintended kind.'[21]

The urgency of intended happiness, intended perfection, pervades Hardy's text, but its poignancy derives from the failures of perfection, the unfulfilled, skewed, and disturbed. That is what allows the reader to recognise and yearn for the shadow plots of achievement and joy which can never fully manifest themselves. The shifts between the perfect and the blighted, between the benign and the grotesque, are mediated through anthropomorphic imagery, which shifts the boundaries between people and objects, 'representing the persistence of the barbaric idea which confuses persons and things'. Carpenter had suggested that evolutionary theory disturbed all such demarcations, showing the vacillations between mollusc and man and the continuance of common forms still capable of change. Darwin expressed deep emotional and intellectual problems through the struggle to control anthropomorphism in 'the face of nature'. Visage and surface, 'physiognomy', elide the distinctions between man and the natural world.

It was at present a place perfectly accordant with man's nature – neither ghastly, hateful, nor ugly: neither commonplace, unmeaning, nor tame; but, like man, slighted and enduring; and withal singularly colossal and mysterious in its swarthy monotony. As with some persons who have long lived apart, solitude seemed to look out of its countenance. It had a lonely face, suggesting tragical possibilities. (*Return*: 35)[22]

Instead of man disjunct from all other aspects of the material order, or at the pinnacle of hierarchy, he must now find a place in a world of 'horizontality', as it comes home to Clym in *The Return of the Native*. 'It gave him a sense of bare equality with, and no superiority to, a single living thing under the sun.'

So the problem of finding a scale for the human becomes a besetting preoccupation of Hardy's work, a scale that will be neither unrealistically grandiose, nor debilitatingly reductive, which will accept evanescence and the autonomy of systems not serving the human, but which will still call upon Darwin's often-repeated assertion: 'the relation of organism to organism is the most important of all relations' (e.g. 14:449). Darwin offers no privileged place to the human, but by appropriating older myth-metaphors such as the tree of life, he might seem to restore a continuity or wholeness to the human. In *The Woodlanders* Hardy re-uses the image of the tree, first in the abbreviated anthropological/ psychological riposte of the old man whose life is literally dependent on the tree which has grown alongside his life's span; then through the entire imagery of work which places the human at the service of the natural world, and most strikingly in passages such as this, in which the human is seen as part of (not fully in control of) natural process. The human body is everywhere suggested in the description, the perfect exists alongside the warped and stunted; sound and touch are scarcely separable:

They went noiselessly over mats of starry moss, rustled through interspersed tracts of leaves, skirted trunks with spreading roots whose mossed rinds made them like hands wearing green gloves; elbowed old elms and ashes with great forks, in which stood pools of water that overflowed on rainy days and ran down their stems in green cascades. On older trees still than these huge lobes of fungi grew like lungs. Here, as everywhere, the Unfulfilled Intention, which makes life what it is, was as obvious as it could be among the depraved crowds of a city slum. The leaf was deformed, the curve was crippled, the taper was interrupted; the lichen ate the vigour of the stalk, and the ivy strangled to death the promising sapling. (82)[23]

Variation is here perceived not as creative divergence, but as marred and interrupted form. The *Unfulfilled* Intention, the 'struggle for life', is evident and botched: as he writes in a later scene, the trees are 'close together, wrestling for existence, their branches disfigured with wounds resulting from their mutual rubbing and blows'. He calls directly here on Darwin's extended description of the 'great tree': 'At each period of growth all the growing twigs have tried to branch out on all sides, and to overtop and kill the surrounding twigs and branches, in the same manner as species and groups of species have tried to overmaster other species in the great battle for life' (171). Similarly, his description of

'Dead boughs scattered about like ichthyosauri in a museum' condenses the time-scale in Darwin's similar description: 'From the first growth of the tree, many a limb and branch has decayed and dripped off; and these lost branches of various sizes may represent those whole orders, families, and genera which have now no living representatives, and which are known to us only from having been found in a fossil state' (172).

But the intervention of the human form disturbs in Hardy's writing the assurance of Darwin's tree. The woodland is simultaneously a scene of decay, deformation, new growth and 'starry moss'. Hardy is acutely alert to diverse time-scales, and to the extent to which the oblivious interaction of these differing scales make up the mesh of event and experience: 'a few short months ago . . . down to so recent a time that flowers then folded were hardly faded yet'. In his journal in December 1865 he notes: 'To insects the twelvemonth has been an epoch, to leaves a life, to tweeting birds a generation, to man a year' (157). And in *Tess* that observation has become both more reductive and more voluptuous. Time-jars are the norm.

In the ill-judged execution of the well-judged plan of things the call seldom produces the comer, the man to love rarely coincides with the hour for loving. Nature does not often say 'See!' to her poor creature at a time when seeing can lead to happy doing; or reply 'Here!' to a body's cry of 'Where?' till the hide-and-seek has become an irksome, outworn game. We may wonder whether at the acme and summit of the human progress these anachronisms will be connected by a finer intuition, a closer interaction of the social machinery than that which now jolts us round and along; but such completeness is not to be prophesied, or even conceived as possible. (67)

Exuberant life is diminished within the scale of the writing which surveys it. The most fortunate creatures are those who dwell entirely within a single time-scale: for human beings empathy with such life can be only momentary. Our habitual experience is of multiple time which brings with it the incommensurate: Mrs Yeobright, on her journey across the heath to renew contact with Clym and Eustacia, sits down beside a pond:

Occasionally she came to a spot where independent worlds of ephemerons were passing their time in mad carousal, some in the air, some on the hot ground and vegetation, some in the tepid and stringy water of a nearly dried pool. All the shallower ponds had decreased to a vaporous mud amid which the maggoty shapes of innumerable obscure creatures could be indistinctly seen, heaving and wallowing with enjoyment. Being a woman not disinclined to philosophize she sometimes sat down under her umbrella to rest and to watch their happiness, for a certain hopefulness as to the result of her visit gave ease to her mind. (285)

The 'ephemerons' live a life of ecstatic enjoyment; the term 'ephemeron' names their time span as brief and yet the effect of the description is of ceaseless activity, unstoppable delight. By naming them 'ephemerons' Hardy calls into play those alternative time-scales which the human must always inhabit – and within our reading here diverse time-codes are at jar. Mrs Yeobright is recovering hope, but the reader (with the foreknowledge of the book's title *The Closed Door*) previsions a time beyond the end of her walk, and that not hopefully. *Human* anxiety and envy are encoded in the half-repudiation of the creatures' enjoyment: 'the maggoty shapes of innumerable obscure creatures could be indistinctly seen, heaving and wallowing with enjoyment'.

The two major emotional and creative problems which evolutionary theory forced on Hardy were to find a scale for the human, and a place for the human within the natural order. Like Darwin, an ambiguous anthropomorphism pervades his writing – an anthropomorphism which paradoxically denies human centrality and gives the human a fugitive and secondary role in his system of reference but not in his system of values.

Egdon is fitted to survive because it is not exceptionally steep or flat, and not subject to man's husbandry. The 'finger-touches' it has felt are 'of the last geological change'.

Those surfaces were neither so steep as to be destructible by weather, nor so flat as to be the victims of floods and deposits. With the exception of an aged highway, and a still more aged barrow presently to be referred to – themselves almost crystallized to natural products by long continuance – even the trifling irregularities were not caused by pickaxe, plough, or spade, but remained as the very finger-touches of the last geological change. (*Return*: 36)

Hardy's reading and his observation alike made him hyperconscious of multiple scale, multiple time, and of the unique problem consciousness created in persuading the human to attempt to live in all of them.

At night, when human discords and harmonies are hushed, in a general sense, for the greater part of twelve hours, there is nothing to moderate the blow with which the infinitely great, the stellar universe, strikes down upon the infinitely little, the mind of the beholder; and this was the case now. (*Two on a Tower*: 83)[24]

The human body is implicit in these descriptions of magnitudes; it comes to the surface of language to reach out, or be struck:

even the trifling irregularities were not caused by pickaxe, plough, or spade, but remained as the very finger-touches of the last geological change . . . At night . . . there is nothing to moderate the blow with which the infinitely great, the stellar universe, strikes down upon the infinitely little, the mind of the beholder.

What to Darwin was in the main wonderful – the sense of history prolonged beyond consciousness, of modes of existence independent of our observation – to Hardy was more often a source of oppression and disruption. He dwelt most happily within bounds, but his writing all has to do with the crossing of bounds – of time, of space, of relationships too. We see the paradox intensely marked in the biographical fact that he disliked to be touched, while his writing is permeated by experiences of touch, texture and temperature. His hypersensitivity to tactual experience is related to the problem of finding a scale for response and experience.

In Hardy's early novel, *A Pair of Blue Eyes*, a scene occurs which is often referred to in discussions of his relation to evolutionary ideas and specifically to Lyell's discussions of geological time; Knight finds himself clinging to a cliff face, about to fall; opposite Knight's eyes was an imbedded fossil, standing forth in low relief from the rock. It was a creature with eyes:

The eyes, dead and turned to stone, were even now regarding him. It was one of the early crustaceans called Trilobites. Separated by millions of years in their lives, Knight and this underling seemed to have met in their place of death. It was the single instance within reach of his vision of anything that had ever been alive and had had a body to save, as he himself had now.

The creature represented but a low type of animal existence, for never in their vernal years had the plains indicated by those numberless slaty layers been traversed by an intelligence worthy of the name. Zoophytes, mollusca, shell-fish, were the highest development of those ancient dates. The immense lapses of time each formation represented had known nothing of the dignity of man. They were grand times, but they were mean times too, and mean were their relics. He was to be with the small in his death.[25]

Man here still feels himself at the summit of creation – the *incongruity* of companionship with minute fossil life thwarts him. Yet kinship is acknowledged, the creature had 'been alive and had had a body to save, as he himself had now'.

Lyell's tone of melancholy puzzlement over the machine of the universe becomes militant in Hardy:

Why the working of this same machinery should be attended with so much evil, is a mystery far beyond the reach of our philosophy, and must probably remain so until we are permitted to investigate, not our planet alone and its inhabitants, but other parts of the moral and material universe with which they may be connected. Could our survey embrace other worlds, and the events, not of a few centuries only, but of periods as indefinite as those with which geology renders us familiar, some apparent contradictions might be reconciled, and some difficulties would doubtless be cleared up. But even then, as our capacities are finite, while the scheme of the universe may be infinite, both in time and space, it is presumptuous to suppose that all sources of doubt and perplexity would ever be removed. (*Principles of Geology*, vol. ii, ch. xxix, p. 144 (10th edition))

The absolute gap between our finite capacities and the infinite time and space of the universe burdens Hardy's texts with a sense of malfunction and apprehension. There is a collapse of congruity between the human and the objects of human knowledge and human emotion. In such a situation finding a place and scale for the human becomes a matter not of the appropriation of space, the colonising of experience, but rather of identification, a willingness to be permeated, to be 'transmissive'. Passivity is naturalised at the level of description as well as of character.

In *The Return of the Native* the topic of the book is the near impossibility of return. In an evolutionary order it is not possible to choose to return to an earlier state. 'In Clym Yeobright's face could be dimly seen the typical countenance of the future' (185). Clym 'the native' comes back to Egdon, wanting to become again an 'inhabitant' but wanting also to educate and develop the other inhabitants. Thereby he becomes an invader – an alien force which disrupts and changes. He wishes to 'revert . . . to ancestral forms' (*The Origin of Species*: 77) but 'by the experiment itself the conditions of life are changed'. His determination to remain in Egdon rather than to move on disrupts his relations to his mother and to Eustacia Vye. At the centre of the book's record, though, is the description of Clym, half-blind, working as a furze-cutter on the heath. In this passage a momentary completeness is achieved.

His daily life was of a curious microscopic sort, his whole world being limited to a circuit of a few feet from his person. His familiars were creeping and winged things, and they seemed to enroll him in their band. Bees hummed around his ears with an intimate air, and tugged at the heath and furze-flowers at his side in such numbers as to weigh them down to the sod. The strange amber-coloured butterflies which Egdon produced, and which were never seen elsewhere, quivered in the breath of his lips, alighted upon his bowed back, and sported with the glittering point of his hook as he flourished it up and down. Tribes of emerald-green grasshoppers leaped over his feet, falling awkwardly on their backs, heads, or hips, like unskilful acrobats, as chance might rule; or engaged themselves in noisy flirtations under the fern-fronds with silent ones of homely hue. Huge flies, ignorant of larders and wire-netting, and quite in a savage state, buzzed about him without knowing that he was a man. In and out of the fern-dells snakes glided in their most brilliant blue and yellow guise, it being the season immediately following the shedding of their old skins, when their colours are brightest. Litters of young rabbits came out from their forms to sun themselves upon hillocks, the hot beams blazing through the delicate tissue of each thin-fleshed ear, and firing it to a blood-red transparency in which the veins could be seen. None of them feared him. (262)

Everything is particular; the pleasures of touch are augmented by our pleasures of sight, which he lacks. The persistent anthropomorphism calls attention to the human and comically, throwaway, dislimns human boundaries; 'unskilled acrobats', 'silent ones of homely hue', 'flies, ignorant of larders and wire-netting'. Man is here familiarised with all other creatures: the weight of the bees who 'tugged at the heath and furze-flowers' is enlarged as under a microscope to equality with the human inhabitant. Bodily temperature is again the medium of pleasure and of experience, and is felt as much *by means of* the young rabbits who 'sun themselves upon hillocks, the hot beams blazing through the delicate tissue of each thin-fleshed ear' as through Clym's presence. The 'entangled' or 'tangled bank' which in Darwin's text is peopled by plants, birds, insects, and worms, here has room also for man, not set apart from other kinds. 'None of them feared him.'

All the separate time- and space-scales for a short while are in harmony. Because Clym's world is 'limited to a circuit of a few feet from his person' and because of the 'monotony of his occupation', he is not distinguished from the rest of the natural order. His coat is now like that of Egdon Heath itself as it was described in the first chapter: 'Civilization was its enemy; and ever since the beginning of vegetation its soil had worn the same antique brown dress, the natural and invariable garment of the particular formation.' The topographical 'features' and 'surface' of the introductory description are here present as human face, but a face almost indistinguishable from the heath ('the minor features of the heath . . . the white surface of the road' are here countered by 'a brown spot in the midst of an expanse of olive-green gorse'). The fullness and the quirkiness of this central description are both equally unforgettable. The reader is offered plenitude, but a plenitude which cannot rest easy with itself for long.

The 'return of the native' can be achieved only within the smallest extent of time and space. The rest of the book shows Clym obliged to reemerge from the pleasures of 'forced limitation'.

In *Tess* there occurs a somewhat similar moment of completeness which openly washes away all 'distinction between the near and the far' and in which 'Tess was conscious of neither time nor space'. Here Hardy brings out the animistic sense that all life is equally alert and equally passive. The atmosphere is so *'transmissive'* 'that inanimate objects seemed endowed with two or three senses, if not five'. 'An auditor felt close to everything within the horizon.' In this soundless landscape Tess moves, hearing only the sound of Angel's strings and drawn towards them:

It was a typical summer evening in June, the atmosphere being in such delicate equilibrium and so transmissive that inanimate objects seemed endowed with two or three senses, if not five. There was no distinction between the near and the far, and an auditor felt close to everything within the horizon. The soundlessness impressed her as a positive entity rather than as the mere negation of noise. It was broken by the strumming of strings . . . The outskirt of the garden in which Tess found herself had been left uncultivated for some years, and was now damp and rank with juicy grass which sent up mists of pollen at a touch; and with tall blooming weeds emitting offensive smells – weeds whose red and yellow and purple hues formed a polychrome as dazzling as that of cultivated flowers. She went stealthily as a cat through this profusion of growth, gathering cuckoo-spittle on her skirts, cracking snails that were underfoot, staining her hands with thistle-milk and slug-slime, and rubbing off upon her naked arms sticky blights which, though snow-white on the apple-tree trunks, made madder stains on her skin; thus she drew quite near to Clare, still unobserved of him. (150)

Viscous substances, rank smells, slime and stickiness: the unweeded garden is a 'profusion of growth' but it is described in language which registers disturbance and repugnance – a disturbance and repugnance which yet yield to voluptuous acceptance. Tess registers but does not describe. She is immersed in this sticky life-and-death, yet not in alienated consciousness of it. The language of description is interposed, but 'transmissive'. Here hyperfecundity, the activity of growth, permeates language, even transgresses language. Resistance to such fullness is felt in the writing, but also calm.

Life in Hardy never falters, but the individuals who live it barely survive the books' length.

In his last two novels, *Tess* and *Jude*, generative plot threatens and squanders individuality. Tess is a late representative of a 'great family'. Darwin's 'great family' of all life is narrowed again to that of privilege. Angel thinks 'The historic interest of her family – that masterful line of d'Urbervilles – whom he had despised as a spent force, touched his

sentiments now' (364). But she is also, through her mother and as vit-
ally, a representative of that fecundity which has allowed those outside
the parkland to endure, while the 'great family' withers away. Hardy
was fascinated by theories of descent – he read Weismann on heredity,
just as earlier he had read *The Origin* and *The Descent*.[26] Angel Clare
imagines himself as the 'new' man and is unable to understand that
Tess is a possible form for the 'new' woman – both survivor and intelligent forerunner. In that sense Tess dies, wasted. But the book (which
is imbued with Max Müller's solar mythology and with sun worship)
properly gives us back the scale of Tess's life. It is for this reason – that
writing still predominates over plot – that we feel Tess's story as less
bleak than that of Jude and Sue.

Tess is jubilant as well as terrible. Jude and Sue on the other hand see
themselves as precursors, and can achieve their full value only *as* precursors of a 'new' order. The death of their children (murdered by little
Father Time in a late-Malthusian tragedy, 'Done because we are too
menny') leaves Jude and Sue as aberrant, without succession, and therefore 'monstrous' in the sense that they can carry no cultural or physical
mutations into the future and must live out their lives merely at odds
with the present.

In the late works plot dominates 'apprehension'. The Romantic
materialism which Hardy shared with Darwin threatens to wither in
the face of the urgency of succession. Society has set too much store by
ideas of succession, heredity and progress. Renewal, and the lateral
range of sensation, are endangered by the insistence on development.

Already in a journal entry in 1876 Hardy had registered something
closer to a hardening than a merging:

If it be possible to compress into a sentence all that a man learns between 20
and 40, it is that all things merge in one another – good into evil, generosity
into justice, religion into politics, the year into the ages, the world into the
universe. With this in view the evolution of species seems but a minute and
obvious process in the same movement.[27]

To Darwin, the plot that his own writing proposed seemed (or needed
to seem) benign. Hardy perceived the malign tautology latent in it: the
'struggle for life', or, even more, 'the survival of the fittest', pre-emptively
extolled the conquerors. Those who survived were justified. But he
shared with Darwin that delight in material life in its widest diversity,
the passion for particularity, and for individuality and plenitude which
is the counter-element in Darwin's narrative and theory. Hardy set out

the contradiction. Like Darwin, he feels the problem of anthropomorphism in describing a natural order not centred on man, but although he often registers grotesque interruption through allusions to the human body, yet his writing conjures the intimacy of the senses by means of which we apprehend the material world.

Plot – that combination of the inexorable and the gratuitous – in *Jude* annuls writing. But in all other of Hardy's works there is, as in Darwin, a strongly surviving belief in the 'recuperative powers' which pervade both language and the physical world.

Notes

INTRODUCTION

1 Thomas S. Kuhn, *The Structure of Scientific Revolutions* (Chicago, 1962): 52.
2 *The Cahier Rouge of Claude Bernard*, tr. H. H. Hoff *et al.* (Cambridge, Mass., 1967): 87.
3 *Essays of George Eliot*, ed. Thomas Pinney (London, 1963): 44–5. Hereafter referred to as Pinney.
4 Quotations from *The Origin* in this study are from the first edition except where specified (*On The Origin of Species By Means of Natural Selection, or the Preservation of Favoured Races In the Struggle for Life*, by Charles Darwin, M. A., Fellow of the Royal, Geological, Linnaean, etc., Societies; author of 'Journal of Researches During H.M.S. *Beagle*'s Voyage Round the World', London, 1859). Darwin revised the work extensively between 1859 and 1878. These changes are all recorded in Morse Peckham's invaluable variorum text (Philadelphia, 1959) and I wish to express my gratitude to him for this work. All subsequent references to his work run (Peckham: page reference). Page references in my text are to the Pelican Classics volume edited with an introduction by John Burrow (Harmondsworth, 1968). This volume prints the text of the first edition.
5 Barry Barnes, *Scientific Knowledge and Sociological Theory* (London, 1974): 166.
6 Paul Ricoeur discusses in general terms the relationships between theory, language and fiction in *Interpretation Theory: Discourse and the Surplus of Meaning* (Fort Worth, Texas, 1976): 67.

As Max Black puts it, to describe a domain of reality in terms of an imaginary theoretical model is a way of seeing things differently by changing our language about the subject of our investigation. This change of language proceeds from the construction of a heuristic fiction and through the transposition of the characteristics of this heuristic fiction to reality itself . . . Thanks to this detour through the heuristic fiction we perceive new connections among things.

7 Jean-Baptiste Lamarck, *Philosophie zoologique* (Paris, 1809); J. B. Lamarck, *Histoire naturelle des animaux sans vertèbres* (1815–1833); Charles Lyell, *The Principles of Geology* (London, 1830–33); Charles Lyell, *The Antiquity of Man* (London, 1864); Robert Chambers, *Vestiges of the Natural History of Creation* (London, 1844). Darwin's opponents resented the identification

of evolutionary theory with Darwinism. St John Mivart, for example, in *Man and Apes* (London, 1873): 2 comments on the injustice of 'popular awards':

Again, the doctrine of evolution as applied to organic life – the doctrine, that is, which teaches that the various new species of animals and plants have manifested themselves through a purely natural process of hereditary succession – is widely spoken of by the term 'Darwinism'. Yet this doctrine is far older than Mr. Darwin, and is held by many who deem that which is truly 'Darwinism' (namely a belief in the origin of species by natural selection) to be a crude and utterly untenable hypothesis.

8 Jacques Barzun, *Darwin, Marx and Wagner* (New York, 1958); Stanley E. Hyman, *The Tangled Bank: Darwin, Marx, Frazer and Freud as Imaginative Writers* (New York, 1962); A. Dwight Culler, 'The Darwinian Revolution and Literary Form', in *The Art of Victorian Prose*, ed. George Levine (London, 1968): 224–6.

9 'There are men who may never have heard of the books or even the name of Darwin, but despite themselves live within the atmosphere created by him and feel its influences.' Francesco De Sanctis, 'Darwinism in Art', 1883, in F. De Sanctis, *Saggi Critici* (Bari, 1953): 3:355–67.

10 Richard Ohmann, 'Prolegomena to the Analysis of Prose Style', in *Style in Prose Fiction*, English Institute Essays, ed. H. Martin (New York, 1959): 23. See also Wolfgang Iser, *The Act of Reading: a Theory of Aesthetic Response* (London, 1978).

11 See chapter 1 for further discussion of this topic.

12 All volume and page references to Lyell are to the first edition of *The Principles of Geology* (London, 1830–3).

13 In 1970 Francis Crick specified the problems remaining in molecular biology as:

a detailed understanding of the replication of DNA and of the unwinding process; the structure of chromosomes, the meaning of the nucleic acid sequences which are not merely the expression of the genetic code but are used for stopping or starting or control mechanisms of one sort or another; the significance of repetitive sequences in DNA; and so on . . . (*Nature*, 280: (1970):615).

14 Michel Serres, *Feux et signaux de brume: Zola* (Paris, 1975).

15 Charles Darwin to Charles Lyell, 12 December 1859, in *Life and Letters of Charles Darwin*, ed. Francis Darwin (London, 1887): 2:37.

16 John Ruskin, *Love's Meinie* (Keston, Kent, 1873): 59.

17 *The George Eliot Letters*, ed. Gordon Haight (London, 1956): 2:109–10. In Notebook 119 Darwin records reading 'some Arabian Nights' in 1840.

18 *The Descent of Man, and Selection in Relation to Sex*, 2 vols. (London, 1870–1).

19 Benjamin Disraeli, *Tancred* (London, 1847).

20 Sigmund Freud, *The Standard Edition of the Complete Psychological Works*, ed. James Strachey (London, 1953–6): 17:140–1.

21 Ibid., 17:143.

22 Darwin first records reading Comte in 1854. Notebook 128: 11 March 1854: 'Philosophies Positive. G. Lewes'. He comments, 'curious'; (G. H. Lewes, *Comte's Philosophy of the Sciences* (London, 1853)). Darwin refers to Comte as early as September 1838 in his notebooks. (See Howard E. Gruber and Paul H. Barrett, *Darwin on Man: A Psychological Study of Scientific Creativity together with Darwin's Early and Unpublished Notebooks* (London, 1974): 291–2 (hereafter referred to as Gruber and Barrett).) Comte's *Cours de Philosophie Positive* (Paris, 1830–5) was reviewed by Brewster in the *Edinburgh Review*, 67 (1838) and Darwin read and commented on this in his notebooks M, N and OUN. Pp. 65–8 of the M Notebook which includes notes on the review are missing. Comte was first translated and condensed by Harriet Martineau in 1853. Surprisingly, since he read most of her work as it appeared, Darwin does not record reading her version. A full English translation did not appear until the 1870s – *System of Positive Policy*, tr. J. H. Bridges, F. Harrison, E. S. Beesly, R. Congreve *et al.* (London, 1875–7). Darwin's 1838 reference to Comte is related to the three successive states of knowledge: 'the theological or fictitious state, the metaphysical or abstract state, and the scientific or positive state'. Darwin remarks: 'So ready is change, from our idea of causation, to give a cause . . . that savages . . . consider the thunder and lightning the direct will of the God (. . . and hence arises the *theological* age of science in every nation according to M. le Comte).' For a full account of his shifting attitudes to Comte see Silvan Schweber, 'The Origin of the Origin Revisited', *Journal of the History of Biology*, 10 (1977): 229–316; esp 241–64.

23 Thomas Henry Huxley, *Science and Hebrew Tradition* (London, 1893): 75–6. The 'Lectures on Evolution' date from 1876. Eric Voegelin, *From Enlightenment to Revolution* (Durham, N.C., 1975) discusses the concepts of 'the authoritative present' and 'the imminentisation of the eschaton' as typifying post-Romantic culture.

24 Herbert Spencer was the other major theorist of evolution in England in the 1850s. In the Preface to *First Principles* he emphasised that his theory of evolution was independent of Darwin and preceded him. He wrote on 'The Development Hypothesis' between 1852 and 1854 and used the term 'evolution' in 'Progress: its Law and Cause' in 1857, whereas most natural historians of the time, Darwin included, preferred the terms 'transformation', 'metamorphosis' or 'mutation'. Spencer's excellence was his power of displacement and connection from one field of study to another. He was not an experimental scientist and was most commonly attacked for his lack of first-hand empirical data in the many fields he surveyed, including those of psychology, sociology and anthropology. For recent appraisals of his work see Robert L. Carneiro, 'Structure, Function, and Equilibrium in the Evolutionism of Herbert Spencer', *Journal of Anthropological Research*, 29 (1973): 77–95, and Derek Freeman, 'The Evolutionary Theories of Charles Darwin and Herbert Spencer', *Current Anthropology*, 15 (1974): 211–37. This article and the fifteen commentaries which accompany it discuss the problem of Darwin's 'social evolutionist' views.

25 Samuel Butler, *Life and Habit* (London, 1878), *Evolution, Old and New* (1879), *Unconscious Memory* (1880), *Luck, or Cunning* (1887).

26 See, for example, Charles Gillespie, *Genesis and Geology: The Impact of Scientific Discoveries upon Religious Beliefs in the Decades before Darwin* (Cambridge, Mass., 1951); *Forerunners of Darwin*, ed. B. Glass, O. Temkin and William Straus (Baltimore, 1959).

27 Georges Canguilhem, 'Du développement à l'évolution au xix siècle' in *Thalès* (Recueil des Travaux de l'Institut d'Histoire des Sciences et des Techniques de l'Université de Paris) (Paris, 1962); Gavin de Beer, *Streams of Culture* (London, 1969); Peter J. Bowler, 'The Changing Meaning of Evolution', *Journal of the History of Ideas*, 36 (1975): 95–114; Steven J. Gould, 'Darwin's Dilemma', *Natural History*, 183 (1974): 16–22; William Coleman, *Form and Function in Nineteenth Century Biology* (Cambridge, 1977).

28 Laurence Sterne, *The Life and Opinions of Tristram Shandy, Gentleman* (London, 1759–67): 5:3.

29 Northrop Frye, *Fables of Identity, Studies in Poetic Mythology* (New York, 1963): 9. Harold Bloom, in *The Anxiety of Influence* (New Haven, 1973), usefully appropriates the evolutionary implications of his chosen kinship metaphor to describe the relations between writers and their precursors.

30 Paracelsus, *Selected Writings*, ed. Jolande Jacobi (London, 1951): 95. Originally published 1530.

31 *The Works of George Herbert*, ed. F. E. Hutchinson (Oxford, 1953): 90.

32 See Geoffrey White, Joseph Juhasz and Peter Wilson, 'Is man no more than this?', *Journal of the History of the Behavioural Sciences*, 9 (1973): 203–12.

33 George Henry Lewes, 'Mr. Darwin's Hypotheses', in the *Fortnightly Review*, 16 (1868): 353.

34 Darwin records reading *Self-Help* on 13 May 1860, and comments 'goodish' (Notebook, 128).

35 See Walter F. Cannon, 'Darwin's Vision in *The Origin of Species*' in *The Art of Victorian Prose*, ed. George Levine (London, 1968): 154–76.

36 *Journals and Papers*, ed. H. House, completed G. Storey (London, 1959): 120.

37 *Zoological Philosophy* (Paris, 1809) tr. Hugh Elliot (tr. first pub. London, 1914, reprinted New York, 1963): 119–20.

38 Florence Hardy, *The Early Years of Thomas Hardy* (London, 1925): 213.

39 Joseph Conrad, *Victory* (London, 1948): 196.

1: 'PLEASURE LIKE A TRAGEDY': IMAGINATION AND THE MATERIAL WORLD

1 Gavin de Beer, *Charles Darwin and Thomas Henry Huxley Autobiographies* (London, 1974), 'An Autobiographical Fragment, Written in 1838': 5. Hereafter *Autobiography*.

2 *Evolution by Natural Selection: Darwin and Wallace*, foreword by G. de Beer (Cambridge, 1958). Contains Darwin's *Sketch* of 1842 and *Essay* of 1844. The 'Big Book' is Darwin's never-completed major work which he put on

one side in order to write *The Origin of Species*. See *Charles Darwin's Natural Selection, being the second part of his big species book written from 1856 to 1858*, ed. from MS by Robert Stauffer (Cambridge, 1975). Texts of the notebooks or major discussions of them are to be found in Gruber and Barratt (*Darwin on Man*, p. 263); Gavin de Beer, ed. 'Darwin's Notebooks on Transmutation of Species', *Bulletin of the British Museum (Natural History) Historical Series* 2 (1960–1) and 3 (1967); Silvan Schweber, 'The Origin of *The Origin* Revisited', *Journal of the History of Biology*, 10 (1977): 229–316. David Kohn, 'Theories to Work By: Rejected Theories, Reproduction, and Darwin's Path to Natural Selection', *Studies in the History of Biology*, 4 (1980): 67–170; Sandra Herbert, 'The Place of Man in the Development of Darwin's Theory of Transmutation: Part I. To July 1837', *Journal of the History of Biology*, 7 (1974): 217–58, and 'The Red Notebook of Charles Darwin', *Bulletin of the British Museum (Natural History) Historical Series* 7 (1980). Darwin's notebooks and reading-lists are among the Darwin Papers in Cambridge University Library. I am grateful to the University Library for permission to use the material.

3 *Autobiography*, 23, 34, 83–4.
4 Donald Fleming, 'Charles Darwin, the Anaesthetic Man', *Victorian Studies*, 4 (1961): 291–336; John Angus Campbell, 'Nature, Religion and Emotional Response: A Reconsideration of Darwin's Affective Decline', *Victorian Studies*, 18 (1974): 159–74. Even John Burrow, one of the most perceptive of commentators on Darwin in general, remarks in his Introduction to *The Origin* (Harmondsworth, 1968): 'He had no delight in words as such, and little feeling for literature, at least by the time he reached middle age, when his taste was chiefly for light novels from which his only requirements were that the heroine should be pretty and the ending happy' (12). He goes on, 'Presumably he would have approved no more of the works of his contemporary, George Eliot, than she did of *The Origin*.' The substance of the present study controverts both those assumptions. Suffice it here to note that Darwin read *Adam Bede* when it first appeared and gave it the rarest of the comments in the book-lists: 'Excellent' (Notebook, 128).
5 'Darwin's Reading and the Fictions of Development', in *The Darwinian Heritage*, ed. D. Kohn (Princeton, 1984). Those interested in Darwin's views on the psychology of reading are referred to this essay.
6 See 'Darwin's Reading' (note 5 above) for discussion of the significance of *The Winter's Tale*, Montaigne's 'Of the Cannibals' and Sir Thomas Browne's *Religio Medici*, in forming the contraries of artificial and natural selection. The essay studies Darwin's reading-lists in detail.
7 In 'Theories to Work By: Rejected Theories, Reproduction and Darwin's Path to Natural Selection', *Studies in the History of Biology*, 4 (1980): 67–170, David Kohn presents evidence which suggests that Darwin was reading Malthus 'during the six days of 28 September to 3 October'. For further discussion of the theoretical relation of Malthus's work to Darwin's see, for example, Peter Vorzimmer, 'Darwin, Malthus, and the Theory of Natural

Selection', *Journal of the History of Ideas*, 30 (1969): 527–42; Robert M. Young, 'Malthus and the Evolutionists: The Common Context of Biological and Social Theory', *Past and Present*, 43 (1969): 109–41; Camille Limoges, *La Sélection naturelle* (Paris, 1970); Sandra Herbert, 'Darwin, Malthus, and Selection', *Journal of the History of Biology*, 4 (1971): 209–17; Peter J. Bowler, 'Malthus, Darwin and the Concept of Struggle', *Journal of the History of Ideas*, 30 (1969): 527–42; Dov Ospovat, 'Darwin after Malthus', *Journal of the History of Biology*, 12 (1979): 211–30. Valentino Gerratana, in 'Darwin and Marx', argues against seeing Malthus as a crucial influence, as does Gruber.

8 Thomas Malthus, *An Essay on the Principle of Population* (London, 1826). (This is the edition that Darwin owned.)

9 *Autobiography*, ed. cit.: 49. He continued to read Milton on his return to England. For example, Notebook 119: 1840: 'March 13th, Minor Poems of Milton and first volume of Wordsworth.' Darwin's response to Wordsworth has been studied by Edward Manier, *The Young Darwin and his Cultural Circle* (Dordrecht, 1978) and Marilyn Gaull, 'From Wordsworth to Darwin', *The Wordsworth Circle*, 10 (1979): 33–48.

10 John Milton, *Poetical Works*, ed. D. Bush (Oxford, 1966).

11 Darwin's version of this passage in the first edition is somewhat more formal: 'one wishes to find a language to express one's ideas': *Journal of Researches into the Geology and Natural History of the Various Countries visited by H.M.S. Beagle, under the Command of Captain Fitzroy, R.N. From 1832 to 1836* (London, 1839): 591.

12 In the B Transmutation notebook Darwin oscillated between the image of the tree and the image of coral: 'Organized beings represent a tree, *irregularly branched* some branches far more branched, – Hence Genera. – As many terminal buds dying, as new one generated' (B22); 'the tree of life should perhaps be called the coral of life, base of branches dead; so that passages cannot be seen. –' (B25). Coral better represents the absolute crumbling away of earlier forms and the impossibility of tracking back, but the tree represents the energy of living form in the process of growth and diversification.

13 Compare Edward Manier in *The Young Darwin and his Cultural Circle* (Dordrecht, 1978) and in 'Darwin's Language and Logic', *Studies in History and Philosophy of Science*, 11 (1980): 305–23.

14 For discussion of Darwin's responses to the controversies created by his work see Peter J. Vorzimmer, *Charles Darwin: The Years of Controversy: The Origin of Species and its Critics 1859–1882* (Philadelphia, 1970); Michael Ghiselin, *The Triumph of the Darwinian Method* (Berkeley, 1969). For an invaluable account of the reception of *The Origin of Species* see Alvar Ellegård, *Darwin and the General Reader. The Reception of Darwin's Theory of Evolution in the British Periodical Press, 1859–1872* (Göteborg, 1958).

15 Pinney: 287–8.

16 Francis Darwin, 'Reminiscences of My Father's Everyday Life' in *The Autobiography of Charles Darwin* (reprinted New York, 1958): 106. First edition 1892.

17 *Autobiography*: 51–2.
18 See Neil Gillespie, *Charles Darwin and the Problem of Creation* (Chicago, 1979).
19 'Cause and Effect in Biology', in *Cause and Effect*, ed. D. Lerner (New York, 1965); Ernst Mayr, *Evolution and the Diversity of Life* (Cambridge, Mass., 1976); Francisco Ayala, 'Teleological Explanations in Evolutionary Biology', *Philosophy of Science*, 37 (1970): 1–15; J. Hillis Miller, *The Disappearance of God* (Cambridge, Mass., 1963) and *The Form of Victorian Fiction* (Notre Dame, 1968); Owen Chadwick, *Secularisation in the Nineteenth Century* (Cambridge, 1975).
20 David Hull, *Darwin and his Critics* (Cambridge, Mass., 1973): 118.
21 See Martin Rudwick, 'Transposed Concepts from the Human Sciences in the Early Work of Charles Lyell', in *Images of the Earth*, ed. L. J. Jordanova and Roy Porter (British Society for the History of Science Monographs I) (Chalfont St Giles, 1979): 67–83: 'Lyell's adoption of the metaphor of linguistic decipherment is important, because it suggests how he was able to escape from the stultifying empiricism and aversion to theorising that characterised his main scientific milieu, the Geographical Society of London' (71). See also his 'The Strategy of Lyell's *Principles of Geology*', *Isis*, 61 (1970): 5–33.
22 Gérard Gorette, *Narrative Discourse*, tr. J. Lewin (Oxford, 1980) most illuminatingly discusses these problems.
23 See Jina Politi, *The Novel and Its Presuppositions* (Amsterdam, 1977); George Levine, 'Determinism and Responsibility in the Works of George Eliot', *PMLA* (1962): 268–79; Barbara Hardy, *The Appropriate Form* (London, 1964), particularly the chapter on *Jane Eyre*.
24 Christopher Heywood, 'French and American Sources of Victorian Realism' in *Comparative Criticism: A Yearbook*, ed. Elinor Shaffer, Vol. I (Cambridge, 1979).
25 While we think of Evolution as divided into astronomic, geologic, biologic, psychologic, sociologic, etc., it may seem to a certain extent a coincidence that the same law of metamorphosis holds throughout all its divisions. But when we recognise these divisions as mere conventional groupings, made to facilitate the arrangement and acquisition of knowledge – when we regard the different existences with which they severally deal as component parts of one Cosmos; we see at once that they are not several kinds of Evolution having certain traits in common, but one Evolution going on everywhere after the same manner (*First Principles*, London, 1862: 545).
26 *The Correspondence of Thomas Carlyle and Ralph Waldo Emerson*, ed. C. E. Norton (Boston and New York, 1883–4): 2:388.
27 Cited Raymond Williams, in an appreciation of Goldmann, *New Left Review*, 67 (1971): 12.
28 Michel Foucault, *Les Mots et les choses* (Paris, 1966) tr. as *The Order of Things* (London, 1970) has been the catalyst for much subsequent discussion of 'epistemes' and his work is a necessary pre-condition for a study such as mine.
29 Cited in Georges Poulet, *La Conscience critique* (Paris, 1971): 248.

2: FIT AND MISFITTING: ANTHROPOMORPHISM AND THE NATURAL ORDER

1 William Wordsworth, *The Poetical Works*, ed. E. de Selincourt and Helen Darbishire (Oxford, 1949): 5:5.

2 Georges Canguilhem, 'The Role of Analogies and Models in Scientific Discovery', in *Scientific Change*, ed. A. C. Crombie (London, 1963): 507–20. Claude Bernard showed that it was mistaken to deduce function from structure: *Leçons de physiologie expérimentale appliquée à la médecine* (Paris, 1856): 2:6. And c.f. Mary Hesse, *The Structure of Scientific Inference* (London, 1974): 209.

3 Charles Bell, *The Hand, Its Mechanism and Vital Endowments As Evincing Design* (Bridgewater Treatises 4) (London, 1833): 33. Darwin admired Bell's works and drew on his *The Anatomy and Philosophy of Expression as Connected with the Fine Arts* (London, 1844) first published in 1806 as *Essays on the Anatomy of Expression in Painting* in the notebooks and *The Expression of the Emotions*, as well as on his discussion of morphology, in *The Origin*.

4 John Ruskin, *Modern Painters*, 3:209: 'The highest creativity is that to which the primrose is for ever nothing else than itself – a little flower apprehended in the very plain and leafy fact of it, whatever and how many soever the associations and passions may be, that crowd around it.' *The Works of John Ruskin*, ed. E. T. Cook and A. Wedderburn (London, 1904): 5:209.

5 Darwin's transmutation notebooks B–E are published in *Bulletin of the British Museum (Natural History) Historical Series* (2) (1960): 23–183, ed. G. de Beer and the pages excised by Darwin in *Bulletin of the British Museum (Natural History) Historical Series* (3) (1967): 129–76. The notebooks on 'Man, Mind and Materialism' and miscellaneous notes labelled by Darwin 'Old and useless Notes about the moral sense and some metaphysical points written about the year 1837 & earlier' are collected and annotated by P. Barrett in *Darwin on Man*, Howard E. Gruber and Paul H. Barrett (London, 1974). See also 'The Red Notebook of Charles Darwin', ed. Sandra Herbert, *Bulletin of the British Museum (Natural History) Historical Series* (7) (1980). Darwin's Reading Notebooks now form an Appendix to Vol. 4 of *The Correspondence of Charles Darwin*, eds. Frederick Burkhardt and Sydney Smith (Cambridge, 1988) pp. 434–573.

6 David Hull, *Darwin and His Critics* (Cambridge, Mass., 1973) and Peter J. Vorzimmer, *Charles Darwin: The Years of Controversy. The Origin of Species and its Critics 1859–1882* (Philadelphia, 1970); P. B. Medawar, *Induction and Intuition in Scientific Thought* (London, 1969). For a defence of Darwin's inductive procedures see John Stuart Mill, *System of Logic, Works*, ed. F. E. L. Priestley (Toronto, 1963–): 2:19, note. Darwin wrote in 1860 to Lyell: 'Without the making of theories I am convinced there would be no observation': *Life and Letters of Charles Darwin*, ed. F. Darwin (London, 1887): 2:315.

7 Peckham, *Victorian Studies*, 3 (1956): 19–40, collected in *The Triumph of Romanticism* (Columbia, S. Carolina, 1970).

8 Darwin wrote sketches of his theory in 1842 and 1844: *Evolution by Natural Selection: Darwin and Wallace* (Cambridge, 1958). He was halfway through a large-scale work on the same subject when he heard that Wallace had reached conclusions similar to his own: *Charles Darwin's Natural Selection, being the Second Part of his big species book written from 1856 to 1858* (Cambridge, 1975). He and Wallace jointly presented their papers to the Linnaean Society in 1858. *The Origin* was written in thirteen months and published in November 1859. Darwin referred to it as an abstract: 'I can here give only the general conclusions at which I have arrived, with a few facts in illustration.'

9 See Neil Gillespie, *Charles Darwin and the Problem of Creation* (Chicago, 1979). Gillespie argues tellingly for Darwin's theism by means of an analysis of his creationist language. See also Pierre Macherey, *Pour une théorie de la production littéraire* (Paris, 1966), or *A Theory of Literary Production*, tr. G. Wall (London, 1978). Macherey polemically substitutes production for creation and argues many of the same difficulties as Darwin without apparently recognising the connection with him. The conceptual mediator is Marx.

10 Darwin pointed out that classification in the case of languages was necessarily genealogical. By the 1870s the evolutionist reading of language development was the prevailing view. See the Müller–George Darwin controversy in the *Contemporary Review*, vols. 25, 26, 27 (1875), especially W. D. Whitney, 'Are Languages Institutions?': 'It is the prevailing belief that the world is filled everywhere with families of related dialects, and that a family of languages, as of individuals or of races, arises by the dispersion and differentiation of a unitary stock' (25: 713–14) and A. H. Joyce, 'The Jelly-fish Theory of Language', (27: 713–23). Compare Darwin's cousin Hensleigh Wedgwood, *The Origin of Language* (London, 1866) and his *Dictionary of English Etymology* (London, 1859–67). Wedgwood held that 'the natural origin of language' was imitative and that this 'accounts for these striking coincidences which are occasionally found in the most remote languages, irrespective of the question whether the common forms of speech are the lingering remnants of a common ancestry'. See also Edward Manier, *The Young Darwin and his Cultural Circle* (Dordrecht, 1978). For further discussion of the analogy between language development and Darwinian evolutionism see below pp. 112–114. A work which develops the connections between humanism, language, and science is Jacques Derrida, *Of Grammatology*, tr. G. Spivak (Baltimore, 1974): grammatology 'ought not to be *one of the sciences of man* because it asks first, as its characteristic question, the question of the name of man' (83). See esp. 'The Supplement of (at) the Origin' (313–16).

11 Hayden White, 'The Fictions of Factual Representation' in *The Literature of Fact*, ed. A. Fletcher (New York, 1976): 21–44 takes Darwin to be a bare empiricist unwittingly betrayed into metaphor. This view leads him to misrepresent Darwin's attitude to analogy. White comments: 'Analogy, he

says again and again, is always a deceitful guide' (38). Darwin does no such thing. He demurs at dependence on analogy but uses it as an argumentative tool precisely because it is essential to his *theory* of common descent:

Analogy would lead me one step further, namely, to the belief that all animals and plants have descended from some one prototype. But analogy may be a deceitful guide. Nevertheless all living things have much in common . . . Therefore I should infer from analogy that probably all the organic beings which have ever lived on this earth have descended from some one primordial form. (455)

12 Elizabeth Sewell in *The Orphic Voice: Poetry and Natural History* (London, 1961) sees Darwin as 'Half a Bacon, that half which was hypnotised by facts and mechanics' (25). She says that Huxley suggests 'a genetic origin for inanimate matter in embryological terms, a lovely reversion to the Baconian metaphor of generations, and quite un-Darwinian' (440). Generation and embryology are, in fact, crucial to Darwin's poetics of nature. The true contrast between Baconian science and language and that of Darwin is in their differing relations to power. Naming and knowledge for Bacon is 'a restitution and reinvesting of man to the sovereignty and power . . . which he had in his first state of creation'. For Darwin the 'first state' is represented by simple organisms; it long precedes naming and offers no possibility of return. Moreover, he emphasises always man's insufficiency.

13 For recent discussions of the relationship of Darwinism to social Darwinism see, for example, Robert M. Young, 'The Historiographic and Ideological Contexts of the Nineteenth-century Debate on Man's Place in Nature', in *Changing Perspectives in the History of Science*, ed. M. Teich and R. M. Young (London, 1973): 344–438; David Freeman, 'The Evolutionary Theories of Charles Darwin and Herbert Spencer', *Current Anthropology* 15 (1974): 211–37 (and numerous commentaries); John Greene, 'Darwin as a Social Evolutionist', *Journal of the History of Biology* 10 (1977): 1–27; 'Darwin and Social Darwinism: Purity and History' in *Natural Order: Historical Studies of Scientific Culture*, ed. B. Barnes and S. Shapin (Beverly Hills and London, 1979): 125–42. See also John Durant, 'The Meaning of Evolution: post-Darwinian Debates on the Significance for Man of the Theory of Evolution, 1858–1908', Unpublished Ph.D. dissertation, University of Cambridge, 1978; Greta Jones, *Social Darwinism and English Thought: the Interaction between Biological and Social Theory* (Brighton, 1980).

14 Marx–Engels, *Werke*, 39 vols. in 41 (Berlin, 1960–8): 29:524; 30:131.

15 Valentino Gerratana gives an excellent account of Marx's relationship to Darwin in 'Marx and Darwin', *New Left Review*, 82 (1973): 60–82. Gerratana underestimates Darwin's reading but well demonstrates the extent to which Darwin deviated from Malthus's social theory. For evidence against the tradition that Marx offered to dedicate *Capital* to Darwin, see Margaret Fay, 'Did Marx offer to dedicate *Capital* to Darwin?', *Journal of the History of Ideas*, 39 (1978): 133–46; Lewis S. Feuer, 'The Case of the "Darwin–Marx" letter: a Study in Socio-Literary Detection', *Encounter*, (October, 1978): 62–78.

16 *Selected Correspondence*, ed. S. W. Ryazanskaya (Moscow, 1965): 128.

17 Struggle, according to the abridged Dr Johnson in Darwin's library, may mean 'To labour, to act with difficulty, to strive, to contend, to contest . . . to labour in difficulties; to be in agonies or distress'. See Manier (p. 170) for discussion of the term; see also B. G. Gale, 'Darwin and the Concept of a Struggle for Existence', *Isis*, 63 (1972): 321–44.

18 *The Life and Letters of Charles Darwin*, ed. F. Darwin (London, 1887): 2:109; 2:263–4; 1:94.

19 Not only theologians but scientists had earlier taken man as central to any system of knowledge, even when emphasising the comparative method: 'Isn't it necessary to examine the nature of animals, compare their structures, study the animal kingdom in general, in order to . . . arrive at the capital science of which man himself is the object?' (Buffon, *Histoire naturelle* (London, 1834), 10:115; 'Man must necessarily be the type; because he is the most complete epitome of the whole range of cases', Auguste Comte, *The Positive Philosophy*, freely tr., Harriet Martineau, (London, 1853): 1:373. Feuerbach's view was closer to Darwin's: 'Man distinguishes himself from Nature. This distinction of his is his God' (*Essence of Christianity*, tr. George Eliot (London, 1854): 106. Compare Marx, 'Theses on Feuerbach No. 11' (written, 1845) in F. Engels, *Ludwig Feuerbach and the End of Classical German Philosophy* (London, 1888).

20 *Science of Language* (London, 1861): 1:357. Gruber's work has demonstrated the continuity of Darwin's interest in psychology and anthropology. His interest in language-systems persisted from the notebooks through to *The Descent of Man*. He sees music as prior to language and links it to the second great determinant of descent, sexual selection.

21 Jacques Derrida, 'Structure, Sign, and Play' in *The Languages of Criticism and the Sciences of Man*, ed. R. Macksey and E. Donato (Baltimore and London, 1970): 264.

22 'The will, which confines the variations in the vegetable structure within a certain range, lest the order of creation should be disturbed by the introduction of an indefinite number of intermediate forms, is apparently the same in its motive, as that which brings back the celestial Luminaries to their original orbits, after the completion of a cycle of changes induced by their mutual perturbations.' Charles Daubeney, presidential address to the B.A.A.S., 1856, in *Victorian Science*, ed. G. Basalla, W. Coleman and R. Kargon (Garden City, New York, 1970): 308.

23 'Instinct and Reason', *Contemporary Review*, (1875): 773. John Morley in the *Pall Mall Gazette*, 20 and 21 March 1871, objected to the implicit anthropomorphism of his argument that beauty is a force in sexual selection:

Why should we only find the aesthetic quality in birds wonderful when it happens to coincide with our own? . . . There is no more positive reason for attributing aesthetic consciousness to the Argus pheasant than there is for attributing to bees geometric consciousness of the hexagonal prisms and rhombic plates of the hive which they so marvellously construct. (Cited *More Letters*, ed. F. Darwin, 1:324–5, note 3.)

24 Darwin saw the danger of deifying Natural Selection:

> One word more upon the Deification of Natural Selection: attributing so much weight to it does not exclude still more general laws, i.e. the ordering of the whole universe. I have said that Natural Selection is to the structure of organized beings what the human architect is to the building. The very existence of the human architect shows the existence of more general laws; but no one, in giving credit for a building to the human architect, thinks it necessary to refer to the laws by which man has appeared. (To Lyell, 17 June 1860. *More Letters*, 1:154.)

25 Lamarck repudiated the idea of Nature as a 'special entity' because the concept includes 'the idea of nature as eternal' and thus goes against the idea of change (*Zoological Philosophy*: 183). Comte scorned the 'mythological personage Nature'. Robert Boyle in *A Free Inquiry Into the Vulgarly Received Notion of Nature* had offered the classic defence of the term: *Works*, (London, 1772): 5: 158–254.

26 Howard E. Gruber, 'The Evolving Systems Approach to Creative Scientific Work: Charles Darwin's Early Thought', in *Scientific Discovery: Case Histories*, ed. T. Nickles (Reidel, 1980): 113–30; Ralph Colp, 'Charles Darwin's Vision of Organic Nature', *New York State Journal of Medicine*, 79 (1979): 1622–9.

27 For fuller discussion see chapter 8 below.

28 See Dov Ospovat, 'Perfect Adaptation and Teleological Explanation: Approaches to the problem of the History of Life in the Mid-Nineteenth Century', in *Studies in the History of Biology*, 2 (1978): 33–56.

29 *Popular Lectures on Scientific Subjects*, tr. E. Atkinson, intro. J. Tyndall (London, 1873): 269–70. 'A Case of Paranoia', in *The Standard Edition of the Complete Psychological Works of Sigmund Freud*, ed. J. Strachey (London, 1953–6): 17:455–8. In paranoia Dr Schreber believed that the world had come catastrophically to an end; Freud quotes the Goethe passage and then comments that 'the paranoiac builds it (the external world) up again . . . by the work of his delusions' (457).

3: ANALOGY, METAPHOR AND NARRATIVE IN *THE ORIGIN*

1 Matthew Arnold, *Letters to Arthur Hugh Clough*, ed. H. F. Lowry (London, 1932): 97.

2 *More Letters*: 1: 176. To W. W. Bates, 22 November 1860.

3 *The Autobiography of Charles Darwin and Selected Letters*, edited by F. Darwin (New York, 1892, reprinted 1958): 101.

4 Mary Hesse in *Models and Analogies in Science* (Notre Dame, Indiana, 1966) emphasises the predictive functions of scientific metaphor:

> In the metaphoric view . . . since the domain of the explanandum is redescribed in terminology transferred from the secondary system, it is to be expected that the original observation language will both be shifted in meaning and extended in vocabulary, and hence that predictions in the strong sense will become possible. (171)

The *narrative* element in analogy is crucial to this function. See below, pp. 74–78.

5 David Lodge, *The Modes of Modern Writing: Metaphor, Metonymy, and the Typology of Modern Writing* (London, 1977) offers a lucid discussion of the relations between metaphor and metonymy.

6 Darwin read Carlyle's works as they appeared (notebook 119) e.g. 'Chartism', January 1840; 'French Revolution', March 1839; 'Past and Present', May 1843; 'Hero Worship', March 1840. Later, in his *Autobiography*, he demurred at Carlyle's arrogance and authoritarianism. This may be because Carlyle's perceived ideological position had shifted.

7 Charles Kingsley, *Madam How and Lady Why* (London, 1870): 144.

8 Claude Bernard, *Introduction à l'étude de la médecine expérimentale*, intro. François Dagognet (Paris 1966), first published 1865. For discussion of Claude Bernard in relation to fiction see my 'Plot and the Analogy with Science in Later Nineteenth-Century Novelists', *Comparative Criticism*, ed. E. Shaffer, 2, (1980): 131–49.

9 P. B. Medawar, *Induction and Intuition in Scientific Thought* (London, 1969): 101–11.

10 A. O. Lovejoy, *The Great Chain of Being: A Study of the History of an Idea* (Cambridge, Mass., 1936); Earl R. Wasserman, 'Metaphors for Poetry' in his *The Subtler Language* (Baltimore, 1959): 169–88, and his 'Nature Moralized: the Divine Analogy in the Eighteenth Century', *ELH*, 20 (1953): 39–76.

11 William Paley, *Natural Theology* (Edinburgh, 1849): 11. Darwin wrote that Paley's method of argument was of the greatest educational value to him (*Autobiography*: 32). See Dov Ospovat, *The Development of Darwin's Theory: Natural History, Natural Theology and Natural Selection, 1839–1859* (Cambridge, 1981). This excellent book unfortunately appeared too late for me to profit from it while preparing and writing this study.

12 Samuel Butler in *Erewhon* (1872) develops Paley's analogy of the watch in 'The Book of the Machines', one of the earliest satirical critiques of Darwinian theory. Astonishingly, he claimed later to have forgotten Paley entirely until reminded of him by Thomson. The Darwin–Butler controversy is discussed in Basil Willey, *Darwin and Butler: Two Versions of Evolution* (London, 1960). Butler's creative response to Darwin is later complicated, and to some extent limited, by his preoccupation with the plagiarism he imputed to Darwin.

13 London, 1736.

14 T. H. Huxley, 'On the Physical Basis of Life', *Fortnightly Review*, N.S. 5, (1869): 129–45.

15 Clerk Maxwell in an early essay (1854), 'Are there real analogies in Nature?', discusses analogical form: 'all the phenomena of nature, being varieties of motion, can only differ in complexity'. 'Self-excenteration' (his neologism) becomes possible only if there are real analogies in nature which do not have to be induced by the mind. See M. Hesse, 'Maxwell's Logic of Analogy' in *The Structure of Scientific Inference* (London, 1974): 209n.; James

Clerk Maxwell, 'On Faraday's Lines of Force' in *The Scientific Papers*, ed. W. D. Niven (Cambridge, 1890) 1:155–229.

16 *Natural Theology*: 132; cf. 139–42.

17 The persisting misunderstanding about transformation and use is seen in Ruskin's heftily aggressive joke about the robin's feathers in *Love's Meinie* (Keston, Kent, 1873):

> I have no doubt the Darwinian theory on the subject is that the feathers of birds once stuck up all erect, like the bristles of a brush, and have only been blown flat by continual flying . . . If you fasten a hair-brush to a mill wheel, with the handle forward, so as to develop itself into a neck by moving always in the same direction, and within continual hearing of a stem-whistle, after a certain number of revolutions the hair-brush will fall in love with the whistle; they will marry, lay an egg, and the produce will be a nightingale.

18 'The theory of determinism, in which the will is regarded as determined or swayed to a particular course by external inducements and formed habits, so that the consciousness of freedom rests chiefly upon an oblivion of the antecedents to our choice.' William Thomson, *Oxford Essays* (1855).

19 T. H. Huxley, 'Lectures on Evolution' in *Science and Hebrew Tradition*, (London, 1893): 73. Lecture delivered in 1876.

20 Cited in Frederic Jameson, *Marxism and Form* (Princeton, 1971): 128.

21 Florence Hardy, *The Early Life of Thomas Hardy* (London, 1928): 219–20, 225.

22 'It expresses a simple fact, without any reference to the nature or cause of this universal action. It affords the only explanation which positive science admits, that is, the connection between certain less known facts and other better known facts.' 'The Fundamental Theory of Hypotheses', in *The Positive Philosophy*, freely translated and condensed by H. Martineau (London, 1853): 1:182.

23 *The Mill on the Floss*, ed. G. Haight (Oxford, 1980): 238.

24 Max Black, *Models and Metaphors* (Ithaca, New York, 1962); Georges Canguilhem, *Etudes d'histoire et de philosophie des sciences* (Paris, 1968); Mary Hesse, *Models and Analogies in Science* (Notre Dame, Indiana, 1966), *The Structure of Scientific Inference* (London, 1974); Donald Schon, *Invention and the Evolution of Ideas* (London, 1967).

25 See Ricoeur, chapter 1, note 6.

26 Michael Polanyi, 'Life's Irreducible Structure', in *Topics in the Philosophy of Biology*, ed. M. Grene and E. Mendelsohn (Dordrecht, 1976): 128–42.

27 Paul K. Feyerabend, 'Problems of Empiricism, Part II' in *The Nature and Function of Scientific Theories*, ed. R. Kolodny (Pittsburgh, 1970): 275–353. See also his *Against Method* (London, 1975).

28 Hesse, *Models and Analogies*: 168–70, 176–7.

29 'Of the Transformation of Hypotheses in the History of Science', *Transactions of the Cambridge Philosophical Society*, 9, (1851): 139–47. Whewell's *History of the Inductive Sciences* (London, 1837) was an early influence on Darwin. See Michael Ruse, 'Darwin's Debt to Philosophy: an Examination of the Influence of the Philosophical Ideas of John F. W. Herschel and William

Whewell on the Development of Charles Darwin's Theory of Evolution', *Studies in the History and Philosophy of Science*, 6 (1975): 154–81.

30 *The Structure of Scientific Inference* (London, 1974): 209n.

31 'The essence of the term species.' Compare Kant's account of Plato in *The Critique of Pure Reason:*

> Plato saw clear proofs of an origin from ideas . . . No one creature, under the individual conditions of its existence, perfectly harmonizes with the idea of the most perfect of its kind – just as little as man with the idea of humanity, which nevertheless he bears in his soul as the archetypal standard of his actions; that, notwithstanding, these ideas are in the highest sense individually, unchangeably, and completely determined, and are the original causes of things.

(Immanuel Kant, *Critique of Pure Reason*, tr. J. M. D. Meiklejohn (London, 1930): 223.)

32 Jean-Louis Lamarck, *Zoological Philosophy*, tr. H. Elliott (New York, 1914, repr. 1963), first published 1809. Gregory Bateson in *Mind and Nature* (London, 1980) develops a related argument about epistemology and evolutionary theory.

33 Robert Chambers, *Vestiges of the Natural History of Creation* (London, 1844).

4: DARWINIAN MYTHS

1 T. H. Huxley, *Man's Place in Nature, and Other Anthropological Essays* (London, 1894): 81–2. First published as an essay, January 1863.

2 For excellent accounts of these problems see William Coleman, *Biology in the Nineteenth Century: Problems of Form, Function, and Transformation* (Cambridge, 1977) and Stephen Jay Gould, *Ontogeny and Phylogeny* (Cambridge, Mass., 1977). For an ontogenic version of evolutionary theory see D'Arcy Thompson, *On Growth and Form* (Cambridge, 1917).

3 Alvan Ellegård, *Darwin and the General Reader: The Reception of Darwin's Theory of Evolution in the British Periodical Press, 1859–1872* (Göthenburg 1958): 239; 240.

4 Charles Kingsley, *The Water Babies* (London, 1863): 86. Page references are to the 1888 edn.

5 Ernst Haeckel, *The Evolution of Man*, 2 vols. (London 1879). August Weismann, *Studies in the Theory of Descent*, ed. R. Meldola, pref. C. Darwin (London, 1882). Gould points out that Von Baer, whose influence lies behind much evolutionary discussion of diversification and of the movement from simplicity to complexity in development, did not subscribe to recapitulation. Both Chambers and Spencer drew on von Baer. Spencer described his discovery of him in 1852: 'This statement that every plant and animal, originally homogenous, becomes gradually heterogenous, set us a process of coordination among accumulated thoughts that were previously unorganized.' *First Principles* (London, 1881): 337. In *Principles of Biology* (London, 1886): 141–2 (written 1863–7) Spencer distinguishes von Baer's work from 'an erroneous semblance of it that has obtained considerable currency . . . that during its development, each higher organism

passes through stages in which it resembles the adult forms of lower organisms'.

6 William Wordsworth, *The Prelude, or, Growth of a Poet's Mind*, ed. E. de Selincourt (Oxford, 1926): 56.

7 Virginia Woolf, in *Moments of Being*, ed. J. Schulkind (London, 1976): 79.

8 For two very different approaches to the subject see *Organic Form: the Life of an Idea* ed. George Rousseau (London, 1972) and Terry Eagleton, *Criticism and Ideology* (London, 1976). See also Sally Shuttleworth, *George Eliot and Nineteenth-Century Science* (Cambridge, 1984).

9 Samuel Taylor Coleridge, *The Statesman's Manual*, Appendix C in *Lay Sermons*, ed. R. J. White, *Collected Works*, VI (London, 1972): 72–3.

10 Ellen Moers in *Literary Women* (London, 1978) reads the work as a nightmare of childbirth. To me it seems rather to be a repudiation of men's claim to an equivalence between creative writing and physical production. Mary Shelley acknowledges Erasmus Darwin in the opening of her 1817 preface: 'The event on which this fiction is founded, has been supposed, by Dr. Darwin, and some of the physiological writers of Germany, as not of impossible occurrence.'

11 In *Aspects of Form*, ed. Lancelot Law Whyte (London, 1968): 41.

12 Ernst Cassirer, *Language and Myth*, tr. S. K. Langer (New York, 1946): 51.

13 Ovid, *Metamorphoses*, Book 15, ll. 252–8. tr. Frank Justus Miller *The Loeb, Classical Library* (Cambridge, Mass. and London, 1916): 383.

14 Joseph Wiesenfarth, *George Eliot's Mythmaking* (Heidelberg, 1977).

15 'On the Fundamental Antithesis of Philosophy', *Transactions of the Cambridge Philosophical Society*, 8 (1850): 170–81.

16 In *Fables of Identity* (New York, 1963): 19–20. See pp. 68–70 above on epistemology and evolutionary theory.

17 *Fables of Identity*: 19–20.

18 To M. Darwin, April 1858: F. Darwin, *Autobiography and Selected Letters* (New York, 1892, reprinted 1958): 194–5.

19 George Stocking, Jr, *Race, Culture, and Evolution: Essays in the History of Anthropology* (New York, 1968); J. S. Haller, *Outcasts from Evolution: Scientific Attitudes to Racial Inferiority, 1859–1900* (London, 1971). Darwin read Tylor, and enjoyed his work. During the period of theory formation in the 1840s Darwin read widely in race-theory: e.g. 'Smith Varieties of the Human Race', 'White Regular Gradations of Man', 'Blumenbach' etc. (Notebook 119). His library included a very great number of anthropological works published during the 1860s which provided material for *The Descent of Man*.

20 The author of one of the most popular discussions of the anthropomorphic implications of Darwinism, Winwood Reade, *The Martyrdom of Man* (1872), was so fired by Du Chaillu's visit to the Royal Institution and British Association that as a young man he set off for his gorilla country and subsequently discovered the speciousness of Du Chaillu's account. Tylor remarks on myths of degeneration: 'Mr Kingsley's story of the great and famous nation of the Doasyoulikes, who degenerated by natural selection into gorillas, is the civilized counterpart of this savage myth' (*Primitive Culture*, 1:377).

21 Robert Ackerman, 'Writing about Writing about Myth', *Journal of the History of Ideas*, 34, (1973): 147–55; Janet Burstein, 'Victorian Mythography and the Progress of the Intellect', *Victorian Studies*, 18 (1975): 309–24.

22 *Lectures on the Science of Language* (first series) (London, 1861): 327.

23 *Lectures on the Science of Language* (second series, 1864): 309–10.

24 *Orlando* (London, 1928): 208.

25 Hallam Tennyson, *Alfred Lord Tennyson* (London, 1897) 1:314.

26 See *Glaucus; or, The Wonders of the Shore* (London, 1855). The fashion for marine biology, recorded also in G. H. Lewes's *Seaside Studies* (London 1859) and George Eliot's Ilfracombe Journals owed much to the work of the naturalist Philip Gosse. See for example, *The Romance of Natural History* (1st and 2nd series) (London: 1860–1) with its emphasis on 'the emotions of the human mind, – surprise, wonder, terror, revulsion, admiration, love, desire . . . – which are made energetic by the contemplation of the creatures around him'. *Omphalos: An Attempt to Untie the Geological Knot* (London, 1857) set Gosse at odds with Kingsley. See Edmund Gosse, *Father and Son* (London, 1907) for the most authentic account of the relations between geology, biology and theology.

27 Erasmus Darwin, *The Loves of the Plants* (Lichfield, 1789–90). The running head for *The Temple of Nature* (London, 1803) was its subtitle 'The Origin of Society'. Darwin's title almost certainly alludes to his grandfather's, whose unashamed anthropomorphism envigorates his natural history. He emphasises profusion and destruction equally: 'the thick ranks of vegetable war' (41); 'births unnumber'd, ere the parents die,/ The hourly waste of lovely life supply' (341).

28 G. H. Lewes, *Studies in Animal Life* (London, 1862).

29 'During my last year at Cambridge I read with care and profound interest Humboldt's Personal Narrative. This work . . . stirred up in me a burning zeal to add even the most humble contribution to the noble structure of Natural life Science' (*Autobiography*: 38).

30 Cited in Brian Stock, *Myth and Science in the Twelfth Century: A Study of Bernard Silvester* (Princeton, 1972): 217–18. *Cosmographia* 2:14:162–5.

31 Edmund Spenser, *The Faerie Queene*, ed. J. C. Smith (Books 1–3) (Oxford, 1909): 428. First published 1590.

32 Spenser, *The Faerie Queene*, ed. Smith (Books 4–7): 455.

33 Max Müller, *Lectures on the Science of Language*, second series (London, 1864): 'Roots formed the constituent elements of all languages . . . To a mature mind . . . simplicity is more wonderful than complexity . . . there is something more truly wonderful in a root than in all the lyrics in the world' (306–7). Lewes transposed Müller's image back into Darwin's metaphor of 'the great tree': 'From these roots closely resembling each other . . . but all more or less different, there have been developed the various stems of the great tree.' 'Mr Darwin's Hypotheses', *Fortnightly Review*, 4 NS (1868): 80.

34 Edward Carpenter, *Civilisation: Its Cause and Cure* (London, 1889): 136–7.

35 Charles Lyell, *The Principles of Geology* (London, 1830), 1:158.

36 Charles Kingsley, *The Water Babies* (London, 1863). My page references are to the 1888 edition.

37 William Paley, *Natural Theology* (Edinburgh, 1849): 238; cf. 182.

38 Alton Locke dreams: 'I was at the lowest point of created life; a madrepore rooted to the rock, fathoms below the tide-mark; and worst of all, my individuality was gone.' Using Chambers's 'scale of development' he becomes in dream successively fish, bird, beast, ape, man.

39 *Fraser's Magazine* (1849). Collected in *Literary and General Essays* (London, 1880): 191.

40 Another influence on *The Water Babies* may have been the story of the wild boy. See Harlan Lane, *The Wild Boy of Aveyron* (London, 1977).

41 Rosemary Jackson in *Fantasy: The Literature of Subversion* (London, 1981) sees the emphasis on cleanliness as repressive (151) but this is to ignore the repressive nature of Tom's dirtying. His blackened skin represents his social oppression. These sensory/ideological contradictions give the book much of its power. See also C. N. Manlove, *Modern Fantasy: Five Studies* (Cambridge, 1975).

42 *Letters*, ed. F. Darwin: 2:171.

43 *Anthropological Review*: 1 (1863): 472. The review notes particularly Kingsley's application of 'Darwinian laws to the supposed "degradation" of the ape from human species'.

44 Peckham: 478.

45 *Evidence as to Man's Place in Nature* (London, 1863): 1.

46 'Where, then, is the difference between brute and man? What is it that man can do, and of which we find no signs, no rudiments, in the whole brute word? . . . the one great barrier between the brute and man is *Language* . . . Language is our Rubicon, and no brute will dare to cross it.' *Lectures on the Science of Language* (First series): 340. The figure of James Burnett, Lord Monboddo, lies behind many of the disputes about animal language. In *Of the Origin and Progress of Language* (Edinburgh, 1773–92) he had argued that the orang outang at least had the capacity for language: 'the Orang Outang is an animal of the human form, inside as well as outside . . . he has the human intelligence, as much as can be expected in an animal living without civility or arts' (1:289, 2nd edition, 1774). Peacock appropriated Monboddo's theories in his satirical 'Sir Oran Haut-Ton' in *Melincourt*.

47 *Man's Place in Nature*: 112.

48 (London, 1855): 532.

49 Mrs Gatty, *Parables from Nature*, first series (London, 1855); second series (London, 1865).

50 Gatty, 1865: 67. Mrs Gatty's rook turns the usual degradationist arguments round on themselves: man has suffered 'a total loss of our language. . . . The sounds he emits now from his bill-less mouth are, in truth, an unmeaning jargon' (80).

51 *Natural Theology*: 242; see p. 81 above.

52 Von Baer had earlier mocked the anthropocentrism of ontogeny by imagining what would happen if birds studied their own development and applied their conclusions to humankind: 'we, as fledglings in the nest, are more advanced than they shall ever be'. Cited S. J. Gould, *Ontogeny and Phylogeny* (Princeton, 1977): 54.

53 *Principles of Geology*: 1: 123.

54 *After London: or Wild England* (London, 1855). My page references are to *After London*, Introduction by John Fowles (Oxford, 1980).

55 Two influential works were Ray Lankester, *Degeneration. A Chapter in Darwinism* (London, 1880) and Max Nordau, *Degeneration*, tr. from the second edition (London, 1913). Allon White, *The Uses of Obscurity: the Fiction of Early Modernism* (London, 1981) well describes the effects of this particular reading of Darwin's implications.

5: GEORGE ELIOT: *MIDDLEMARCH*

1 *Galaxy*, 15 (1873): 424–8.

2 R. H. Hutton, *Spectator*, 49 (1876): 1131–3.

3 *Middlemarch. A Study in Provincial Life* (London, 1872). All page references are to the Cabinet Edition (London, 1878). References run volume, chapter, page. Much material from scientific and philosophical sources is collected in John Clark Pratt and Victor A. Neufeldt, eds., *George Eliot's Middlemarch Notebooks, A Transcription* (Berkeley and Los Angeles, 1979).

4 Sidney Colvin, *Fortnightly Review*, N.S. 13 (1873): 142–7.

5 Edward Dowden, *Contemporary Review*, 29 (1877): 348–69.

6 For discussions of the importance of scientific ideas in George Eliot's work, see U. C. Knoepflmacher, *Religious Humanism and the Victorian Novel: George Eliot, Walter Pater, Samuel Butler* (Princeton, 1965); Bernard Paris, *Experiments in Life* (London, 1965); W. J. Harvey, 'The Intellectual Background of the Novel; Casaubon and Lydgate' in *Middlemarch: Critical Approaches*, ed. B. Hardy (London, 1967); Michael York Mason, 'Middlemarch and Science: Problems of Life and Mind', *Review of English Studies*, 22 N.S. (1971): 151–69; J. Hillis Miller, 'Optic and Semiotic in *Middlemarch*' in *The Worlds of Victorian Fiction*, ed. J. H. Buckley (Cambridge, Mass., 1975): 124–45; Rosemary Ashton, *The German Idea* (Cambridge, 1980); George Levine, 'George Eliot's Hypothesis of Reality', *Nineteenth Century Fiction*, (1980): 1–28.

7 For a fuller discussion of concept-interchange see my 'Anxiety and Interchange: *Daniel Deronda* and the Implications of Darwin's Writing', *Journal for the History of the Behavioural Sciences*, 19 (1983): 31–44.

8 *Problems of Life and Mind* (London, 1874): 261. 1st edition: 1873.

9 All Tyndall's work emphasised 'The Scientific Use of the Imagination' (the title of his 1870 address to the mathematical and physical section of the B.A.A.S.). His spirited defence of *The Origin* in his 1874 presidential address roused much controversy because of its agnostic frame of reference. Rede Lecture: *On Radiation* (London, 1865): 60–1.

10 *Fortnightly Review*, 5 N.S. (1869): 132.

11 Ibid. 143.

12 Lewes first wrote extensively on Darwin in the *Pall Mall Gazette* in 1865. His review of *The Variation of Plants and Animals* pleased Darwin. The articles in *The Fortnightly Review*, 3 and 4 N.S. (1868): 353–73; 611–28; 61–80; 492–509, seem to have been a watershed in George Eliot's understanding of the implications of Darwin's thought. See also *The Physical Basis of Mind* (London, 1877), particularly the chapter on 'Evolution': 79–136.

13 'Mr Darwin's Hypotheses': 494.

14 'If the time should ever come when what is now called Science, thus familiarized to men, shall be ready to put on . . . a form of flesh and blood, the Poet will lend his divine spirit to aid the transfiguration.' *The Lyrical Ballads, 1798–1805*, ed. G. Sampson (London, 1940): 26. See my essay 'Darwin's Reading and the Fictions of Development' in *The Darwinian Heritage*, ed. D. Kohn (Princeton, 1985) for discussion of this connection.

15 *Time in Science and Philosophy*, ed. J. Ziman (Prague, 1971), especially I. Prirogine, 'Time, Structure, and Entropy': 89–99; Stephen Toulmin and June Goodfield, *The Discovery of Time* (London, 1965). See the next chapter for discussion of this problem in *Daniel Deronda*.

16 See Strother B. Purdy, *The Hole in the Fabric: Science, Contemporary Literature, and Henry James* (Pittsburgh, 1977) on the non-Euclideanism of life and of narrative structures.

17 *The Mill on the Floss*, ed. G. Haight (Oxford, 1980): 238.

18 *The George Eliot Letters*, ed. G. Haight (9 vols., Oxford, 1954–78): 3:214, Hereafter *Letters*.

19 Letter to Mrs Stuart, 1874: *Letters*: 6:81.

20 *Daniel Deronda*, Cabinet Edition: 1:11:166–7.

21 *Theophrastus Such*, Cabinet Edition: 248–55.

22 There is probably a covert comparison in George Eliot's first reaction to Darwin. Lewes's *The Physiology of Common Life* had recently appeared. In a letter to Barbara Bodichon she comments: 'it really promises to be a useful book, and, I think, especially useful as an educator, even apart from the specific knowledge it conveys, because it looks at the questions discussed in a philosophic spirit – a very rare quality in books on natural science. We have been reading Darwin's book on the "Origin of Species" just now.' *Letters*: 3:227.

23 *Letters*: 5:458–9.

24 Claude Bernard, *An Introduction to the Study of Experimental Medicine* (New York, 1957): 15. First published 1865. G. H. Lewes was much influenced by Bernard's work. For a fuller discussion see Paul Q. Hirst, *Bernard, Durkheim, and Epistemology* (London, 1975); Frederic L. Holmes, *Claude Bernard and Animal Chemistry* (Cambridge, Mass., 1974); Gillian Beer, 'Plot and the Analogy with Science in Later Nineteenth-Century Novelists' in *Comparative Criticism II*, ed. E. S. Shaffer (Cambridge, 1980).

25 *Principles of Geology*: 1:73.

26 *Problems of Life and Mind* (London, 1874–9): 1:471–2.

27 *Studies in Animal Life* (London, 1862): 155.

28 *Introduction à l'étude de la médecine expérimentale.* Lewes's copy is in Dr Williams's Library, London.

29 *The Foundations of a Creed* (London, 1873–5): 1:26. Huxley's review of *The Origin* in *The Westminster Review*, 73 (1860): 541–70 uses a rose-coloured version of the metaphor: 'Harmonious order governing eternally continuous progress – the web and woof of matter and force interweaving by slow degrees, without a broken thread, that veil which lies between us and the Infinite.' (Reprinted in *Darwiniana* (London, 1893): 59.)

30 John Tyndall, *On Radiation* (London, 1865): 9–10.

31 Alexander Bain, *Mind and Body: the Theories of their Relation* (London, 1873): 27.

32 I. J. Beck, *The Method of Descartes* (Oxford, 1952), especially ch. 11. Compare Willard van Quine and Joseph Ullian in *The Web of Belief* (New York, 1970).

33 Cited by Robert Chambers, *Vestiges of the Natural History of Creation* (London, 1844): 11–12.

34 See Terry Eagleton, *Criticism and Ideology* (London, 1977) for an interesting discussion of some ideological functions of the web. He links it more closely to organicism than I do. For a witty and provocative discussion of spinning, weaving and yarning in George Eliot, see Sandra H. Gilbert and Susan Gubar, *The Madwoman in the Attic: The Woman Writer and the Nineteenth Century Literary Imagination* (New Haven and London, 1979), especially pp. 519–28.

35 Darwin said that Julia Wedgwood was one of the few who perfectly understood his work. 'The Boundaries of Science: a Second Dialogue', *Macmillan's Magazine*, 4 (1861): 241.

36 Anskar's thousandth anniversary fell in 1865 and an account of his life was prepared for the occasion by L. Dreves, *Leben des heiligen Ansgar* (Paderborn, 1864).

37 *Sacred and Legendary Art* (London, 1848): xxii.

38 *Sacred and Legendary Art*: 2: 184–9.

39 *Letters*, 4:49.

6: GEORGE ELIOT: *DANIEL DERONDA* AND THE IDEA OF A FUTURE LIFE

1 *Essays of George Eliot*, ed. T. Pinney (London, 1963): 413 et seq. George Eliot here emphasises, like Mill, 'an invariable order of succession' between phenomena, not 'the ultimate or ontological cause of anything'. John Stuart Mill, *A System of Logic* (London, 1841): Bk 3, ch. 5, note 2: in *Collected Works of John Stuart Mill*, ed. F. E. L. Priestley (Toronto, 1963): 7:326.

2 Pinney: 31.

3 See George Levine's classic article 'Determinism and Responsibility in the Works of George Eliot', *P.M.L.A.* 77 (1962): 268–79.
4 Charles Darwin, *The Descent of Man and Selection in Relation to Sex* (London, 1901): 3. First edition 1871.
5 *Daniel Deronda*, Cabinet Edition, 1: 10:144. All references are to the Cabinet Edition and run: volume, chapter, page.
6 *Descent*: 43.
7 It was announced in an advertisement in *The Leader* on 18 June 1853.
8 *Letters*: 1:136; 1:93.
9 *Letters*: 8:52 ([?] 8 July 1852).
10 Francis Galton, Darwin's cousin, adumbrated eugenic theory through his researches into *Hereditary Genius* (London, 1865) and *Natural Inheritance* (London, 1889).
11 John Hedley Brooke, 'Natural Theology and the Plurality of Worlds: Observations on the Brewster–Whewell Debate', *Annals of Science*, 34 (1977): 221–86; William C. Heffernan, 'The Singularity of Our Inhabited World: William Whewell and A. R. Wallace in Dissent', *Journal of the History of Ideas*, 39 (1978): 81–100.
12 See Alexander Welsh, 'Theories of Science and Romance, 1870–1920', *Victorian Studies*, 18 (1973): 134–54; George Levine, 'George Eliot's Hypothesis of Reality', *Nineteenth Century Fiction*, 35 (1980): 1–28; W. K. Clifford, *Lectures and Essays*, ed. L. Stephen and F. Pollock (London, 1879): 1:149.
13 For a different reading of the problem of origins in *Daniel Deronda* see Cynthia Chase, 'The Decomposition of Elephants: Double-Reading *Daniel Deronda*', *P.M.L.A.*, 93 (1978): 215–27. See also Thomas Pinney, 'More Leaves from George Eliot's Notebook', *Huntington Library Quarterly*, 29 (1965–6): 353–76 and K. K. Collins, 'Questions of Method: Some Unpublished Late Essays', *Nineteenth Century Fiction*, 35 (1980): 385–405. These two essays publish G.E. notes and essays on such topics as origins and social evolution which supplement the material in Pinney, Baker, and Pratt.
14 Baker 3: 75. At their first meeting, at this same period, 23 March 1875, Thomas Hardy and Leslie Stephen discussed: 'theologies decayed and defunct, the origin of things, the constitution of matter, the unreality of time . . . [Stephen said that] the new theory of vortex rings had "a staggering fascination" for him.' Florence Emily Hardy, *The Early Life of Thomas Hardy* (London, 1928): 139.
15 R. A. Proctor, 'The Past and Future of Our Earth', *Contemporary Review*, 25 (1874): 74–99. George Eliot and G. H., Lewes subscribed to the *Contemporary Review* and knew Proctor personally. Haight writes: 'The germ of *Daniel Deronda* planted in September 1872 when George Eliot was watching Miss Leigh at the roulette table in Homburg, began to grow at once. She made notes on "Gambling Superstitions" from an article in the *Cornhill*.' (R. A. Proctor, *Cornhill*, 25 (1872): 704–17.)
16 Claude Bernard, *An Introduction to the Study of Experimental Medicine*, tr. H. C. Greene (New York, 1949): 50.

17 Hans Vaihinger, *The Philosophy of 'As If'* (London, 1924; 2nd edn 1968). Original printing Berlin 1911.

18 Wolfgang Iser, *The Act of Reading* (London, 1978): 225.

19 Ernst Mayr, 'Teleological and Teleonomic, A New Analysis', in *Methodological and Historical Essays*, ed. R. S. Cohen and M. W. Wartofsky (Dordrecht and Boston, 1974): 96. August Weismann in *Studies in the Theory of Descent* (first German publication 1875) (London, 1882): 694 cited von Baer: 'The Darwinian hypothesis, as stated by its supporters, always ends by denying to the processes of nature any relation to the future, i.e. any relation of aim or design.'

20 Edward Said, *Beginnings* (New York, 1975) especially 'The Novel as Beginning Intention'.

21 J. G. Herder, *Abhandlung über den Ursprung der Sprache* (Berlin, 1772). See Helene M. Kastinger Riley, 'Some German Theories on the Origin of Language from Herder to Wagner', *Modern Language Review*, 74 (1979): 617–32. See also Morris Swadesh, *The Origin and Diversification of Language* (Chicago, 1971); Richard Dorson, *The British Folklorists, A History* (Chicago, 1968); Burton Feldman and Robert D. Richardson, *The Rise of Modern Mythology 1680–1860* (Indiana, 1972).

22 In 1866 William Thomson took up Helmholtz's vortex theory. G. E's notes from Croll include a long account of Helmholtz's contraction theory which implied the inevitable cooling of the sun. Darwin wrote in his *Autobiography* of his dismay 'at the view now held by most physicists, namely that the sun with all the planets will in time grow too cold for life' (53–4).

23 *Letters*: 6:301–2.

24 Pinney: 409.

25 Paul Broca. *On the Phenomenon of Hybridity in the Genus Homo*, ed. C. Carter Blake (London, 1864): 62. Darwin recorded reading race-theorists in his reading-lists throughout the 1840s and 1850s. The early numbers of the *Anthropological Review* are dominated by articles on various aspects of race-theory, sparked off by the new interest in 'species'. For discussions of Victorian race-theory see John Haller, *Outcasts from Evolution* (Urbana, Ill., 1971); G. W. Stocking, *Race, Culture and Evolution* (New York, 1978); John Burrow, *Evolution and Society* (Cambridge, 1996). Burrow offers a lucid analysis of the reception and transformation of evolutionist ideas in social terms in England.

26 *The Variation of Plants and Animals under Domestication* (London, 1868) discussed 'blending' and 'reversion'. In 1864 Darwin wrote to Hooker: 'The tendency of hybrids to revert to either parent is part of a wider law . . . namely, that crossing races as well as species tends to bring back characters which existed in progenitors hundreds and thousands of generations ago.'

27 *Westminster Review*, 59, 1853: 388–407.

28 Compare Peter Dale, 'Symbolic Representation and the Means of Revolution in *Daniel Deronda*', *The Victorian Newsletter* (1981): 25–30.

29 *Physics*, 5, 40, 217b35–218a3.

7: DESCENT AND SEXUAL SELECTION: WOMEN IN NARRATIVE

1 James Sully, *Sensation and Intuition: Studies in Psychology and Aesthetics* (London, 1874): 5–6; 9–10. See particularly the essay on 'The Relation of the Evolution Hypothesis to Human Psychology'. The second, and greatly enlarged, edition of Herbert Spencer's *Principles of Psychology* appeared in 1870–2.
2 The image of 'foreign' language combines the etymological and racial elements in evolutionary discourse: cf. *Origin*; 97: 'a breed, like a dialect of a language, can hardly be said to have had a definite origin'. See also Colin MacCabe, *James Joyce and the Revolution of the World* (London, 1978) on unknown languages in *Daniel Deronda*.
3 Notebook 707 records stories of such transformation of idea into matter. See Baker: 1:114, 139.
4 *Letters*: 4: 364.
5 Mathilde Blind, *The Ascent of Man* (London, 1889).
6 Elinor Shaffer, *Kubla Khan and the Fall of Jerusalem* (Cambridge, 1975), reads Deronda as a Messiah-figure within an established eschatological tradition.
7 W. B. Carpenter (1874): 152.
8 Pinney: 403.
9 *Expression of the Emotions in Man and Animals*, preface by Konrad Lorenz (Chicago and London, 1965): 237.
10 Sören Kierkegaard, *The Concept of Dread*, tr. W. Lowrie (London, 1944).

8: FINDING A SCALE FOR THE HUMAN: PLOT AND WRITING IN HARDY'S NOVELS

1 *Expression of the Emotions*: 360–1.
2 Florence Emily Hardy, *The Early Life of Thomas Hardy 1840–1891* (London: 1928): 253. Hereafter *Early Life*.
3 *Early Life*: 268.
4 *Early Life*: 301–2.
5 Thomas Hardy, *Tess of the D'Urbervilles: A Pure Woman Faithfully Presented*, ed. P. N. Furbank (London, 1975): 316. All page references are to this edition.
6 At the end of his life Hardy listed thinkers important to him as 'Darwin, Huxley, Spencer, Comte, Hume, Mill', cited Carl J. Weber, *Hardy of Wessex: His Life and Literary Career* (New York, 1965): 246–7. In the *Early Life* he claimed to have been 'among the earliest acclaimers of *The Origin of Species*': 198. See Peter Morton, '*Tess of the D'Urbervilles*: a Neo-Darwinian Reading', *Southern Review*, 7 (1974): 38–50; Roger Robinson, 'Hardy and Darwin' in *Thomas Hardy: the Writer and his Background* (New York, 1980): 128–50; Elliot B. Ghose, 'Psychic Evolution: Darwinism and Initiation in *Tess*', *Nineteenth Century Fiction*, 18, (1963): 261–72; Perry Meisel, *Thomas Hardy: The Return of the Repressed* (New Haven and London, 1972); Bruce Johnson,

'The Perfection of Species' and Hardy's Tess', in *Nature and the Victorian Imagination*, ed. G. B. Tennyson and U. C. Knoepflmacher (Berkeley, 1978): 259–77. Meisel and Johnson are particularly impressive in their grasp of the implications of Darwin's thought for Hardy.

7 *The Return of the Native*, ed. Derwent May (London, 1975). All page references are to this edition.

8 *Early Life*: 285–6.

9 For discussion of Darwin's debt to Wordsworth see Edward Manier, *The Young Darwin and his Cultural Circle* (Dordrecht, 1978): 89–96; Marilyn Gaull, 'From Wordsworth to Darwin', *The Wordsworth Circle*, 10 (1979): 33–48.

10 *Tess*: 146, 174.

11 *Early Life*: 279.

12 'The Dorsetshire Labourer', *Longman's Magazine* (1883).

13 Cited in Gordon S. Haight, *A Century of George Eliot Criticism* (London, 1966): 192.

14 *The Mayor of Casterbridge*, ed. I. Gregor (London, 1976).

15 Florence Hardy, *The Later Years of Thomas Hardy* (London, 1930).

16 H. Orel, ed., *Thomas Hardy's Personal Writings* (London, 1967): 39.

17 John Bayley, *An Essay on Hardy* (Cambridge, 1978) discusses the unaccording, oblivious quality of Hardy's writing.

18 Derrida, *Of Grammatology*: 264.

L'immédiateté rompue est donc la face triste, *négative*, nostalgique, coupable, rousseauiste, de la pensée du jeu dont *l'affirmation* nietzschéene, l'affirmation joyeuse du jeu du monde et de l'innocence du devenir, l'affirmation d'un monde de signes sans faute, sans vérité, sans origine, offert à une interprétation active, serait l'autre face.

19 'Natural selection will not produce absolute perfection.' Darwin cites the bee's sting, which causes its death.

20 *Early Life*: 163 (1 January 1879).

21 R. H. Hutton, writing in 1854, shows how the problem of 'essence' in taxonomy had already entered literary language: 'Just as science finds the type of a class of flowers which actual nature seldom or never does more than *approach*, so that in a certain sense science knows what the flower *ought* to be, while nature never quite produces it.' He then discusses Shakespeare's Cleopatra as an example. *Prospective Review*, 10 (1854): 476.

22 See the discussion above: pp. 105–8.

23 *The Woodlanders*, intro. David Lodge (London, 1975): 82.

24 *Two on a Tower*, intro. F. B. Pinion (London, 1976): 83.

25 *A Pair of Blue Eyes*, ed. Ronald Blythe (London, 1976): 222.

26 August Weismann, *Studies in the Theory of Descent* (London, 1882). Hardy said that he read him in 1890 'having finished adapting *Tess of the d'Urbervilles* for the serial issue'. *Early Life*: 301.

27 *Early Life*: 146–7.

Select bibliography of primary works

Secondary works are detailed in the footnotes and indexed under authors' names and topics. Editions listed in the bibliography are in a few cases those we know Darwin to have used, rather than first editions or modern standard editions.

Agassiz, Louis, *An Essay on Classification* (London, 1859).
　Life and Correspondence, ed. Elizabeth Cary Agassiz, 2 vols. (London, 1885).
Bain, Alexander, *The Emotions and the Will* (London, 1859).
Basalla, G., Coleman W. and Kargon, Robert H., eds., *Victorian Science: A Self-Portrait from the Presidential Addresses to the British Association for the Advancement of Science* (New York, 1970).
Bell, Charles, *Essay on the Anatomy of Expression in Painting* (London, 1806), 3rd rev. edn (London, 1844).
　The Hand, Its Mechanism and Vital Endowments as Evincing Design (Bridgewater Treatises, 4) (London, 1833).
Bernard, Claude, *Introduction à l'étude de la médicine expérimentale* (Paris, 1865); *An Introduction to the Study of Experimental Medicine*, tr. H. C. Greene (New York, 1949).
　The Cahier Rouge of Claude Bernard, tr. H. H. Hoff et al. (Cambridge, Mass., 1967).
Broca, Paul, *On the Phenomenon of Hybridity in the Genus Homo*, ed. C. C. Blake (London, 1864).
Butler, Samuel, *Erewhon: or, Over the Range* (London, 1872).
　Life and Habit; an essay after a completer view of evolution (London, 1878).
　Evolution, Old or New: or the Theories of Buffon, Dr. Erasmus Darwin and Lamarck, as compared with that of Mr. Charles Darwin (London, 1879).
　Unconscious Memory (London, 1880).
　Luck or Cunning as the Main Means of Organic Modification? (London, 1887).
Carpenter, Edward, *Modern Science: a Criticism* (Manchester, 1885).
　Civilization, Its Cause and Cure; and other essays (London, 1889).
Carpenter, W. B., *Principles of Human Physiology*, 1st edn (London, 1842): 9th edn (London, 1881).
　Principles of Mental Physiology (London, 1874).
Chambers, Robert, *Vestiges of the Natural History of Creation* (London, 1844).

Clodd, Edward, *Pioneers of Evolution from Thales to Huxley with an Intermediate Chapter on the Causes of the Arrest of the Movement* (London, 1897).
  Myths and Dreams (London, 1885).
Coleridge, Samuel Taylor, *Poetical Works*, 3 vols. (London, 1829).
  Lay Sermons: 1. The Statesman's Manual, 2. Blessed are ye that sow beside all waters, ed. D. Coleridge (London, 1852).
Comte, Auguste, *Cours de philosophie positive*, 6 vols. (Paris, 1830–42).
  Positive Philosphy, tr. and condensed by H. Martineau, 2 vols. (London, 1853).
  System of Positive Polity, tr. J. H. Bridges, F. Harrison, E. S. Beesly, R. Congreve, 4 vols. (London, 1875–7).

CHARLES DARWIN

Works
Journal of Researches into the Geology and Natural History of the Various Countries Visited during the Voyage of H.M.S. Beagle Round the World (London, 1839).
'On the tendency of species to form varieties, and on the perpetuation of varieties and species by natural means of selection', Charles Darwin and Alfred Wallace, *Journal of the Proceedings of the Linnaean Society of London, Zoology*, 3 (1859): 45–62.
On the Origin of Species By Means of Natural Selection, or the Preservation of Favoured Races in the Struggle for Life (London, 1859).
On the Origin of Species, A Variorum Edition, ed. Morse Peckham (Philadelphia, 1959).
The Origin of Species, ed. John Burrow (Harmondsworth, 1968).
The Variation of Plants and Animals under Domestication, 2 vols. (London, 1868).
The Descent of Man and Selection in Relation to Sex (London, 1871).
The Expression of the Emotions in Man and Animals (London, 1872).
Formation of Vegetable Mould through the Action of Worms, with Observations on their Habits (London, 1881).
Evolution by Natural Selection: Darwin and Wallace, ed. G. de Beer (Cambridge, 1958), contains the *Sketch* (1842) and the *Essay* (1844).
Charles Darwin's Natural Selection, being the Second Part of his Big Species Book written from 1856 to 1858, ed. R. Stauffer (Cambridge, 1975).

Edited notebooks and letters
Darwin, F. (ed.), *The Life and Letters of Charles Darwin, including an Autobiographical Chapter*, 3 vols. (London, 1887).
Darwin, F. and Seward, A. C. (eds.), *More Letters of Charles Darwin: a record of his work in a Series of hitherto unpublished letters*, 2 vols. (London, 1903).
de Beer, G. (ed.), *Charles Darwin and Thomas Henry Huxley Autobiographies* (London, 1974), follows Nora Barlow's unexpurgated text and includes 'An Autobiographical Fragment, Written in 1838'.
  'Darwin's Notebooks on Transmutation of Species', *Bulletin of the British Museum* (Natural History) Historical Series, 2 (1960–1); 3 (1967).

Darwin on Man A Psychological Study of Scientific Creativity Together with Darwin's Early and Unpublished Notebooks, ed. Howard Gruber and Paul Barrett (London, 1974).

Barrett, P. (ed.), *The Collected Papers of Charles Darwin* (Chicago, 1977).

Vorzimmer, P. J. 'The Darwin Reading Notebooks (1838–1860)', *Journal of the History of Biology*, 10 (1977): 107–53.

Herbert, S. (ed.), 'The Red Notebook of Charles Darwin', *Bulletin of the British Museum (Natural History) Historical Series*, 7 (1980).

Darwin, Erasmus, *The Botanic Garden; or, The Loves of the Plants* (London, 1791).
Zoonomia; or, The Laws of Organic Life, 2 vols. (London, 1794–6).
Phytologia; or, The Philosophy of Agriculture and Gardening With the Theory of Draining Morasses, and with an improved construction of the Drill Plough (London, 1800).
The Temple of Nature; or, The Origin of Society, a poem, with philosophical notes (London, 1803).

Disraeli, Benjamin, *Tancred: or, the New Crusade*, 3 vols. (London, 1847).

GEORGE ELIOT

The Works of George Eliot, Cabinet edition, 20 vols. (Edinburgh and London, 1878–80).

Haight, G. S. (ed.), *The Letters of George Eliot*, 9 vols. (London, 1954–78).

Pinney, T. (ed.), *Essays of George Eliot* (London, 1963).

Pinney, T., 'More Leaves from George Eliot's Notebook', *Huntington Library Quarterly*, 29 (1965–66): 353–76.

Baker, W. (ed.), *Some George Eliot Notebooks: an Edition of the Carl H. Pforzheimer Library's George Eliot Holograph Notebooks, MSS707-11* (Salzburg, 1976, 1980).

Pratt, J. C. and Neufeldt, V. A., *George Eliot's* Middlemarch *Notebooks* (Berkeley and Los Angeles, 1979).

Collins, K. K., 'Questions of Method: Some Unpublished Late Essays', *Nineteenth Century Fiction*, 35 (1980): 385–405.

Feuerbach, Ludwig, *The Essence of Christianity*, tr. M. Evans (i.e. George Eliot) (London, 1854).

Freud, Sigmund, *The Standard Edition of the Complete Psychological Works of Sigmund Freud*, tr. under editorship of J. Strachey, 24 vols. (London, 1953–74).

Gatty, Margaret, *Parables from Nature*, 1st and 2nd ser. (London, 1855–65).

Gosse, Edmund, *Father and Son: A Study of Two Temperaments* (London, 1907).

Gosse, Philip Henry, *A Manual of Marine Zoology for the British Isles* (London, 1855–6).
Omphalos: an attempt to untie the geological knot (London, 1857).
The Romance of Natural History, 1st series (London, 1860); 2nd series (London, 1861).

Haeckel, Ernst, *The History of Creation*, tr. and revised by E. Ray Lankester, 2 vols. (London, 1876).

The Evolution of Man, 2 vols. (London, 1879).

The Riddle of the Universe at the Close of the Nineteenth Century, tr. J. McCabe (London, 1900).

Hardy, F., *The Early Life of Thomas Hardy 1840–91* (London, 1928).

Later Years of Thomas Hardy, 1892–1928 (London, 1930).

Hardy, Thomas, *The New Wessex Edition of the Novels of Thomas Hardy*, ed. P. N. Furbank, 14 vols. (London, 1975).

Complete Poems, ed. J. Gibson (London, 1976).

Helmholtz, Hermann, *Popular Lectures on Scientific Subjects*, tr. E. Atkinson; intro. J. Tyndall (London, 1873).

Abhandlungen zur Thermodynamik, ed. M. Planck (Leipzig, 1921).

Epistemological Writings, tr. M. F. Lowe; ed. R. S. Cohen and Y. Elkana (Dordrecht, 1977).

Huxley, Thomas Henry, *Collected Essays*, 9 vols. (London, 1892–5).

Autobiographies of Charles Darwin and Thomas Henry Huxley, ed. G. de Beer (London, 1974).

Jameson, Anna, *Sacred and Legendary Art*, 2 vols. (London, 1848).

Legends of the Madonna, as represented in the fine arts (London, 1852).

Jefferies, Richard, *After London; or, Wild England* (London, 1885).

Kant, Immanuel, *Critique of Pure Reason*, tr. J. M. D. Meiklejohn (London, 1860).

Kingsley, Charles, *Alton Locke, tailor and poet* (London, 1850).

The Water-Babies (London, 1863).

Lankester, Ray, *Degeneration. A Chapter in Darwinism* (London, 1880).

Lamarck, Jean-Baptiste, *Philosophie Zoologique* (Paris, 1809).

Zoological Philosophy, tr. H. Elliot, 1st edn (London, 1914); (reprinted N.Y., 1963).

Histoire Naturelle des animaux sans vertèbres (Paris, 1815).

Lewes, George Henry, *Comte's Philosophy of the Sciences* (London, 1853).

Sea-side Studies (London, 1858).

The Physiology of Common Life (Edinburgh, 1859–60).

'Mr. Darwin's Hypotheses', *Fortnightly Review*, 3 and 4 new series (1868): 353–73; 611; 628; 61–80; 492–509.

Problems of Life and Mind, 4 vols. (London, 1874–9).

Lubbock, John, *Prehistoric Times as Illustrated by Ancient Remains and the Manners and Customs of Modern Savages* (London, 1865).

The Origin of Civilisation and the Primitive Condition of Man (London, 1870).

Lyell, Charles, *Principles of Geology*, 3 vols. (London, 1830–1833).

The Geological Evidences of the Antiquity of Man (London, 1863).

Malthus, Thomas, *An Essay on the Principle of Population; or, A View of Its Past and Present Effects on Human Happiness*, 6th edn, 2 vols. (London, 1826).

Marx, Karl, *Karl Marx and Frederick Engels; Selected Correspondence* (Moscow, 1956).

Early Writings, tr. and ed. T. B. Bottomore (London, 1963).

Maudsley, Henry, *Body and Mind* (enlarged edn) (London, 1873).

The Pathology of Mind (London, 1879).

Maxwell, James Clerk, *Scientific Papers*, ed. W. D. Niven, 2 vols. (Cambridge, 1890).

Mill, John Stuart, *A System of Logic, Ratiocinative and Inductive*, 2 vols. (London, 1843); 5th edn (London, 1862).

Nature, the Utility of Religion, and Theism. Three Essays (London, 1874).

Milton, John, *Poetical Works* (London, 1822), a single-volume edition close in date to Darwin's travels.

Poetical Works, ed. D. Bush (London, 1966).

Mivart, St John, *Man and Apes* (London, 1873).

Monboddo (James Burnett, Lord), *Of the Origin and Progress of Language* (Edinburgh, 1773–6).

Müller, Friedrich Max, *Lectures on the Science of Language*, 1st and 2nd series (1861–64).

Chips from a German Workshop, 4 vols. (London, 1867–76).

Introduction to the Science of Religion (London, 1873).

Nordau, Max, *Degeneration*, tr. from 2nd edn of the German (London, 1895).

Ovid, *Metamorphoses*, with an English tr. by F. J. Miller (London, 1916).

Proctor, Richard, 'Gambling Superstitions', *The Cornhill Magazine*, 25 (1872): 704–17.

'The Past and Future of Our Earth', *Contemporary Review*, 25 (1874): 77–79.

Myths and Marvels of Astronomy (London, 1878).

Reade, Winwood, *The Martyrdom of Man* (London, 1872).

Ruskin, John, *The Works of John Ruskin*, Library edition, ed. E. T. Cook and A. D. O. Wedderburn, 39 vols. (London, 1902–12).

Schopenhauer, Arthur, *Über den Willen in der Natur* (Frankfurt, 1836).

Shelley, Mary, *Frankenstein: or, The Modern Prometheus* (London, 1818).

Spencer, Herbert, *Essays: Scientific, Political and Speculative*, 3 vols. (London, 1858).

First Principles (London, 1862).

The Principles of Biology (London, 1864).

The Principles of Psychology 2nd edn (London, 1870).

Descriptive Sociology; or, Groups of Sociological Facts (London, 1873).

Spenser, Edmund, *Poetical Works*, ed. J. C. Smith and E. de Selincourt (Oxford, 1912).

Sully, James, *Sensation and Intuition: Studies in Psychology and Aesthetics* (London, 1874).

Tylor, Edward, *Researches into the Early History of Mankind and the Development of Civilization* (London, 1865).

Primitive Culture, 2 vols. (London, 1871).

Tyndall, John, *On Radiation: the Rede Lecture* (London, 1865).

Essays on the Use and Limit of the Imagination in Science (London, 1870).

Address delivered before the British Association assembled at Belfast, with additions (London, 1874).

Wallace, Alfred, *Contributions to the Theory of Natural Selection*, 2nd edn (London, 1871).

Wallace, Alfred, et al., *Forecasts of the Coming Century* (London, 1897).

Wedgwood, Hensleigh, *On the Developement (sic) of Understanding* (London, 1848).
 A Dictionary of English Etymology, 3 vols. (London, 1859–67).
 The Origin of Language (London, 1866).
Weismann, August, *Studies in the Theory of Descent*, tr. and ed. R. Meldola, Preface by C. Darwin (London, 1882).
 Essays upon Heredity and Kindred Biological Problems, tr. and ed. E. B. Poulton, S. Schönland, and A. E. Shipley (Oxford, 1889).
Wordsworth, William, *The Excursion, being a portion of The Recluse, a poem* (London, 1814).
 Lyrical Ballads by Wordsworth and Coleridge. The text of the 1789 edn with the additional 1800 poems and the prefaces, ed. R. L. Brett and A. R. Jones (London, 1963).
 Poetical Works, ed. E. de Selincourt, 2nd edn, 5 vols. (Oxford, 1952).

Index

273